ANALYZING BACH CANTATAS

ANALYZING BACH CANTATAS

Eric Chafe

New York Oxford

Oxford University Press

2000

To my wife, Patricia,

in love and hope.

Oxford University Press

Oxford New York
Athens Auckland Bangkok Bogotá Buenos Aires Calcutta
Cape Town Chennai Dar es Salaam Delhi Florence Hong Kong Istanbul
Karachi Kuala Lumpur Madrid Melbourne Mexico City Mumbai
Nairobi Paris São Paulo Singapore Taipei Tokyo Toronto Warsaw

and associated companies in
Berlin Ibadan

Published by Oxford University Press, Inc.
198 Madison Avenue, New York, New York 10016

Oxford is a registered trademark of Oxford University Press

Library of Congress Cataloging-in-Publication Data
Chafe, Eric Thomas, 1946–
Analyzing Bach cantatas / Eric Chafe.
p. cm.
Includes bibliographical references.
ISBN 0-19-512099-x
1. Bach, Johann Sebastian, 1685–1750. Cantatas. 2. Cantatas, Sacred—Analysis,
appreciation. 3. Bach, Johann Sebastian, 1685–1750—Harmony.
4. Bach, Johann Sebastian, 1685–1750—Religion.
I. Title.
ML410.B13C38 1998
782.2'4' 092—dc21 98-15109

1 3 5 7 9 8 6 4 2

Printed in the United States of America
on acid-free paper

Acknowledgments

I HAVE BENEFITED GREATLY FROM THE ASSISTANCE, advice, and encouragement of many persons in writing this book. My decision to study Cantata 77 came about in part as the result of a 1993 invitation from Alexander Goehr, then composer-in-residence at Tanglewood, to speak to his composition seminar on the *durus/mollis* idea in Baroque music. That occasion forced me to think about the relationship between my earlier studies of Bach and Monteverdi. The outcome was that in spring 1994 I gave a paper on Cantata 77 at a meeting of the American Bach Society in Atlanta. On that occasion Martin Petzoldt encouraged me to pursue the line of reasoning that appears in chapters 7 and 8 of this book. Professor Petzoldt very kindly sent me a copy of parts of his unpublished *Habilitationsschrift* on the Bach cantata texts, a work that was of enormous value to me in preparing that study. Once the notion of writing a book on the analysis of Bach cantatas had jelled in my mind, I received financial assistance from Brandeis University in the form of Mazer Faculty Grants that enabled me to get student research assistance; Kathryn Carlson and Dana Dalton helped me considerably in this regard. A grant from the National Endowment for the Humanities and financial assistance from Brandeis University gave me a year off in 1992–93, during which I studied and wrote on the Bach cantatas exclusively. Most of what I wrote that year will, in fact, appear in a future study, but the opportunity to devote a year to study of the Bach cantatas was certainly a major impetus for this book. Renate Steiger very kindly read the final manuscript and made several valuable suggestions and supportive comments.

During the writing of this book, my wife, Patricia, was stricken suddenly and unexpectedly with a subarachnoid aneurysm, after which there were many medical complications that blocked her recovery for a long time (nearly two years at the point of writing). Writing this book was one of the activities that most sustained me during that time, a testimony to the tremendous power of Bach's music to uplift the spirit. In addition, I counted on many friends and colleagues in various ways for support. Their help was, and is, far too extensive for me to begin to acknowledge it here. They know who they are, and I hope they know as well how grateful I am. Among them one must be singled out because her instant response to the emergency that occurred in early 1996 (when I was, unfortunately, on the West Coast) may literally have saved my wife's life. My good friend and former student Wendy Heller took charge when I called her to say that my wife had sounded ill on the phone, recognizing the gravity of the situation, getting Pat to the hospital immediately, and following up in many ways, both before and after I returned home. This is the perfect occasion for me to express not only my gratitude for that but also my pride in having had such an outstanding student, colleague, and friend. Finally, two of the prepublication reviewers of the manuscript of this book, Robin Leaver and Richard Taruskin, lifted the veil of anonymity from their reviews. Their comments, which I followed as closely as possible, were of great help to me in preparing the final draft. Finally, I am grateful to Bärenreiter Music Corporation for permission to reproduce the facsimile editions of "Dies sind die heil'gen zehn Gebot" in Example 7.1.

Contents

Introduction

My chief purpose in writing this book was to stimulate as wide as possible a range of scholars, professional musicians, students, and other Bach lovers to become deeply involved with the Bach cantatas, including the less well-known ones. Many of the latter, in fact, count, like their more famous counterparts, among the very highest achievements of Western musical art. Nevertheless, studies of individual Bach cantatas that are both illuminating and detailed are few in number; and those that endeavor to integrate the analysis of both text and music along with their substantial historical backgrounds are fewer still. I have attempted, therefore, to introduce what I believe to be the most necessary areas of knowledge for anyone engaged in analyzing Bach cantatas. It will be clear from my title and chapter headings that I view analysis as a process through which we attain understanding, a means to an end, not an end in itself; and that I believe that process, like the works themselves, involves the interaction of musical and extramusical qualities.

If we take seriously our knowledge that the Bach cantatas were written for occasions and ends that transcended music alone, then to study them historically necessitates our involvement with the theological content of their texts and, just as important, with the principles according to which that content was formulated so as to speak directly to the individual listener. What such a listener lacked in terms of the aesthetic consciousness of later eras was compensated for by his or her receptiveness to the web of intentions that bind the works to their cultural and religious surroundings. The foremost of those intentions was that the cantata mirror what might be described as the dynamic character of the faith experience in terms of an unfolding sequence of affections and forms. Since that process was widely conceived as one of increasing understanding on the part of the believer, the cantata was basically a form of internalized *paysage moralisè*, a term referring to the third of the traditional four senses of hermeneutics, the moral or tropological sense, which normally focused on the faith concerns of the individual. In this sense, the listener and the idealized "believer" of the cantata texts were to be one and the same, the aesthetic and religious experiences intertwining for the duration of the work.

In Chapters 1 and 2, therefore, I have attempted to introduce the most essential religious and musical contexts for the relationship of Bach's cantatas to the Lutheran hermeneutic tradition. Those contexts involved very deep-rooted patterns of thought and perception that conditioned the hearing of musical relationships, no matter how "autonomous" the latter may appear out of context. Since scripture and its interpretation formed the backbone of Luther's work and of the tradition he initiated, the first such context is, of course, the set of principles according to which the Lutheran tradition interpreted the scriptures, which underlies the texts of numerous Bach cantatas and their primary goal, that of bridging the gap between scripture and faith. In addition, the liturgical year, organized so as to provide a spectrum of weekly readings from scripture as well as to mirror the eras of salvation history in its changing seasons, provided another context within which the characters and designs of many cantatas and even sequences of cantatas were molded. In producing annual cycles of cantatas Bach operated solidly within these two frames of reference, perhaps even intending his first Leipzig cycle to exemplify the very question of the interpretation of scripture—represented in the biblical motto beginnings of many of those cantatas-by musical means. And that music could be drawn into the process of scripture interpretation was self-evident in the tradition that emanated directly from Luther's well-known view that music was "next to theology" in its capacity to refresh and illuminate the spirit. That tradition, which I have dubbed the Lutheran "metaphysical" tradition in music theory, because its chief exponents viewed music in analogy with hermeneutics, completes the threefold spectrum of contexts for Bach's cantata oeuvre that occupies the first two chapters.

In order to illustrate how the principles of Lutheran hermeneutics operate in one particular work, I have devoted chapter 3 to a study of Cantata 21, "Ich hatte viel Bekümmernis," a relatively early work with an unusually wide range of movement types and an overall design that regulates them in a highly purposive manner. Since Cantata 21 derives most of its text from the scriptures and since it changes overall from C minor (part 1) to C major (the final chorus of part 2), bringing out conspicuous parallels and points of transformation between its two major divisions, it deals directly with the connection between scripture and the faith experience of the contemporary believer. At the same time, it raises questions concerning the relationship of Bach's tonal structures to the theological content of his cantatas that are central to his work as a whole. Cantata 21 (1714) was written very closely in time to the emergence of the tonal paradigm—the musicalischer Circul or circle of keys (1711)—that replaced what I have called elsewhere the "modal-hexachordal" system of the Middle Ages and Renaissance. Understanding how the work reflects that particular context provides a key to understanding Bach's tonal "hermeneutics" in general.

The fourth chapter then turns to the sphere of historical music theory to pick up on one of the running themes of this study: Bach's interaction with modal melodies, especially with those that contain anomalous events—such as their ending with a change of mode—and the influence of those melodies on multimovement cantata designs. Whereas chapter 2 introduces the figures of Johann Kuhnau and Andreas Werckmeister in order to illustrate the speculative or "metaphysical" aspect of music theory in the Lutheran tradition (Werckmeister) as well as the pragmatic approach to the question of allegory in musical composition (Kuhnau), chapter 4 addresses the question of modal chorale harmonization as perceived by theorists such as Werckmeister, who represents the generation before Bach, and Bach's pupil Johann Philipp Kirnberger, who represents the generation after. Although Kirnberger was directly influenced by Bach, his perspective is less applicable to Bach's work than Werckmeister's, owing to the weakening of the living tradition of modal composition in the late eighteenth century. I begin with Kirnberger, whose distinction between Bach's "strict" and "varied" chorale settings raises questions that demand our understanding something of the seventeenth-century background for modal composition. Since a comprehensive survey of that subject is out of the question in a study of this scope, I have selected several figures, such as Lucas Osiander, author of the earliest set of four-part note-against-note harmonizations of Lutheran chorale melodies (1586), and Athanasius Kircher, perhaps the most influential seventeenth-century music theorist (1650), in order to describe the effect that the rise of modern tonality had on modal composition. Against that background I turn to Bach's setting of "Das alte Jahr," printed by Kirnberger as an example of Bach's "varied" treatment of the modes, with a view toward indicating how the concerns of pre-Baroque tonal theory conditioned a modern-style chorale harmonization. I then introduce Werckmeister's views on certain chorales that he considered problematic from the standpoint of their correct modal harmonizations. Whereas what we might call Kirnberger's "liberal" attitude toward modal composition reflects the ideals of the era of Enlightenment empiricism and the new "critical" hermeneutics, Werckmeister's approach is permeated by the ideals of pre-enlightenment hermeneutics and the "metaphysical" tradition in music theory, both of which remain very much alive in Bach's work. That the perspectives of both men are relevant for Bach is testimony to Bach's unique ability to synthesize and coordinate the most disparate ideals as if in a form of contrapuntal interaction.

The experience of having reflected in an earlier book (*Monteverdi's Tonal Language*, New York: Schirmer, 1992) on the tonal language of the seventeenth century has conditioned my approach to tonal questions applying to Bach at virtually every step, and especially those questions that apply to his modal harmonizations. Understanding the way that our modern concepts of relative major and minor keys, of key relationships, and of dominant/subdominant polarity within the key arose from the older theory is, in my view, essential to understanding how the relationship of music and theology conditioned Bach's cantata designs. The series of developments and transformations that bridged the tonal usages of the sixteenth century and those of the eighteenth has yet to be set forth with anything like the degree of breadth and comprehensiveness it requires; and such a study is probably still a long way off. Nevertheless, it is necessary to enter the labyrinth, to use one of Werckmeister's tonal metaphors, and, I hope, emerge with insight into the older ways of hearing and conceptualizing tonal qualities that were of great importance to Bach, even though they virtually disappeared altogether in the mainstream musical styles of the late eighteenth century.

One such quality to which I give considerable attention in this book is the sense that the two modulatory directions—the sharp or dominant and the flat or subdominant—were to a very considerable degree perceived as opposite in their affective characters, the former direction widely associated with the idea of ascent and the latter with descent. This idea is not at all new or unique to Bach, of course, or even to Baroque music. It derives from the hexachord theory of the Middle Ages and Renaissance, which took on harmonic-tonal characteristics in the seventeenth century. Its applicability varied from composer to composer and work to work, but in the oeuvre of a composer such as Monteverdi, which was centered on text–music relationships, it represented a very powerful tool for text expression. And, despite the archaism of the modes and hexachords in the eighteenth century, the new paradigm of the circle of keys, and the concept in which it was rooted, the *ambitus* of the six most closely related keys to any given "tonic" exhibited very close lines of descent from the older theory. For a composer of such extraordinarily meditative bent as Bach, therefore, it was possible for the basic principles behind the old modal and hexachord theory to expand into the framework of the circle of keys, even to appear to merge with those of the newer tonal styles. This is particularly so in the case of Bach's modal settings. In Bach's music the aforementioned associations of the sharp and flat modulatory directions could operate at several levels—chord progressions and cadences (both of which are directly descended from seventeenth-century practice) as well as key relationships, both within the tonal spectrum of the "ambitus" and throughout the larger tonal scope of the circle of keys. I will take up these aspects of his tonal "hermeneutics" throughout this book, drawing on a select number of theoretical writings and considering a range of Bach cantatas in which those questions are prominent.

One of the principal issues to which we must be constantly on the alert in Bach's modal settings is the quality that Werckmeister and others in the Lutheran "metaphysical" tradition perceived as the disparity between *sensus* and *ratio*, or, in musical terms, between the ear and the mind. That disparity emerges, for example, in those modal settings—most often Mixolydian and Phrygian—whose final cadences sound as though they end on the dominant rather than the "tonic." In such settings "tonal" hearing encourages us to rely on the ear rather than received opinion, a viewpoint that emerged throughout the seventeenth century and became dominant in the generation after Werckmeister—that is, Bach's generation. Werckmeister perceived clearly and decried the tendency in his time toward translating the modes into the modern major and minor keys, while Bach's contemporary Johann David Heinichen proclaimed that the *musicalischer Circul* had rendered the modes obsolete. Another contemporary, Johann Mattheson, concurred, adding as well that the new outlook had vindicated the senses—that is, elevated hearing above received opinion. One generation later still, Kirnberger, who attests to Bach's deep involvement with the modes, perceives Bach's achievement in this regard as one of simply expanding their harmonic content for the purpose of "charming" the ear. As I will argue at various points in this book, our tendency to resolve the disparity between modal and tonal hearing, or between the "correct" modal final and its tonal interpretation (often as a dominant), in favor of the absoluteness of tonal hearing is the legacy of this change from the time of Werckmeister to that of Kirnberger. Standing between the two, Bach understood, like no one else that we know of, the potential of the modes not only to enrich the harmonic content of chorale settings but also to deepen the power of music to raise questions that have close analogues in the realm of text setting. Although it is possible to view Bach's stance as a resistance to the tendency of his time to absorb the modes into the framework of tonal hearing, it is probably more accurate to describe his work in terms of its probing every musical parameter for its capacity to increase the expressive subtlety of music.

In chapter 5 I turn to several cantatas utilizing chorales that Werckmeister took up in the *Harmonologia Musica* as examples of melodies whose modes were frequently misinterpreted and wrongly harmonized. This chapter attempts to reveal the depth of Bach's involvement with the question of modal harmonizations and the influence of such chorales on the musico-theological designs of entire cantatas. Chapter 6 extends the principles applied in chapter 5 to two chorale cantatas whose overall forms, deriving from parallels between music and theological content in their chorale melodies, closely mirror the chief concerns of Lutheran hermeneutics. The result in these and other works was that the cantata became a multivalent expression of the process of meditation itself, analogous to the principles of scripture interpretation. Such works seem to establish links between the faith experience of the contemporary believer and the underlying content of scripture, which was exactly Luther's foremost hermeneutic principle.

For chapters 7 and 8 I have chosen to examine one cantata, BWV 77, "Du sollt Gott, deinen Herren, lieben," in close detail. Cantata 77 incorporates several of the broad themes of Lutheranism—Law versus Gospel, love of God and love of one's neighbor, human imperfection, and the hope of eternity—presenting them in a cantata design featuring two chorales, beginning and ending the work, with modal anomalies of the kind that Werckmeister addressed in the *Harmonologia Musica.* Its final chorale, in particular, raises questions of completeness versus incompleteness to an extraordinary degree. Although Cantata 77 is relatively well known for the numerological qualities of its opening movement, its tonal characteristics are far more interesting and can, in fact, be traced back to the tonal character of the ancient melody that became associated in the Reformation era with Luther's chorale paraphrase of the Ten Commandments. I therefore devote sections of chapter 7 to the chorale melody, its history, text, and tonal qualities, and to the theological character of the text of Cantata 77 and its relationship to its known model, a cantata text by Johann Oswald Knauer. In the last of these topics I have been greatly aided by Martin Petzoldt's work on Cantata 77 and, indeed, by Petzoldt's approach to the analysis of Bach's cantata texts generally. In chapter 8 I attempt to show how Bach responded to the theological and historical elements in Luther's chorale, including its modally anomalous melody, creating in the process a work of enormous harmonic and tonal expressivity and subtlety. Bach seems virtually to re-create or revive, and to amplify, qualities in the old melody that had been developed by composers as far back as Heinrich Isaac and Paul Hofhaimer, more than two centuries before. At the same time, Bach renders Cantata 77 into a mirror of those aspects of Lutheran theology that center on the relationship of God and humankind in the Old and New Testament views. Ultimately, the numerological and other symbolic elements in the opening chorus relate to the Old Testament perspective on the Law as the key to that relationship, while the tonal qualities of the movement allegorize the perspective of the New Testament and the Gospel as its true interpretation.

Finally, I have chosen to end this study with another cantata from the 1723–24 Leipzig cycle, "O Ewigkeit, du Donnerwort" (Cantata 60), written eleven weeks after Cantata 77 for the twenty-fourth Sunday after Trinity, one of the more pronounced of the eschatologically oriented feast days that come toward the end of the liturgical year. In certain respects Cantata 60 is opposite in its dynamic character to Cantata 77, while in others—especially its expressing its overall direction in terms of the chorales that begin and end the work—it reveals similar techniques. Its final chorale, "Es ist genung," is one of the most famous in Bach's work, owing to Alban Berg's incorporating it into his 1935 violin concerto, where it serves as a symbol for the eschatological character that Berg intended as the program for that work. In an immediate sense, Berg was drawn to that particular chorale because of the very complex, dissonant, and chromatic harmonization, especially that of its opening phrase. In Bach's work those qualities are the outcome of a process of reflection on the inner character of the faith experience as well as on fundamental musico-allegorical properties of the tonal system. Berg's seizing on certain of those qualities in his work, especially in the organization of its tone row, attests to his own intention of reflecting on fundamental tonal qualities, now in a basically atonal context.

From the preceding summary of the contents of this book the reader will perceive that I have attempted to weave together several themes, of which the most prominent are: (1) the ways in which traditional hermeneutics influenced the texts and overall designs of the cantatas; (2) the viewing of cantatas in relation to their placing within the liturgical year; (3) the influence of modal chorales on the designs of entire cantatas, including nonchorale cantatas; and (4) the role of "tonal allegory" in relation to the foregoing themes. In spite of this volume's title, I have not attempted to answer the question of what analysis is. The primary reason for that is my belief that analysis is by no means the quasi-objective operation that some musicians believe it to be, but one that is very much conditioned by the music-theoretical and aesthetic assumptions of the analyst. I resist the notion that analysis is the application of one or another of those systems—Schenkerian voice leading, Riemannian functional harmony, and Fortean pitch-class set theory being the leading ones—that center primarily on pitch relationships and therefore articulate a belief in some form of absolute music. The illusion of rigor that such systems create is owing directly, though not entirely, of course, to their exclusiveness. Systems of analysis that are inclusive with regard to "extramusical" aspects of the works have not been forthcoming, and there is some sense among musical scholars that the idea of such a system is questionable, if not actually a contradiction in terms. I do not believe that; but I am aware that some readers will question my use of the term "analysis" rather than "interpretation." I have used it for that very reason.

Among the themes listed in the preceding paragraph, I have considered the last one at length in an earlier study (*Tonal Allegory in the Vocal Music of J. S. Bach*, Berkeley: University of California Press, 1991). Furthermore, my subsequent book, *Monteverdi's Tonal Language*, addresses very similar questions in the music of the early seventeenth century. And a primary involvement of mine since that book has been to set forth in some detail the tonal structure of Wagner's *Tristan und Isolde* with respect to the question of tonal allegory and Wagner's Schopenhauerian conception of allegory in general. It is perhaps inevitable, therefore, that this book articulates the view, common to those studies, that musical allegory is one of the primary impulses behind the composition of music and that it is a far deeper presence in composition than is generally acknowledged. In fact, I would go so far as to assert that if the aforementioned inclusive system of analysis ever comes forth it will either give a very prominent place to or actually *be* a theory of musical allegory. It is necessary, therefore, to make clear that musical allegory is not equivalent to what many scholars working in the music of the seventeenth and eighteenth centuries understand by the term "musical rhetoric." There are affinities between the two, certainly; and allegory, in fact, can be said to encompass musical rhetoric. But rhetoric, as it was conceived by Baroque theorists and as it is generally applied by scholars today, is centered on what I would describe as incidental "pointing" devices—that is, it does not attempt to link its designative devices in a sequence analogous to the idea of a sustained metaphor, which is the most compelling description of allegory. Rhetoric is, generally speaking, the "surface" manifestation of the allegorical impulse, which controls both the immediate surface detail and the techniques by means of which the composer organizes large-scale aspects of the work into a sequence of quasi-narrative character. This does not mean, however, that allegory always involves a "story" or "program" that we must learn to "read" in order to grasp the composer's intentions accurately. Rather, allegory describes the unifying aspects of the work, including even those that are not known to be designative in intent. Those unifying qualities, however, are by no means limited to the purely musical relationships that are generally described in terms of the "organic metaphor" and its implications of autonomy. As long as human beings live variegated lives that involve the participation of both intellect and feeling and as long as music is a part of the larger scheme of things, it will be impossible to reduce music to an ideal of absoluteness or autonomy; and in that view of life allegory will mirror, as is often said, the finiteness of human existence. It was all the more compelling to seventeenth-century artists of all kinds on that account.

I have selected the cantatas included in this book so as to provide a spectrum of works ranging from Bach's Weimar period to the period of the 1730s, when, so far as we know, Bach's cantata composition might have fallen off considerably. The majority of the cantatas, however, have been chosen from the peak of his activity as cantata composer, the Leipzig cycles of 1723–24 and 1724–25. I have decided not to focus on the best-known works, although a few of those I discuss fall into that category. Instead, the principle of inclusion is heavily weighted toward providing a selection of works that exhibit unusual clarity of musico-allegorical design, along with those that, while following the same basic principles, demand much closer study before they yield to the interpretative scalpel. The ordering of the discussions is not chronological, nor does it follow any single pattern, such as that of the liturgical year. Nevertheless, I have attempted to mirror both those principles to some degree, more as reminders to the reader and occasional articulations of those principles than as a set procedure. Thus, the first cantata I discuss in any detail is an early one (Cantata 21, written no later than 1714), while the last (Cantata 60, written in 1724) comes near the end of the liturgical year. I hope the reader will understand and accept my subjective ordering as the outcome of many years' involvement with the Bach cantatas, in the process of which I have found that the juxtaposition of varied works is one of the most interesting means of identifying the principles that bond them in terms of the vision Bach announced relatively early in his career: that of producing a "well-regulated church music to the glory of God." That vision never wavered, nor did the principles behind it, and finding it in works of very different characters is one of the best approaches to defining its nature. I hope, too, that the reader will come to perceive that I have attempted to follow a logical thread of ideas in the ordering of this book even though it does not follow a single ordering principle.

In this book I have not shied away from drawing directly on discussions of works and ideas that I have set forth in my 1991 study of tonal allegory in Bach, although, in nearly all cases I have treated the earlier discussions as springboards to discussions of wider scope and greater detail. And, of course, I have taken the opportunity to discuss works not taken up in that book. As I mentioned in the acknowledgments, I was fortunate, in 1992–93 to have the support of a grant from the National Endowment for the Humanities, plus additional financial assistance from Brandeis University, which together enabled me to devote that year to study of the Bach cantatas. The result was that I put together a group of separate Bach studies in book form, under the title *Studies in the Interpretation of J. S. Bach's Cantatas.* In that book I devoted individual chapters to the liturgical year and its influence on Bach's cantata cycles. It was, and still is, my ambition to study the cantatas within the year in a manner that reveals the many ways in which the cyclic aspects of the year manifested themselves in the cantata cycles. In the process of writing, however, it soon became evident to me that such a study was beyond the scope of a single volume of reasonable length. Also, I felt more and more that to address questions of analysis relating to the placement of the cantatas within the liturgical year was a more pressing need that could be taken up in a shorter study. I have therefore recast parts of that earlier study as the present one, setting aside for the time being those parts of the book that were not centered primarily on analytical issues. I have been guided by my knowledge that the Bach cantatas comprise one of the central bodies of work in the Western musical canon and by my desire to encourage as many music lovers as possible to explore that field for the many startling discoveries they are sure to make. My hope is that many of those discoveries will involve the ways in which one of the greatest of all musical minds attempted to mirror both the dogma and the mystery of religious experience in musico-allegorical terms.

Finally, it is necessary to add a word as to how the reader should use this book. First of all, I must emphasize that, in keeping with my aim of addressing an audience ranging from those who are inexperienced with the Bach cantatas to those who are very experienced with the works, I have not written this book simply to be read through, but rather as a guide to the works I discuss and an introduction to the analysis of the Bach cantatas in general. This is, therefore, neither a reference book nor a textbook in the usual sense, but one to be read closely in conjunction with getting to know the works themselves, through listening and familiarity with the texts (and study of the scores, when feasible). Since the amount of detail involved in my discussions of the various cantatas I consider varies greatly from work to work, some readers may wish to select those cantatas whose discussions demand relatively little in the way of technical knowledge. I would recommend that all readers begin with the first two chapters, then read the first section of the third, an introduction to

Cantata 21. The remainder of chapter 3, a commentary on the individual movements, treats Cantata 21 at a level of detail that demands considerable musical sophistication from the reader. Likewise, chapter 4 will be difficult for readers who are not versed in music theory, including that of the seventeenth and eighteenth centuries (although I have attempted to make it comprehensible to musicians in general). Chapters 5 and 6 take up a series of cantatas in varying levels of detail. I do not intend that the reader attempt to read these discussions in sequence. Although they are linked by the themes introduced above, some of the cantatas that are not well known, such as Cantata 153, have required rather elaborate extended discussions, whereas discussions of other cantatas are relatively straightforward. The reader will need to decide how much of each discussion is appropriate to his or her level of musical understanding. In general, I have provided introductory comments at the outset of each segment, which are intended to serve as a starting point for investigation of the works. And Cantata 77 is taken up in two separate chapters, the first of which (chapter 7) deals with the history of the chorale and its versions, the theological character of the work, and its textual model, while the second demands, once again, that the reader possess some experience in music theory.

Despite these caveats, the book is readable in sequence by advanced undergraduates, graduate students, and musicians generally who are willing to examine the cantatas themselves and not simply let the book serve as a series of descriptive analysis-commentaries that substitute for the works. The latter approach will prove deadly and tedious very quickly, whereas learning the works will provide a basis for understanding one of the core segments of the Western musical repertoire and one whose Christian theological outlook is more challenging than ever in our predominantly secular age.

ANALYZING BACH CANTATAS

ONE

The Hermeneutic Matrix

Littera gesta docet, quid credas allegoria,
Moralis quid agas, quo tendas anagogia.

(The letter teaches actions, allegory what you believe,
the moral what to do, the anagogical where you are going.)

Basic Principles

J. S. Bach's interaction with tradition, embodied in countless aspects of his oeuvre —his settings of the modal chorale melodies of the Lutheran church, to name but one—is one of the most interesting sides of his work. Bach's capacity to evoke and revitalize past musical styles often involves specific religious contexts for which a sense of temporal distinctions is central. Thus, many cantatas become the meeting ground for archaic and modern styles whose relationship, were it not for closely parallel textual qualities, might be judged inexplicable. In such works heterogeneity of style often mirrors the variegated layers of the verbal texts and their diverse origins (Old Testament, New Testament, chorale, and "madrigal" poetry). The various organizing principles provided both by those texts and by certain large-scale musical devices such as tonality reflect the ways in which Lutheran hermeneutics, sometimes very learnedly, sometimes very simply, articulated the essential unity of theological meaning. Within such a belief system, stylistic heterogeneity is secondary to the overarching unity of scripture and its spiritual working on the believer.

The idea that there *was* an essential unity of theological meaning, and hence of scripture, on which it was founded was, of course, a first principle of pre-Enlightenment hermeneutics, the matrix in which Bach's cantata texts were formed. So, too, was the idea that scripture, despite its truth as a historical record of God's dealings with humanity, served a basic purpose: the salvation of humankind. Viewed both as "salvation history" and as the catalyst to faith in the contemporary believer, scripture lent itself to objective or methodological as well as spiritual or inspired readings. Lutheranism's great reliance on scripture, therefore, had the effect that hermeneutics —the science of text interpretation—became one of the foremost tools for articulating and defending the basic tenets of the faith. As such, its influence was far more widespread than we imagine today, extending into the literary and visual arts and, it goes without saying, into such adjuncts of the liturgy as the Bach cantatas, whose texts often utilize the selfsame means as hermeneutics in relating the content of scripture to the faith experience of the contemporary believer. And from the musical standpoint the Bach cantatas serve an analogous purpose. They strive, that is, toward the interpretation and enhancement of the message of scripture—which may be cited directly or in paraphrase—by means that involve both the introduction of an array of musical transliterational devices for the purpose of underscoring the text itself (pictorialisms and symbolic devices, for example) and the organization of the musico-dynamic aspects of the works so as to stir the affections or emotions of the believer (*Gemütsbewegung*, in the language of the time). Analogous, perhaps, to what Luther called the "external" and "internal" clarity of scripture, the musical interpretation of the text in Bach's cantatas had outer and inner dimensions, the latter attempting to create a parallel dynamic to the faith experience of the believer as detailed in the text.[1] In order to understand how these aspects of the Bach cantatas affect questions of analysis we need first of all to understand the principles of scripture interpretation themselves.

As I have indicated, the ancient concept of scripture as "salvation history"—that is, the notion that God had a plan for the salvation of humanity that was revealed progressively throughout the successive eras of biblical history—was essential to Lutheran hermeneutics, as it had been to the interpretative principles employed in the Middle Ages. It presupposed, of course, that the Old and New Testaments constituted a single entity with a single purpose and that this unity of content and purpose controlled the meaning of individual passages in scripture. According to this conception, differences, even disparities, between the Old and New Testaments reflected the fact that the revelation of God's plan was more complete in later than in earlier eras. Since Old Testament events could therefore be understood as typological prefigurings of what was fully revealed only in the New Testament, they acquired new significance in light of the latter, which centered on the work of Jesus. Even antitheses between the two testaments took on new meaning. Thus, the figures of Adam, the prototype of fallen man, and Moses, the lawgiver, were answered by the figure of Christ, the prototype of the new risen man and the giver of the Gospel. The Fall of Adam was overcome by the resurrection of Jesus, Mount Sinai had a parallel in the Sermon on the Mount, and God's chosen people of Israel had a counterpart in the Christian church, interpreted as the new Zion. Above all, Law and Gospel constituted two separate, but ultimately complementary, aspects of God's revelation, corresponding to the fact that God presented Himself in very different forms in the Old and New Testaments. In this framework the third entity in the Trinitarian conception of the deity, the Holy Spirit, represented the era of the church and, as the author of the scriptures, the key to faith in postbiblical times. Through the Spirit the history of salvation became a contemporary matter. Central to the articulation of such a large-scale unity of the content of scripture, therefore, was the belief that scripture possessed both literal and spiritual meanings, the latter expressed in the three so-called "spiritual" senses of hermeneutics. When subjected to allegorical, tropological, and anagogical (eschatological) interpretation, the events of biblical history moved outside their own historical time frames and became imbued with new levels of meaning for later generations.

As is well known, Luther generally opposed the traditional fourfold interpretative scheme of medieval hermeneutics described in the motto that heads this chapter, preferring a simpler "literal-prophetic" sense that was Christologically oriented.[2] Luther's objections centered on the fact that "allegorical" interpretations of scripture had traditionally been directed toward Law and works and the institutions of the church rather than faith.[3] Since, as Luther believed, the purpose of scripture was the salvation of humanity, its meaning must be oriented toward the contemporary believer; its "objective" truth was inseparable from its working on the individual. In his hermeneutics the juxtaposition of Law and Gospel represented the pivot of faith, the shift from recognition of one's sinful nature to acceptance of God's forgiveness and love. Luther called this process the "analogy (or allegory) of faith," describing it as the means by which faith bridged the gap between Old Testament events and the experience of the contemporary believer. History, correctly interpreted according to the analogy of faith, had an inner dimension that paralleled the workings of Law and Gospel on the individual. Thus, the story of the fall and rebuilding of Jerusalem (Isaiah 1:21–28; 4:2–6) not only was literally true but also embodied the fact that under the Law the human condition was dominated by recognition of sinfulness and destruction, whereas under the Gospel the conscience was restored:

> Faith must be built up on the basis of history, and we ought to stay with it [history] alone and not so easily slip into allegories, unless by way of metaphor we apply them to other things in accordance with the method [analogy] of faith. So here Jerusalem can allegorically be called our conscience, which has been taken and laid waste by the terror of the Law and then set free out of the remnant and the sprouts, and the restored conscience is saved by the Word of the Gospel, through which we grow up into mature manhood by the knowledge of God (cf. Eph. 4:13). Such allegory must be used in accordance with the Word of the Law and the Gospel, and this is the explanation of different matters by the same Spirit. . . . This is the summary of Scripture: It is the work of the law to humble according to history, externally and internally, physically and spiritually. It is the work of the Gospel to console, externally and internally, physically and spiritually. What our predecessors have experienced according to history externally and physically, this we experience according to our own history internally and spiritually.[4]

This passage, which I have cited and discussed elsewhere, is a central statement regarding the principles behind Lutheran hermeneutics.[5] According to the method or analogy of faith, the proper way to interpret scripture spiritually, or allegorically, involves the perception of a "dynamic" of descent (destruction, the Law) followed by ascent (rebuilding, the Gospel), which will be found to underlie countless individual scriptural passages. The particular one that Luther discusses—the destruction and rebuilding of Jerusalem—had a special importance in the Lutheran liturgy in many places, including Leipzig, as we will see; and one of Bach's cantatas on that subject even mirrors Luther's principles directly.[6] With the aid of the analogy of faith Luther related scripture to the faith experience of the believer. And in analogous ways the Bach cantatas set out to achieve very similar goals.

Within Luther's hermeneutics, therefore, the medieval four senses were not so much rejected as they were reoriented according to the dialectical relationship of

Law and Gospel and the analogy of faith. As a result many residues of the medieval scheme persisted through the era of Lutheran orthodoxy, but generally in freely flexible forms.[7] Nowhere, perhaps, do we see this more clearly than in the case of certain of Bach's settings of cantata texts by Erdmann Neumeister, who, as both a prominent theologian-pastor and a prolific author of cantata poetry, bridges the exigencies of methodologically oriented scripture interpretation and those of devotional texts for musical purposes. While at Weimar (1708–17) and even during his Leipzig period, Bach set a substantial number of Neumeister texts that are carefully constructed so as to bring the principles of traditional hermeneutics into the foreground. None does this more directly than the Neumeister cantata text that Bach set in 1714 for the beginning of the liturgical year, Advent Sunday. That work, "Nun komm, der Heiden Heiland" (Cantata 61), which Bach reperformed in 1723 as the Advent cantata of his first Leipzig cantata cycle, exhibits an unusually straightforward degree of correspondence between the hermeneutic principles behind its text and the musical devices with which Bach responded to Neumeister's design. Neumeister's text illustrates principles set forth by him in his treatise on the celebration of Advent, Christmas, and the New Year (*Christlicher Unterricht wie die h. Adventszeit, das h. Christ-Fest und das Neue Jahr gotgefällig zu feiren sey*). As Jaroslav Pelikan points out, Neumeister speaks in that book of the threefold advent of Christ—in the flesh at His birth, in the means of grace through word and sacrament, and in judgment at the end of time.[8] "Nun komm, der Heiden Heiland," however, interprets the coming of Jesus in a fourfold scheme that parallels the four senses of hermeneutics even more closely: first as His coming in the flesh to Israel (the incarnation, represented in the opening chorus, "Nun komm, der Heiden Heiland"), then as His coming in the spirit to the church (the tenor aria, "Komm, Jesu, komm zu deiner Kirche"), then as His coming to the individual believer through faith (soprano aria, "Öffne dich, mein ganzes Herze, Jesus kömmt und ziehet ein"), and, finally, as His coming to the believer at the end of time (final chorale, "Komm, du schöne Freudenkrone"). And, as I have shown elsewhere, Cantata 61 mirrors these "senses" in its movement sequence and its patterned series of styles and keys, the latter "ascending" by thirds from movement to movement.[9]

Although Bach was not often presented with texts that display the principles of scripture interpretation so clearly, those principles underlie the texts of a great many of his cantatas, sometimes in their entireties, sometimes in part. And they are particularly prominent in some of Bach's earliest cantatas, a fact suggesting that Bach, like other Lutheran musicians of the time, such as Johann Kuhnau and Johann Andreas Werckmeister (see the following chapter), was well grounded in hermeneutics and that this grounding probably conditioned his goals as composer of church music. Thus, as I have described elsewhere, the design of the Mühlhausen cantata, "Gottes Zeit ist die allerbeste Zeit" (the so-called "Actus Tragicus," Cantata 106), utilizes several levels of musical and textual organization to represent its central theme—death under the Law and the Gospel—in as broad and comprehensive a theological context as possible.[10] Within that context the chronological aspect of the text mirrors the eras of "salvation history"—the time of Israel, time of Christ, and time of the church—which center on the time and person of Jesus, while certain of the musical details expand the central antithesis of Law and Gospel to a structured framework analogous to the unity of scripture and the inner dynamic of faith (the moral or tropological sense of traditional hermeneutics). The "Actus Tragicus" thus projects its unity of theological meaning in terms of the Christocentric unity of scripture. And in other Bach cantatas, as in the "Actus Tragicus," sequences of texts that represent the eras of the Old Testament, the New Testament, and the church also correspond to the historical, tropological, and eschatological senses of hermeneutics, articulating what has been called the "circle of Luther's theology"—Law, Gospel, and faith—as a dynamic process within the believer.[11]

Law and Gospel represent, on the one hand, God's demands from humanity and, on the other, His promise of salvation. The purpose of the Law, as Luther constantly reiterated, is to reveal to humankind the seriousness of sin and eternal damnation; through the Law the sinner can recognize his transgressions against God, come to the awareness of his sinful, contaminated nature, and take the first step toward his salvation: repentance and faith. The Law is thus the measure of human sinfulness, for which God's punishment since the Fall of Adam is death, whereas the Gospel offers eternal life as the believer's reward for his faith. Luther's writings, therefore, describe a two-stage process of faith, the first dominated by the awareness and acknowledgment of sin (*Sündenerkenntnis*, brought about by the Law) and the second shifting to the believer's deriving comfort from his awareness of God's love and his own response of love (*Tröstung des Gewissens*, brought about by the Gospel). The dynamic character of this faith process was the pattern of destruction followed by restoration, or descent by ascent, the dynamic that underlay the only true means of allegorizing the message of scripture as we have seen. God, therefore, presents Himself in two very different guises that align closely, but by no means absolutely, with the pictures of God in the Old Testament and of Jesus in the New. The theme of destruction (the work of the Law) and restoration (the work of the Gospel) is one of the most characteristic features of Lutheran theology, deriving as it does from the dialectic of God's wrath (*Zorn*) and His mercy (*Barmherzigkeit* or *Erbarmen*) toward humanity.

Luther's interpretation of God's two sides and the meaning of Law and Gospel derives largely, of course, from St. Paul. And it incorporates other, later, interpretations, the most significant being the "satisfaction" theory of redemption set forth by Anselm of Canterbury in the eleventh century.[12] According to that theory, God demands satisfaction from humanity according to the dictates of the Law. Humankind, however, is incapable of satisfying God's just demands—that is, of justifying itself before God—and must, therefore, undergo the punishment of death for its sinfulness. At this point, however, God's other, merciful and forgiving side enters the picture in the person of Jesus, Whose innocent death, motivated by God's love for humanity, satisfies God's demand for justice for those who believe. The satisfaction theory, therefore, translates very naturally into forensic or juridical imagery, with God represented as a strict judge (*Richter*), the sinner as a wrongdoer brought before the court (*Gericht*) and condemned for having broken the law, and Jesus as an innocent friend of the prisoner, Who accepts the punishment Himself in order that the wrongdoer go free. In the language of Bach's cantata texts, Jesus "stills" or calms God's anger.

Luther's theology is very deeply rooted in the satisfaction theory, which he set forth in many of his writings, often making use of the forensic imagery I have described.[13] The Passion story was, of course, a focal point for such ideas and imagery; and Luther's writings on the Passion set forth the satisfaction theory with particular clarity. Transmitted through the period of Lutheran orthodoxy, these writings have been shown to underlie many of the texts of Bach's *St. Matthew Passion* and, in addition, much of the large-scale musico-allegorical design of that work.[14] Also, although the era of Lutheran orthodoxy was, if anything, even more committed to the satisfaction theory than Luther himself, Luther's views did not go wholly unaltered by the emphases of the Pietism of seventeenth- and eighteenth-century Germany; and by the time of Bach's activity as cantata composer love—both that of God for humankind and that of humanity's response to Jesus' sufferings—had come more into the foreground than before, serving as the dramatic focal point of the trial scene of the *St. Matthew Passion*, for example, in the aria "Aus Liebe will mein Heiland sterben." The tremendous musical contrast between this aria—delicate-sounding by virtue of Bach's instrumentation for soprano and flute, with two oboes *da caccia* as a substitute for the *basso continuo*—and the cry for death in the two ponderously chromatic "Laß ihn kreuzigen" choruses makes this one of the most vivid passages in the work, placing the opposition of judgment and love at the very heart of the message of the passion.[15]

The theological ideas just introduced are seldom very far in the background in Bach's cantatas, even when the direct subject matter as defined by the Gospel and Epistle readings for the day might not seem to invite them. Luther's view that the basic content and purpose of scripture was contained in the dialectical relationship of Law and Gospel ensured that the message of hope and salvation for the believer —almost always a direct concern of Lutheran cantata texts—was framed in such terms. On particular occasions during the year, however, the core themes of Lutheran belief came into the foreground, especially on certain Sundays during the Trinity season when the Gospel and Epistle readings centered on questions of Law and Gospel, faith and justification. Perhaps no other cantata illustrates the ideas just described so well as Cantata 9, "Es ist das Heil uns kommen hier," written in 1732–35 for such an occasion, the sixth Sunday after Trinity. "Es ist das Heil," based on one of the most widely known chorales of the early Reformation period, sets forth a complete summary of Lutheran doctrine regarding the roles of Law, Gospel, and faith in salvation.[16] The introductory chorus (the first verse of the chorale) makes clear the opposition of good works and faith and the efficacy of the latter only:

Es ist das Heil uns kommen her	Salvation has come here unto us
Von Gnad und lauter Güte.	Through grace and pure goodness.
Die Werk, die helfen nimmermehr,	Works no longer help us,
Sie mögen nicht behüten.	They cannot protect us.
Der Glaub sieht Jesum Christum an,	Faith looks unto Jesus Christ,
Der hat g'nug für uns all getan,	Who has accomplished enough for us all,
Er ist der Mittler worden.	He has become our mediator.

In the sequence of movements that follows, three bass recitatives (nos. 2, 4, and 6) set forth the roles of Law, Gospel, and faith, respectively. The first of these describes the purpose of the Law—to make known humanity's sinful nature—and the incapacity of humanity to fulfill it:

Gott gab uns ein Gesetz,	God gave us the Law,
Doch waren wir zu schwach,	But we were too weak
Daß wir es hätten halten können;	To be able to keep it;
Wir gingen nur den Sünden nach,	We walked only in the ways of sin,
Kein Mensch war fromm zu nennen;	And no one could have been called pious;
Der Geist blieb an dem Fleische kleben	The Spirit remained bound to the flesh
Und wagte nicht zu widerstreben.	And did not venture to resist.
Wir sollten im Gesetze gehn,	We should have proceeded according to the Law,
Und dort als wie in einem Spiegel sehn,	And seen in it as in a mirror,
Wie unsere Natur unartig sei:	How our nature was unruly:
Und dennoch blieben wir dabei;	And nevertheless we persisted;
Aus eigner Kraft war Niemand fähig,	Of his own strength no one was capable
Der Sünden Unart zu verlassen,	Of abandoning the evil of sin,
Er möcht 'auch alle Kraft zusammenfassen.	Even if he summoned together all his forces.

The tenor aria that immediately follows, "Wir waren schon zu tief gesunken," gives voice to the condition of fallen humanity, after which the second recitative narrates how the necessary fulfillment of the Law occurred through Jesus' innocent death; faith in Jesus is the key to salvation:

Doch mußte das Gesetz erfüllet werden;	Yet the Law had to be fulfilled;
Deswegen kam das Heil der Erden,	Therefore the Savior of the earth came,
Des Höchsten Sohn, der hat es selbst erfüllt	The son of the most high, Who fulfilled it Himself
Und seines Vaters Zorn gestillt.	And stilled His Father's anger.
Durch sein unschuldig Sterben	Through His innocent death
Ließ er uns Hülf erwerben.	He ennabled us to attain help.
Wer nun demselben traut,	Whoever, then, trusts in Him,
Wer auf sein Leiden baut,	Whoever builds on His sufferings,
Der gehet nicht verloren.	He will not be lost.
Der Himmel ist vor den erkoren,	Heaven is appointed for the one
Der wahren Glauben mit sich bringt	Who brings true faith with him
Und fest um Jesu Arme schlingt.	And wraps himself firmly in Jesus' arms.

This recitative is followed by a soprano-alto duet with flute and oboe d'amore in which Bach uses canonic imitation between the vocal and instrumental pairs to represent the doctrine of justification by faith. This movement alone abandons the narrative third-person mode to address God personally:

Herr, du siehst statt guter Werke	Lord, instead of good works, Thou lookest
Auf des Herzens Glaubensstärke,	On the strength of faith in the heart,
Nur den Glauben nimmst du an.	Only faith do You accept.
Nur der Glaube macht gerecht,	Only faith justifies,
Alles andre scheint zu schlecht,	Everything else glows too weakly
Als daß es uns helfen kann.	To be able to help us.

Finally, the third recitative summarizes the roles of Law, Gospel, and faith in the believer's hopes for the afterlife:

Wenn wir die Sünd' aus dem Gesetz erkennen,	If we recognize sin from the Law,
So schlägt es das Gewissen nieder;	Then it strikes down our conscience;
Doch ist das unser Trost zu nennen,	Yet it is to be accounted as our comfort,
Daß wir im Evangelio	That in the Gospel
Gleich wieder froh	We are made happy
Und freudig werden;	And joyful at once;
Dies nun stärket unsern Glauben wieder.	This strengthens our faith all the more.
Drauf hoffen wir der Zeit,	Therefore we hope for the time
Die Gottes Gütigkeit	Which God's goodness
Uns zugesaget hat . . .	Has promised us . . .

Bach's means of musically representing these stages, which correspond to the Old Testament, New Testament, and present-day eras, are manifold, involving melodic direction, vocal ranges (the recitatives are all for bass, while the two arias articulate a rising pattern from tenor to soprano and alto), styles, and instrumentation. Regulating the overall design, however, is the tonal plan, which, as I have shown elsewhere, modulates downward along the circle of keys from E major (the opening chorus) to B minor (the ending of the first recitative) and E minor (the aria "Wir waren schon zu tief gesunken") and then upward through B minor and A major (the second recitative and the soprano-alto duet) to close in E once more (the third recitative and final chorale). Behind the fourteen-movement chorale itself (which was reduced to seven movements for the cantata) lies the image of Jesus as Alpha and Omega, beginning and end, a symbol for His encompassing the whole of time, now interpreted as "salvation history." In this cantata, therefore, we confront a quintessential expression of the core ideas of Lutheran hermeneutics, which the author of the chorale text took pains to make clear by means of an appendix that gives exact identifications of the many scriptural passages on which its ideas were founded.[17]

Behind the simple tone of the "Actus Tragicus" lies a complex and highly purposeful design that encompasses the core ideas of Lutheran hermeneutics; "Es ist das Heil" sets forth these principles far more directly and learnedly. But both cantatas utilize overall tonal designs that involve modulation in the flat direction and back for the purpose of mirroring the underlying shape of descent–ascent or destruction followed by restoration. And both cantatas feature a chronological or "historical" dimension in that the narratives encompassed in their movement sequences move forward in time through the Old and New Testament eras to the present time of the contemporary believer and his hopes for salvation. These two aspects of the works—the one centered on an affective "dynamic" within the believer and the other on an external or objective historical narrative—constitute a basic means by which many Bach cantatas represent the believer's internalizing the content of scriptural history. Not all Bach cantatas are as patterned in this respect as "Es ist das Heil" and the "Actus Tragicus," of course; nevertheless, they often present their theological content in ways that reveal dependence on the thought patterns of traditional hermeneutics. Owing to Lutheranism's great emphasis on scripture, those patterns were deeply ingrained in many aspects of the religious life. In fact, certain prominent features of Bach's cantata cycles might even have been conceived so as to embody such principles directly. Many of the cantatas of the 1723–24 cycle, for example, begin with biblical mottoes or otherwise feature such mottoes prominently. As their designs unfold, the means by which the mottoes are drawn into the faith experience of the contemporary believer often involve interpretive processes analogous to those of traditional hermeneutics—Old Testament/New Testament parallels and juxtapositions, literal and figurative, or "objective" and "subjective" levels of meaning, points of insight and transformation, and the like—and many such processes have distinct counterparts in Bach's music. These works take the word of God as their starting point and the internal understanding of that word as their basic theological goal.[18] In the chorale cantatas God's word is mediated by the traditional hymns of the Lutheran church, but the interpretative intent is no less prominent, as we saw in "Es ist das Heil."

Aspects of the Liturgical Year

Bach's projecting the idea of unified annual cycles in many of the cantatas of his first two years in Leipzig—even though he was unable to realize his intentions fully in that respect (as also in the case of his other annual cycle, the *Orgelbüchlein*)—attests to the fact that the liturgical year itself was a form of theological expression on the largest scale, one that had evolved over many centuries before it attained the form that it had in the late Middle Ages. Beginning at the darkest time of the year, the liturgical year aligns the coming of God's light into the world (the incarnation) with the turning of the sun at the winter solstice (Christmas), the coming of that light to the Gentiles with the New Year (Epiphany), the Passion and resurrection of Christ with the spring equinox and the coming of the Holy Spirit, and the revelation of the Trinity with the summer solstice.[19] Encompassing and regulating the smaller cycles of the day, the week, and the season, the liturgical year itself symbolized the vastly larger time spans that corresponded to the eras of salvation history. Its alignment with the civil and geophysical years encouraged the perception of order, recurrence, and confidence in the renewal of God's promises and blessings to humanity, expressions of which tended to emerge on those feast days that clustered around the turning points of Advent (the liturgical year), Christmas (the geophysical year), and Epiphany (the civil year).

In addition to the hermeneutic principles just outlined, therefore, the liturgical year provides one of the principal contexts for our understanding of the Bach cantatas. And the placing of cantatas within the liturgical year often, as we will see, had great influence on how their texts were constructed. Themes such as destruction/restoration and the dialectic of God's wrath and His mercy were, like the concept of salvation history and the metaphor of light and darkness, so central to the thought patterns of the Christian church from antiquity that they not only recur frequently in individual cantatas but also condition the character of the liturgical year at many points. Since the liturgical year was centered on the regular reading of scripture, its seasonal unfolding and especially its most prominent turning points exhibit parallels of various kinds with the principles that underlay the ordering, understanding, and interpretation of the sacred texts. From its beginnings at Advent to its closing at the end of the Trinity season, the liturgical year exhibits both a chronological dimension that closely parallels the eras of salvation history and what we might call a dynamic character that emerges with particular force at the principal climaxes and turning points (Advent/Christmas, Good Friday/Easter, Pentecost/Trinity). On the largest scale, the liturgical year divides basically into two "halves," of which the first is the so-called Proprium Temporale or "proper of the time" (of Christ), which summarizes the principal stages of Jesus' life and work in a series of changing seasons that extend from the anticipation of His birth (Advent) to His death, resurrection and postresurrection appearances, and the coming of the Holy Spirit (Good Friday, Easter, Pentecost). In the Lutheran liturgy Trinity Sunday ends this sequence, celebrating the completed revelation of God's triune nature and serving as a kind of symbolic "doxology" to the first half of the year. In a very broad sense, the dynamic of the Temporale can be described as a pattern of descent (extending from the incarnation to Jesus' death and burial) followed by ascent (Jesus' resurrection and ascension), after which the coming of the Holy Spirit at Pentecost, traditionally viewed as the "birthday of the church," describes another symbolic incarnation, or descent, that returns the liturgical focus of the year to the perspective of the church on earth.[20]

After Pentecost and Trinity the second half of the year is taken up entirely with the series of Sundays in (or after) Trinity, which may, exceptionally, extend to as many as twenty-seven and which can be considered to represent the era of the church, in contrast to the era of Jesus that precedes it. Since it does not follow a chronological sequence ordered according to the principal events in Jesus' life, the Trinity season as a whole takes up a wide range of themes, many of which center on Christian life, on the believer's fear of judgment, on the antithesis of present life and eternity, and on faith and the necessity of undergoing tribulation in the world in preparation for the second coming and the Last Judgment. The character of the season, therefore, centers on questions of doctrine and faith in a varied mix, a significant number of the weekly Gospel readings featuring parables and miracle stories that invite metaphoric interpretations of the world as a "hospital" for the spiritually sick, a "desert" in which the spiritually hungry are in need of manna, a testing ground for love and mercy toward one's neighbor, and the like. In short, the Trinity season seems to explore the human condition, its weakness, wavering, sinfulness, and mortality, emphasizing these qualities so as to demonstrate the need for both fear of God's judgment and trust in His mercy.

Since the Trinity season centers on the concerns of Christian life, in the ordering of Lutheran chorale collections according to the liturgical year, the catechism chorales, which represented a basic expression of the core doctrines of the faith, were often associated with the early weeks of the Trinity season. Lucas Osiander's *Fünfftzig Geistliche Lieder und Psalmen* of 1586, for example, begins with chorales for Advent and Christmas (nos. 1–9), followed by chorales for Easter (nos. 10–13), Ascension Day (no. 14), Pentecost (nos. 15–16), and Trinity Sunday (nos. 17–18), then uses a chorale for the feast day of John the Baptist (June 24) as a pivot to the sacrament of Baptism (no. 19), which then becomes the beginning of a catechism sequence (nos. 20–24 comprise chorales on the Nicene Creed, the Lord's Prayer, the Ten Commandments, and the communion, respectively). In this ordering the first half of the year limits the chronological summary of the life of Christ to the three principal feast days of the liturgy, Christmas (with Advent), Easter (with Ascension Day), and Pentecost (with Trinity Sunday), while the second half associates the early Trinity season with the basic doctrines of the church.[21]

In Bach's work this quality can be seen most clearly in the *Orgelbüchlein*, which was planned as a large collection of organ chorale preludes for the entire year. The *Orgelbüchlein* is a compendium, so to speak, of well-known chorales for virtually every feast day, beginning with Advent and progressing through to the end of the Trinity season, with the usual selection of miscellaneous chorales at the end. Directly following the chorales for Trinity Sunday, Bach places settings (or blank pages intended for settings) of the catechism chorales, beginning with "Dies sind die heil'-gen zehn Gebot" and two other chorales on the Ten Commandments, then "Wir glauben all' an einen Gott" (the Creed), "Vater unser im Himmelreich" (the Lord's Prayer), "Christ, unser Herr, zum Jordan kam" (Baptism), "Aus tiefer Noth schrei' ich zu dir," and several other penitential chorales and, finally, "Durch Adams Fall," "Es ist das Heil," "Jesus Christus, unser Heiland, der von uns den Zorn Gottes wand," and a group of other chorales on the communion and justification.[22] The close relationship of this succession to the six catechism chorales of *Clavierübung*, Part 3, is unmistakable ("Dies sind die heil'gen zehn Gebot," "Wir glauben all' an einen Gott," "Vater unser im Himmelreich," "Christ, unser Herr, zum Jordan kam," "Aus tiefer Not," and "Jesus Christus, unser Heiland"). The latter collection is limited to twenty-one chorale preludes grouped into two basic subdivisions within a set of twenty-seven pieces. The first nine pieces (after the introductory organ prelude) comprise two sets of three chorale preludes on the Trinity (Kyrie, "Gott Vater in Ewigkeit," "Christe, aller Welt Trost," and Kyrie, "Gott heiliger Geist," each in *stile antico* and *stile moderno* settings) followed by three settings of the Gloria "Allein Gott in der Höh' sei Ehr." This part of the collection thus articulates the Trinititarian nature of God. The second subdivision then sets Luther's six chorales on the catechism, each in a long and a short setting, beginning with "Dies sind die heil'gen zehn Gebot." Bach's intention, perhaps, was to overlap the ordering of the traditional Missa Brevis (Kyrie and Gloria) with the ending of the first half of the liturgical year (Trinity) and the catechism with the beginning of the second half. According to this view, the chorale sequence in *Clavierübung*, Part 3, centers on the shift between the time of Christ and the time of the church. Another, older, chorale collection that is set up in similar fashion is that which has been published as *The Neumeister Collection of Chorale Preludes from the Bach Circle*.[23] In that collection, which follows the ordering of the liturgical year, we find, at the point corresponding to Trinity Sunday, a grouping of three verses of "O Herr Gott Vater in Ewigkeit" (by Johann Michael Bach), whose second verse is headed "Christe" and its third "O Gott heiliger Geist." After this grouping, which resembles Bach's three Trinitarian settings of "Allein Gott in der Höh' sei Ehr" in *Clavierübung*, Part 3, follow other settings associated with Trinity Sunday ("Vater unser im Himmelreich," "Der du bist drei in Einigkeit," and two settings of "Allein Gott in der Höh' sei Ehr"). Then, after a setting of "Mag ich

Unglück nicht widerstehen" (trust in God), follow settings of the catechism chorales "Dies sind die heil'gen zehn Gebot," "Wir glauben all' an einen Gott," and "Aus tiefer Not schrei' ich zu dir." From this standpoint the beginning of the Trinity season in Bach's chorale cantata cycle can be said to exhibit a residue of such ordering principles in that it favors chorales on the sacraments. The third cantata of the cycle, Cantata 7, "Christ, unser Herr, zum Jordan kam," for the feast of John the Baptist, centers, of course, on Baptism, while the second and fourth are based on penitential chorales (Cantata 2, "Ach Gott, vom Himmel sieh' darein," on the second Sunday after Trinity, and Cantata 135, "Ach Herr, mich armen Sünder," on the third) and the seventh, Cantata 9, "Es ist das Heil," for the sixth Sunday after Trinity, on justification (often associated with the Lord's Supper).[24]

As it continues, the Trinity season is characterized by themes that involve antithesis, of which the most prominent are God's judgment versus His mercy and the qualities of tribulation versus consolation, fear versus hope, and faith versus doubt in the believer's conscience. A running theme is the believer's rejection of the world versus his anticipation of eternity. Those themes come ever more sharply into focus during the eschatologically oriented last weeks of the season as the believer's longing to leave the world intensifies and his thoughts turn upward again: the sixteenth Sunday after Trinity focuses on death and resurrection, the twentieth on anticipation of the Kingdom of God, the twenty-fourth on the fleeting character of human life and the fear of eternity, the twenty-fifth on the second coming of Christ and the end of the world, the twenty-sixth on the Last Judgment and the coming of a "new heaven and new earth," and the twenty-seventh on preparation for the final consummation. In those final weeks there are basically two views of eternity and the end of the world, the one centered on fearful visions of the Last Judgment (the twenty-second, twenty-fifth, and twenty-sixth Sundays after Trinity) and the other on the picture of eternity as a heavenly banquet (the twentieth and twenty-seventh Sundays after Trinity). Although the ending of the Trinity season anticipates the end of the world and the onset of eternity, it nevertheless merges into Advent and the beginning of the liturgical year over again with anticipation of the birth of Christ, which was traditionally viewed as a turning point, marking a new era in the history of salvation. Ultimately, God's response to the many cries for help throughout the season is the incarnation of Christ and the turning of the liturgical year from darkness to light at Christmas (as expressed in the analogy of the turn to longer days at the winter solstice).

Thus, the liturgical year constitutes a huge cycle that encompasses references to the time of Israel awaiting the coming of the Messiah (Advent), the time of Christ (the Temporale), the time of the church (the Trinity season), and the anticipation of eternity (the final weeks of the Trinity season). Hence the appropriateness of the very similar sequence of stages in Cantata 61 as an introduction to the year as a whole. Since Advent dealt traditionally with Jesus' coming in the flesh (past), in the spirit (present), and in judgment at the end of time (future), it is at this time of the year that the overlap of historical eras that is associated with the different senses of hermeneutics is most marked. At Advent and Christmas, therefore, the fulfillment of Old Testament prophecy in the events of the New Testament merged with tropological and eschatological perspectives on those events to articulate the bond between past, present, and future in the experience of the believer.

The qualities just described can be clearly seen in the cantatas that Bach produced for the period that encompassed the turning of the liturgical, geophysical, and civil years. In 1723, for example, the change from the last weeks of Trinity to Advent involved a series of cantatas in which fears of eternity, death, and judgment give way to hope and *Trost*. This is especially apparent in the last three Trinity cantatas, in which various forms of *Anfang/Ende* (beginning/ending) symbolism figure prominently. That symbolism links the turning of the liturgical year to the distant past (usually represented by an Old Testament viewpoint) and the future as embodied in the believer's fear of judgment and hopes for eternal life. Thus, "O Ewigkeit, du Donnerwort" (O Eternity, thou word of thunder, BWV 60), for the twenty-fourth Sunday after Trinity, is a dialogue between "Fear" and "Hope," in which Hope finally overcomes Fear. At the outset the chorale verse sung by the alto (Fear) depicts eternity as a beginning without end ("O Anfang sonder Ende") while the figure of Hope (tenor) awaits God's salvation—"Herr, ich warte auf dein Heil" (Lord, I await Thy salvation: Genesis 49:18)—in a reference to Jacob's last words to his sons before his death, his announcement of what would befall them in the "last days" (Genesis 49:1), now, metaphorically, the last weeks of the liturgical year. The counterpart of Jacob's "testament" is the comforting words from Revelation (14:13)—"Selig sind die Toten, die in dem Herren sterben, von nun an" (Blessed are the dead who die in the Lord, from henceforth)—which Bach assigns to the figure of Jesus instead of Hope in the final dialogue, thereby confirming the onset of a new era ("von nun an"). This symbolic progression from the first to the last book of the Bible prepares for the eschatological final chorale, "Es ist genung," which represents in a single setting the transformation from fear of death to the anticipation of a blessed death.[25] On the following week, "Es reiffet euch ein schrecklich Ende" (A terrifying end is prepared for you: BWV 90) centers on the opposition between warnings of God's judgment, graphically represented in the two arias, and God's protection of the elect, which comes to the fore in the final recitative and chorale. Thus, the "schrecklich Ende" that is prepared for the sinner stands in opposition to the proclamation that God's blessings are renewed from day to day—"Des Höchsten Güte wird von Tag zu Tag neu"—which sounds like a comforting response to the fearful "Anfang sonder Ende" of Cantata 60.

Finally, for the twenty-sixth and last Sunday after Trinity, 1723, Bach reworked a Weimar cantata he had originally written for the second Sunday in Advent, 1716, "Wachet! betet! betet! wachet!" (BWV 70a/70), in which the juxtaposition of God's judgment and His mercy in terms of the sinful and the elect is even more prominent. Since the second Sunday in Advent was traditionally occupied with Jesus' second coming, as judge of the world, it overlapped closely with the end of the Trinity season, rendering Bach's recasting "Wachet! betet!" for the Sunday *before* rather than *after* Advent Sunday a relatively straightforward matter. Bach expanded it from a one-part cantata in six movements to two parts that comprise eleven movements.[26] In the Weimar version a chorus and chorale in C frame a series of four arias in a, e, G, and C. For the Leipzig version Bach retained the basic sequence of keys; but in dividing the work between the E minor and G major arias, in adding three recitatives and a concluding G major chorale to the first part and a fourth recitative to the second part, he created not only a more imposing work with which to end the liturgical year but also one in which the juxtaposition of the damned and the elect dramatizes and intensifies the themes of destruction and restoration, fear and hope, that run throughout the late Trinity season.

Once again, ending and beginning imagery is very prominent, the former associated with fear and the latter with hope. The opening chorus, in C, urges readiness for the coming end of the world—"Wachet! betet! betet! wachet! Seid bereit allezeit, bis der Herr der Herrlichkeit dieser Welt ein Ende machet" (Watch! pray! pray! watch! Be prepared at all times, until the Lord of Lords makes an end of this world)—after which the first recitative sets God's judgment of the "verstöckten Sünder" against the "Anfang wahrer Freude" that He shows to the "erwählte Gotteskinder." The first aria, in a, then compares the believer's oppressed state of mind to that of Israel in Egypt, likening the world to Sodom before the destruction and urging the faithful to awaken to the reality of the coming end: "Wenn kömmt der Tag, an dem wir ziehen aus dem Ägypten dieser Welt? Ach! laßt uns bald aus Sodom fliehen, eh uns das Feuer überfällt! Wacht, Seelen, auf von Sicherheit, und glaubt, es ist die letzte Zeit!" (When will the day come on which we will depart from the Egypt of this world? Ah! let us flee at once from Sodom before the fire comes upon us! Awaken, souls, from your security, and believe that it is the end of time!) From this point on the movement sequence represents an increasingly positive series of affections that culminate in the chorale ending part 1. The second recitative/aria pair, in E minor, describes the conflict of flesh and spirit that surrounds the believer in the world, anticipating Jesus' second coming and announcing that His word will continue even after the destruction of the world. Next, the G major recitative envisions God's protection of the elect and His restoration of them to a "himmlisch Eden." And, finally, the concluding chorale, "Freu' dich sehr, o meine Seele," also in G, voices pure joy in the believer's anticipation of the afterlife, its triple meter and very secure tonal design seeming to affirm the certainty of his salvation.[27]

The sequence of movements just described represents a progression that begins with images of destruction in the past (the Old Testament narratives of Israel in Egypt and the destruction of Sodom and Gomorrah), moves through expressions of the believer's conflict in the present (centered on the New Testament text "the spirit is willing, but the flesh is weak," cited near the close of the second recitative) and his trust in God's word, and ends with his anticipating the joy of eternity in the future. The sequence is, of course, indebted to the pattern of traditional hermeneutics, and its character is that of the replacing of fear by hope. After the very positive ending of part 1, the G major aria "Hebt euer Haupt empor und seid getrost, ihr Frommen" (Lift your heads up high and be comforted, ye pious), begins part 2 by reaffirming the believer's hopes for eternal life; the line "ihr sollt in Eden grünen, Gott ewiglich zu dienen" (you shall flourish in Eden, eternally to serve God) refers back to the G major ending of the last recitative in part 1: "Indem er sie in seiner Hand bewahrt und in ein himmlisch Eden setzet" (while He protects you in His hand and places you in a heavenly Eden). Eden, then, is a metaphor for the believer's restoration and reconciliation with God in eternity. Drawing its principal melodic line from the melody of the chorale "Was frag' ich nach der Welt," this aria centers its optimistic outlook on eternity. The accompanied recitative and aria that follow, both in C, then return to the theme with which the cantata began, the coming end of the world, treating that theme in terms of the antithesis between the destruction itself and the believer's hopes for salvation. The recitative, for bass, trumpet, and strings, introduces the eschatological chorale "Es ist gewißlich an der Zeit" in the trumpet, while the voice and other instruments take up the contrast between God's wrath and His mercy. The aria projects the antithesis of destruction and restoration by means of a tripartite design featuring *adagio* outer sections that express the believer's hopes for salvation and a *presto* representation of destruction in the middle section. And the final chorale, again in C, places the believer's longing for "Jesus and His light" above that for heaven and earth, proclaiming that Jesus has reconciled the believer to God and freed him from judgment.

In summary, then, "Wachet! betet! betet! wachet!" presents the theme of destruction and restoration in terms of the antithesis of God's judgment and His mercy, the former associated with the end of the world and the latter with the second coming of Jesus the redeemer, bringing light to the world, freeing the believer from God's judgment (Egypt, Sodom), and restoring the faithful to the new "Eden." In part 1 Bach represents the believer's progression from the "Ägypten dieser Welt" to the "himmlisch Eden" with the aid of the tonal motion from a to G, which culminates in the believer's joyful anticipation of eternal life. In the work as a whole, however, this progression is enclosed within a quasi-symmetrical C major framework centered on the antithesis of destruction and restoration. In "Wachet! betet!" the literal, or descriptive, aspect of the idea of destruction figures much more prominently than in other cantatas, in which the idea of spiritual destruction is closely associated with tribulation and suffering rather than with apocalyptic visions of the end (as in Cantata 21, to be taken up in the following chapter). Nevertheless, the idea of a progression from the sphere of worldly torment (Egypt) to that of joy (Eden) emerges unmistakably in the Leipzig version of the work.

For the beginning of the new liturgical year, one week later, with "Nun komm, der Heiden Heiland," Bach once again represented a progression that culminated in the believer's anticipation of eternity, and this time Bach drew closer parallels among the eras of salvation history, the "senses" of hermeneutics, and the inner experience of the believer (see note 9). The latter work not only represents the progression through the separate eras and tropological stages in an ordered sequence but also draws upon the same four keys as "Wachet! betet!"—a, C, e, and G—aligning them in a rising-third pattern that, in contrast to the distinct sense of symmetry and closure in "Wachet! betet!," seems to represent an upward, tonally "open" progression from the physical advent of Jesus to His coming at the end of time. In both cantatas the tonal motion from a to G represents a form of spiritual "ascent." But the "open" tonal design of Cantata 61 seems to mirror the idea of a new beginning, whereas the "closed" design of Cantata 70 reflects its ending the liturgical year.

In "Wachet! betet!" the A minor aria "Wenn kömmt der Tag, an dem wir ziehen aus dem Ägypten dieser Welt?" alludes to a "day" that will put an end to the "letzte Zeit" of worldly tribulation. In this respect it echoes the opening recitative, which speaks of a "day" that is immanent and that will witness both God's judgment of the sinful and the "Anfang wahrer Freude" that He will provide for the elect. The G major ending of part 1 anticipates the "Freude" in question, even though the cantata ends in C. In the final recitative of part 2 the believer cries out again, now for the "seligster Erquickungstag" that will lead him forth to the awaited fulfillment. In the present life Jesus provides a "light of consolation" that enables the believer to view the end of life with joy, awaiting the time when Jesus will provide the light of fulfillment (the final chorale). In the following week "Nun komm, der Heiden Heiland" announces the coming of Jesus' light in terms of His blessing the church with the onset of a "new year": the first recitative ends, "Du kömmst und läßt dein Licht mit vollem Segen scheinen" (You come and let your light shine with full blessing), and the aria that follows begins, "Komm, Jesu, komm zu deiner Kirche und gib ein selig neues Jahr" (Come, Jesu, come to Your church and give us a blessed new year). These metaphors, derived in an immediate sense from the Epistle for Advent Sunday (Romans 13:11–14: an exhortation to the community to "awake out of sleep, for now is our salvation nearer than we believed [v. 11]. The night is far spent, the day is at hand: let us therefore cast off the works of darkness, and let us put on the armor of light" [v. 12]) would, of course, have been understood by anyone in Bach's congregation as means by which the liturgical year, closely aligned with the geophysical and civil years, reenacted the meaning of past events, such as the captivity and exodus of Israel, as God's leading forth the faithful from the darkness of the world to the light of eternity (the new Eden or the promised land).

The particular "day" when the light would appear was, of course, Christmas Day, closely aligned since ancient times with the winter solstice. And Bach's 1723 cantata for Christmas Day, "Christen, ätzet diesen Tag" (Christians, etch this day: BWV 63), responds to the "coming" that is anticipated in Cantatas 70 and 61 by emphasizing Christmas Day as the long-awaited time of fulfillment.[28] "Christen, ätzet diesen Tag," also written in Weimar, once again describes the theme of Israel's release from captivity as a figure of Jesus' birth and the release of humanity from sin and death. And it uses the metaphor of an inscription that commemorates a great event (in this case the incarnation) to bring out the idea of the *present* as the pivot between the past and future ages, a theme that Bach then turns into the idea of musical structure as metaphor for the idea of the monument on which the inscription is engraved.[29] "Christen, ätzet diesen Tag" is symmetrically organized, to an even greater extent than Cantata 70; and, like Cantata 70, its C major outer movements frame pivotal movements (arias) in a and G. Between them a tenor recitative describes Christmas Day as the turning point from the suffering with which Israel was tormented and burdened to pure salvation and grace, the latter brought about by the "lion from David's stem," whose "bow" and "sword" restore humanity to its former freedom (i.e., before the fall, the "himmlisch Eden" of "Wachet! betet!"). Thus, in three successive Weimar cantatas associated with the turning of the liturgical year 1723 Bach utilized tonal motion from a to G in conjunction with "the world" and the anticipation of eternity (Cantata 70), Jesus' coming in the flesh and at the end of time (Cantata 61), and the fulfillment of God's promise to Israel (Cantata 63). In viewing Jesus' birth as the fulfillment of Old Testament prophecy regarding the Savior of Israel, "Christen, ätzet diesen Tag" interprets the turning of the geophysical year as a mirroring in microcosm of the turning of the ages, just as in juxtaposing the fearful end of the world to the joyful new beginning, "Wachet! betet!" mirrors its position at the end of the liturgical year. The *Anfang/Ende* symbolism would then reappear in association with the turning of the civil year on New Year's Day in the aria "Jesus soll mein alles sein, Jesus soll mein Anfang bleiben, . . . Jesus macht mein Ende gut" (Jesus shall be everything to me, Jesus shall remain my beginning, . . . Jesus makes my end good), where it is oriented directly toward the believer's eschatological hopes.[30] And on the following day (January 2, 1724) Cantata 153, for the Sunday after the New Year, interpreted the flight of the Holy Family to Egypt (New Testament) as a reenactment of the captivity of Israel in Egypt (Old Testament), a figure of the believer's spiritual tribulation in the present (the "Ägypten dieser Welt" of "Wachet! betet!"), and an anticipation of his release from the world in the future.[31] In this way the entire season from late Trinity through the New Year drew on a community of ideas that reflected the ways in which hermeneutics interpreted the antitheses of scripture in terms of the believer's inner experience of salvation history (i.e., the analogy of faith).

What, I hope, this all-too-brief summary of the turning of the year in 1723–24 makes clear is that Bach's cantatas often bring out cyclic elements within the seasons of the liturgical year, mirroring its parallels and antitheses in a variety of ways that may differ from work to work and year to year, but that will usually be clearly discernible in their texts, movement layouts, key sequences, and the like. Cantatas 70, 61, and 63 were all written in Weimar, but in different years and order from their grouping in the Leipzig cycle of 1723–24. Whether or not Bach might have planned to form a cycle from his Weimar cantatas even while he was composing them is unknown, but such a plan would be in character. Certainly, in putting together his first Leipzig cycle Bach drew many of his Weimar cantatas into coherent sequences that, as we have seen with Cantatas 70, 61, and 63, aid in articulating large-scale cyclic elements in the liturgical year as a whole.

Thus, one of the most common themes of the late-Trinity, Advent, and Christmas seasons was the metaphoric interpretation of the turning of the liturgical, geophysical, and civil years in terms of the turning point of history and of faith that came with the incarnation of Jesus. Any one of several feast days—the twenty-sixth Sunday after Trinity, Advent Sunday, the three days of Christmas, the Sunday after Christmas, New Year's Day, the Sunday after New Year's Day, and Epiphany Sunday—might take up this theme, modifying it according to the more particular character of the feast day in question. In general, the idea of "time" is very prominent in the cantata texts written for those feasts, where it is often expressed in terms of the eras of salvation history and the internalizing of that history in the faith experience of the believer. And in turn, Bach's cantatas for those feast days often derive their overall designs from the underlying metaphor of the old year as the time of Israel and the new as the time of Christ, utilizing in some cases chorales that change their mode or time signature, juxtaposing archaic and modern styles, and the like. Cantata 61 undoubtedly provides the clearest, most patterned instance of how the four senses of scripture can be aligned with past, present, and future times as well as with the inner dynamic of faith, a process in which the coming of Jesus to the world, the church, and the believer takes place at several levels. But, in fact, we find similar sets of ideas underlying many other cantatas as well. Thus, while "Christen, ätzet diesen Tag" utilizes its symmetrical design to emphasize the meaning of Christmas Day as the turning of the ages, Cantata 121, "Christum wir sollen loben schon," for the second day of Christmas on the following year, draws, as we will see (chapter 5), an implied analogy between the unfathomable mystery of the incarnation and the turning of the sun at the winter solstice, and Cantata 64, "Sehet, welch eine Liebe," for the third day of Christmas, 1723, emphasizes instead something closer to the division into worlds "above" and "below" rather than present and future, a theme that is more in keeping with its Johannine Gospel reading. Cantata 28, "Gottlob! Nun geht das Jahr zu Ende," for the Sunday after Christmas, 1725, juxtaposes modern and archaic styles in order to project the idea of looking backward to God's past blessings and forward to the hope of their renewal simultaneously. Most of Bach's cantatas for New Year's Day tend to express the idea of beginning/ending equivalence in association with the name Jesus, whereas those for the first Sunday in the new year associate the New Testament narrative of the flight of the holy family to Egypt with the Old Testament story of the captivity of Israel in Egypt in order to underscore the central theme of the believer's longing for release from the world. All these works are very carefully designed so as to mirror the temporal levels of their texts in musical terms.

In the case of the *Christmas Oratorio* the idea of a cycle of six cantatas performed on the most prominent feast days of the season led Bach to articulate the division between the old and new years as one with analogies to the division between the literal (narrative) and spiritual (interpretative) senses of hermeneutics. The first three cantatas of the cycle take up the Gospel narrative of the birth of Christ, thereby emphasizing the literal-historical sense. Their key sequence—D–G–D—associates the subdominant region of the *ambitus* with the human sphere, the second cantata utilizing high and low pitch spheres to differentiate the response of the shepherds from the message of the angels and modulating to *its* subdominant as it brings out the humble circumstances of Jesus' birth (the "finstre Stall"). The third cantata, "Herrscher des Himmels," then returns to D, moving to the dominant as it articulates the meaning of Jesus' birth for the salvation of humanity: "Herr, dein Mitleid, dein Erbarmen tröstet uns uns macht uns frei" (Lord, Your compassion, Your mercy comfort us and make us free). The fourth cantata, for New Year's Day, then abandons the narrative of the circumcision in the Gospel for the day, in order to center on the name of Jesus, introducing a shift in tone in the *Christmas Oratorio* that is analogous to the shift from the literal to the spiritual sense of hermeneutics. That cantata, in fact, leaves room, as do other Bach cantatas for New Year's Day, for an expression of how the believer's internalizing the meaning of the incarnation affects his understanding of death. The idea of beginning/ending equivalence emerges in terms of how the new relationship with God that was inaugurated by the birth of Jesus transforms the believer's understanding of last things, especially his own death. The shift in the tonality of this cantata (F) away from the "tonic" key, D, of the cycle as a whole enables the movement in question, an "echo" aria, to introduce a juxtaposition of the dominant minor and major keys (c–C) at the point where this theme appears, one of the pivotal moments of the oratorio as a whole in terms of its internal aspect (the echo representing Jesus as a comforting presence within the heart, answering the believer's fears and uncertainties). In this context the key of F seems to represent the believer's personal response to the incarnation as the key to the new year. The Epiphany cantata that constitutes the fifth movement of the cycle then affirms the return to D by means of its dominant, A, developing the metaphor of Jesus as "light," after which the D major sixth cantata takes up the interpretation of Jesus as *Christus victor*, defeating the forces of evil and restoring humanity to God's grace.

In articulating the latter theme at its close the *Christmas Oratorio* expresses the dominant viewpoint on the atonement for the principal feast days of the Temporale. The characters of the two halves of the liturgical year are thus very different from each other, the climactic feast days of the Temporale centering on the principal events of the atonement—the incarnation, death, and resurrection of Christ—and the series of Sundays in the Trinity season taking up the concerns of the believer in the world, all of which rotate around the conflict between faith and "the world." The Temporale is, of course, the oldest part of the liturgy, Easter and the so-called "great fifty days" between Easter and Pentecost having been established in early Christian times as the original liturgical cycle, with the cycle of Christmas and Epiphany following not long afterward. Trinity and the Trinity season, on the other hand, emerged only in the later Middle Ages. As a result the different characters of the two halves of the year reflect to a considerable extent the two contrasted views of the atonement that dominated, respectively, the period of the early church and the Greek Fathers and the era of the Latin scholastic writers from the eleventh century on. As theologian Gustav Aulén set them forth more than sixty years ago, the former view of the atonement, in Aulén's terms the "classic" view, depicted Jesus' work as the defeat of the forces of evil—sin, death, and the devil—the triumphant work of God in reconciling the world to Himself through the incarnation, death, and resurrection of Jesus, Who is depicted as the *Christus victor*.[32] Aulén's second, or "Latin," view of the atonement, on the other hand, was closely identified with the satisfaction theory as set forth by Anselm of Canterbury, the dominant vision of the late Middle Ages. Luther, in Aulén's view (which has been substantially criticized), revived the "classic" view, which was the true core of his theology, while retaining the terminology of the satisfaction theory as a conventional survival that no longer expressed the content of that theory itself. Other authors, however, have taken the position that, as Paul Althaus puts it, "Luther combines the classical and the Latin concepts—to use Aulén's terms—but in such a way that he decisively follows the Latin line."[33] Aulén recognized, however, as have all other writers on the two views of the atonement, that the theological outlook of the period of Lutheran orthodoxy (and even of Luther's own contemporaries) was essentially that of the satisfaction theory, in which the human element, especially penitence, came decidedly to the fore. There is no dispute, therefore, concerning its prominence in Bach's time. What is very interesting, however, is that *both* views of the atonement coexisted in Bach's work, as is easily seen from the utterly different settings of the two surviving passions. The *St. John Passion* clearly articulates the idea of the Passion as Jesus' victory over the forces of evil, whereas the *St. Matthew Passion* centers on the satisfaction theory as it was understood in Bach's time.[34] In addition, Bach's oratorios and cantatas for the principal feast days of the Temporale articulate the "classic" view, while a large number of Trinity cantatas take up the satisfaction theory in relation to the recurrent theme of God's judgment and mercy.[35]

In the foregoing discussions I have attempted to show that the manifold forms of the Bach cantatas demand that we recognize their derivation from specific extramusical contexts such as the underlying principles of scripture interpretation and the liturgical year. Themes, modulatory sequences, key relationships among movements, and even relationships among individual Bach cantatas can all be shown to exhibit patterns, such as that of descent followed by ascent, that are shared by numerous aspects of human life. In a considerable number of cantatas and cantata movements, such as the design of Cantata 61, those patterns reflect principles established for many centuries in Christian thought with particular clarity. Extending those principles to works in which the patterns are less straightforward involves leaps of imagination, to be sure, but nothing that strains our understanding of the principles themselves.

TWO

The Lutheran "Metaphysical" Tradition in Music and Music Theory

NOT ONLY DO WE ENCOUNTER THE principles described in the preceding chapter in seventeenth- and eighteenth-century Lutheran theological writings, such as the aforementioned Neumeister treatise, but they also figure prominently in the writings of certain Lutheran music theorists. In fact, many such writers articulated a vision of the meaning of music that might reasonably be called the Lutheran "metaphysical" tradition in music theory, in that they perceived an alliance between music and theology that was rooted in Luther's own views on music, especially his placing music "next to theology."[1] From there it was no great leap to found an extensive "allegorical" conception of music on the idea that the major triad constituted a mirroring of the Trinity in nature (three notes, one chord). The involvement of such writings with the idea of musical "allegory" as both a mirror of God's design and purpose in the creation—that is, an embedded feature of music reflecting eternal (Lutheran) truths—as well as with a more pragmatic and arbitrary process, involved in musical composition, provided composers of church music with a theological basis and sense of purpose for the coordination of heterogenous musical styles.

Among those theorists who might be identified with the tradition just described none was more committed to a conception of music that united practical, allegorical and theological emphases than Andreas Werckmeister, organist at Halberstadt and himself a Lutheran pastor. Werckmeister's writings range from treatises on highly speculative aspects of music, such as the *Musicae mathematicae hodegus curiosus* (1686) and *Musicalische Paradoxal-Discourse* (1707), to a detailed study of musical temperament (the *Musicalische Temperatur* of 1691) and a manual for the testing of organ construction and design (the *Erweiterte und verbesserte Orgel-Probe* of 1698). Even in the more pragmatically oriented of his works, however, the speculative theological approach is never far from the center of his interests. And Werckmeister clearly viewed this aspect of music in analogy with hermeneutics. The *Mu-*

sicae mathematicae, a classic statement on music's divine origin and its reflections of that origin, contains a detailed appendix, titled "Anhang von der allegorischen und moralischen Music," in which Werckmeister sets forth numerous allegorical interpretations of the harmonic series (and, occasionally, other elements of music). The words "allegorischen" and "moralischen" refer, of course, to the second and third of the traditional four senses of hermeneutics as described in the motto heading chapter 1. Werckmeister's last treatise, *Musicalische Paradoxal-Discourse*, returns directly to this theme, proclaiming that such knowledge serves the modern practice of music in its purpose of honoring God as well as stimulating "mathematical, historical and allegorical reflection" in those who "love God and church music."[2]

Like many others in the Lutheran "metaphysical" tradition, Werckmeister clung to the scriptural pronouncement that the universe was created by God "according to number, weight and measure," holding that the numerical proportions that underlay the primary musical consonances, the so-called "harmonic" numbers, reflected God's work and nature. Not only was the unison an image of God Himself and the major triad (the *trias harmonicas*) an image of the Trinity, but even the proportions of constructions in the Old Testament, such as Solomon's temple and Noah's ark, and the lengths of time of the various biblical eras were all based on the same numerical ratios as the musical consonances. They therefore represented hidden reflections of God in history, prefigurings of the New Testament revelation. Within this scheme the concept of "salvation history" had a place that related to music, in that the harmonic music of the Christian church represented a basic part of God's revelation of His nature and the work of salvation accomplished through Christ. Through music one could confirm the content of scripture, in both its "hidden" and its directly revealed aspects. The major and minor triads represented the divine and the human, respectively, while the minor third within the major triad represented the humanity of Jesus. Although such allegories were rooted in the harmonic numbers and the basic consonances, even musical features such as temperament, chromatic and enharmonic styles, and the like were subject to allegorical explication. In general, their "meaning" was derived from the fact that the numerical ratios involved stood a great distance from the Pythagorean harmonic numbers. Thus, in the *Musicae mathematicae* Werckmeister proclaimed musical temperament a mirroring of the necessity of mortality, an idea that he followed up in the twenty-fifth chapter of the *Musicalische Paradoxal-Discourse*, "Wie die *Temperatur* vollkommen, und unvollkommen sey, und mit dem Christenthum könne verglichen werden." Since the harmonic numbers and the musical consonances to which they corresponded represented the sphere of God, which was one of perfection, the impossibility of a pure and perfect temperament became an allegory of the unavoidable imperfection of human life, while the diatonic scale of the clarino octave on the trumpet was, in Werckmeister's words, a "mirror and prefiguration of eternal life," which is certainly the association it has in many Bach movements (such as the "Et expecto resurrectionem mortuorum, et vitam venturi saeculi" of the *Mass in B Minor* and the final chorus of "Ich hatte viel Bekümmernis," to be taken up in the following chapter). In this way basic Lutheran ideas, such as the theology of the cross, the opposition of Law and Gospel, and the disparity between God and humanity, could be related directly to music, with number as their mediating element.

Throughout his work Werckmeister affirms, directly or indirectly, the intimate connection between this kind of musical allegory and biblical hermeneutics, founding that relationship on scriptural authority as well as Luther's view of music. At the same time, such allegorical explication was, of course, a manifestation of the Baroque dictum that music be representational, that *Oratio* or word (understood in the broadest sense to encompass verbal-logical procedures) take precedence over *harmonia*, as Monteverdi had expressed it.[3] In the seventeenth century the allegorizing of the harmonic triad as an emblem of the Trinity in nature reflects the fact that the triad had, since around 1600, been recognized as an entity that could be indicated in the shorthand of figured bass notation. But the triad had, of course, expressed a major part of the goal of music in the fifteenth and sixteenth centuries; and the many tuning systems that emerged during that era represented, in a global sense, the search for absolute purity—just intonation as an ideal that could never be attained. The central style of the sixteenth century had founded its conception of consonance and dissonance on the so-called harmonic numbers; purity of intonation, the purging of dissonance from counterpoint and of chromatic accidentals from the notation, went hand in hand with the ideal of a continuous triadic sonority to project the kind of union of *sensus* and *ratio* that was achieved in painting through perspective, in which the numerical proportions went hand in hand with the "natural" way of seeing things. The culture and art of the fifteenth and sixteenth centuries are permeated by such ideals, which we recognize in the musical attributes of *harmonia* and the *ars perfecta*.

With the seventeenth century we encounter for the first time in music history an age that preserved the style of the preceding era as a historical phenomenon, the *stile antico* or *prima pratica*. And the very fact of its preservation, thereby introducing a fundamental bifurcation of the language and perception of music, is itself, as Manfred Bukofzer set forth so eloquently, a primary characteristic of the music we call Baroque.[4] The new music of the seventeenth century recognizes in countless ways that the old ideal of perfection has become historical, a lost paradise as it were. An inevitable result of the new focus on affect or *Gemütsbewegung* was a tacit acknowledgment that imperfection was embedded in the very nature of music. And that change in outlook inevitably raised the question of whether *sensus* or *ratio* should have priority in deciding matters such as consonance and dissonance. For Werckmeister and most of his generation the means by which the musical consonances were verified was number, or *ratio*, not the ear, or *sensus*, while for the next generation, that of Mattheson and Heinichen, the reverse was true, an expression of the eventual victory of the empiricist enterprise of the seventeenth and eighteenth centuries. This difference in outlook, however, is less important than the existence of the debate itself, which is symptomatic of a vast array of questions that attest to the emergence of the new rationalism after around 1600. From the beginning of the "Baroque" era the split between sense and intellect attests to the perception of a divided human nature. When, therefore, Werckmeister juxtaposes ideals of perfection and imperfection in the triads and in temperament, he is acknowledging the compromise on which music is founded—that music necessarily introduces imperfect intervals and dissonances because it has fallen, like humankind, from its original purity. The human condition necessitates temperament, which becomes the fundamental allegory of the separation of humanity from God. Rationalism is therefore suspect unless it remains close to the original revealed truths of scripture and their reflection in the harmonic numbers and musical consonances on which music is founded. In the Baroque era the new rationalism, which ultimately created the great systems of Enlightenment science and philosophy, can be heard everywhere throughout music in the endless subdivisions and categories that the Renaissance style had relegated to a subordinate position. In this sense, the Renaissance style can be said to have been predicated on the search for unity and wholeness, the Baroque style on the inevitability of heterogeneity.

The tradition that Werckmeister represents viewed music as a gift from God to humanity, its purpose being, as Werckmeister never tired of reiterating, the twofold one of giving honor and glory to God and of serving humanity (one's "neighbor").[5] This view, which appears in numerous German Lutheran music treatises in the seventeenth and eighteenth centuries and was cited twice in somewhat different forms by Bach himself, derived from those passages in the scriptures where Jesus had given as the summary of the Law that one love God with all one's heart and one's neighbor as oneself.[6] It therefore affirmed the bond that Luther had proclaimed between music and theology. In fact, it is a distinct possibility that Bach conceived of his first Leipzig cantata cycle, perhaps even his church music in general, in such terms. His affixing the catchphrase "to honor almighty God alone and to instruct the neighbor" on a collection of organ music organized according to the liturgical year (the *Orgelbüchlein*) suggests as much, while his signing the words "Soli Deo Gloria" (glory to God alone) and "Jesu Juva" (Jesus help) to many of his cantata manuscripts attests to the same dualism of God in His majesty and the human condition in need of aid from Jesus. That dualism, as we will see, underlies the text (and possibly also the music) of the Ten Commandments chorale, "Dies sind die heil'gen zehn Gebot," which Bach brought into association with the "great" commandment to love God and one's neighbor in Cantata 77. Bach's well-known statement regarding the *Endzweck* of music on his resignation from Mühlhausen likewise speaks of the "final purpose" of church music as giving glory to God, while the much-disputed term "well-regulated" (*wohlbestallte*), might be taken to suggest a purpose that is more down-to-earth, so to speak.[7]

If Bach did conceive of his cantata cycles as expressions of the Lutheran purpose of music, we might well expect him to proclaim that purpose at the time of his taking up his duties in Leipzig. And since, as is well known, Bach began his tenure as Leipzig *Thomaskantor* in the late spring of 1723, he had to begin his cantata cycles in the middle of the liturgical year—that is, with the first Sunday after Trinity rather than Advent Sunday. In other words, the two halves of the liturgical year—the Temporale and the Trinity season—were reversed in Bach's cycles. And while it is distinctly possible, likely in fact, that Bach ultimately reordered his cycles so as to begin with Advent, the fact that their composition was six months out of phase affected the ways in which Bach articulated the beginning of the Trinity season. Thus, as I have pointed out elsewhere, Bach's cantatas for the first and second Sundays after Trinity in 1723 appear very much to have been intended as a musico-theological "message" for his new community.[8] For these Sundays, his first official performances in the two principal Leipzig churches, Bach created a pair of fourteen-movement works, "Die Elenden sollen essen" (Cantata 75) and "Die Himmel erzählen die Ehre Gottes" (Cantata 76), in which there is a distinct progression of ideas that culminates in the dualism of God's glory and the meaning of love for humanity.

The beginning of the Trinity season is an ideal time for such a message, since it returns the focus of the liturgical year to the time of the church and the believer's concerns over life on earth. While "Die Elenden sollen essen" deals with the antithesis between worldly tribulation and the spiritual riches, centered on love of God, that lead to eternal life, "Die Himmel erzählen die Ehre Gottes" juxtaposes the glory of God as proclaimed throughout nature (part 1) to the Christian community on earth as the "treue Schar" who proclaim and increase God's glory through faith, love, and holiness. As the heavens proclaim the glory of God in nature, the faithful represent "heaven on earth," praising the love of God by practicing love for one another until the time when the "heaven of pious souls" will proclaim the praise of God in eternity:

So soll die Christenheit	So shall we Christians
Die Liebe Gottes preisen	Praise God's love
Und sie an sich erweisen:	And prove it among ourselves:
Bis in die Ewigkeit	Until in eternity
Die Himmel frommer Seelen	The heaven of pious souls
Gott und sein Lob erzählen.	Proclaims of God and His praise.

Thus, Cantata 76 interprets "heaven" in three senses, the first purely physical, drawing on an Old Testament text, the second in terms of the church on earth, and the third eschatologically. The key to recognizing God's proclaiming His presence is hearing the voice of God in Jesus Christ, the "light of reason" (part 1), while loving and giving honor to God (part 2) involve loving one's neighbor (or one's "brother," in the Johannine language of Cantata 76). The overall progression of ideas is from the Old Testament God and the glory of God the creator to His revelation in Jesus (part 1), the community of the faithful, and the anticipation of the afterlife (part 2), the familiar sequence of traditional hermeneutics. Ultimately, the eschatological goal of Cantata 76 and many other Bach works was that of praising God in His own sphere, "Lobet Gott in seinen Reichen," as the Easter Oratorio proclaims, or "Lob, und Ehre, und Preis und Gewalt sei unserm Gott von Ewigkeit zu Ewigkeit," in the case of Cantata 21, performed on the week following Cantata 76. In such large-scale musical devices as the overall change from major to minor and from the presence of trumpet as the emblem of God's glory in part 1 to the sound of the viola da gamba in part 2 only, where it is associated with human love, Cantata 76 mirrors both its place in the liturgical year and the Lutheran view of the purpose of music.

In fact, the message of Cantata 76 is so close to the purpose of music in the Lutheran tradition that it seems appropriate to view Bach's Leipzig cantata cycles as his carrying out the kind of intention that he had placed on the title page of the *Orgelbüchlein.* After anticipating eternity and the "Himmel frommer Seelen" in its penultimate movement, Cantata 76 ends with a statement regarding life on earth, thus returning the perspective of the work to that of the community carrying out God's work in good deeds of brotherly love. Other cantatas, however, such as "Ich hatte viel Bekümmernis" (Cantata 21, performed, as I mentioned, on the following week), point upward, ending with the anticipation of eternity. And this contrast in the endings of the two cantatas can itself be considered a reflection of the dualism of God and the neighbor (humanity). On the week following the performance of "Ich hatte viel Bekümmernis" Bach reperformed another Weimar cantata, "Barmherziges Herze der ewigen Liebe" (BWV 185), that named love of God and one's neighbor as the "Christen Kunst" and that remained wholly within the human perspective. The dominance of minor keys in Cantata 185 is very telling in this respect, while the lone major-key aria owes its hopeful tone to the fact that its text deals with the believer's reward in eternity for works of love in the present. The cantata that provides us with the clearest statement regarding love of God and love of one's neighbor, however, is the one that I have chosen for close study at the end of this book, Cantata 77, "Du sollt Gott, deinen Herren, lieben," for the thirteenth Sunday after Trinity, 1723. That work, as we will see, follows a broad tonal outline that is opposite in one important respect to that of Cantata 21: not only does it change from major to minor—undoubtedly as a means of representing the shift from God to humanity (the neighbor)—but it also has a form of "incomplete" ending that suggests ideas regarding the dualisms of perfect/imperfect, complete/incomplete, divine/human, and above/below that Werckmeister incorporated into his vision of a musical hermeneutics centered on the major and minor triads.

It seems, therefore, that the Lutheran vision of the dual purpose of music defined important characteristics of music itself, especially those that relate to music's dualistic aspects (major and minor keys, strict and free styles, high- and low-pitch spectra, and the like) and the theological dualisms—such as God and the neighbor and Law and Gospel—that were perceived as relating to them. And Bach, as I have pointed out elsewhere, proclaimed his adherence to its basic precepts in a number of allegorical canons whose inscriptions and musical techniques represent aspects of Bach's style in microcosm, as it were.[9] Those canons, several of which utilize titles that Bach may have derived from Werckmeister (or even from Luther via Werckmeister), cover a spectrum of tonal devices and styles: the triad ("Trias harmonica"), the diatonic key and the principle of solmization ("Mi/Fa et Fa/Mi est tota Musica"), modulation ("In fine videbitur cujus toni. *Symbolum.* Omnia tunc bona, clausula quando bona est"), chromaticism ("*Symbolum.* Christus Coronabit Crucigeros"), and the circle of minor keys ("Canon a 2. Per tonos").[10] One even refers to the process of interpretation itself: "Quaerendo invenietis" (He who seeks will find). In the music of these canons the principle of antithesis—major versus minor, inversion (ascent versus descent), chromaticism versus diatonicism, and the like—reigns supreme, while the inscriptions draw connections between the musical devices Bach employs and the kinds of theological ideas with which they are often associated, both in the Lutheran metaphysical tradition and throughout Bach's cantata oeuvre. In particular, the two canons that Bach headed with the word "Symbolum" refer to central Lutheran ideas, the theology of the cross and the importance of dying a blessed death—that is, in faith.

Although certain musical dualisms, such as that of major and minor, were widely perceived to mirror the spheres of God and humankind and countless compositions were conceived in such terms, no such blanket antitheses could ever account for the complexity of music. And, in fact, the associational qualities of major and minor triads and keys in the seventeenth and early eighteenth centuries were viewed in more complex terms than the simplistic happy/sad dualism to which they are often reduced. Behind the German terms for major and minor (*dur* and *moll*), which were widely adopted only during this time period, lay the ancient terms *durus* (hard) and *mollis* (soft), which had described a much broader set of meanings throughout the Middle Ages and Renaissance.[11] Of these, the one that remained alive into Bach's time was that of the medieval-Renaissance hexachords or transposition scales, which determined the system of solmization by means of which many generations of musicians conceived of the tonal aspects of music. And in that system the qualities of "hardness" and "softness" that the terms evoke were not primarily aligned with major and minor modes, but with relatively sharp and flat tonal regions. As a result, in the early seventeenth century the associations we think of most readily for the major and minor modes were often reversed: those madrigals from his fifth and sixth books in which Monteverdi shifts between the *cantus mollis* and *cantus durus* treat the latter pejoratively in relation to the former, even though there is a pronounced sense of minor–major shift.[12]

Although the modern major/minor paradigm had come into existence long before Bach's time, residues of the older hexachordal model persisted into the eighteenth century and provide us with clues to Bach's treatment of the major and minor modes. Bach's early cantata "Gott ist mein König" (BWV 71), for example, ends with successive movements in C major, C minor, and C major again, the first of these, an alto aria, beginning and ending with the words "Durch mächtige Kraft," which Bach sets in C, accompanied by trumpets and drums in military style and with a thematic connection to the theme of the C major opening chorus, "Gott ist mein König." Cantata 70 is built around the antitheses of God's power and human weakness, on the one hand, and the change from youth to old age as the principal manifestation of human weakness, on the other. When, therefore, the penultimate movement turns to c and changes its instrumentation from trumpets and drums to strings and woodwinds, including the unique sonority of a pair of recorders with a chordal cello obbligato, we have no difficulty in understanding the text of this movement—"Du wollest dem Feinde nicht geben die Seele deiner Turteltauben" (Psalms 74:19: O deliver not the soul of thy turtledove unto the multitude of the wicked)—as a representation of human weakness, a plea for God to protect the faithful. Bach emphasizes a rising and falling semitone idea throughout the movement that derives, as he reveals at the end, from an archaic-sounding chant line. When the chant line finally emerges, reiterating the tone c' fourteen times in syllabic style in all four vocal parts before rising to d♭', then circling above and below the final c' we hear the C major chord begin to sound like the dominant of f. And when the final movement begins, in a triadic C major that eventually reintroduces the trumpets and drums, we may well hear the words with which it begins, "Das neue Regiment," not principally as articulating a minor–major shift (which has been undercut by the ending of the preceding movement), but as restoring C major after the "weakening" effect of the ending of the preceding movement. In other words, Bach has composed out a *mollis–durus* shift that is broader in scope than the minor–major shift to which later tonal theory would reduce the key juxtaposition. In association with the text, that shift aids in conveying ideas of weakness versus strength, archaic versus modern styles, human versus divine attributes, and the like.

In fact, even the new tonal paradigm, the circle of major and minor keys, retained at first clear lines of descent from the older hexachord theory.[13] And from that standpoint both wide-ranging modulation and a spectrum of keys that formed a closed circle were sufficiently unfamiliar to many musicians to elicit pejorative associations from time to time. Thus, despite its forward-looking aspects, Bach's *Well-tempered Clavier* can be considered a response to the fact that when the circle of keys and the tuning that made it possible were in their relative infancy (around 1700) certain keys were considered "difficult," not only because they might not be perfectly tuned but also because key relationships and modulatory principles were often not well understood. Werckmeister addressed this question in many of his writings, describing the new pitch system as a labyrinth into and out of which very few could find their way. Johann Caspar Ferdinand Fischer's *Ariadne musicae*, an earlier set of keyboard fugues that limited itself to only nineteen of the twenty-four major and minor keys, invokes this association. As a metaphor for the complexity that accompanied the new tonal topography, the labyrinth also characterized the distance separating human life and its need for tonal imperfection and compromise from the divine sphere of the old harmonic numbers. In composing "allegorical" canons, as much as in harmonizing modal chorale melodies, Bach stood with his feet in two worlds, a quality that is by no means unique to him but is certainly more intensely projected by him than is true of any other composer of his time. On the one hand, he carried the implications of the musical circle to their logical point of completion, developing in the process a harmonic style that was capable of the utmost refinement in expressive modulatory devices that depended on the musical circle; on the other hand, he adhered to principles that were centuries old, bringing them to new life within the broad tonal palette of his time. Along with those principles went a host of metaphoric viewpoints on tonality and a range of procedures that link Bach with the traditions of literally centuries earlier, among which none was more compelling than those that had been embodied in the terms *durus* and *mollis*. In certain of Bach's compositions the ancient meanings are reanimated in ways that attest to a very rare ability to think the elements of music through in terms of their historical content. As we will see, the Lutheran chorale repertoire was of enormous stimulation to him in this regard.

For those not accustomed to thinking of music in terms of its allegorico-theological dimensions, interpretations that depend on such archaic associations —which were never, of course, introduced solely for designative purposes (i.e., without regard for their musical logic)—may well appear arbitrary, read into the work rather than inherent in it or representing any form of demonstrable intent of the composer's. It is certainly true that we can never hope to have a direct verbal statement from Bach himself on such a question; and the extent to which we may draw upon the writings of his immediate predecessors is, of course, open to responsible questioning. Nevertheless, there is no dearth of writings by seventeenth- and eighteenth-century Lutheran music theorists that resonate particularly strongly with Bach's work in any number of ways. Among those authors I have singled out Andreas Werckmeister and Bach's predecessor in Leipzig, Johann Kuhnau, elsewhere, because these two men stood out for their skill in writing on the "allegorical" aspects of music, their involvement with both theory and practice, and, above all, the many demonstrable affinities in both those areas with Bach's work. Of the two, Kuhnau speaks more directly on the question of musical allegory in composition, including a series of remarks on the introduction *by the composer* of various tonal aspects of music, including modulation, for what we would call "allegorical" purposes. Since both Kuhnau and Werckmeister made explicit connections between musical allegory and biblical hermeneutics, we are virtually compelled to recognize that at the very least an intellectual climate that was conducive to the musical allegorizing of theological subjects obtained in Bach's world. And, given Bach's often very intensive developing of music's many inherited features, it would be most unusual for him to have produced upward of two hundred church cantatas without employing the kinds of musical allegory described by Werckmeister and Kuhnau. In fact, parallels to their writings can easily be found throughout Bach's oeuvre. And they generally reveal the depth and intricacy we are accustomed to find in his treatment of other traditional aspects of music. That Bach's work has very much the aspect of transforming tradition means that the "historical" sources we draw upon to illuminate his work will inevitably seem very modest in scope, in comparison with even the historical aspects of that work. What may well sound naive or simplistic in Baroque writings on musical allegory emerges in Bach's compositions as what Theodor W. Adorno called "allegorical expression heightened to the utmost"—that is, a highly intensified version of the dialectic of music's archaic, traditional, even conventional aspects and the unique complexity and expressivity of Bach's modern harmonic-contrapuntal language.[14]

On the question of the sharp (*durus*) and flat (*mollis*) modulatory directions, for example, we may observe that Werckmeister, in his last treatise, the *Musicalische Paradoxal-Discourse* of 1707, sets forth four examples of triadic progression by thirds, describing the sharpward motion as an ascending progression and the flat motion as a descending one.[15] And it is clear that Werckmeister is speaking of *tonal* ascent and descent progressions, for the melodic direction in two of his examples descends when he speaks of the ascending progression and vice versa. The two aspects (melodic and tonal motion) will often go hand in hand, of course, especially if the composer desires to project the idea of ascent or descent as an allegorical device. Thus, in his modulating canon from the *Musical Offering* Bach combines sharpward motion through the minor circle of keys with ascent in pitch, introducing both to illustrate the allegorical heading "as the modulation ascends so may the glory of the king." Likewise, the treatise that Bach used to teach his pupils the thoroughbass rules, and from which he borrowed the catchphrase regarding the purpose of music I cited earlier, Friedrich Erhardt Niedt's *Musicalische Handleitung*, part 1, gives as basic schemes of modulation two examples that pass through "circles" of keys or cadences by thirds, the first one following the pattern C, a, F, d, B♭ (b if the piece is major), G, e, and C and the second the pattern C, e, G, b, d, F, a, and C; the editors of the English translation describe these, logically, as "descending" and "ascending" patterns.[16] At the close of the section Niedt adds: "All of this is useful as well, when one piece is finished and the next one is to be begun right away in another key," a remark that suggests that the patterning of harmonic sequences and keys within individual movements holds for movement sequences as well. Although Heinichen's discussion of the patterning of key relationships in his *musicalischer Circul* rejects the simple one by thirds that Niedt describes, his rejection clearly implies that the pattern of tonal motion by thirds was well established. And there is a sense in Bach's work that patterns of "ascent" and "descent" by thirds and fifths are basic, almost archetypical ones that operate not only at the level of chord progressions and the brief sequential patterns that extend such progressions (such as those in Niedt's examples) but also to the patterning of movement keys as well.[17]

My purpose in citing such instances of the ways in which tonal qualities were traditionally perceived is not at all to argue that such qualities constitute inevitable truths regarding the Western tonal system or even its seventeenth- and eighteenth-century manifestations (even though Werckmeister described the examples just cited in exactly those terms: "wie sie von Natur auff einander folgen"), but, rather, to suggest that many of the ways in which Baroque theorists and composers conceived and described tonality (i.e., mode, modulation, harmonic progressions, and the like) were inherited from much older theory still—basically, in fact, the modal and hexachordal theory of the Middle Ages and Renaissance. For us, therefore, many of those archaic means of understanding tonality have value not for their serving those of our analytical needs that derive from the idea of autonomous or "absolute" musical art, but for their pointing to the allegorical aspect of the composer's intention in any given work. The two perspectives will often, but not always, coincide.

Some of the clearest and best-known statements on the principles of "tonal allegory" in the seventeenth and eighteenth centuries come, of course, from Johann Kuhnau, Bach's predecessor as Leipzig *Thomaskantor*.[18] In the preface to his collection of programmatic keyboard sonatas, the *Biblische Historien* of 1700, Kuhnau is careful to distinguish between the erroneous belief of some musicians that individual modes can be assigned specific fixed associations and his own view that differences in modal types and structures (*Systema*)—that is, the relative placement of tones and semitones—and even transpositions of the modes produce differences in their effects.[19] The major and minor modal types, for example, "are particularly different in that the former possess something perfect and cheerful, while the others represent sadness and melancholy and, because of the lack of about a half comma or some other little fraction, longing." Kuhnau also distinguishes between musical representation that is immediately recognizable because the sound of the music resembles the sound that is imitated (e.g., birdcalls and nature sounds generally) and representation that "aims at an analogy" with what is being represented. The latter category involves a comparison "in *aliquo tertio*"; in other words, the representation and what is represented are related through some third thing to which they both relate—that is, an intellectual mediation or abstraction. Of this latter kind of representation Kuhnau offers many examples, a significant number of which involve modulatory tonal devices. Thus, Kuhnau speaks of his representing King Saul's "violent paroxysm of madness with fifths following closely on one another, likewise his great melancholy and pensiveness through the apparent exceeding of the mode in the theme," and of his depicting Jacob, "the bridegroom, in love, contented but at the same time fearing a misfortune, by means of a graceful melody with several somewhat foreign tones and cadences mixed in." Likewise, Laban's deceit gave rise to a deception of the ear ("Verführung des Gehörs") that involves unexpected progression from one mode into another, while Gideon's doubt inspired Kuhnau to introduce "several subjects here and there that always begin a second higher, according to the manner of unsure singers, who seek their notes in such an uncertain manner."

Kuhnau makes clear that only through analogy (*Argumentum Similitudinis*) can such devices make their effect. And such "argument" demands a "good interpretation" (*Interpretation*). For just as verbal texts occasionally need a good explication (*Auslegung*, the word commonly used for scriptural exegesis), so the musician may be excused for "clarifying the dark concept he represents to others with the aid of words." The example Kuhnau offers of the latter kind of representation is, perhaps, the most interesting in his preface. Kuhnau speaks of his having heard a program sonata titled *La Medica*, in which, after representing the lamenting of the patient and his relatives as well as their application to the doctor for help in their distress, "there finally came a *Gique* under which appeared the following words: The patient is getting on well but has not yet fully recovered." Kuhnau opposes those who scoffed at such an interpretative nicety as an incomplete recovery, maintaining that the tonal character of the final movement of the sonata had indeed represented its subject accurately: "The sonata was in *d-minor*, but in the *Gique* one could always hear modulations toward *g-minor*. When at last the final [cadence] went back to *d* the ear did not derive satisfaction from it but would rather have heard it in *g*."[20] In other words, Kuhnau describes the subtle device of "weaking" the tonic key at the final cadence by means of prior emphasis on the subdominant, exactly the quality that, as we will see, obtains in certain of Bach's modal chorale harmonizations.

Kuhnau now wraps up his discussion with a statement that indicates his basic position on musical representation in general: "Now in conclusion, concerning the affections of sorrow and joy, it is easy to represent them through music, and words are not necessary for this unless one wishes to suggest a particular person, as was the case in my sonatas, so that, for example, the lament of the sad *Hezekiah* may not be taken for that of a weeping *Peter*, a lamenting *Jeremiah*, or some other afflicted person."[21] With this last remark Kuhnau asserts that musical qualities are analogous not to the particular content of the biblical stories but to what we might call their dynamic affective qualities. Taken in light of his earlier remark that the composer's clarifying his "dark concept" with the use of words was analogous to the exegesis of verbal texts and the fact that Kuhnau almost always explicates the content of his stories in a fashion that speaks to the experience of the contemporary listener, his biblical "histories" can be understood as specific versions of music's more general capacity to mirror human emotion. This quality is analogous to the interpreter's relating particular scriptural passages whose literal meanings are entirely different from one another to the spiritual experience of the believer by means of their sharing the underlying descent/ascent dynamic of the analogy of faith.

About a decade later Kuhnau gave his perspective on how the composer might set one such text by analogy to biblical hermeneutics. In the preface to his cycle of cantatas, written for Leipzig in 1709–10, Kuhnau proclaimed that understanding the principles of hermeneutics was necessary for the composer of church music, describing the following devices, all in the setting of the first two verses of the first psalm: repetition of the word "dem" (in the words "wohl dem" or "blessed is he") in "unexpected keys, which bring the hearers to attention," taking the word "waldelt" (wanders) figuratively to refer to the "twisted circumlocutions" of the ungodly, then setting it with many passages that "wander outside the scale," setting the word "Rath" (council) in "remote and unforeseen keys" ("since a council often comes to an unpredictable decision"), moving away from the right key and "erring" into foreign tonalities for the word "Sünder." Kuhnau's terms clearly describe modulatory devices. The single sentence "Blessed is the man that walketh not in the counsel of the ungodly nor standeth in the way of sinners" exhibits four such devices in addition to others described by Kuhnau that do not involve tonal allegory. Finally, as I have discussed elsewhere, Kuhnau describes what was undoubtedly a larger scale of tonal allegory, his setting the words "sondern hat Lust zum Gesetz des Herrn," which represent a sudden shift of tone between the first and second verses of the psalm, in a "completely different key, with mi transformed into fa, or fa into mi."[22] In this document Kuhnau distinguishes between the *sensus figuratus* and the *sensus proprius* of the text, as well as differentiating the *sensus*, *scopus*, and *pondus* as interpretive objectives. Comparison of multiple translations of the Bible prompts the composer to recognition of the varied levels of meaning in the text, stimulating his imagination. If musical allegory is to be thought of as the extending of figurative devices to a sequence, analogous to the idea of "extended metaphor" in literary allegory, then Kuhnau's remarks indicate just that for the tonal aspects of his setting of the first psalm.

Perhaps the closest of Bach's works to Kuhnau's *Biblische Historien* is his early *Capriccio on the Departure of His Beloved Brother*, a program sonata with titles that represent principally the various affections associated with a trip and the response of friends to the departure. Bach might, in fact, have modeled his work on Kuhnau's, as has often been supposed. The allegorical dimension of the sonata involves more than tonality, of course; nevertheless, the tonal dimension is conspicuous and easily related to the program headings of the movements. In the first movement Bach perhaps intended to represent the "Schmeichelung der Freunde" (coaxing of the friends) as they attempt to dissuade his brother from departing by means of both the ornamental style of the melody and the very secure B♭ tonal design (which does not "wander" or make any significant departures from the original key—other than to cadence in the dominant at about the midpoint of the movement). In contrast, the second movement, a "representation of various events (*Casuum*) that might befall him in foreign parts," takes the words "in der Fremde" figuratively to set up a series of modulations that extend the initial d/g fifth relationship of its fugue theme into progressively flatter regions (as far as B♭ minor) (Ex. 2.1). Bach wrote this movement as a fugue whose theme falls a sixth from its initial pitch, then ascends by step without really creating the sense of a return to the starting pitch. The answering entries are a fifth *lower*, not higher, and they pass through the voices from top to bottom in turn (soprano, alto, tenor, and bass). As a result this five-measure unit shifts from its initial g to the subdominant, c (with *Tierce de Picarde*). At this point Bach transposes the set of entries down a tone, so as to interpret the c–C as the dominant of f and to lead the sequence of four entries down to b♭. Again he transposes the pattern down a tone, but this time the tonality leads to E♭ *major* instead of minor. The overall pitch and modulatory scheme of the twelve entries of the theme, however, is always

Example 2.1. *Capriccio on the Departure of His Beloved Brother*, second movement

downward by fifths: d–g and g–c within the first set, c–f and f–b♭ within the second, B♭–E♭ and E♭–A♭ in the third. After the twelfth entry, on e♭ in the bass, cadences on A♭, Bach introduces a final set of three—beginning on c' in the alto, f in the tenor, and B♭ in the bass (the last one incomplete), leading the final measures of the movement to a close on the dominant of f. In this movement the ornamental character of the theme and the four-part polyphony combine with the shifting modulatory character to suggest the possibility that Bach's brother will get lost in foreign parts. In this context the "falling" modulations (not only in terms of fifth levels but also in terms of pitch, since from the first to the last entry the starting pitch of the theme drops over two octaves from d" in the soprano to B♭ in the bass) illustrate the word *Casuum* of the programmatic heading ("Ist eine Vorstellung unterschiedlicher *Casuum*, die ihm in der Fremde könnte verfallen"), which means both "falling" and "accident"; the verb *verfallen* likewise expresses this idea. Bach therefore seems to make a clear association between the increasing flat accidentals, the falling pitch levels, and the increasing flattening of the harmony.

The C ending of this movement (with *Tierce de Picardie*) then serves to set up the key (f) of the next movement, an *adagissimo* ground-bass movement, titled "Ist ein allgemeines Lamento der Freunde." The protracted appoggiatura-laden descending lines of the melody, the chromaticism, and the key (all widely associated with lamenting movements, such as the opening chorus of Cantata 12, "Weinen, Klagen, Sorgen, Zagen," and the F minor Sinfonia for harpsichord) can be considered to represent this movement as the "nadir," so to speak, of a tonal descent/ascent design for the sonata as a whole (Ex. 2.2). Within the fourth movement—"Now the friends come up and take their departure, since they now see that it cannot be otherwise"—Bach leads the tonality progressively from the "deep" flat region to F *major* (Ex. 2.3); and with the return of B♭ in the next two movements the "drama" of dissuasion, lamentation, and acceptance yields to "objective" representation of the post horn and the coach's departure in an aria and fugue, both of which are conspicuously free of the modulatory devices of the preceding movements. Written within a very few years after the publication of Kuhnau's *Biblische Historien*, Bach's *Capriccio* recalls a number of Kuhnau's works, both in style and in its programmatic intent. Its tone, however, is tongue-in-cheek, as the title *Capriccio* was perhaps meant to convey. In this respect its allegorical dimension is all the more suggestive that Bach could expect its "message" to be understood. There is, in fact, a strong affinity between the tonal design of this work and that of the "Actus Tragicus," which is Bach's own version of a "biblical history." This sonata represents, in fact, a tonal allegory of the type that can be found in many Bach cantatas, what I have called "descent/ascent" cantatas, in which the modulatory design mirrors theological ideas such as the opposition of Law and Gospel.

Whether accurately or not, the modulatory devices in the second movement of Bach's *Capriccio* have occasionally been interpreted as introducing the howling "wolves" of mean-tone temperament, so that Bach's brother might not only get lost but also be threatened by a more permanent form of "departure." In other words, the modulatory design could be taken as to represent the inevitability of worldly tribulation, as Werckmeister had described the necessity of temperament. In this light, we may note that another piece of highly modulatory character, the *Kleines*

Example 2.2. *Capriccio on the Departure of His Beloved Brother*, third movement, mm. 1–17, 41–49

harmonisches Labyrinth (BWV 591) for organ (which may not be a work of Bach's), utilizes the extraordinary modulatory style and contrapuntal complexity of its fugal middle section to represent the kind of "allegory" Bach intended in the second movement of the *Capriccio*. Werckmeister and others associated the idea of the musical "labyrinth" with extravagant modulatory and contrapuntal devices (*Harmonologia Musica*, pp. 44, 119). As I have argued elsewhere, many of Bach's canons have this "allegorical" character, which is often associated with tonal devices of the kind Werckmeister described in his treatises. I have also suggested a conceptual connection between Kuhnau's idea of "deceiving" the ear and similar ideas of Bach's.[23] It is well known that the key sequences and titles of certain of Bach's keyboard collections resemble those of Kuhnau. It is not necessary, of course, to con-

Example 2.3. *Capriccio on the Departure of His Beloved Brother*, fourth movement

clude that Bach held the same views on musical allegory as Kuhnau or Werckmeister, but that Bach knew such views is probably beyond dispute, and that he could evoke them, as he did so many other aspects of German Baroque music, seems a very safe bet.

Rather than discuss Kuhnau's and Werckmeister's comments on musical allegory any further, I will now cite a source of a somewhat different kind. That source, the funeral oration written by Johann Melchior Göze for Werckmeister's death in 1707, traces to a theologian rather than a practicing musician, but it clearly seems to imply some knowledge of music, especially the allegorical relationship of music and theology that Werckmeister emphasized throughout his work.[24] I am not suggesting that we use such a document literally to interpret any of Bach's works; its value is rather to illustrate and lead us into a way of thinking that was shared to a very considerable degree by Bach. And it has the virtue of compressing in a relatively circumscribed space a chain of ideas that leads from the very general pronouncements on music and religion that are found in countless Lutheran music treatises of the time to more particular associations of general relevance for the question of tonal allegory in practice.

On the third page of his oration Göze turns to the traditional subject of music as described in the scriptures, moving from there to Luther's view that music is a "noble gift of God that comes very near to theological knowledge."[25] From there the sequence of ideas leads to a statement of the purpose of music as "zu Gottes Ehre und der menschlichen Gemüther Vergnügung," which Göze affirms was exemplified in Werckmeister's work. The way in which Göze sets forth this theme is interesting. Unlike other famous musicians, Werckmeister's honoring God in music did not take the form of playing a golden or silver organ—that is, it did not strive to emulate God's glory—but rather took that of playing the "attractively built organ of our St. Martin's" (in Halberstadt) with "so many harmonies to rejoice the heart, as an artist pleasing to God lovingly sets psalms and hymns of praise."[26] Göze then cites "the famous and well-known Spaniard, Savedra," who "in his emblems represents very thoughtfully a musical instrument strung with many strings with this inscription: *Majora minoribus consonent*!" Göze comments with the couplet: "Man sehe doch hier groß und klein / will übereingestimmet seyn" (One sees even here that great and small / will be harmonized together), passing over the obvious musical interpretation of "majora minoribus" as major and minor to describe the consonant harmony in terms of the relationship of *Obrigkeit* and *Unterthanen* (authority and subjects) and then, finally, of God and humankind:

> And certainly it does not only sound well in ordinary life when government and subjects live together in a fine harmony, but also when we mortal human beings learn to adapt ourselves obediently according to the will of our God and accord with it in good patience, even though He sometimes stretches the strings a little high. The melodies of God, which he harmonizes with us, do not always proceed from the *cantus mollis* [aus einem *B molli*]. The Ionian mode, since it always proceeds only in joy and pleasure, will not always ring out; thus the Dorian mode, since the sun only shines for our pleasure, is often very belatedly tuned. Often instead the Mixolydian mode is heard, so that we must call from the depths and ask, "Has God then forgotten to show His grace and hidden His countenance in anger?" O how very often was the departed [Werckmeister] met in this way by God's will, when his dear God sometimes harmonized a song with him in the *cantus durus* [aus dem *B. duro*]. When He let his first wife and child die, when without warning He took away many valued friends in death.[27]

While we obviously would not wish to attribute to a theologian with, perhaps, no practical experience in music the depth of musical understanding demanded for an adequate assessment of the role of musical allegory in Kuhnau or Werckmeister, much less Bach, it is possible that Göze's remarks directly represent an outlook derived from Werckmeister. The sequence of associations in his oration, progressing from scriptural references to music through Luther's view of music and the orthodox Lutheran view of the purpose of music and from there to statements on musical expression and allegory, is one that we find in Werckmeister's and other music treatises of the Lutheran tradition up to Bach's time. Göze's linking the terms *durus* and *mollis* with God's wrathful and merciful sides, simplistic as it may sound in the context of twentieth-century analytical interests, was no mere rhetorical punning, but a musical association of a kind that can be found in early-seventeenth-century music, including that of Monteverdi.[28] Rooted in the hard and soft hexachords, it had an ancient pedigree that undoubtedly also underlay Luther's remarks on his choice of tones for the German Mass, the sixth (F) for the Gospel "because Christ is a friendly Lord and His sayings are dear" and the eighth (G) for the Epistle "because Paul is a serious apostle."[29] Although Bach would hardly have needed any such model for his own allegorical designs, the kind of thinking about the larger significance of music that Göze's remarks represent was certainly familiar to him and makes a fair claim to be considered a major part of his intention in such works.[30]

And those intentions are often subtler than we realize. The relationship Göze describes between God and humankind and between *Obrigkeit* and *Untertanen*, for example, is the subject matter of Bach's several cantatas for the changing of the town council, in Leipzig as well as Mühlhausen. Those cantatas, like "Gott is mein König," generally project a very festive character, primarily in association with praise and thanks to God, but also in keeping with the idea that worldly government derives its authority from God and serves, as an aria from Cantata 119, "Preise, Jerusalem, den Herrn," puts it, as God's image (*Ebenbild*) on earth. Cantata 119 is unusually festive in the styles and instrumentation of its cornerstone choruses: the opening movement is an ABA form French Overture with chorus in its fugal section and the seventh is a similarly disposed ABA choral fugue with orchestral introduction and a contrasting (texted) middle section; both movements are scored for three trumpets and kettledrums, two recorders, and three oboes, in addition to the strings, chorus, and *basso continuo.* The image of stability and majesty dominates not only these movements but also the fourth movement, a bass recitative accompanied by strings and *basso continuo* and framed by fanfares for the trumpets and kettledrums. The cantata develops the analogy between Leipzig and Jerusalem, Leipzig as the "new Zion," praising God and thanking Him for His blessings, which, as the central recitative makes clear, are transmitted through "kluge Obrigkeit und durch ihr weises Regiment"—that is, through government and the Leipzig town council. Both the bass recitative and the second of the large chorus introduce a widely used fanfare theme of the time that Bach associates in his cantatas with majesty (usually God's majesty); in Cantata 119 he introduces it in order to suggest the transmission of authority from God to His people through the duly appointed worldly government.[31] Between the C major choral "pillars" appear two recitative/aria pairs, the first in the dominant major (G) and the second in the dominant minor (g). The key of the latter may well appear surprising since its text deals with worldly authority as God's gift to His people, even the image of God Himself ("Die Obrigkeit ist Gottes Gabe, ja selber Gottes Ebenbild"). And the movement has occasionally been interpreted as satirical in tone. But, in fact, the flat minor tonality is exactly Bach's means of representing the important idea that such government is human, not divine, and our accepting and obeying it is exactly because of its sanction by God. The middle section of the aria amplifies the idea just described by turning to C minor—that is, the tonic minor of the C major of the choral "pillars"—for the line "Wer ihre Macht nicht will ermessen, der muss auch Gottes gar vergessen: wie würde sonst sein Wort erfüllt?" (Whoever will not accept its authority must also abandon God's: how otherwise would His word be fulfilled?) Behind this idea lies, of course, a very similar "tonal allegory" to the representation of Jesus' humanity in the incarnation by means of modulation to flat-minor regions. As in "Gott ist mein König," behind the turn to flat-minor keys in "Preise, Jerusalem, den Herrn" lies an acknowledgment of human weakness, even in the person of worldly authority. Bach invokes the ancient, broader meaning of the terms *durus* and *mollis* to lend the figurative aspect of his tonal design a meaning we might not otherwise suspect.

Nevertheless, Göze's remarks, which also imply a *durus* character for the Mixolydian mode, much as they may suggest something of the character of the opening chorus of Cantata 77, for example (see chapter 8), cannot be held to be in any way prescriptive for "tonal allegory." At the same time, however, knowledge of the ancient theoretical background of the hexachords suggests an association for the change from b' to b♭' in the chorale on which that movement is based, "Dies sind die heil'gen zehn Gebot," that Bach amplifies, as we will see, to a larger tonal scale that includes, but is not limited to, the modern association of *durus* and *mollis* with major and minor.[32] Göze's juxtaposition of Mixolydian and Dorian even suggests the tonal dualism in the melody of the Ten Commandments chorale (i.e., the change from G Mixolydian to G transposed Dorian; see chapter 7). Even his casual remark that God "sometimes stretches the strings a little high" can be related to the idea of the D Mixolydian version of the chorale melody in "Dies sind die heil'gen zehn Gebot" as an unattainable ideal (see chapter 8).

It would be erroneous, however, to claim that the allegorical vision of music defined by Werckmeister and others of the time completely represented Bach's intentions for the composition of church music or that Bach composed regularly according to a designative "system" that was invariable. Neither Göze's nor Werckmeister's views were intended to represent unquestioned facts; in general, the attempt to set up one-to-one correspondences between musical events and theoretical pronouncements is rightly viewed with suspicion. Also, in important ways Bach's generation turned its back on many of the more speculative aspects of music that Werckmeister represented, as the confrontation between Johann Mattheson and Johann Heinrich Buttstedt illustrates. In their public dispute over the validity of such traditional aspects of music theory as solmization and the modes, the forward-looking Mattheson certainly emerged as the victor over the conservative Buttstedt. At the same time, however, there were others, notably Johann Joseph Fux, who disagreed with Mattheson; and it would be equally if not more erroneous not to recognize that Mattheson himself stood very close to the Lutheran musical tradition. Certainly, a new skepticism was arising, one that would ultimately reject the traditional perception of music as the mirroring of God in nature just as in the field of biblical hermeneutics it would call into question the unity of scripture.[33] But for a musician of such a complex turn of mind as Bach (and not least where music and its relationship to "word" was concerned) the new pragmatism scarcely offered a worldview that was rich enough to compensate for all that was provided by the old traditions. Complexity is, in fact, a very important issue, especially in the case of Bach, who was criticized in his own time for exactly that quality. Many of Bach's early works, such as the "Actus Tragicus," have a seventeenth-century manner that may appear "simple," at least in tone. But in them we often find a complexity of allegorical design that adds dimensions to the music that are seldom, if ever, to be encountered in the works of other composers. In Bach's work the ability to revive past styles and the urge to reinvigorate and modernize went hand in hand with an "allegorical" bent that was spiritually very close to the seventeenth-century "metaphysical" tradition in music theory to generate forms that are susceptible to both historical and contemporary analytical modes.

THREE

Cantata 21, "Ich hatte viel Bekümmernis"

ONE OF THE WAYS IN WHICH MANY individual Bach cantatas mirror the pattern of traditional hermeneutics is their ending, like the liturgical year itself, with emphasis on the anticipation of eternity (i.e., the eschatological perspective). In such works eternity represents the goal of faith, the believer's overcoming all ties to the world. Since, in this perspective, "the world" constitutes the principal obstacle to faith, a common design for many cantatas is that of a progression from tribulation to *Trost*, from faith "in opposition to experience" to faith "realized in experience."[1] The Bach cantata that most exhibits this character and that can therefore be considered a quintessential representation of the inner dynamic of faith is the Weimar cantata "Ich hatte viel Bekümmernis" (BWV 21), which was performed for the first time that we know of on the third Sunday after Trinity, 1714. The opening chorus of that work, "Ich hatte viel Bekümmernis in meinem Herzen; aber deine Tröstungen erquicken meine Seele," announces the antithesis of tribulation and consolation as its central theme, drawing on a scriptural passage (Psalms 94:19: "I had much tribulation in my heart; but Your consolations revive my soul") that was associated in the period of Lutheran orthodoxy with the opposition of worldly tribulation and Jesus.[2] That opposition, as we will see, is central to the design of Bach's cantata.

"Ich hatte viel Bekümmernis" is known today in what is basically its final eleven-movement form, which was already in place in 1714 and underwent only relatively minor modifications between 1714 and its reperformance as the third cantata of Bach's first Leipzig cantata cycle of 1723–24. But the work had a history that preceded the attainment of its final form in Weimar, although the exact details of that history are unknown. The most likely, but by no means unequivocally established, core of the earlier version would have comprised the present movements 2 through 6 plus movement 9, whereas the final chorus, no. 11, presumably originated in another earlier work, and movements 1, 7, 8, and 10 were added in 1714 (the movement's final version is outlined in Table 3.1). It is highly probable that the 1714 ex-

Table 3.1. Cantata 21, "Ich hatte viel Bekümmernis." Weimar, 1714. Third Sunday after Trinity.

Movement	Genre	Instrumentation	Text incipit	Key
			Part One	
1	Sinfonia	Ob., str., b.c.	Untexted	c
2	Chorus	SATB chorus, ob., str., b.c.	Ich hatte viel Bekümmernis in meinem Herzen; aber deine Tröstungen erquicken meine Seele	c
3	Aria	Sop., ob., b.c.	Seufzer, Tränen, Kummer, Not	c
4	Recitative	Sop., b.c.	Wie hast du dich, mein Gott, in meiner Furcht und Zagen denn ganz von mir gewandt?	c–f
5	Aria	Sop., str., b.c.	Bäche von gesalz'nen Zähren	f
6	Chorus	SATB chorus, ob., str, b.c.	Was betrübst du dich, meine Seele . . . daß er meines Angesichtes Hilfe und mein Gott ist.	f–c
			Part Two	
7	Recitative dialogue	Sop., bass, str., b.c.	Soul: Ach Jesu, meine Ruh', mein Licht, wo bleibest du? Jesus: O Seele, sieh! ich bin bei dir.	E♭–B♭
8	Dialogue aria	Sop., bass, str., b.c.	Soul: Komm, mein Jesu, und erquicke Jesus: Ja, ich komme und erquicke	E♭
9	Chorus with chorale	SATB chorus	Sei nun wieder zufrieden, meine Seele/ Was helfen uns die schweren Sorgen?	g
10	Aria	Sop., b.c.	Erfreue dich, Seele, erfreue dich, Herze	F
11	Chorus	SATB chorus, tpt.1, 2, 3, timp., ob., str., b.c.	Das Lamm, das erwürget ist . . . Lob, und Ehre, und Preis und Gewalt sei unserm Gott von Ewigkeit zu Ewigkeit. Amen, alleluja!	C

pansion of the work was carried out with the aid of one or more poetic and theological sources.[3] And it is possible that a still earlier form of the work involved the three minor-key choruses with psalm texts, Nos. 2, 6, and 9, but the evidence to indicate any more than this is scanty. Although I will be discussing the work only in its final form, what we do know of its compositional history, principally the background for its text, is of considerable interest for our understanding of the theological and aesthetic character of the cantata. Rather than discuss it separately, however, I will introduce it in the context of an introduction to the overall form and theological intent of the work.

In that context, it must be observed that "Ich hatte viel Bekümmernis" is only loosely reflective of the Gospel and Epistle readings for the third Sunday after Trinity (the parables of the lost sheep and lost silver piece in Luke 15:1–10 and the advice to leave one's cares to God in 1 Peter 5:6–11). Instead, the text seems to take its primary impetus from the more general idea of "joy in heaven" over the repentance of the sinner in the excerpt from Luke as well as from Peter's hope that "in due time"

God will "exalt" the believer who has humbled himself and that "the God of all grace Who hath called us unto His eternal glory by Christ Jesus, after that ye have suffered a while, make you perfect, stablish, strengthen, settle you." These ideas and the ending verse of the Epistle "To Him be glory and dominion for ever and ever. Amen" all fit with the character of the final choral doxology of Cantata 21, which is one of the most eschatologically oriented movements in Bach's oeuvre, ending with the joyful, transformational rather than fearful vision of eternity. This emphasis, and the fact that Cantata 21 also draws a substantial part of its theological content from a parable for an entirely different Sunday (see following discussion) may explain why Bach put the designation "per ogni tempo" on the title page.[4]

The discussion of Cantata 21 that follows is based in part on my description of the work in an earlier study.[5] For the present context I will emphasize ways in which I believe Cantata 21 represents the patterns of traditional hermeneutics and the spiritual goal that those patterns were created to attain: the believer's progression from scripture, history, and the physical world to a "spiritual" view of existence centered on his hopes for a future life. As is true of the "Actus Tragicus" and many other Bach cantatas, the musico-theological design of "Ich hatte viel Bekümmernis" is rooted in the ground of pre-Enlightenment hermeneutics, the bridge between scripture and faith. The designation "per ogni tempo" should undoubtedly, therefore, be understood as an indication of the "universality" of its theological message.

Cantata 21 divides in its basic eleven-movement Weimar and Leipzig versions into two parts, the first part (nos. 1–6) using two choruses based on psalm texts as cornerstones (no. 2, following an instrumental introduction, and no. 6) and centering its affective content on tribulation, while the second part (nos. 7–11) describes a progression in the believer's understanding, urging faith, consolation, and joy and moving forward toward a choral doxology based on a text from Revelation with the character of an eschatological vision (see Table 3.1).[6] Thus, the bipartite division articulates the two views of faith alluded to above. Part 1 is entirely in minor (c and f), whereas four of the five movements of part 2 (all but no. 9, which presumably belonged to the earlier version) are in major, the key sequence as a whole outlining a progression by adjacent key-signature levels (three flats, two flats, one flat, and no flats—i.e., E♭, g, F, and C) to the concluding chorus in the tonic major.[7] In part 1 a central movement sequence that comprised a recitative surrounded by two arias represents the tortured cry to God from an individual believer in the depths of despair, forsaken but clinging to the hope that God will respond. It is surrounded in turn by the two C minor psalm choruses, which seem to "universalize" the believer's faith struggles. The character of this first division of the work, which forms, along with movement no. 9, most of the presumed core of the pre-1714 version of the work, is indebted to the tone of the most tormented of the psalms.[8] Only in the final sections of the two choruses is there any hope, as the believer, questioning his tribulation and unrest, affirms faith in God: "Ich hatte viel Bekümmernis in meinem Herzen; *aber deine Tröstungen erquicken meine Seele*" (no. 2); "Was betrübst du dich, meine Seele, und bist so unruhig in mir? Harre auf Gott, denn ich werde ihm noch danken, *daß er meines Angesichtes Hilfe und mein Gott ist*" (no. 6: "Why do you torment yourself, O my soul, and why are you so full of unrest? Seek after God, for I will give Him thanks, *for He is the help of my countenance and my God*") (italics

must note that the eschatological vision of the final chorus is also one with pronounced connections to the Passion, since its central image is of the "lamb that was slaughtered"—that is, the Jesus of the Passion—Who now resides in glory.

Cantata 21 prefigures the aspect of the final chorus just described in the duet aria of part 2 (no. 8), in which Jesus announces that the believer's salvation will come through His wounds and the "fruit of the vine" ("Hier aus dieser Wundenhöhle sollst du erben Heil durch diesen Saft der Reben"), a reference to the believer's symbolic acceptance of the meaning of the Passion through the Eucharistic wine.[16] The text of this duet, indebted to the love imagery we often associate with Pietism but which was very much a feature of Lutheran orthodoxy as well, calls for Jesus to "sweeten" the believer's soul and heart—"Ach, Jesu, durchsüße mir Seele und Herze!"—an obvious antithesis to the "salty tears" described in part 1.[17] As a result, the changing of water into wine as the "hour" in which Jesus manifested His glory was also interpreted as His coming to the believer through faith and *Trost.* The final line of the Gospel narrative, cited earlier, brings out the Johannine theme of the importance of the disciples' (and eventually others') recognition of Jesus' divinity (often associated with His "signs" or miracles) as the catalyst to faith. In John's theology, faith has a transforming quality that leads to the idea of "realized eschatology"—the sense that eternity is present now in the person of Jesus through faith. While Lutheranism views eschatology primarily as "future eschatology"—that is, as a future event —the centrality of faith, especially the aspect of faith that is "realized in experience," nevertheless partakes of that transformational quality, which is inseparable from the secure anticipation of eternity, the "certainty of salvation."[18] This quality emerges in Cantata 21 at the beginning of part 2, where Jesus' appearance to the believer through faith (nos. 7 and 8) provides the assurance of salvation.

The text of Cantata 21, therefore, views Jesus' "hour" as His coming to the believer through faith and *Trost*, through the sacrament (the Eucharistic wine as symbol of the Passion), and in glory at the end of time, a series of stages comparable to those we have found in Cantata 61. As some scholars have pointed out, such methods of text construction reflect the interpretative procedures associated with pre-Enlightenment hermeneutics and its basic premise of the unity of scripture.[19] At the same time they bring out the alignment of those senses with salvation history—that is, the eras of the Old Testament, New Testament, the church, and the contemporary believer. Works such as the "Actus Tragicus" and "Ich hatte viel Bekümmernis," therefore, endeavor to represent not just the antitheses but the bond between those eras and their corresponding textual types and theological outlooks. In the "Actus Tragicus" Bach's primary means of depicting the unity of scripture and of God's time involves a symmetrical design featuring parallels between Old and New Testament texts.[20] In Cantata 21 it involves parallels that give greater emphasis to the process of transformation. Behind the "Weinen"/"Wein" metaphor, therefore, lies not only the antithesis between the world and the spiritual life but also the unifying quality of faith; tribulation is a necessary part of the process of faith, even though it appears opposed to it. Thus, imagery involving wine in the Lutheran tradition generally involves several levels of interpretation that correspond to the senses of traditional hermeneutics. The basic meaning behind those levels is the simultaneity of worldly tribulation and the hope of eternal life, which appears in the poem carved on the so-called "Bach-Goblet" (owned by the composer) in the antithetical lines "ruffet 'Ach'" and "hofft auf Leben."[21] Likewise, in Cantata 21, the reiterated "Ach" of the part 1 recitative—"Ach! kennst du nicht dein Kind? Ach! hörst du nicht die Klagen . . . allein, mein Weh und Ach, scheint jetzt, als sei es dir ganz unbewußt" ("Ah! don't You know Your child? Ah! do You not hear the cries . . . my woe and torment appear now to be completely unknown to You")—is a symbol not only of tribulation but also of faith. After its questioning in the G minor chorale of no. 9, presumably the final movement of the "original" version of the cantata ("Was hilft uns unser Weh und Ach?"), its transformation into rejoicing in "Erfreue dich, Seele" (the "Ächzen"/"Jauchzen" juxtaposition) represents the realization of a faith that was present in part 1, but was not as yet the source of positive affections for the believer (principally love, *Trost*, and "himmlische Lust," as the middle section of "Erfreue dich, Seele" makes explicit).

From this standpoint, Cantata 21, part 1, with its virtually unchanging C minor tonality, represents the believer's long period of waiting for the manifestation of God's *Trost*, while the tonally ascending movement sequence of part 2 describes the progression from Jesus' coming to the believer in faith and the Eucharist to a vision of the "hour" when He would come in glory. The second duet refers to Jesus' wounds and the Eucharistic wine as the source of the believer's salvation, the aria "Erfreue dich, Seele" calls for the transformation of tears into wine, and the final chorus, "Das Lamm, das erwürget ist," represents the final "hour" at which Jesus manifests His glory.

In this light, the transformation that occurs in the final two movements of part 2 culminates a three-stage process that is substantially indebted to the story of the wedding at Cana and that can be considered to embody the core theological message of the work. Part 1 constitutes the first stage, in which Old Testament texts predominate and an atmosphere that centers on worldly tribulation (or "faith in opposition to experience") culminates in the extravagant water/tears imagery of "Bäche von gesalz'nen Zähren." In part 1 Bach draws on a complex of more-or-less well-known musical styles and rhetorical devices in order to represent not just the inevitability of worldly tribulation but also the sense that the crux of such torment is its relation to the individual believer's faith struggles. After the central sequence of three tortured solo movements, the voice of the psalmist returns in the final chorus to affirm the need to hold onto one's faith even in times of torment and unrest. The central recitative focuses on the believer's feelings of forsakenness, which "Bäche von gesalz'nen Zähren" extends to the metaphor of his struggling against "Sturm und Wellen," like a ship without mast or anchor in an ocean of tribulation. The beginning of the final chorus of part 1 (whose text derives from the same psalm as that of "Bäche von gesalz'nen Zähren") then marks a turning point, away from the believer's complete absorption in tribulation and toward a questioning of the meaning and value of suffering: "Was betrübst du dich, meine Seele, und bist so unruhig in mir?" The solution, given in the remainder of the chorus, is turning to God: "Harre auf Gott, denn ich werde ihm noch danken, daß er meines Angesichtes Hilfe und mein Gott ist." This point marks the end of the first stage.

Part 2 begins the second stage with two momentous changes that were apparently introduced only when the work was expanded to eleven movements in 1714:

the introduction of the first major-key movement in the cantata and the appearance of the voice of Jesus in dialogue with the soul in a duet recitative and aria pairing. The believer's faith contact with Jesus is his response to the "Harre auf Gott" at the end of part 1. After the believer cries out in darkness, "Ach Jesu, meine Ruh', mein Licht, wo bleibest du?" (Ah, Jesu, my rest, my light, where are You?), Jesus speaks directly to his soul, providing the response of *Trost* from God that was lacking in the part 1 recitative and leading the dialogue to an announcement that the eschatological "Stunde" will soon come. The duet aria that follows then takes up the Eucharistic imagery described here previously. In the choral movement that follows, the believer, represented in the psalm text of the "free" choral parts, addresses his soul directly, searching for inner peace ("Sei nun wieder zufrieden, meine Seele"), while two verses of the chorale "Wer nur den lieben Gott läßt walten" ("Was helfen uns die schweren Sorgen" and "Denk' nicht in deiner Drangsalshitze") affirm the possibility of abandoning tribulation and fixing one's hopes on eternal life. In relation to the Old Testament character of the part 1 texts and the personal encounter with Jesus at the beginning of part 2, the simultaneity of the psalm and chorale texts in this movement can be considered to represent the church's support of the believer, with the first collective voice in the cantata. This movement, perhaps the final movement of an earlier form of the cantata that was solely in minor keys, articulates a second point of culmination in the work.

After this, the believer once again addresses his soul directly, in "Erfreue dich, Seele," the only aria for voice and *basso continuo* alone, which now proclaims his abandonment of tribulation for joy and his coming to understand that God's *Trost* is manifested in Jesus' comforting him with the joyful anticipation of eternity ("himmlische Lust"). The final chorus, from the book of Revelation, then elevates that quality to the level of a collective vision of eternity, completing the f/F and c/C parallels between the endings of the two parts. Although the tears–wine metaphor is shared by Cantatas 21, 155, and 13, "Erfreue dich, Seele" renders the sense of "Verwandlung," or transformation, all the greater in that it juxtaposes words that are identical or very close in sound, whereas their meanings are opposite: "Weinen/Wein," "Ächzen/Jauchzen."[22] In the final two movements the "hour" of *Trost*, which was anticipated musically in Jesus' "Die Stunde kömmet schon" at the end of the recitative dialogue with the soul, is manifested openly.

In "Die kräfftige Erquickung unter der schweren Angst-Last," Martin Petzoldt argues convincingly for a compositional chronology of Cantata 21 in which the sequence of movements that comprised the conjectured earlier form of the work—2 through 6, plus 9, the movements that are in minor keys—was expanded in 1714 by movements 7 and 8 (both in E♭), ten (in F), and eleven (in C). The "new" movements, as I have attempted to show, would have added the entire New Testament aspect of the work and the only set of movements with major keys. And, as Petzoldt indicates, their references to poems of Paul Gerhardt and Johann Rist (and, I would argue, to the idea complex of the wedding at Cana as well) served as a support and "theological legitimation" for the overall textual plan for the work's final form.[23] Textual parallels between the newer major-key solos mirror both their chronological proximity and their theological interrelatedness. Presumably, then, the minor, Bible-texted choruses (nos. 2, 6, and 9) could have constituted the work's earliest group of movements, expanded at some later time by the addition of recitatives and arias to the sequence that comprises the present nos. 2–6 and 9, while no. 11 (the final chorus) had a separate origin, and nos. 7–8 and 10 and the introductory Sinfonia (no. 1) were the last additions to the design. The overall conception came only in 1714. Owing in part, perhaps, to the fact that Bach was dealing extensively with preexistent compositions, he now focused his attention on the overall design, introducing the very impressive tonal plan, whose progression by successive key-signature levels to the final vision of eternity (Johann Arndt's *visio beata* and *gaudium aeternum*, as described in note 6) mirrors the increasing confidence of the believer's faith and his anticipation of eternal life. In this design there remains one further question, however: namely, the very striking musical parallels between the final choruses of parts 1 and 2, in c and C, respectively. Those parallels suggest much more than a fortuitous circumstance, an accidental similarity between two separate earlier compositions, and bid fair to be considered the primary poles in the work's transformational character. While source-critical evidence offers as yet no secure answer to this situation, our understanding the musico-theological and aesthetic character of the work depends on their relationship.

The two-part design of Cantata 21, even if it was not the original conception of the work, features other parallels and oppositions between the two halves, all of which are analogous to how the conception of scriptural unity encompasses the antitheses between the Old and New Testaments. Undoubtedly, the most striking relationship of this kind is that between the two final choruses. But the two recitatives seem also to have been intended to relate to each other, in that the believer's forsaken cries to God in the part 1 recitative are answered by Jesus' comforting response to the soul in the recitative dialogue that begins part 2. The nature of these parallels is taken up later in this chapter. Note, however, that the modulatory design of the part 1 recitative leads to the F minor tonality of "Bäche von gesalz'nen Zähren" and the opening section of "Was betrübst du dich." In turning to the subdominant for the only shift away from C minor in the whole of part 1, the ending of the first recitative represents a form of tonal "descent," a "weakening" of the tonic that permits us to view the tonal design of part 1 as an instance of the type I have described elsewhere as descent followed by ascent, the tonal dynamic that Bach often associated with the idea of destruction followed by restoration. In contrast, the part 2 recitative anticipates the process of "ascent" (sharpward motion through the circle of keys) that leads to the F and C tonalities of the final two movements. The latter design is one that Bach used in works such as "Nun komm, der Heiden Heiland" (Cantata 61) and "Weinen, Klagen, Sorgen, Zagen" (Cantata 12) to represent progressions from relatively worldly or historical to spiritual or eschatologically oriented perspectives.

In bringing out the parallel between the final two movements of parts 1 and 2, the two-part division of Cantata 21 draws the return from f to c that takes place in the final chorus of part 1 into the ascending, or progressively sharpening, pattern of part 2. The advantage of viewing the key sequence in this way is that the key of f in part 1, which might be described as the "nadir" of the work, spiritually as well as tonally, initiates the process of "restoration" that culminates in the transformation at the end of part 2. In this light, the tonal design of Cantata 21 parallels the three stages described previously. The first stage ends with the return to c from its subdominant region, the second with motion to the dominant region of the c *ambitus*, and the third with the transformation to the tonic major. The affective progression articulated by these stages is closely bound up with the relationship between solo and choral movements, the former affording Bach the greatest scope to address personal, individual concerns, while the latter tend to "universalize" those concerns.

COMMENTARY ON THE INDIVIDUAL MOVEMENTS

Part 1

No. 1: Sinfonia (c)

In part 1 the instrumental Sinfonia and the first chorus serve as an introduction to the cantata as a whole. The Sinfonia, although untexted and therefore of imprecise, or generalized, rhetorical character, prepares for the very dramatic point at which the chorus enters with its threefold iteration of the word "ich" before even the principal theme enters. The latter gesture and the incessant text repetitions that Johann Mattheson pointed up in the first chorus (as well as in the third and eighth movements) introduce an obsessive quality that dominates the believer's outlook on tribulation in much of part 1.[24] In this context, the Sinfonia plays a role that we encounter in many other movements of this type throughout the Bach cantatas: that of conveying the pathos that surrounds the believer's path through life. Basically a trio-sonata adagio for oboe, strings, and *basso continuo*, featuring highly ornamented oboe and violin lines and a written-out accompanimental texture in the second violin and viola, it continually builds and resolves dissonances in an ornate but melancholy oboe/violin dialogue over a walking bass. The oboe, frequently the voice of pathetic affections in pieces of this kind, takes the lead, as it will in the first aria, "Seufzer, Tränen, Kummer, Not." It is perhaps not so surprising, therefore, that in the midst of the movement (mm. 11–12) we hear what sound like passing anticipations of the tortured melodic line of that aria. Toward the end of the movement Bach introduces a series of unexpected interruptions of the basic rhythmic motion (deceptive cadences and pauses), all of which (but especially that of mm. 15–16) delay the approach to the final cadence by irregular amounts. Just before the final measure, the oboe detaches itself from the accompanying parts, playing a brief trill, then shooting upward in a diminished-seventh-chord arpeggio, whose uppermost tone, a♮'', seems momentarily to break with the downward tendency of the many a♭''s heard throughout the movement. Perhaps Bach intended the soloistic effect to represent, like the lone soprano solo that ends the central movement complex of the "Actus Tragicus," an expression of the believer's longing for release. After this gesture, the one-measure approach to the final C minor cadence of the Sinfonia restores the predominant motion of the movement, as if to canonize the inevitability of tribulation, to which the beginning of the opening chorus then gives explicit voice (carrying forward the walking bass and dissonance–resolution patterns of the Sinfonia). The change from what is basically a chamber music style to a full chorus of unusually single-minded thematic character (at least in its principal section) dramatizes the aforementioned "universalizing" quality, while the subsequent progression through the sequence of three solo movements to the concluding C minor chorus develops its implications in terms of the first stage of the faith process described previously.

No. 2: Chorus, "Ich hatte viel Bekümmernis in meinem Herze" (c)

Even though the text repetition cited by Mattheson in "Ich hatte viel Bekümmernis" would apply equally well to many other Bach works, the fact that Mattheson chose movements from this particular cantata is nonetheless significant. In the first chorus Bach not only repeats the initial four words a second time within the theme itself but also lends them an emphatic character with tone repetitions that overlap the entrances of the theme in the various voices, thereby ensuring that the reiterations themselves (and the dissonance–resolution patterns they introduce) form part of the core meaning of the movement. Along with Bach's carrying over the walking-bass idea from the Sinfonia, these details contribute to the establishing of a framework from which the individual consciousness, obsessively projected in the many repetitions of the word "ich," cannot free itself. When, finally, Bach breaks with the first half of the text, in order to make a sudden shift of tone for "Aber [this word set apart as an adagio interruption of the cadence of the preceding section] deine Tröstungen erquicken meine Seele [now continuing vivace]," not only the new tempo but also a marked change in harmonic style and vocal texture forecast the believer's hopes from God. Bach sets up a circle-of-fifths harmonic pattern that leads after nine measures to a very optimistic E♭ cadence, preceded by three measures in which the chorus and doubling instruments move entirely in running-sixteenth-note sequences. This very palpable sense of *Erquickung* then continues for a further seven measures, during which Bach allows the circle-of-fifths harmonies to lead back to C minor (and a further set of text repetitions cited by Mattheson). Finally, Bach shifts to andante (presumably the original "walking bass" tempo of the movement) as the final measures settle on c. At the close, a sudden but brief rhythmic animation in the chorus (with a new "leaping" idea) suggests an attempt to hold onto the *Erquickung* even though the tempo and key have returned to their initial states.

No. 3: Aria "Seufzer, Tränen, Kummer, Not" (c)

In the chorus, therefore, the optimism of God's *Trost* and *Erquickung*, associated with E♭, is "contained" within the pervasive C minor framework, which continues in the aria "Seufzer, Tränen, Kummer, Not" (sighs, tears, grief, need), a veritable litany of suffering (after the four words just cited, we hear of "ängstlich's Sehnen," "Furcht und Tod," "Jammer," and "Schmerz": anxious longing, fear and death, sorrow, and pain). In this respect, "Seufzer, Tränen" resembles the opening chorus of Cantata 12, which features a similarly obsessive catalog of tribulation (and a ground-bass design to represent the sense of the unrelieved character of worldly suffering): "Weinen, Klagen, Sorgen, Zagen, Angst und Not sind der Christen Tränenbrot" (weeping, laments, cares, hesitance, anxiety and need are the Christian's bread of tears).[25] The text repetitions Mattheson cited in "Seufzer, Tränen, Kummer, Not" reflect the fact that the aria has no contrasting textual or thematic material and no real "B" section, a vital part of Bach's intention of projecting the sense of endlessly prolonged torment. Within a framework that conveys a quality of slow, inexorable motion, Bach carefully prepares his cadences, only to deflect several of them at the last moment, thereby heightening the sense of anxiety and uncertainty. Above all, however, the various fragmented melodic units of the oboe and soprano lines, with their tortured augmented and diminished intervals, suggest, like the text repetitions, an analogue of tribulation "knawing" unrelievedly on the believer's "beklemmtes Herz" (constricted heart).

No. 4: Recitative (c/f)

After this comes the only recitative in part 1, in which, as I mentioned, the believer voices feelings of isolation from and rejection by God. This movement is a perfect representation of the idea of "faith in opposition to experience." Beginning with a questioning of God, the soloist then turns to a bitter complaint, with which the movement ends. The recitative consequently divides into two "halves," each of eight measures' duration, the first of which further divides into two four-measure units ending with Phrygian cadences to A (i.e., V of d) and G (V of c), respectively, while the second moves to the subdominant, f, ending on the dominant of that key. The overall tonal direction of the recitative therefore, is, that of a progressive flattening, the final cadence setting up the F minor key of the second aria and of the beginning section of the final chorus (which also features two Phrygian cadences to C—i.e., V of f). To complete the believer's anxious questioning of God (closing the first "half" of the recitative), Bach has the first violin ascend by step from b♮' to g", while the *basso continuo* descends, also by step, from c to G: "Wie hast du dich, mein Gott, in meiner Noth, in meiner Furcht und Zagen, denn ganz von mir gewandt?" (first phrase) "Ach! kennst du nicht dein Kind? Ach! hörst du nicht die Klagen von *denen, die dir sind mit Bund und Treu verwandt?*" (second phrase; italics mine) (Why have You, my God, in my need, in my fear and hesitation, turned completely away from me? Ah! do You not know Your child? Ah! do You not hear the laments of *those who are joined to You in covenant and faith?*). The contrary-motion passage (italicized) unobtrusively conveys the above/below quality involved in the "Bund und Treu" between God and the believer for a reason that will become clear only in the lone recitative in part 2, where Bach will amplify the idea considerably. To begin the final segment of the recitative, Bach immediately turns to E♭, as the text alludes to the believer's past hopes from God: "Du warest meine Lust" (You were my joy). This, however, gives way immediately, as the soprano leaps up the minor seventh to d♭", reiterating it in a manner that is typical of the first part of Cantata 21 as a whole, before descending to the F minor cadence: "und bist mir grausam worden!" (and have become gruesome to me!). The remainder of the recitative is in f, with a substantial emphasis on its subdominant (b♭): "Ich suche dich an allen Orten, ich ruf', ich schrei' dir nach,—allein, mein Weh und Ach, scheint jetzt, als sei es dir ganz unbewusst" (I seek You in all places, I call, I cry out for You,—however, my woe and torment appear now to be completely unknown to You).

The role of such subdominant (flat) modulations in Cantata 21 (of which we will consider others in the following discussion) is typical for Bach's work as a whole. Very often they align with textual passages centering on the general qualities of human weakness that underlie the Lutheran conception of "the world" as a place of tribulation and the crisis of faith that life in the world involves. As we will see, the weakening of tonic cadences by means of emphasis on the subdominant is one of Bach's most striking and effective means of representing the human condition in need of aid from God; and Bach does not shy away from ending movements and even entire cantatas with such "weakening" effects.[26] In fact, often when the opportunity arises Bach takes advantage of the tonally "weak" character of the final cadences of particular chorales (especially those in the Phrygian mode) so as to project the disparity between the "correct" modal final and our tendency to hear it as a dominant. In the Phrygian mode this duality may be associated with rhetorical questions, since what we hear as a dominant (the questioning aspect) is nevertheless the true final of the mode (the answer), analogous to the fact that rhetorical questions are really statements in disguise. The believer's tormented questioning of God in the first recitative of Cantata 21 is, in fact, rooted in the ground of a faith whose "realization" is the principal subject matter of the work.

The ending of the central fugue-solo-chorale complex of the "Actus Tragicus" provides a perfect instance of the weakening of a final cadence in association with the believer's cry to God for aid. There the subdominant emphasis in the f–F cadence of the central movement represents the means by which the believer, in crying to God, overcomes his fear of the inevitability of death (the choral text "Es ist der alte Bund: Mensch du musst sterben" [It is the old covenant: Mankind, you must die] which stops abruptly on the dominant of f). Influenced by the subdominant harmony, however, the "weak" ending of the soprano solo, "Ja, komm, Herr Jesu, komm," encourages our hearing the final b♭'–a' semitone as tonic and leading tone in the key of the movement that follows, b♭. And that particular instance brings out the fact that Bach may use the "subdominant" quality of a movement cadence as a feature in a larger design, one that makes more extensive modulation in the flat direction for the purpose of highlighting the descent–ascent dynamic that fits particularly well with the idea of destruction followed by restoration.

No. 5: Aria, "Bäche von gesalz'nen Zähren" (f)

Paradoxically, the b♭ solo of the "Actus Tragicus" represents both the flattest region of the work (the "nadir," so to speak) and a turning point that will eventually restore the principal key of the cantata, E♭. And, also paradoxically, in Cantata 21 the increased melodic and rhythmic fluidity and full string sound of the F minor aria "Bäche von gesalz'nen Zähren" come as a relief (especially when compared with the fragmented character of "Seufzer, Tränen, Kummer, Not"), even though the aria text describes the "brooks of salty tears" and the "rushing floods" that threaten the believer's destruction. Owing to the character of Bach's setting, instead of gnawing at his heart the believer's tears in this aria provide a measure of release that the text itself does not voice. The aria's middle section moves toward B♭ minor via its subdominant, e♭, as the believer feels himself weakening ("und dies trübsalsvolle Meer will mir Geist und Leben schwächen": and this sea of tribulation will weaken my spirit and my life) and sinking into the depths as if into hell itself ("Hier versink' ich in den Grund, dort seh' ich der Hölle Schlund": Here I sink into the depths, there I see the jaws of hell), after which the return of the principal section provides once again a measure of alleviation. Behind the imagery of this movement lies, perhaps, another Bible story in which water was interpreted allegorically: the story of the flood. Like the destruction and restoration of Jerusalem, the captivity and exodus from Egypt, the changing of water into wine at Cana, and other such stories, the flood story was interpreted allegorically as prefiguring the believer's hopes for release from worldly tribulation. On the third Sunday after Trinity the year after the first Leipzig performance of "Ich hatte viel Bekümmernis" Bach took up another widespread transformational metaphor that involved water, the comparison of the believer's tears to rain, after which the sunshine represented Jesus' comforting the soul: "Mein Jesus tröstet mich! Er läßt nach Tränen und nach Weinen die Freudensonne wieder scheinen" (Cantata 135, movement 5: My Jesus comforts me! He lets the sun of joy shine forth again after tears and after weeping).

No. 6: Chorus "Was betrübst du dich, meine Seele" (f/c)

In the recitative that directly precedes the aria just cited from Cantata 135, a striking series of modulations in the subdominant (flat) direction depicts the believer's weakening under the continual tears and tribulation, after which the aria begins the process of restoration. In Cantata 21, that process begins in earnest in the final chorus of part 1, which, still in f at first and still featuring Phrygian cadences to C, questions the value of spiritual tribulation and unrest: "Was betrübst du dich, meine Seele und bist so unruhig in mir?" With the reference to unrest, the music moves through two full diatonic circles of fifths (C, F, B♭, E♭, A♭, d°, G, C, f–F, B♭, E♭, A♭, d°, G, and c), before settling on another prominent Phrygian cadence, this time to G (V of c), after which it winds its way through E♭ ("Harre auf Gott, denn ich werde ihm noch danken") to c for the beginning of the concluding fugue: "daß er meines Angesichtes Hilfe, und mein Gott ist."

The fugue itself will be taken up later in this chapter in relation to the C major fugue that ends part 2. Note here that the return to C minor in conjunction with the positive ending of the text of this movement, although it can be considered a restoration of the believer's faith after the intense fears of destruction in the F minor aria, represents no more than a provisional resolution, in that the promised *Erquickung* of the soul does not as yet appear. The fugue remains in the adagio tempo and in minor, and it retains clear affinities to the opening section of "Ich hatte viel Bekümmernis," especially in the repeated-tone character of its subject. Whereas the circle of fifths in the second section of the opening chorus had led to a very positive cadence in E♭ before returning to c, that of the final chorus remains in c throughout its two cycles. As in the first chorus (and even in the first recitative), the brief introduction of E♭ (at "Harre auf Gott") points to a positive outcome that awaits part 2 for its full realization.

Part 2

No. 7: Recitative dialogue (E♭/B♭)

If part 1 of "Ich hatte viel Bekümmernis" is occupied with "faith in opposition to experience," it is the task of part 2 to provide its counterpart, "faith realized in experience," the believer's coming under the influence of *Trost*, the "point at which faith and experience intersect," love, which gives confidence to faith, and joy, the "feeling quality" of faith.[27] These qualities come out first in the recitative and aria duets that constitute the first two movements of part 2, and they are reiterated in the middle section of the penultimate movement, "Es brennet und flammet die reineste Kerze der Liebe, des Trostes in Seele und Brust, weil Jesus mich tröstet mit himmlischer Lust" (The purest candle of love, of consolation, burns in the soul and breast, since Jesus comforts me with heavenly longing). In contrast to the angst-ridden tone of part 1, therefore, part 2 begins more hopefully, in major (E♭), with a recitative dialogue between the soul and Jesus (no. 7). With the secure establishment of E♭ at the beginning of part 2, God's response, so long withheld in part 1, introduces a tone of comfort, effecting a vital change in the believer's consciousness. First the soul cries out in darkness, "Ach Jesu, meine Ruh', mein Licht, wo bleibest du?" (Ah Jesu, my rest, my light, where are You?) And after Jesus' initial response of consolation, "O Seele, sieh! ich bin bei dir" (O soul, see! I am with you), the soul continues to reiterate its cry of doubt and forsakenness: "Bei mir? hier ist ja lauter Nacht" (With me? here it is pure night). Jesus' "Ich bin dein treuer Freund, der auch im Dunkeln wacht" (I am your true friend, Who watches even in the dark) prompts a plea from the soul for Jesus to shine forth with the "Licht des Trostes" (light of consolation), and the recitative ends with the promise of eternity, alluding to the "hour" at which that *Trost* will appear (drawn from the Gospel narrative of the wedding at Cana, as mentioned above): "Die Stunde kommet schon, da deines Kampfes Kron dir wird ein süßes Labsal sein." Whereas in part 1 the lone recitative was centered amid a quasi-symmetrical sequence of movements of predominantly tortured character and it addressed a God who did not answer, the only recitative of part 2 stands at the beginning of a movement sequence that becomes progressively more positive as it approaches its final goal, and in it God finally responds. Its text refers back to the *Trost* that was anticipated in the text of the opening chorus ("aber deine Tröstungen erquicken meine Seele"), while that of the duet aria that follows realizes the promised *Erquickung* of the soul (see the following discussion). The beginning of part 2 therefore represents a turning point, the comforting appearance of Jesus constituting a response to the believer's feelings of desolation in the part 1 recitative.

The antithesis of light and darkness is, of course, a principal means by which the coming of Christ was related both to the turning of the geophysical year at Christmas (the winter solstice) and to the shift from the era of Israel to that of the new Zion, the old year of sorrow and fallen man to the new year of faith in eternal life.[28] At the same time, Luther described faith as a process of groping in the darkness, of moving away from all other experience only to experience Christ.[29] In this E♭ major recitative Bach represents the light–darkness antithesis by tonal means, setting up a secure E♭ in which the soprano's initial motion toward the dominant ("mein Licht, wo bleibest du?") prompts a comforting response in the tonic from the bass, "O Seele, sieh! ich bin bei dir." This passage is "enclosed," as it were, by a slowly ascending B♭ major scale on the first violin and an E♭ major scalar descent (from e♭ to G) in the *basso continuo*. An even more prominent use of this rhetorically motivated contrary motion device occurs in the first recitative of Cantata 12, "Weinen! Klagen! Sorgen! Zagen!," written in Weimar just eight weeks before the 1714 Weimar performance of "Ich hatte viel Bekümmernis."[30] Bach assigns the first violin of that recitative an ascending C major scale (c"–c'''), while the *basso continuo* outlines a C *minor* descent from c to C. Its obvious purpose is to illustrate the antithesis behind the text—"Wir müssen durch viel Trübsal in das Reich Gottes eingehen" (we must undergo much tribulation to enter into the Kingdom of God)—as a simultaneity: the believer must undergo worldly tribulation and live in the hope of eternity at the same time. In Cantata 12 this inner conflict, which resembles that between the soul and Jesus in the corresponding recitative from Cantata 21, marks the beginning of a progression "upward" from the tribulation of its opening movement to the final *Trost* that represents the believer's closest approach to the anticipation of eternity in the present life, just as it does in Cantata 21.[31] We can hardly fail to be reminded of the contrary-motion ending of the first segment of the recitative in part 1, at the point where the believer lamented that, owing to his feeling no response to his suffering, his relationship of "Bund und Treu" with God was unfulfilled. In that movement, as here, the contrary motion of the "tonic" cadence was centered between phrases that cadenced in the dominant and subdominant regions. But the overall tonal motion of the earlier recitative was flatward, shifting to the subdominant, and its affective direction was increasingly pessimistic, just the opposite of what we will find to be the overall tonal and affective direction of the part 2 recitative (whose B♭ ending is anticipated in the rising scale of the first phrase). It is here, in other words, that the "Bund und Treu" are revealed (and, in fact, Jesus refers to Himself here as the believer's "treuer Freund").

In the recitative dialogue Bach establishes the security of the E♭ tonality by the simplest possible harmonic means, using the registral and directional qualities of the vocal and instrumental lines to highlight those pitches that define the tonal "space" bounded by the subdominant, dominant, and tonic. Thus, at the outset the soprano's decorative d♭" on "Jesu" colors the subdominant harmony with a personal, supplicatory quality, while the violin's d♮" and the steady rhythm of its rising B♭ scale project a more "objective" affirmative tone. Likewise, after the soprano's further descent, decorating the a♭'–g' semitone on "meine Ruh'," the violin continues up through a♮" to b♭", holding the latter tone for nearly two measures to overlap the soprano and bass solos. This point of dominant emphasis coincides with the soprano's questioning phrase "mein Licht, wo bleibest du?," which now moves upward to end on the highest tone of its phrase, f" (Ex. 3.1).

The bass's response to this dominant arrival is first to outline the B♭ triad, ending with a leap upward from f to d' ("O Seele, sieh'") as the *basso continuo* moves down to A♭, then to resolve the upward motion to the tonic, E♭, in the lower octave ("ich bin bei dir"), preceding its cadential e♭ by the a♭–g semitone (an echo of the soprano's "meine Ruh'"). The upward-looking gestures and the motion toward the

Example 3.1. Cantata 21: Recitative beginning part 2

Example 3.1. (*continued*)

—*continued*

Example 3.1. (*continued*)

dominant give way to the tonic in the lower register. This point marks the ending of the initial phrase pairing and the widest point in the registral expansion of the outermost parts. Following this very optimistic beginning, however, the soprano immediately questions both the tonic cadence and the bass's leap upward to d' on "sieh" by leaping up a minor seventh from e♭' to d♭" ("Bei mir?"), as the string parts all drop suddenly in pitch in invervals ranging from a tenth to a twelfth. These gestures mirror the soul's essential feeling of unworthiness, which Bach amplifies as the soprano line continues, dropping a seventh at the end from b♭' to c' as the harmony turns to the subdominant ("hier ist ja lauter Nacht!"). The device is, of course, very similar to the beginning of the third segment of the part 1 recitative, where, after the half close on G and the contrary-motion phrase that ended the first segment, Bach had briefly settled on E♭ ("Du warest meine Lust"), after which the soprano had leaped upward from e♭' to d♭", there also to deflect the tonality to the subdominant, f ("und bist mir grausam worden!").

In such passages Bach affirms tonal associations that are, in fact, very telling not only for the individual movement and for the tonal design of the cantata as a whole but also for what we might with much justice call the tonal "hermeneutics" of his work in its entirety. In the opening phrase of the part 2 recitative the soprano's "mein Licht" initiates an ascent that coincides with the first violin's arrival on the high b♭" and the harmonic arrival on the dominant ("wo bleibest du?"); in its second phrase the soprano, following the strings, drops suddenly downward as the harmony reaches the *sub*dominant on "Nacht." In other words, the soprano perceives Jesus' sphere as that of the light above, in contrast to the human sphere of the darkness below. Between the two lies Jesus' urging the soul to look upward (the rising leap on "sieh'") and His articulation of the tonic in the lower register for "ich bin bei dir," the union above/below, light/darkness, and divine/human. Jesus' presence in the world of darkness is a spiritual incarnation, the turning point to what will ultimately bring about the elevation of humanity.

Subsequent events in the part 2 recitative confirm this interpretation. Following the soprano's turn to the subdominant, the bass's second response draws the A♭ back into the sphere of another phrase that closes in E♭, which it sets up with another upward leap, now of the major seventh from e♭ to d' ("Ich bin dein treuer Freund, der auch im Dunkeln *wacht*"), before dropping suddenly in pitch for the cadence ("wo lauter Schalken seind": where pure rogues are). This phrase leads first to the c' ("Freund") on which the soprano had ended, after which the upward leap to d' relates back, of course, to the bass's f–d' leap on "Seele, sieh'." At the same time it responds to both the soprano's rising e♭'–d♭" leap on "bei mir" and its subsequent b♭'–c' drop on "lauter Nacht." While the f–d' leap urges a form of enlightenment on the soul ("O Seele, sieh'"), the e♭–d' leap ("im Dunkeln wacht") responds to the soprano's "lauter Nacht" by affirming Jesus' presence in the world below (so that the ensuing E♭ cadence confirms the earlier one at "Ich bin bei dir"). The ending of Jesus' phrase, "wo lauter Schalken seind," weakening the E♭ cadence by dropping suddenly into the low vocal register and ending on the pitch B♭ is another expression of the world of darkness in which the believer dwells.

This first point of arrival on E♭ in the *basso continuo* is further weakened by its metric placement (the fourth beat of the measure) and, above all, by the soprano's crying immediately for Jesus' intervention, which it still conceives in terms of the light from above: "Brich doch mit deinem Glanz und Licht des Trostes ein!" (Break forth with Your glance and light of consolation!) With this outcry the soprano intensifies the association of the world above with the visual imagery of the text ("sieh'," "wacht"), representing the breaking forth of the "light of consolation" as an arrival from outside the world of darkness. Deflecting the E♭ cadence to a G^6 chord, it sets up a C major cadence to complete the line. The soprano itself, however, sings the pitch e♭" directly before the C^6 chord of the cadence. Jesus' response, "Die Stunde kommet schon," which refers, via the story of the wedding at Cana, to the transformation that comes in the final movements of Cantata 21, outlines the C major arpeggio, making clear that the C is a gift from "above" by moving via a slow circle-of-fifths progression in arioso style to B♭, on which the movement ends ("da deines Kampfes Kron' dir wird ein süsses Labsal sein": when the crown of your struggles will be a sweet refreshment to you). The melody of "Die Stunde kommet schon, da deines Kampfes Kron'" refers back to that of "Du warest meine Lust, und bist mir grausam worden" from the part 1 recitative, a detail suggesting, perhaps, that the anticipation of C in part 2 is equivalent to the anticipation of E♭ in part 1. Both passages continue in the flat direction, the former to f and the latter through an F^4_2 chord to B♭. The circle-of-fifths progression draws the soprano's introduction of the dominant of c/C back into the framework of E♭, indicating that the "Stunde" in question is a future event. Together with the more animated rhythmic style, the circle of fifths introduces a decided tone of consolation in response to the soprano's cry of angst. Jesus' comforting presence and promise of eternity reconcile the soul to life in the world of darkness.

No. 8: Aria Duetto (E♭)

After this point there are no further recitatives, and the completion of the circle of fifths with which this dialogue ends comes with the E♭ duet that follows (no. 8). The return to E♭ leaves the promised C major ("Die Stunde kommet schon") for the final chorus, which will be reached through the series of stages that follow the recitative. The E♭ duet brings about the soul's "conversion" to hope, as Jesus responds to its iterations of despair:

[Soul] "Komm, mein Jesu, und erquicke"
(Come, my Jesu, and revive,)

[Jesus] "Ja, ich komme und erquicke"
(Yes, I come and revive)

[Soul] "und erfreu' mit deinem Blicke."
(and rejoice with Your glance.)

[Jesus] "dich mit meinem Gnadenblicke."
(you with my glance of grace.)

[Soul] "Komm, mein Jesu, und erquicke"
(Come, my Jesu, and revive,)

[Soul] "diese Seele, die soll sterben und nicht leben,"
(this soul, which will die and not live,)

[Jesus] "Deine Seele, die soll leben und nicht sterben,"
(Your soul, which will live and not die,)

[Soul] "und in ihrer Unglückshöhle"
(and in its pit of misfortune)

[Jesus] "hier aus dieser Wundenhöhle"
(here from this wounded cavity)

[Soul] "ganz verderben."
(completely disintegrate.)

[Jesus] "sollt du erben"
(shall you inherit)

[Soul] "Ich muß stets in Kummer schweben,"
(I must continually live in torment,)

[Jesus] "Heil durch diesen Saft der Reben."
(salvation through this fruit of the vine.)

[Soul] "ja, ach ja! ich bin verloren,"
(yes, ah yes! I am lost,)

[Jesus] "Nein, ach nein! du bist erkoren,"
(No, ah no! you are chosen,)

[Jesus] "sollt du erben"
(shall you inherit)

[Soul] "nein, ach nein! du hassest mich."
(no, ah no! You hate me.)

[Jesus] "ja, ach ja! ich liebe dich."
(yes, ah yes! I love you.)

In this dialogue the antithesis between the soul's "Ich muß stets in Kummer schweben" and Jesus' "sollt du erben Heil durch diesen Saft der Reben" anticipates the "Weinen"/"Wein" juxtaposition of "Erfreue dich, Seele." Jesus' assurance of love climaxes this first principal section of the duet, enabling the soul, in a middle section that Bach assigns to a quicker tempo (the promised *Erquickung*), to anticipate, now in phrases that are no longer continually broken and interrupted, the fulfillment of its hopes: "Ach Jesus, durchsüße mir Seele und Herze!" (Ah Jesus, send Your sweetness through my soul and heart!) As it sings forth, Jesus joins with "Entweichet ihr Sorgen, verschwinde du Schmerze" (Dissipate, you cares, disappear, you pains), the music increasingly intertwining their lines into a traditional symbol of union—close, quasi-canonic imitation. After this, the truncated return of the opening lines at the end serves as a reminder that fulfillment is yet to come, while indicating that the soul has now taken the path to that fulfillment in its acceptance of Jesus' promise.[32] In this it provides a symbolic representation of the working of the Gospel through the inner, or tropological, understanding of God's word. The intimate character of duets such as this one between the soul and Christ is often described as Pietistic because of the imagery of love, which is sometimes more overt than here, speaking of "burning flames," kisses between Jesus and the soul, and the like. While the language is indeed indebted to the subjective emphases of Pietism, it is probably more accurate to understand such movements in terms of their representation of the shift from a literal or external understanding of God's word in scripture to the inner prompting of faith and its recognition by the believer. There was certainly an increasing emphasis on love during the seventeenth and early eighteenth centuries, and that emphasis accounts for much of the imagery in Bach's cantata texts. At the same time, however, we must recognize that love was also central to Luther's theology, where, as here, it is an essential part of the experience of faith.[33]

No. 9: Chorus with Chorale (g)

After the two dialogues between the soul and Jesus, in the next two movements the believer addresses his soul directly. First the G minor chorus responds to the unrest expressed in "Was betrübst du dich" with Psalms 116:7—"Sei nun wieder zufrieden, meine Seele, denn der Herr tut dir Guts" (Return unto thy rest, O my soul, for the Lord hath dealt bountifully with thee)—while two verses of the hymn "Wer nur den lieben Gott läßt walten" (Whoever allows God alone to rule) urge the believer to abandon tribulation for trust in God. This, the only minor-key movement in part 2, seems to look backward and forward simultaneously (in part the outcome of its presumed origins, discussed earlier), drawing an equivalence between the Old Testament and chorale texts. "Sei nun wieder zufrieden" is the first triple-meter movement in the cantata, its slow, even quarter-note motion representing the calming effect described in the text. Its most striking musical gesture comes at the beginning of the movement, before the entrance of the chorale *cantus firmus*, as the soprano and bass sing the beginning of the text "Sei nun wieder zufrieden" to long descending scalar lines in steady quarter-note rhythm, after which the alto enters to sing the beginning of the line in inversion. The dualism of descending and ascending lines continues throughout the movement in a manner that is easily and immediately audible against the tenor chorale melody (for the second verse the chorale melody shifts to the soprano). It is as if, after the encounter with Jesus in the two duets, the believer, dominated by the dualism of suffering and hope, death and life, is aided in the search for inner peace (the psalm text) by the church (the chorale), which urges him to abandon "Kreuz und Leid"—that is, the state of mind that dwells on sorrow, or faith "in opposition to experience." Now that God has answered the tormented prayers of part 1, the believer need only await the promised time to come, which will bring about a change, leading each individual to his or her goal. The second chorale verse ends: "Die folgend Zeit verändert viel und setzet jeglichem sein Ziel" (The time to come will change much and will assign to every person his purpose).

No. 10: Aria "Erfreue dich, Seele" (F)

The F major aria "Erfreue dich, Seele, erfreue dich, Herze" (no. 10) moves closer to that goal, representing the believer's joy and completely reversing the affective character of the cantata as set forth throughout the whole of part 1. Toward the end of "Sei nun wieder zufrieden, meine Seele" the *basso continuo* had introduced a scalar eighth-note passage that now seems, by hindsight, to have anticipated the *basso continuo* patterns of the aria. And the wide-ranging scalar lines and two-octave ascending and descending arpeggios of the *basso continuo* line of "Erfreue dich, Seele" both anticipate the thematic material of the final chorus and, along with the fast triple meter and running sixteenth notes, create an atmosphere of uncontainable elation. Not only does the transformation of tears into wine suggest a continuation of the Eucharistic imagery of the E♭ *Aria duetto*, but also the soprano now echoes Jesus' words of comfort from that movement—"Entweiche nun, Kummer, verschwinde, du Schmerze!"—as if to proclaim that it (the "soul") has accepted Jesus' promise. Likewise, the text of its middle section, as described here previously, brings love, *Trost*, and the joyful anticipation of eternity into close conjunction. In all this the soul seems to indicate its anticipation of meeting Jesus face-to-face. The final chorus then elevates the believer's hopes to the level of what is clearly a vision of both the promised "Stunde" of the E♭ recitative and the "folgend Zeit" of the G minor psalm/chorale chorus.

No. 11: Chorus "Das Lamm, das erwürget ist" (C)

Above all, the final choruses of the two parts of Cantata 21 appear to have been created to elevate the sense of transformation to a universal level in which the idea of Old Testament/New Testament parallels and antitheses is absorbed into the final vision of eternity. Apart from the fact that the Psalms and Revelation texts emphasize,

Example 3.2. Cantata 21: Themes of closing choruses, parts 1 and 2

on the one hand, trust in God from one in a state of torment and unrest and, on the other, the joyful state of mind of one who has received the comforting message of the Gospel, the designs of the two movements—preludes and "permutation" fugues in C minor and C major, respectively—could hardly fail to invite comparison; and such a comparison could likewise hardly fail to center on their parallels and differences. The two fugue themes themselves embody the essential nature of the differences in microcosm (Ex. 3.2). The C minor theme projects an extraordinary sense of descent from the dominant to the tonic, but that descent does not involve modulation from the dominant to the tonic; instead, the line descends through the minor triad from the fifth to the tonic, leaps up to the minor sixth degree, from which it falls to the fifth, then the tonic again, then rises to the fourth degree, and descends through the scale to close on the tonic. There are, in fact, three descents to the tonic within the theme, the first through the triad, the second down the fifth, and the third down the scale. Picking up from the tonic (either at the pitch on which the theme ended or at an octave displacement), the tonal answer then continues the descent idea down from tonic to dominant; putting the theme and answer together, therefore, we find that they articulate a continuous descent idea that is particularly evident when the voices enter at successively lower pitch levels (as they do at one point in the movement). In striking contrast, the C major theme ascends through the major triad to the octave above before "modulating" to the dominant, a design that invites a progressively ascending pattern in the subject–answer pairings. Since the two fugues are almost entirely constructed upon regularly spaced entries that alternate between the tonic and dominant, the C minor fugue seems to articulate the idea of continual descent, even though the starting pitches of the vocal entries may rise, while the C major fugue unmistakably articulates the idea of continual ascent, which Bach emphasizes by organizing the pitches of the successive vocal entries into regular ascent patterns.

In addition, the layout of the C major fugue, while similar to its earlier counterpart in some respects, seems to make a point out of several vitally important differences. The character of the theme itself is virtually the opposite in affective character, introducing a "dynamic" element that suggests change and forward progression owing to its shifting the tonal center up a fifth, from which point the answering voice begins. And each time a pair of voices sounds in succession the third tone of the "tonal" answer—c instead of d (as in the primary form of the theme)—and the subsequent leap up the fifth to g introduce qualites of affirmation (the fifth leap), resolution (the return to c through the major triad from the fifth above), and fulfillment (the strong dominant–tonic or antecedent–consequent tonal design) that are completely missing in the C minor theme. Bach amplifies these qualities in the pattern of the successive vocal entries, which now ascend twice through bass, tenor, alto, and soprano voices in turn, the first time with solo voices and the second with chorus and instruments. The second set creates the effect of increasing intensification in the way that the two instrumental choirs underscore each successive entry of the theme, the strings and oboe by introducing rhythmic emphasis on the strong beats as the voice sings the words "Lob, [und] Ehre, [und] Preis, [und] Gewalt" (Praise, [and] honor, [and] worth, [and] power) and the trumpets by echoing these points of emphasis one beat later. Bach carries this pattern through the four chorus entries before assigning the theme to the trumpets themselves at the highest register of the piece, the clarino octave (the ninth entry of the theme). The tremendous sense of mounting excitement throughout this entire passage culminates in the cry "Alleluia" from all four voices of the chorus at the midpoint of the fugue, which coincides with the beginning of the trumpet entry.

Then, for the tenth entry of the theme, on G in the strings and oboe, Bach uses the real instead of the tonal answer, so that the rising-fifth modulatory character of the theme brings about a shift to D (minor), in which the eleventh entry sounds. For this single minor-key version of the theme he has the chorus cry out the beginning of the theme, "Lob, und Ehre, und Preis, und Gewalt," in rhythmic homophony, thereby breaking the pattern of permutation. The theme modulates up a fifth, as usual; and from this A minor Bach moves via the circle of fifths (a, D, G, C, and F) to the subdominant, F, in which he sounds the theme in the soprano for the second successive time (the twelfth entry), a detail that renders the shift up the third from d to F more palpably as an ascent. Throughout the four and a half "extra" measures of the circle of fifths the chorus sings sixteenth-note triadic descent patterns to the word "Amen," while the oboe and strings shoot upward in rocketlike ascent figures derived from the beginning of the fugue theme. The F major version of the theme likewise modulates up a fifth, returning the tonality to C for the final two entries, the thirteenth and fourteenth, on C in the basses echoed by instruments as before and on G in the trumpets.

In what I have described, Bach first sets up a pattern of rotation by means of which the entries of the theme sound strictly in alternation between tonic and dominant as they did in the C minor fugue, but now with important differences, not least among which is his breaking the pattern with the tenth entry. Even before this point, however, the strikingly different character of the C major fugue theme, above all its major key, its ascending rather than descending melodic direction, and its open (C–G) rather than closed (c–c) tonal design, influenced a very different overall form, and one that suggests a counterpart of, or response to, the earlier chorus. The C minor theme articulates a form of closure rhythmically as well as tonally, since the four reiterated g's with which it begins set up a duple or quadruple metric pattern that remains throughout the theme, despite the syncopation toward the end. This theme comprises four half-note units in two measures, so that the pattern of counting in four with which it begins continues throughout the successive entries of the theme—all two measures apart (or four for each subject–answer pair)—until the end of the movement. In its reiterated tones this theme seems to recall that of "Ich hatte viel Bekümmernis." In contrast, the C major theme comprises two "halves," the one articulating a two-measure pattern centered on the words "Lob," "Ehre," "Preis," and "Gewalt" and the other a one-and-one-half-measure pattern centered on "sei unserm Gott von Ewigkeit zu Ewigkeit." The rotation of this theme thus begins after three and a half measures, and each subject–answer pair lasts seven measures rather than four. The series of four vocal entries thus expands to fourteen measures for the soloists and another fourteen for the chorus and instruments. After these twenty-eight measures Bach gives forth the theme six more times to a total of fourteen for the movement as a whole. The first of these six (no. 9) is the climactic first sounding of the theme in the trumpets, the second (no. 10) is the "real" answer on G, the third and fourth (nos. 11 and 12) are the entries on d and F, and the fifth and sixth (nos. 13 and 14) are the bass and trumpet entries on C and G. The metric character of the theme and the permutational aspect of the movement, therefore, might have suggested to Bach a play with the number fourteen as a multiple of seven, especially since the "free" introductory part of the chorus lists seven attributes of the lamb immediately before the fugue begins ("Kraft," "Reichtum," "Weisheit," "Stärke," "Ehre," "Preis," and "Lob": power, riches, wisdom, strength, honor, worth, and praise). The theme itself might be considered to embody the number seven in the four metric units that coincide with the four attributes of the lamb with which it begins and the three metric units that follow before the rotation of the theme begins. Already this difference between the two fugues points up a degree of assymmetry in the latter that is not present in the former. And the breaking of the tonic–dominant rotation pattern from the tenth to the eleventh entry of the theme of the C major fugue, as well as the four and a half "free" measures it entails, suggest that, as in the theme itself, Bach intended that the form of the movement depart from the near-absolute regularity of the earlier fugue.

The numbers four and seven were associated in certain numerological schemes with the world (four) and heaven or eternity (seven), respectively. The chapter from Revelations from which the text of the final chorus of Cantata 21 was drawn contains a plethora of references to the number seven, above all the book of seven seals that only the "lamb" of that verse could open. Although Bach might never have had any such associations in mind for his two choruses, the metrical differences between the two fugues and their themes nevertheless bring out qualities of the kind that those associations represent. Likewise, the highly vivid character of the secondary thematic material of the C major fugue—the long sixteenth-note descent and static alternating pattern of the first countersubject, the ascent–descent arpeggio pattern of the second, and the upward-shooting arpeggio of the third—projects dramatic qualities that are absent from its C minor counterpart. If we consider the emblematic character of the thematic material of the C major fugue, we might conclude that Bach intended it in part to represent a vision of God in His sphere by drawing on widespread associations of majesty. The introduction of three trumpets for this movement suggests an allegory of the Trinity, as it does in many other Bach works. And just as the major triad was taken in the Lutheran tradition to symbolize the Trinity, the symmetrical ascent–descent figure with which the trumpets begin the movement has associations with God in majesty in other Bach cantatas, most notably Cantata 71, "Gott ist mein König," which begins with virtually the identical motto in the trumpets.

The expansion of this idea to an ascent–descent arpeggio for the third segment of the theme, on "Alleluia," and the rising fifth that follows it, introduce a further thematic association of a similar kind. This related theme appears in other of Bach's works, often in pronouncedly eschatological contexts.[34] In the opening chorus of what is, next to Cantata 21, probably the most eschatologically oriented of all Bach's works, "Wachet! betet! betet! wachet!" (Cantata 70, discussed briefly in "Aspects of the Liturgical Year" in chapter 1), this theme appears fourteen times in the trumpet in conjunction with a vision of God's coming as judge to make an end of the world (Ex. 3.3). The number fourteen might well have symbolized for Bach the idea of the "A" and "O" (Alpha and Omega), Jesus as the beginning and ending of existence, creator and judge. This interpretation derived from the book of Revelation, where the first and last letters of the Greek alphabet served as a metaphor for Jesus' control over life and death; from there it was carried over into the first and fourteenth letters of the Latin and German alphabets. The number fourteen thus took over associations of the number seven in Revelation. Possibly, therefore, Bach attempted in the final chorus of Cantata 21 to extend the numerological aspect of Revelation to a theme whose rotation would set up patterns that involved metric units that articulated multiples of seven. The number seven is audible in the C major fugue, first as the seven attributes of the lamb, then as the seven half-measure units of the theme, the seven measures of each subject–answer pair, the fourteen-measure units of a complete set of thematic entries, the two fourteen-measure units in which the rotation pattern sounds, the fourteen statements of the theme, and, finally, the fifty-six (8×7) measures of the fugue as a whole. In this way the rhythmic character of the theme would extend to more "abstract" patterns concerning the layout of the movement. If so, then the number fourteen would relate to the appearance of Jesus and the promise of eternal life that appears only in part 2 of the cantata, while the numbers associated with the C minor chorus that ends part 1 (there are ten vocal entries of the two-measure theme and a total of fifteen altogether for voices and instruments) might be taken to refer to the world (four) and the Law (ten). In the C major fugue the breaking of the permutation pattern with the tenth entry and the tonic–dominant rotation pattern *after* the tenth entry might have been intended to symbolize the end of the Law. The presence of two permutation fugues in the same cantata suggests, perhaps, the nature of God as controller of the universe (widely conceived as a clockwork mechanism in the eighteenth century); at least some of Bach's other permutation fugues are connected with the idea of God as "king" (e.g., the first movement of Cantata 182, "Himmelskönig, sei willkommen"). With such speculations, however, we move beyond the audible aspects of the work and into the sphere of interpretative uncertainty. Ultimately, the major, ascending triadic character of the chorus is the most important key to its theological role in the cantata: that of a New Testament (Gospel) response to the Old Testament message of part 1. Nevertheless, one of the principal goals of works such as this is to draw the *whole* person—usually conveyed by the word "heart" in Bach's sacred texts—into the sphere

Example 3.3. (a) Cantata 70: Theme of first chorus. Trumpet, m. 1. (b) Cantata 21: Theme from final chorus. Bass, mm. 15–16

of its musico-theological meaning, an intent that necessitates the participation of both sensual and intellectual understanding even in the affective process.

In the final version of the cantata, the placing of the two choruses at the ends of the two divisions invites us to compare the sequences they summarize and complete. The relationship between these two choruses might even have been the core idea in the design of the final form of the work. And if the C major chorus was heard in any earlier and shorter cantata, the C minor–major shift could only have been more palpable by virtue of proximity. It is at least worth speculating further that the "ascending" character of the theme of the C major chorus as embodied in its melodically ascending arpeggio and its "modulation" up the fifth from tonic to dominant influenced the overall tonal design of part 2. The five successive entries of the theme that precede the final answer—each moving up a fifth according to the pattern of the subject (C to G, G to d, d to a, F to C, and C to G)—suggest an ascent through the supertonic (d) and the subdominant (F) to the C–G–C of the final subject–answer pairing. If indeed the final form of this cantata came about via expansion of an original choral framework by the addition of recitatives and arias, then the motion from subdominant to tonic in the last two movements of both parts (f–c in part 1; F–C in part 2) might have suggested to Bach the idea of a progression through a rising series of keys in part 2 in analogy to the increasingly positive series of affections from torment (the f and c of part 1), doubt changing to hope (nos. 7 and 8 in E♭), consolation (no. 9 in g), joy (no. 10 in F), and fulfillment (no. 11 in C). As mentioned earlier, in part 2 the only minor-key movement is no. 9, which, whether or not it might have served as the culminating movement of an earlier version of the work, represents the church's response to the state of mind depicted in part 1 of the cantata. After this movement the reduction of the scoring to an aria for voice and *basso continuo* (the only continuo aria in the cantata) suggests, along with the shift to F major and a quick triple meter and the patterns of triadic ascent in the bass line, that the transformation from sorrow to joy is founded on the confidence of the believer's faith. The sudden entrance of full scoring, now with the addition of the trumpets, projects a "universal" quality, confirming the subjective experience as a reality.

Summary

Cantata 21 thus articulates a quasi-chronological progression from a state of mind derived from Old Testament lamentation (part 1: nos. 1–6) to the believer's faith encounter with Jesus (part 2: nos. 7–8), the role of the church's sustenance (no. 9) in bringing about the believer's inner transformation from tribulation to joy (no. 10), and, finally, a more universal anticipation of eternity (no. 11). A basic turning point occurs between parts 1 and 2, after which the sequence of affective states in part 2 can be said to represent the growth of faith in the individual. The most obvious reflection of the turning point is the appearance of the figure of Jesus in dialogue with the soul at the beginning of part 2, while the foremost dimension of its overall musical design is the shift from the C minor tonality that dominates part 1 first to the relative major, E♭, with which part 2 begins, then, by the stages just described, to the C major that ends part 2. The final choruses of the two parts seem to summarize and embody the essential nature of that shift. At the same time, the C major chorus in itself suggests the simultaneity of the sensual and the abstract by means of the audible and inaudible (numerological) aspects of its musical design.[35]

What I have described is the fullest form of the work that has come down to us, in which there is a marked sense of division between two completely contrasted states of mind and of progression from the one to the other. If it is true that this version was preceded by one or more earlier and shorter versions, then a primary thrust of the expansion was its clarifying the Old Testament/New Testament juxtaposition and the progression from the psalmist in tribulation to the contemporary believer trusting in the truth of God's revelation. The most significant alteration (apart from the possible addition of the final chorus) was, of course, the introduction of the figure of Jesus in dialogue with the soul in the recitative–aria pairing that begins part 2, since it points up the change from Old to New Testaments in the most immediate manner (part 1 had made no reference to Jesus or the New Testament). In the recitative the anonymous poet, as we have seen, develops the imagery of darkness versus light, one of the most common means of representing the change that came with the birth of Christ. Thus, the Old Testament texts of the first part of Cantata 21 with their emphasis on suffering and extended periods of doubt and waiting yield to the encounter with Jesus, which represents a new stage in "salvation history" from the perspective of the individual believer.

The possible expansion of an original chorus-dominated version of Cantata 21 in the ways alluded to earlier in this chapter would have vastly increased the role of the individual believer in the sequential design of its final version. Old Testament, New Testament, and chorale and madrigal texts, representing to some degree the historical eras from which they derive (the time of Israel, time of Christ, and time of the church), bring out the interaction of the contemporary believer with history, so that scripture, being internalized, is transmuted, as it were, into the faith experience. That experience in its manifold variations is the "dramatic" subject matter of all Bach's sacred cantatas. Bach, that is, is always concerned with an internal drama, the experience of faith, especially in its relationship to the events that prefigure and trigger it. The triggering of faith is often symbolized, in Cantata 21 as well as the "Actus Tragicus," by the coming of Jesus. In both works the soprano cries out for that event: "Ja, komm, Herr Jesu, komm" in the middle movement of the "Actus Tragicus," "Komm, mein Jesu, und erquicke" in the dialogue sequence that begins part 2 of Cantata 21. Jesus' coming, however, is a multilayered event, for it was traditionally interpreted in terms of His coming in the flesh (Christmas), His coming in the Spirit (grace and faith), and His coming at the end of time (the general resurrection). Thus, as we have seen, the Weimar cantata "Nun komm, der Heiden Heiland" (BWV 61), takes up the four basic aspects or "senses" of the coming of Jesus as its principal subject matter.[36] Its text places the faith encounter with Jesus directly before the movement that represents the personal acceptance of Jesus' incarnation in the human heart, whereas the texts of the "Actus Tragicus" and of Cantata 21 attempt to place the encounter with Jesus at the center of movement sequences that favor Old Testament texts before that event and New Testament and chorale texts after it.[37] In this way Jesus occupies the central or pivotal point in chronological time while the "time of Israel" and the "time of the church" that precede and follow it represent seemingly antithetical stages that can be unified only under the conception of "God's time" as the expression of what from the human perspective is perceived as the history of salvation. Thus, the "Actus Tragicus" contains a symbolic dividing point in the empty bar that follows the central movement, in which the eras of the Old Testament, New Testament, and church come into direct conjunction, while Cantata 21 divides into two parts, placing the most momentous leap forward in the faith experience of the contemporary believer at the beginning of the second half. In the central movement complex of the "Actus Tragicus" the believer cries out for the coming of Jesus in words from the ending of the book of Revelation ("Ja komm, Herr Jesu, komm"), thus lending the sequence as a whole the character of a progression from suffering (the Old Testament text "Es ist der alte Bund: Mensch du musst sterben"), through comfort (the untexted instrumental chorale "Ich hab' mein Sach' Gott heimgestellt"), to anticipation of eternity. The New Testament part of the work follows this centralized representation of the faith encounter with Jesus, giving Luther's eschatological chorale, "Mit Fried' und Freud' ich fahr' dahin," pride of place at the end of the movement sequence that precedes the concluding doxology. In Cantata 21 the break between the two parts represents the gap between tribulation and faith, while the anticipation of eternity is reserved for the final chorus, also from Revelation.

Cantata 21, therefore, deals with the progression of affective states more overtly than does the "Actus Tragicus," and in this respect the addition of recitatives and arias to the conjectured original movement sequence reflects Bach's seizing on the potential of the "modern" operatic style at Weimar for the first time in his cantata oeuvre. In this sense Cantata 21 represents, even in its presumed compositional history, the progression from a cantata type that centered largely on Old Testament texts and clung to archaic (seventeenth-century) movement types to one that afforded more scope to the representation of the affective states of the individual believer by means of up-to-date recitative and aria styles. In the final analysis, that compositional history (which is in any case unknown) is much less important than our recognition that the interaction of older and newer elements in Bach's work goes along with numerous other style distinctions to articulate a higher union that Bach clearly seems to have associated with the overarching unity of scripture and theological meaning, its doctrinal and personal emphases.

FOUR

Modal Questions

In a well-known passage from the second part of his treatise *Die Kunst des reinen Satzes in der Musik*, Johann Philipp Kirnberger, addressing the question of setting the Lutheran chorales in major-minor versus modal style, cites his former teacher, J. S. Bach, as having deemed "the method of composing according to the old church modes as necessary." Presumably, Kirnberger's calling Bach "the most sensitive of the newer composers" in this passage refers particularly to this ability.[1]

Quite apart from Kirnberger's remarks, it is probable that we are all prepared to grant that Bach's interaction with modal melodies was a profound one, but one that was not historically oriented to the same degree or in the same way as our own study of modal music. We do not usually consider that Bach's harmonization of modal melodies was attempting a historically faithful revival of the styles of the sixteenth or seventeenth centuries, for example.[2] Nevertheless, Kirnberger indicates that Bach drew style distinctions in his treatment of modal melodies when he prints Bach's G Mixolydian setting of "Komm, Gott Schöpfer" as an example of the "strictest treatment," following it by Bach's setting of the melody "Das alte Jahr vergangen ist." The latter setting illustrates a manner in which "because of the more attractive and flowing modulation sometimes the minor sixths and sevenths, sometimes the major, are introduced into the harmonic accompaniment." Kirnberger characterizes this latter type of harmonic treatment of the modes as "incontestably the most complete, because it retains throughout the greatest charm and the highest variety for the ear."[3]

If we compare the settings of "Komm, Gott Schöpfer" and "Das alte Jahr vergangen ist" printed by Kirnberger, the most immediately obvious harmonic difference between them is in the area of accidentals—that is, of deviation from the pure diatonic tones of the *cantus naturalis*, in which both settings are notated. On the one hand, "Komm, Gott Schöpfer" contains a single c♯'' in the melody line, the *subsemitonium* or leading tone to a d cadence; and in the harmony Bach introduces a brief f♯' as lower neighbor in a plagal cadence to G. Otherwise, the setting is pure "white note" music.[4] On the other hand, "Das alte Jahr" not only varies the sixths and sevenths, as Kirnberger indicates (in fact, it features all twelve tones of the chromatic scale, including the enharmonic equivalents e♭ and d♯), but also, like Bach's three other settings of this melody, begins in what from the viewpoint of modern tonality is the key of D minor and ends on an E major chord preceded by its dominant, B (or, in the case of one Bach setting, the transpositional equivalent of those keys a tone higher). Its *ambitus* (e'–d") and spectrum of cadences (on f', f', a', f', e', and g♯') are capable of more than one modal interpretation; but if the unusual final pitch, g♯', is not to be interpreted as a *subsemitonium*—that is, a leading tone or dominant—then the mode of the final cadence at least would most likely be interpreted as Phrygian E ending on the raised third. Since the first, second, and fourth phrases of the melody end on f', Bach's harmonizing them in d is not surprising; and since the third phrase ascends by step from a' to d" (through c♯") and ends with a stepwise descent from c♮" to a', Bach's E/A harmonization of its cadence fits entirely within the D minor frame of reference. Phrase 5, ending on e', also articulates a clear D minor half close. The shift to e/E is therefore a matter that involves the sixth and final phrase only; Bach makes it clear from the initial B^{6}_{5} harmony and confirms it with everything else in the phrase, especially the final B^7–E cadence, which introduces the half-diminished supertonic seventh chord in e as its antepenultimate harmony. The tonal shift at the end of Bach's setting might be interpreted in a variety of ways: as a modulation from D minor to E minor with the *Tierce de Picardie* on the final harmony or as a shift of mode from Dorian or Aolian D to Phrygian or Aolian E or even to A Aolian or minor ending on the dominant[5] (Ex. 4.1).

Kirnberger does not specify the mode of Bach's setting of "Das alte Jahr," perhaps because it was simpler to take the piece as an example of modern tonal variety than to attempt to resolve its tonal complexities in terms of mode. And in his discussion of the untransposed modes none contains an authentic cadence to E, even though the list of cadences for each mode is rather large and the discussion itself is prefaced by a remark on the modulatory variety of the modes. If Bach had harmonized the ending with a plagal cadence to E (as Telemann does in his 1730 chorale collection, for example), we would undoubtedly conclude that the setting shifted its mode from D Dorian to E Phrygian.[6] And all Bach's cadences would conform to Kirnberger's and to modal tradition generally. As it is, however, Bach's setting raises questions that the concept of mode alone will not resolve but that are of great importance, nevertheless, for his settings in general. To understand those questions we need to consider something of the seventeenth-century background for modal composition. The discussion that follows will attempt to outline aspects of the seventeenth-century tonal system that carried over into the eighteenth-century circle of keys and influenced Bach's compositional style in settings such as "Das alte Jahr," to which I will return in "Bach and Modal Tradition."

The Seventeenth-Century Background

Traditionally—that is, in most sixteenth- and seventeenth-century theory—a B–E cadence lay outside the normal framework of the modes, which respected the

Example 4.1. Bach's harmonization of "Das Alte Jahr vergangen ist" as printed by Kirnberger

boundaries of the medieval-Renaissance gamut, its three basic hexachords and two key signatures: the *cantus durus* or *naturalis* (the untransposed system), centered on the C hexachord (i.e., the pitches C, D, E, F, G, and A), and *cantus mollis* (the transposed system), centered on the F hexachord (F, G, A, B♭, C, and D).[7] Although the hexachord on G was available in the *cantus durus*, the pitch F♯, necessary to an authentic cadence to E (as the fifth of the B major chord), appeared in neither the G hexachord nor the *cantus naturalis/durus*. And since the true *cantus durus* (i.e., the equivalent of a one-sharp system centered on the G hexachord and including the adjacent D hexachord) was very sparingly used, the entire tonal system of the early seventeenth century was, from our perspective, biased in the flat direction.

Although the hexachord was traditionally a melodic concept, in the late-sixteenth and early-seventeenth centuries it became linked, in practice if not in theory, with the *harmonic* content of each of the two *cantus*—that is, with a spectrum of triads formed on the pitches of the scale. The Lutheran chorale tradition provides us with a clear instance of this development. The earliest Reformation-era chorale harmonizations to place the melody in the uppermost voice, those of Lucas Osiander's *Fünfftzig Geistliche Lieder und Psalmen* (Nuremberg, 1586), adhere with absolute regularity (one is tempted to say "strictness") to the principles behind the harmonic interpretation of the hexachords that I have set forth elsewhere with reference to Monteverdi in particular.[8] That is, Osiander, employing almost exclusively root-position triads in four-part note-against-note harmonization of the traditional melodies, uses only the *cantus mollis* and *cantus naturalis/durus* as signatures, and within that framework he introduces triads on the pitches of only two hexachords per system: the two-flat (B♭) and one-flat (F) hexachords in the *cantus mollis* and the one-flat and natural (C) hexachords in the *cantus durus.* And since the triads that constitute a single harmonically conceived hexachord comprise the pitches of *two* melodic hexachords, the original one and the one a fifth above, each of Osiander's two *cantus* contains the *pitches* of *three* melodic hexachords, B♭, F, and C in the *cantus mollis* and F, C, and G in the *cantus durus.* Within a single *cantus* the sharpest hexachord does not support a spectrum of triads but, rather, supplies the fifths of the triads of the hexachord one degree flatter. In melodic terms, therefore, Osiander's *cantus durus* is equivalent to the gamut with its three basic hexachords, and his *cantus mollis* represents transposition of the entire gamut at the fifth below. Osiander's strictly followed flat/sharp harmonic boundaries, then, are B♭/g and e/E triads for the *cantus naturalis/durus* settings and E♭/c and a/A triads for the *cantus mollis*; never once does a B major or minor triad appear in his harmonizations. His harmonic limits, therefore, define a somewhat narrower range than does the music of Monteverdi, which, as I have described elsewhere, often introduces the triads of the C hexachord (i.e., C, d/D, e/E, F, G, and a/A) into the *cantus mollis* and sometimes introduces those of the G hexachord (i.e., the b/B triads as well) into the *cantus durus.*[9]

Osiander's settings are of the kind we often loosely call modal, meaning that they feature many root-position triads with variable major and minor thirds, frequent open-fifth sonorities, and, above all, harmonic progressions that are not ordered hierarchically or "functionally" so as to generate a strong sense of tonal direction and of key. Although in these respects they are far less "tonal" than Monteverdi's works from at least the third book of madrigals (1592) on, they often employ the harmonic-tonal possibilities of the modal-hexachordal system in an "expressive" manner in relation to the chorale texts. A number of settings, for example, feature harmonic devices such as the raised third on minor triads and even, occasionally, the reverse.[10] And some settings, such as that of the German chorale version of the Twenty-third Psalm ("Der Herr ist mein getreuer Hirt," no. 30 in the collection), shift between the sharp and flat regions of the *cantus* for text-expressive purposes.[11] None of these devices, however, violates the tonal boundaries I have described. Thus, despite their conspicuous differences, the practices of both Osiander and Monteverdi (and, of course, of countless others) reveal that the widening of the tonal range of late-sixteenth- and early-seventeenth-century music was regulated by the expanded concepts of the gamut, *cantus* and hexachord.

And, in fact, Osiander's settings reflect the aforementioned "flat bias" in another detail: in relation to the circle-of-fifths ordering of the hexachordal degrees (e.g., B♭, F, C, G, D, A, and E in the *cantus durus*), Osiander harmonizes the sharpest of the melodic modal finals for each of the two *cantus,* e' for the *cantus durus* and a' for the *cantus mollis,* with triads that are a fifth below those finals—that is, with A major and D major chords, respectively. As a result, those melodies that would normally be classed as Phrygian and Hypophrygian in the two systems are rendered into the Aolian and Hypoaolian modes. It is not difficult to see that in a system of three melodic and two harmonic hexachords the sharpest pitches must often be harmonized as the fifths of the triads, thereby flattening the harmonization in relation to the mode of the melody. Nevertheless, it was often possible for the melodic final in question to have been "correctly" harmonized, and in one single case it is so harmonized. This lone exception is the penultimate setting in the collection, Luther's "Mitten wir im Leben sind" ("In the midst of life we are in death"), which is in Phrygian (often designated Hypophrygian) E in the *cantus durus.* Of the fourteen phrases of each verse of this chorale, however (including the two repeated phrases of the *Stollen*), nine end on the pitch e', and of those nine only one phrase, the last, is harmonized with the E major chord—in a form of Phrygian cadence that sounds distinctly open-ended (i.e., like a dominant ending).[12] In fact, the only E major chord in the setting is that of the final cadence. That detail, as well as the fact that Osiander reserves the only final cadence to E of the entire collection for the ending of this particular chorale, is undoubtedly significant in light of the fact that "Mitten wir im Leben sind" is intensely centered on death and the cry to God for mercy and aid, which culminates in the final "Kyrie eleison."[13] And since Osiander's collection follows the ordering of the liturgical year, it ends, in fact, with Luther's *two* eschatological chorales, following "Mitten wir im Leben sind" by "Mit Fried und Freud ich fahr dahin," Luther's chorale paraphrase of the Song of Simeon. But whereas the first of these chorales is dominated by fear of death, hell, and sin, the second is just the opposite: an expression of the believer's readiness to die in peace and joy. And Osiander's setting of "Mit Fried und Freud" ends the collection by bringing out a very different tone from that of "Mitten wir im Leben sind" in terms of the "hexachordal" quality of the harmonization. That is, the setting begins in the *cantus durus* (or *naturalis*) Dorian mode with the pitch B♮ figuring prominently in the first three phrases (there are no B♭s and the first two phrases end with E–a cadences). In the fourth phrase, however, Osiander makes a shift of the kind that I have described as that from the natural to the one-flat hexachord in the music of Monteverdi: beginning on an F major chord, he introduces the harmonies of the F hexachord (F, g, a, B♭, C, and d), ending with a Phrygian cadence pattern to a (B♭, g, and a chords). And from this point on the harmonies remain completely within the flat region of the *cantus* to the end. The reason for the shift seems obviously associated with the text from the fourth phrase to the end, "sanft und stille, wie Gott mir verheißen hat, der Tod ist mein Schlaf worden"; that is, Osiander brings out the *mollis* quality of the text in his setting, as so many other composers of the time did in the most diverse kinds of works.[14] Thus, at the end of his collection Osiander provides us with the two contrasted eschatological viewpoints that normally occur at the end of the liturgical year, fear and joy, mirroring them in terms of the *durus* and *mollis* hexachords of the *cantus naturalis*, just as he had mirrored the line "He leadeth me in green pastures" with a shift to the flat hexachord in his setting of the Twenty-third Psalm (see note 11).

In the seventeenth century the expansion of the harmonic content of the modes remained at first within the range of the two primary *cantus* (the "natural" and one-flat key signatures) and their associated hexachords, now generally three per system: B♭, F, and C in the *cantus mollis*, F, C, and (less often) G in the *cantus durus.* But the fact that the concept of the hexachord was now linked with a spectrum of triads represented the beginning of a process that would ultimately lead to the eighteenth-century circle of keys and the reinterpretation of the hexachords and modes together as the major-minor scale types. In Germany that process was reflected in everything that surrounded the terms *durus* and *mollis*, whose meanings changed through the course of the century from their traditional hexachordal associations to the names of the major and minor keys.[15] Although there was considerable ambivalence and contradiction regarding the affective associations of the two terms, the substantial overlap in the two sets of meanings made clear that what was involved was a shift in perspective according to which the older meanings were by no means forgotten. Thus, in the late seventeenth century Andreas Werckmeister, one of the principal advocates of the major and minor keys, still occasionally designates them with the terms *cantus durus* and *cantus mollis*. Disliking the association of the pejorative term *dur* with the major keys, he adheres to an old tradition in using the term *dur* to describe sharp-minor triads and *moll* for flat-major; and he speaks of the major (*dur*) key as comprising the Ionian and Mixolydian modes, the minor (*moll*) as comprising the Dorian and Aolian.[16] The last of these usages attests to the process by which the number of modes per system lessened as the number of available systems (key signatures) increased during the seventeenth century.[17] Its completion (i.e., the eventual reduction of the modes to two types represented by the seven-tone major and minor scales) marked the end of traditional modal theory as anything but a purely "historical" phenomenon, as Bach's contemporaries Johann David Heinichen and Johann Mattheson were quick to point out.[18] The major and minor keys (which were capable of varying the sixths and sevenths, as Kirnberger said of Bach's "Das alte Jahr") took over the roles of both the modes and the hexachords simultaneously, swallowing up the subtle distinctions among the individual modes.

Nevertheless, within traditional discussions of the modes, still widely accepted as the basis for the modern keys, the choice of B♭ or B♮, the ancient B *molle* or *rotundo* and B *durum* or *quadratum*, was more important than we nowadays realize. Not only did it determine the only two key signatures in common use before the second quarter of the seventeenth century, but it also expressed the nature of harmonic tonality within each of those key signatures as well. Traditionally, modal distinctions had rested on the placement of the "mi/fa" semitone, which, in the circle-of-fifths ordering of the tones of the hexachord, had expressed the coming together of the flattest and sharpest degrees (i.e., F and E in the C hexachord). In the harmonically conceived hexachord those degrees became the sharpest and flattest *triads*—e–E and F (or d^6)—whose coming together in the so-called Phrygian cadence served to identify the hexachord as a discrete tonal unit (a tonal "circle," whose point of closure was the meeting point of its sharpest and flattest tonal elements). In a framework that comprised two harmonically conceived hexachords, such as either of Osiander's two *cantus*, described previously, or of three such hexachords, as in much of Monteverdi's music, the sharpest and flattest triads, B♭–g and E–e or B♭–g and B–b (in the case of the *cantus durus*) may expand the old "mi" against "fa" idea to the level of the juxtaposition of discrete harmonic regions of the *cantus*. Monteverdi's earlier music increasingly features such differentiation of sharp and flat tonal regions, which reach their peak in the tonal juxtapositions of the recitative dialogues in acts 2 and 4 of *Orfeo*. When these tonal disparities are drawn into the framework of individual keys, as they increasingly are in Monteverdi's later music (i.e., the well-known g–E juxtapositions of *Orfeo* "functioning" as the subdominant and the dominant of the dominant in d, rather than merely as harmonizations of the pitches

B♭ and B), then we are on the threshhold of our concepts of the tonic, dominant, and subdominant and the differentiation of the sharp, flat, and natural regions with separate key signatures.

As the range of key signatures expanded in the seventeenth century, the principles that underlay the hexachords and *cantus* extended by transposition to other pitch levels. Largely because of modulation and the new hierarchical ordering of key relationships in late-seventeenth- and early-eighteenth-century music, however, the greatly increased interaction of key-signature levels in any given tonal piece could not be adequately accounted for with either hexachordal or modal concepts.[19] The "mi–fa" idea remained as a theoretical explanation for key-signature shifting (increasing flats conceptualized as changing "mi" into "fa" and vice versa) and even juxtapositional key changes, but it was ultimately superseded by the newer concepts that surrounded key relationships in music of wider tonal range. At the same time, however, since most eighteenth-century theorists still discussed the modes in their traditional *cantus durus/cantus mollis* contexts and many eighteenth-century composers (including Bach) set large numbers of chorales in the untransposed modes, awareness of the ancient symbolic associations of "mi–fa" shifting and its primary symbol, the B *molle/quadro* alternative, remained a continuing presence in their chorale harmonizations. As a result, it is possible, in certain compositions, such as the opening movement of Cantata 77, discussed in chapter 8, for the traditional modal-hexachordal qualities of an ancient chorale melody to expand to the level of the modulatory procedures of the newer tonal music, right before our eyes, so to speak, and from there to determine the tonal design of an entire cantata. Bach may even associate such an expansion with the theological qualities of his texts; in the opening movement of Cantata 77, for example, they suggest an allegory of the reinterpretation of Old Testament theology by that of the New—that is, a mirroring of the basic underlying principles of biblical hermeneutics.

To the extent that the B–E cadence such as that which ends "Das alte Jahr" (a setting that would normally be viewed as in the *cantus naturalis/durus*) was accepted in seventeenth-century modal theory, it was associated with the Phrygian/Hypophrygian modal pairing in certain of the newer systems, in which we sometimes find descriptions of the modes that reflected modern practice. Athanasius Kircher, for example, attempts to account for all the ways in which the modes were viewed in his time, supplying not only the traditional eight- and twelve-mode systems of the Middle Ages and Renaissance along with a discussion of their transpositions but also schemes in which the tonal practices of his time constitute a palpable presence. In one such scheme the Phrygian mode appears as what we now call the A harmonic-minor scale and the Hypophrygian as a kind of plagal version of that mode, but with a semitone above the final of its authentic counterpart (i.e., e, f, g♯, a, b♭ [*sic*], c, d, and e), while in another the Hypophrygian mode is equivalent to the modern key of E minor. The existence of two such completely disparate views of the same mode is a key to understanding the distinction between modal and tonal usages in seventeenth-century tonality. Of these two versions of the mode, the former makes a more obvious attempt to reconcile aspects of modern practice with modal tradition, providing semitones above both E and A, while the pitch G♯ supplies both the leading tone to A and the major third of the final E. As I have suggested elsewhere, because of its introduction of the foreign tone b♭ (even though Kircher clearly places the mode in the *cantus durus*), this version of the Hypophrygian mode was probably influenced by Giacomo Carissimi's *Jephthe*, which features transposable units in which what we now call the Neapolitan-sixth chord appears as a means of harmonizing the semitone above the cadential harmony.[20] Since this mode has no B (as the root of a triad; hence no dominant), however, its final, E, will sound like the dominant of a in most situations. This mode, therefore, exhibits striking tendencies toward the "subdominant." In his other modern version of the mode, however, Kircher harmonizes a short phrase with the B–E cadence, announcing, nevertheless, that this cadence did not really belong to the mode (or, more accurately, to the untransposed system of the modes—the *cantus naturalis/durus*—in which F♯ was not an essential pitch).[21] In this version of the mode the B–E cadence represented expansion of the modal-hexachordal framework to the level of a true *cantus durus* that was not equivalent to the *cantus naturalis*.[22]

Kircher's modern modal systems, like that of Adriano Banchieri half a century earlier, bear witness to the tendency of early-seventeenth-century music to expand its tonal-harmonic content into a wider range of hexachordal or transpositional levels.[23] The anomalies within Kircher's two modern versions of the E Hypophrygian mode are bound up with the fact that within the untransposed system (the *cantus naturalis/cantus durus*) the E mode (whether designated Phrygian or Hypophrygian) is the sharpest on the circle of fifths. As a result, it has no dominant within the *cantus* and is therefore unstable tonally, tending "backward" toward A, unless, as in Kircher's E minor version of the mode, it acquires stability by appropriating its dominant (i.e., the pitch F♯ as fifth of the B major chord) from the one-sharp system (the true *cantus durus*). In the process of acquiring that stability it becomes equivalent to the Aolian mode, furthering the process of simultaneous tonal expansion and modal reduction that led to the circle of keys. In this respect, the presence or absence of the B♭ and B triads is the most telling detail in Kircher's two modern Hypophrygian modes. Owing to the presence of B♭ rather than B, the former might, in fact, be said to constitute a mode that is interpreted in terms of two *cantus* (*mollis* and *naturalis*) and two finals (E and A), while the latter, owing to the B triad, is E minor (Aolian) in the *cantus durus*, pure and simple. Expansion of the tonal system of the early seventeenth century in the sharp direction—overcoming the aforementioned flat bias—was the process that led to the circle of keys.

And the opening up of the sharp system went hand in hand with the emergence of what I have called the "dominant dynamic" as a fundamental principle of tonal form (in the music of Monteverdi, for example). Its effect on the perception of the modes was incalculable. For once strong articulation of the dominant of the mode (often with the aid of *its* dominant) became virtually a sine qua non of tonal form, the modes, several of which exhibited the aforementioned "subdominant" character, had to adopt the characteristics of the modern keys, including pitch modifications to their melodies so as to fit with the new harmonic qualities. This process marked the end of strict—that is, sixteenth-century-style—modal composition as anything but a historical phenomenon. Both of Kircher's modern versions of the Hypophrygian mode are of value to our understanding of "Das alte Jahr," and Bach's modal composition generally, in that they highlight important issues that surround the carryover of the modal-hexachordal system of the early seventeenth century into the circle of major and minor keys of the early eighteenth.

The principal bond between the two systems was, of course, the primacy of fifth relationships, not only between the hexachords of the *cantus* and the key signatures of the circle of keys but also between the ordering of the modes *within* the hexachord or *cantus* (system) and that of the major and minor keys within the circle. Thus, behind the scalar grouping of the modes within a single *cantus*—on the pitches c, d, e, f, g, and a in the *cantus durus*—there was a strong sense of a "tonal" ordering by fifths (F, C, G, d, a, and e) in which each of the two subgroups of major and minor modes (F, C, and G and d, a, and e, respectively) exhibited features of a flat/natural/sharp ordering. Within the flattest of the major and minor modes of the *cantus durus*, F (Lydian) and d (Dorian), the pitch B was frequently altered to B♭, largely to correct the F–B tritone (particularly since F was a prominent cadence degree in both modes). The effect was to render those modes equivalent to the C (Ionian) and a (Aolian) modes. The corresponding modification in the pitch content of the two sharpest modes, however—that is, the substitution of F♯ for F to "correct" the B–F diminished fifth in G Mixolydian and E Phrygian—was at first not carried out with anything like the same degree of frequency. And whereas flattened pitches, conceptualized as the changing of "mi" into "fa," often introduced long-range tonal effects—transposition, or what we now call modulation, in the flat direction—sharpened pitches, conceptualized as the changing of "fa" into "mi," served primarily in the role of the so-called *subsemitonium modi* at cadences, generally a purely local effect. Thus, as already mentioned, the flat bias within the system as a whole was at first very pronounced, especially when viewed from the perspective of later tonal music. Not only did the Lydian and Dorian modes tend toward the *cantus mollis*, but also the Mixolydian and Phrygian modes exhibited a "subdominant" character: that is, owing to the pitch F, their finals tended to sound like the dominants of the modes a fifth below. At first, therefore, the system tended to expand far more readily in the flat than the sharp direction. Eventually, however, the rise of the new dominant-oriented conception of tonal form encouraged expansion of the system in the sharp direction, so that the pitch F♯ became more and more an integral element of the *cantus durus*. And this in turn caused the G and e modes to represent the sharp region of the *cantus*, as the F and d modes did the flat. The resultant expansion of the key signatures of the six "diatonic" finals to three and the reduction of their modal types to two demanded a new model for ordering the system.

That new ordering, the regrouping of the major and minor modal types into "relative" major/minor pairs—F/d, C/a, G/e—did not appear as a basic concept of music theory until the early eighteenth century. In late-sixteenth- and early-seventeenth-century music, therefore, the lack of a true *cantus durus*, or one-sharp system, meant that the system was not symmetrical around a center that corresponded to a tonic area with what we would call dominant and subdominant "sides" of the key. With Johann David Heinichen's first presentation of the circle of keys (1711), the transpositional levels associated with the three principal hexachords of the system expanded to become the dominant and subdominant areas of what was now called the *ambitus* of the relative major and minor keys: a spectrum of six keys, three major, three minor, retaining the finals of the authentic modes of the twelve-mode system in the *cantus durus* (or *cantus naturalis*), but organized according to the adjacent fifth levels of the three hexachords (F–d, C–a, and G–e in Heinichen's ordering) and expressed in terms of three key signatures. Heinichen made clear that this new interpretation of the *ambitus* of the key was the basis of his *musicalischer Circul*.[24] This three-system symmetry could then continue to expand by transposition (one of the secondary systems of the *ambitus* becoming the central system of the next) until the full circle of twelve major and twelve minor keys was closed. During the period of expansion the addition of flats or sharps to the key signature was still conceptualized as changing "mi" into "fa" and vice versa.[25] As long as the basic transposition scale (the hexachord) had been limited to six tones that contain but one semitone, the modes could all be described within a single key signature, and the placement of the semitone—the "mi" and "fa" degrees of the scale—would define their primary differences. With the expansion of the three hexachords of the system to the three systems of the *ambitus* and of the six-tone hexachord to the seven-tone major scale (which now contained two "mi–fa" semitones, thereby also legitimizing the tritone as a third form of "mi–fa," formerly the "mi" *contra* "fa"), the "mi–fa" idea came to express a wide range of tonal events that relate generally to the directional (modulatory) tendencies of raised and lowered pitches.[26] In Bach's work those tendencies might in some instances expand to the level of the tonal designs of entire cantatas.

In devising means of reinterpreting the modal qualities of the Lutheran chorale melodies, Bach was aided considerably by the fact that the tonal language of his time retained close links to the modal-hexachordal traditions. Conservative theorists still adhered to the concept of mode, and, in general, the understanding of tonal relationships was still very much indebted to the hexachords and solmization, even in the earliest presentations of the major and minor keys. The immediate effect of the new tonal expansion—diversity in the description of the modes, as we saw in Kircher's examples—carried over into Bach's time in the form of relatively "strict" and "free" tonal styles. In Bach's work we can speak, in fact, of *three* distinct viewpoints on the modes, all of which appear to varying degrees in Kircher's treatise, and three potential styles of modal composition. The first corresponded to the old medieval-Renaissance tonal system, which was basically a system of white-note music (what Kirnberger calls the "strictest treatment" in Bach's styles of modal composition), and the third corresponded to the treatment of the modes as modern keys with the full resources of modern tonal music. Between them, however, was the most interesting one, which descended from the transitional period of modal composition in the seventeenth century. In this style the modern major and minor keys do not replace the modes; yet many of the resources of tonal composition come into play. As a result, there is a far greater interaction of modal and tonal styles in pieces that belong to this category than to those of the other two types. The modes are reinterpreted in terms of the new tonality; and in relation to pieces in the other two categories there are many more anomalies, above all in the area of whether or not the modal final sounds like a "tonic" key. We may often sense a tension between the older and newer styles, each accommodating to the other only with difficulty. And we may often have difficulty determining exactly what the mode was intended to be. As we will see, not only was Bach fully aware of this kind of modal composition, but also he made it a primary one in his music, exploiting its obvious musico-allegorical potential to the utmost.

From the standpoint of traditional modal usage, then, Bach's setting of "Das alte Jahr" must be deemed to have shifted not only its mode but also its *cantus*. In Kircher's terms, it made a *mutatio modi* as well as a *mutatio toni*.[27] In shifting from the *cantus naturalis* to the *cantus durus* (i.e., in the sharp rather than the flat direction), by changing its "fa" degree (f) into "mi" (f♯), it exhibits a tonal dynamic that can be considered the opposite of that of a melody such as the Mixolydian chorale "Dies sind die heil'gen zehn Gebot" (to be taken up in chapter 7), which shifts at the end from the *cantus naturalis* to the *cantus mollis*, changing "mi" (b) into "fa" (b♭). And the theological qualities associated with the two chorales are also very different, the one ("Das alte Jahr") becoming increasingly positive and directed toward the anticipation of eternity (see the following discussion), while the other becomes "weaker" at the end as it expresses humanity's need for God's mercy. Describing such complex harmonizations in terms that descend from the hexachord theory of the Middle Ages and Renaissance may well sound inadequate to Bach's fully chromatic tonal language, nothing more than a historical residue that, despite Bach's setting the old catchphrase "Mi–Fa et Fa–Mi est tota Musica" as a canon, no longer expressed anything vital for modern composition. And, in fact, the very first reference to Bach in print appears within a treatise that proclaimed on its title page that solmization and the modes were not "tota Musica" but "todte Musica."[28] Nevertheless, Kirnberger's praise of Bach's sensitivity to modal composition is certainly not hollow; and, in fact, Kirnberger himself recognized, intuitively at least, that the difference that resulted from substituting b♭ for b (i.e., "fa" for "mi") in a chorale harmonization, changing D Dorian into D Aolian, for example, was an affective shift that corresponded to the qualities associated with the terms *durus* and *mollis*.[29]

Bach and Modal Tradition

Anyone who has studied and played even a modest number of Bach's chorale settings, whether those for organ or those for four-part choir, whether relatively simple or highly elaborated, knows for a certainty that Bach never ceases to probe the ways in which harmony can be molded, as it were, so as to convey particular affective qualities of their texts. Bach often seizes on opportunities provided by the ancient chorale melodies to devise ways of reflecting the meaning of their texts in his settings, even though we may have considerable difficulty in ascertaining exactly what mode he intended. In setting chorales with varied strophes, Bach often had to project a particular affect that would not fit with every individual strophe. In the case of "Das alte Jahr," however, the six verses of the chorale articulate a single closely interwoven complex of ideas that center on a metaphoric interpretation of the old year as the embodiment of humanity's recognition of its sinful nature, its need for God's protection and forgiveness, and the new year as humanity's hopes for God's grace and salvation. Within this context the believer's thanks to God for protection of His "arme Christenheit" from danger in the old year, for the gift of His "heilsam Wort," for standing by the faithful, and, above all, for the forgiveness of sin and the gift of His grace lead, over the first four strophes, toward the believer's hopes of eternal life in the last two. The overall direction in the chorale as a whole is therefore a positive one in which the final two verses focus on the anticipation of eternity, with no further references to the old year and its association with human sinfulness. Thus, the new year becomes a metaphor for the idea of a new beginning in the broadest sense.

Das alte Jahr vergangen ist, Wir danken dir, Herr Jesu Christ, Das du uns in so großer G'fahr Behütet hast diß ganzer Jahr.	The old year is past, We thank Thee, Lord Jesus Christ, That You through such great danger Have protected us the entire year.
Wir bitten dich, ewigen Sohn Des Vaters in dem höchsten Thron, Du wollst dein arme Christenheit Ferner bewahren allezeit.	We pray Thee, eternal Son Of the Father on the throne most high, That You Your poor Christianity Will continue to preserve always.
Entzeuch uns nicht dein heilsam Wort, Welch's ist der Seelen Trost und Hort: Vor falscher Lehr, Abgötterey, Behüt uns, Herr, und steh uns bey.	Do not take from us Your holy word, Which is the soul's comfort and refuge: From false teaching, idolatry, Guard us, Lord, and stand by us.
Hilf, daß wir von der Sünd ablahn, Und fromm zu werden fangen an: Kein'r Sünd im alten Jahr gedenk, Ein gnadenreich neu-Jahr uns schenk;	Help that we turn away from sin, And begin to be pious: Do not think of sin in the old year, Give us a new year rich in grace,
Christlich zu leben, seliglich Zu sterben, und hernach fröhlich Am jüngsten Tag wied'r aufzustehn, Mit dir in Himmel einzugehn,	So that we live like Christ, Die blessedly, and hereafter Rise again in joy on judgment day, To enter with You in heaven,
Zu danken und zu loben dich Mit allen Engeln ewiglich. O Jesu! unsern Glauben mehr, Zu deines Namens Lob und Ehr.	To thank and to praise Thee With all the angels eternally. O Jesu! increase our faith For the praise and honor of Your name.

Although the melody of "Das alte Jahr" contains six phrases, each strophe has only four lines, of which the first and last lines were repeated (to different music) so that the overall pattern was aabcdd. Each of the first four strophes follows a pattern in which, after a positive expression in the second line, the third makes reference to the weakness and sinfulness of the human condition ("G'fahr," "arme Christenheit," "falscher Lehr, Abgötterey," and "Sünd"); the fourth line then overcomes the disparity with thanks or a prayer for God's protection. This pattern is mirrored in the melody, which involves first the shift from d to a for phrase 3 (line 2), then the more extensive shift from d to e for phrase 6 (line 4). The positive ending of each strophe has its counterpart in the eschatological character of the last two verses of the chorale as a whole.

In light of what I have just described, the tonal shift at the end of "Das alte Jahr" can be said to mirror the textual antitheses of the old versus the new year, the sinful human condition versus God's grace, and the present life versus eternity. In the setting printed by Kirnberger (Ex. 4.1) Bach seems to have conceived the tonal dynamic as one of flat–sharp motion that involves two stages, the first occupying phrases 1 to 3, in which the move from d to a takes place, and the second phrases 4 to 6, in which motion from d to E occurs. Although it will appear oversimplified from the standpoint of present-day analytical procedures, it is possible to describe this motion in terms of the shift from B♭ to B or, more generally, in terms of the three hexachords of the old modal-hexachordal system. The first phrase features B♭ exclusively and the second mostly B♭, although it introduces B♮ at one point in the bass. The third phrase, however, eliminates B♭ altogether, as it moves decisively toward a, introducing the chromatic descending tetrachord from a to e in the bass. The effect is comparable to that which I have described elsewhere within the work of Monteverdi, where this kind of tonal shifting represents the emergence of the aforementioned "dominant dynamic" as a ruling principle of tonal form.[30] With the fourth phrase (setting the lines that refer to the sinful human condition and that, therefore, look backward to the qualities associated with the old year), the B♭ reappears to replace the B♮ in the harmonization (even though the *melody* contains two b♮s and no b♭'); and a lone e♭' in the alto gives the subdominant, g, a newly increased level of emphasis. The fifth phrase then replaces B♭ with B again, ending on A once more, but now within the context of D minor. After this, phrase 6 effects the final shift of mode and *cantus*, bringing in the B major chord immediately and suggesting a degree of stability by moving the bass line into the lowest register of the piece. The resultant shift to e–E and the *cantus durus* seems to parallel the believer's hopes for eternal life.

All four of Bach's known harmonizations of "Das alte Jahr vergangen ist" end with an authentic final cadence to E (or its transpositional equivalent).[31] In the most interesting of these settings, that of the *Orgelbüchlein*, Bach provides us with indications of what the shift of mode might have represented for him (Ex. 4.2). Beneath an elaborated version of the chorale melody in the uppermost voice, the three lower parts incorporate chromatic ascending and descending tetrachords and pentachords that both articulate the initial D minor tonal framework of the setting and suggest that the idea of the "old year" is a metaphor for the human condition, its "imperfection and mortality," as Werckmeister described the basic allegory behind tempered music. In phrase 3 the ascending chromatic tetrachord moves into the soprano voice, revealing its derivation from the melody of that phrase. As it moves toward the cadence to a–A, this phrase takes on a more optimistic character than the preceding two, introducing a very positive-sounding D major triad; but the immediate return to d for another variant of the opening phrase (phrase 4) places the sequence as a whole solidly within the context of d. The sounding of the tone f above the dominant harmony (A) in each of the first four phrases seems to introduce an element of imperfection and sorrow, even of inevitability. Within this context there can be no sense of transcendence or even of hope, and the a–A of the third phrase is absorbed into the D minor framework entirely. In phrase 5 Bach's utilizing only ascending chromaticism in the lower parts—leading the individual units toward the tones c, g, d, and a in turn—introduces a form of tonal ascent that, in combination with the secondary dominants in the harmony, hints at the possibility of a hopeful outcome. That outcome is virtually overwhelmed, however, by the chromaticism itself and the immediate turning of the hint of D that comes at the end of the phrase

Example 4.2. "Das alte Jahr vergangen ist" from the *Orgelbüchlein*

into a half close in d (the f♯'–f' shift before the cadence is very telling, as a shift from b' to b♭' had been at the beginning of phrase 4).[32] Furthermore, in this setting the sixth phrase does not turn to e/E until the very end, basically only for the final cadence, at which point the soprano line moves upward above the dominant of e/E in a sequence of "sighing" appoggiaturas that reach the highest tone of the piece, f♯", symbol of the shift of system, before dropping to the a'–g♯' of the final E cadence. Ultimately, the ending suggests a quality of yearning to accompany the metaphor of the old year as a symbol of human life, tortured and nearing its end.

In contrast to the setting printed by Kirnberger, this one from the *Orgelbüchlein* seems to mirror both the recognition of a sinful past in the text of the chorale as a whole and the hope for a future that will overcome the believer's state of torment. In keeping with that hope, the last phrase begins by referring back to the beginning of phrase 4, but with a few significant modifications, just before it settles on the dominant of E for the final cadence; this, presumably, is Bach's means of indicating that the old tonal context has now been replaced by a new one (first changing b♭' to b', then f' to f♯' as B becomes established as the dominant in the bass). With the shift of mode, this setting, which is far subtler than I have indicated, conveys a considerable sense of the meaning behind the ending of the chorale text. It does not attempt, however, to convey the affect of the final lines as a realized experience, but rather to place the believer's hopes in the context of his awareness of mortality, so to speak.

Bach's treatment of chorale melodies that change their mode, end on the "wrong" degree of the scale, or contain pitches outside the normal modal (or transpositional) framework is an interesting facet of his work, and one that is immensely revealing of his interaction with tradition. It is also an area in which we have the opportunity to witness his recognition that many modal melodies reflected their texts in ways that could be translated into the broad harmonic terms of his eighteenth-century harmonic-tonal language—that is, their modal anomalies could serve as the basis of allegorical tonal designs, such as the movement sequences of individual cantatas.[33] In the case of "Das alte Jahr vergangen ist" we do not know the cantata (if any) to which Bach's chorale settings belonged. But if I am right in suggesting that Bach perceived the shift of key at the end of those settings as a reflection of the change from the old year to the new and its metaphoric interpretations in terms of the eras of salvation history and the experience of faith (tribulation versus fulfillment), then there is certainly precedent for such an idea in other of Bach's works for New Year's Day. The original form of the chorale that appears most often in Bach's New Year's Day cantatas, "Jesu, nun sei gepreiset," changed not only its mode but also its time signature for the final phrases, two obvious means of representing the change to the new year.[34] In Bach's time it had become customary, at least in some places (including Leipzig), to end "Jesu, nun sei gepreiset" by repeating the text of the last two lines to the music of the first two, thereby returning to the original mode (and meter) at the end; the effect intended by this change was to articulate the idea of beginning–ending equivalence—that is, to emphasize the idea of continuity above that of change between the old and new years.[35] A similar "tonal allegory" appears in the *Christmas Oratorio*, whose fourth cantata, for New Year's Day, is set in the key of F, following the D major framework of the preceding three cantatas (in D, G, and D, respectively); the fifth and sixth cantatas (in A and D) then return to the D frame of reference.[36] The idea of the six cantatas of the oratorio as a tonal "cycle" hinges on the fact that the original key returns to "overcome" the change between the third and fourth cantatas. A similar balance between change and continuity might even perhaps have been intended by Bach in the *Orgelbüchlein*, where he follows "Das alte Jahr vergangen ist" by "In dir ist Freude," a setting that is sharply contrasted to "Das alte Jahr" (chromaticism versus triadic diatonicism, minor versus major, quadruple versus triple meter, rhetorically conceived pathos versus physical exuberance, and the like), yet whose G major tonality can also be thought to confirm the shift to the *cantus durus* at the end of "Das alte Jahr."

A few pages earlier on in the *Orgelbüchlein*, Bach set another modally anomalous chorale that also had liturgical associations of a new beginning, the Christmas chorale "Christum wir sollen loben schon," whose originally Gregorian melody, untransposed, begins on d' and ends on e' (*ambitus* d'–c", beginning on d' and ending on e', with melodic cadences on e', c", a', and e'), thereby suggesting a shift from D minor to A minor (ending on either the tonic or the dominant of a) or from D Dorian to E Phrygian.[37] While many harmonizations of this melody end on an A major chord, thereby suggesting a close on the dominant of the original d, in his setting from the *Orgelbüchlein*, as well as in the chorale motet setting that begins his chorale cantata setting of "Christum wir sollen loben schon" (BWV 121), and the cantonal setting that ends that work, Bach harmonizes the melody so as to emphasize the tonal shift to the dominant, a, via *its* dominant, E (or their transpositional equivalents), which first enters within the final phrase (at about its midpoint) and ultimately serves as the final chord.[38] The E ending has, as so many Phrygian cadences do, the character of an ending on the dominant. As in the case of "Das alte Jahr," Bach brings out rather than covering up the modal anomaly, although in "Das alte Jahr" the shift of mode more clearly effects a "modulation" to e. In the case of "Christum wir sollen loben schon" Bach might have taken the overall rise of a tone in its melody and the resultant shift of mode as a reflection of the fact that this chorale expresses the idea of the new beginning that came with Jesus' birth.[39] Behind Luther's paraphrase of its original text, "A solis ortus cardine," was an association between the birth of Christ and the rising sun (since Christmas occurs about the time of the change to longer days at the winter solstice). As we will see, Bach's chorale cantata on "Christum wir sollen loben schon" draws the modal shift into a compelling "allegorical" design for the work as a whole.

Thus, it was not at all uncommon for the modal qualities of chorale melodies to reflect the texts with which they were associated, although they are never perfectly consistent in this regard. When such a mirroring of the text occurs, however, Bach often seizes on the modal qualities of the chorale, amplifying them in ways that parallel the expansion of the theological content of the chorale text in the modal qualities of the cantata as a whole. In the case of Luther's penitential hymn "Aus tiefer Not schrei' ich zu dir," for example, the first line of the E Phrygian melody mirrors the word "deep" by falling a fifth from b' to e' on the beginning of the word "tiefer," then the idea of the sinner's crying in torment to God by the rising fifth e' to b' (so that the melody suggests the word "aus" of the text), the word "Not" by the semitone above the b', and the entreaty "schrei' ich zu dir" by the falling and rising third with which the line ends. The descent of a third to "ich" and the subsequent rise of a third for "zu dir" are typical details by which the melody mirrors the ideas of penitence and supplication. And for a composer as sensitive as Bach to the tonal qualities of modal melodies, the "subdominant" tonal quality of the Phrygian mode—that is, the sense that in harmonic settings the modal final (E) sounds like the dominant of the key a fifth below (A)—has the additional potential of conveying a broad sense that the melody as a whole represents the weakened condition of the sinner.

In fact, the melody of "Aus tiefer Not" inspired Bach to some very distinct "allegories" of the qualities in question, such as the famous *stile antico* organ chorale prelude in the *Clavierübung*, whose strict style and complex polyphonic writing—including a double pedal part—seem to have been designed to represent the strictness of God's demands and the depths of the sinner's earthly struggles and entanglements. Also, as I have described elsewhere, Bach's chorale cantata on "Aus tiefer Not" (BWV 38) expands on both the melodic-directional and tonal qualities of the Phrygian melody to create a design based on tonal "descent" by fifths from the first through the fifth movements, followed by a return "ascent" to its original tonality in the last movement.[40] In fact, the tonal character of the entire work tends continually in the subdominant direction, that motion coinciding with the increasing stages of the believer's sinking into the depths of tribulation. In that work the basic idea of destruction followed by restoration—or descent followed by ascent—is the key to the entire design. In this way the tonal plan of the cantata mirrors the idea conveyed in the opening phrase of the chorale.

Tonally the Phrygian/Hypophrygian pairing was the "weakest" among the spectrum of modes at a single transpositional level—that is, the most likely to sound as though it ended on the dominant, especially when the concluding harmony was major. As mentioned, certain of Bach's cantatas that utilize Phrygian-mode chorales derive important features of their tonal designs from the very fact that the Phrygian mode contains a disparity between the correct modal final and the way that final is heard tonally. In that the final often sounds like a dominant, the setting as a whole may project a sense that its harmonic content undermines or "weakens" the final—that is, that the harmony functions in relation to the final just as the emphasis on the subdominant did with respect to the tonic in the program sonata described by Kuhnau in the preface to his *Biblische Historien*. Kuhnau's view that the final of that sonata represented incomplete recovery from illness even has a parallel in one of Bach's cantatas, "Es ist nichts gesundes an meinem Leibe," whose Phrygian aspects (embodied in the opening movement, an elaborate setting of the Phrygian melody "Herzlich tut mich verlangen") are associated with sickness as a metaphor for sin. In this respect, the mode type that often sounds as though it ends on the dominant and that may suggest Phrygian, Hypophrygian, or Aolian interpretations—especially when it is associated with such chorales as "Ach Herr, mich armen Sünder," "Herzlich tut mich verlangen," "Erbarm dich mein, o Herre Gott," "Ach Gott, vom Himmel sieh' darein," and "Aus tiefer Not"—can be considered the mode of human weakness for Bach. Tonality itself, represented in the quality of hearing (*sensus*), becomes a metaphor for the inability of the believer to live up to God's demands (the correct modal final).

The quality just described has manifold forms in Bach's work, one of its most outstanding manifestations being the design of Cantata 77, to be taken up in chapters 7 and 8. In that work the outermost movements are settings of chorale melodies —"Dies sind die heil'gen zehn Gebot" and "Ach Gott, vom Himmel sieh' darein"— in the two modes, the Mixolydian and Hypophrygian, that constituted, as mentioned, the sharpest among the modal spectrum and were therefore the ones that tended most strongly in the subdominant direction. As a result, the "subdominant" tendency of the design of this cantata as a whole is one of its most outstanding qualities, and one that Bach develops in relation to its theological theme—love of God and love of one's neighbor—in ways that are very telling for his work as a whole.

From this standpoint, we must recognize that modal composition offered Bach the opportunity to broaden the tonal character of his music, in addition to deepening its ability to mirror the theological content that lay behind the chorale texts. Many of the questions that arise from study of Bach's modal harmonizations, however, cannot be answered from the standpoint of the concept of mode, which, as Heinichen and Mattheson recognized, had been rendered obsolete by the circle of major and minor keys. What remained for a composer such as Bach, who believed in the continuing viability of "modal" composition, was to reinterpret the modes in a living way, recognizing their fundamental differences from the modern major-minor keys and intensifying those differences within the context of the modern tonal system. In many cases, that entailed a process of "translation" according to which melodic characteristics that arose from the placement of the semitone in the individual modes—the semitone above the final in the Phrygian mode, the flat leading tone in the Mixolydian mode, the raised fourth and its "correction" to a perfect fourth in the Lydian mode, the variable sixth degree of the Dorian mode, and the like—were probed as deeply as possible for their tonal implications.

"Durch Adams Fall"–Andreas Werckmeister on the Hypophrygian Mode

Werckmeister, we remember, took an extensively "allegorical" approach to music, perceiving allegory itself as an interpretative means by which musical meaning could be uncovered in processes analogous to hermeneutics. Such meaning belonged to music as a gift of God and a reflection of God's ordering the universe according to "number, weight and measure." At the same time even those aspects of music that reflected the imperfection of human life—such as enharmonicism, temperament, dissonance, and the like—had their place in Werckmeister's allegorical vision. And since the purpose of music was to give glory to God and sustenance to one's neighbor, the chorales of the Lutheran church had a special role, that of conveying the basic tenets of the faith in directly affective, succinctly expressed mergings of poetry and music. Luther looked upon their capacity to uphold the believer in his faith as evidence that music was "next to theology" among the gifts of God. Werckmeister was alert, however, to the fact that many of the oldest chorales had undergone substantial modification from the time of their composition, believing that those modifications—which he interpreted as the result of historical accidents, misunderstandings, and the like—had altered the originally intended relationship of the music to the text. This was particularly evident in the case of chorales that ended on the "wrong," or apparently wrong, degree of the scale, thus confusing the mode and causing them to suffer erroneous harmonizations at the hands of insensitive organists. His remarks alert us to qualities in the old melodies that Bach seized upon in certain cantatas in which those chorales figure prominently. I will take up the cantatas themselves in the following chapter.

In the *Harmonologia Musica* Werckmeister discusses a melody associated with "Durch Adams Fall" that he places in the Hypophrygian mode, although "one cadences very frequently on the Dorian, since the Dorian closes in D."[41] He then remarks, "Nun aber heisset es allemahl: *In fine videbitur cujus Toni.* Dieses Lied aber hält in A. aus," proceeding to argue that it cannot be Dorian, "since no melody closes in its *Clausula minus principali,*" that is, the dominant.[42] Continuing, he adds that

> in this tune, however, no particular confusion should be judged in that regard, because its melody is somewhat altered. For I have also found in ancient chorale books that the formal cadences of this chorale are formed completely differently from the way they are made now; for the ♮ is not found in it, whereas the ♭ is completely differently and sorrowfully introduced, since it is a lamenting song on the destruction of human nature. Thus "Ach Gott, vom Himmel sieh' darein"; likewise "O grosser Gott von Macht" and others of a similar kind. These must all be expressed with a sorrowful affect in the Hypophrygian mode, as their texts demand.[43]

Werckmeister's remarks are interesting on a number of counts. They provide testimony, if we need it, that a chorale setting should follow an *Affekt* and mode that are suitable to the expression of its text; they indicate that such expression is related to tonal features of the setting such as the choice of B♭ or B; they suggest that in some chorales the original link between the text and mode was obscured by later alterations to the melodies; and they attest to the fact that a chorale might reveal its mode only at the end. Since, in Werckmeister's view, no melody ended on the dominant, any melody that seemed to end that way either had been "corrupted" somehow or had had its mode misinterpreted. Misinterpretation of the mode of "Durch Adams Fall" as Dorian rather than Hypophrygian had led to the impossible situation that its final cadence was treated as the dominant rather than the correct final. Werckmeister's reference to an original version of "Durch Adams Fall" that had no B♮s and that treated the B♭s differently from the modern version suggests that this tonal difference aided in clarifying the Hypophrygian character of the melody.

Since Werckmeister did not print the chorale melodies he discusses, we cannot be absolutely certain of the versions of "Durch Adams Fall" to which he is referring. It is most likely from his discussions, however, that he is describing the following melody, which was widely associated with "Durch Adams Fall" in his time[44] (Ex. 4.3). This latter tune is not, in fact, the one used by Bach. Notated in the *cantus durus*, it was basically in a: *ambitus* d'–c"; cadences on g', e' (Phrygian: i.e., preceded by f'), g', e' (Phrygian), g', e' (Phrygian), g', and a'. One variant of this melody, however, ended on d' rather than a' and another with the Phrygian cadence on e', which had already been used to end three earlier phrases. Transposed to the *cantus mollis*, therefore, that

Example 4.3. "Durch Adams Fall" (1524) from Zahn, *Die Melodien der Deutschen Evangelischen Kirchenlieder*, with two alternate endings for the final phrase

melody would have ended on d' in its principal version (with g as a variant ending); and it would have contained several Phrygian cadences to a, with one version ending that way. Only the last of these versions would fit Werckmeister's description of a melody ending on A and featuring b♭ throughout. It matches closely the two other Hypophrygian melodies Werckmeister mentions–"Ach Gott, vom Himmel sieh' darein" and "O grosser Gott von Macht" (see Ex. 5.7 and and Ex. 5.8).

In the passage that immediately precedes his discussion of "Durch Adams Fall" Werckmeister claims that transposed Hypophrygian and Phrygian should both be harmonized with the same basic cadence to A in the *cantus mollis*.[45] This accords with the fact that "Ach, Gott vom Himmel" and "O grosser Gott von Macht" were sometimes designated Phrygian in the seventeenth and eighteenth centuries. Werckmeister's distinction between the two modes seems, reasonably, to have been based on their melodic *ambitus*: in the Phrygian mode the final lay at the bottom of the range; in the Hypophrygian it lay in the middle. Bach's *cantus mollis* versions of "Ach Gott, vom Himmel," however, harmonize the final a' with a D major chord, while his one setting in the true *cantus durus* (i.e., melodically in B Hypophrygian in the one-sharp signature) ends with an E major chord.[46] They therefore do not represent the Hypophrygian mode as Werckmeister conceived it but, rather, appear to end on the dominants of the modes whose finals are a fifth below the final harmony: a in the *cantus durus* or one-sharp signature, g in the *cantus mollis* or one-flat signature. This usage fits with the common designation of "Ach Gott, vom Himmel" as Aolian ending on the dominant. But if we respect Bach's key signatures, the mode of the chorale would represent transposed Hypodorian, not Hypoaolian, creating very nearly exactly the situation that Werckmeister objected to when he proclaimed that "Durch Adams Fall" could not be Dorian since no mode ended on the dominant.[47]

Bach's settings of Werckmeister's Hypophrygian melodies, however, are not uniform in their tonal qualities. Some end with authentic cadences (i.e., A–D in the *cantus mollis*), while others end in a manner that seems intended to emphasize the sense of an incomplete ending on the dominant. Also, the harmonizations just mentioned waver between f♯ and f♮ in the *cantus durus*, or one-sharp key signature, and e♮ and e♭ in the *cantus mollis*, to the extent that this quality must be considered a primary part of Bach's intent. In the case of the setting of "O grosser Gott von Macht" that ends Cantata 46 the wavering is much greater than usual; and, in fact, Bach originally notated the first recorder part in the one-flat signature, then changed it to two flats, notating the entire setting in the latter signature.[48] This gesture fits with the fact that whereas the melody, like that of "Ach Gott, vom Himmel," contains the pitch e but no e♭, the harmonization favors E♭ over E until the final A–D cadence. It appears, therefore, that while the mode of these melodies can be readily determined, Bach's conception of the mode in terms of melody and harmonization together is a more complicated matter and must be considered on the basis of the individual setting.

Bach's *Phrygian*-mode settings, however—that is, those settings in which the final is at the bottom of the *ambitus*—do not exhibit this "problem." In them the cadential harmony matches the melodic final. The endings of the *Stollen* and the *Abgesang* of "Erbarm' dich mein, o Herre Gott" and "Mitten wir im Leben sind," for example, have the same melodic descent of a fourth as "Ach Gott, vom Himmel"; and Bach's harmonizations, in Phrygian E in the *cantus durus* (and therefore Phrygian A if transposed to the *cantus mollis*), fulfill Werckmeister's prescriptions exactly. The same is true of Bach's Phrygian harmonizations of "Aus tiefer Not," "Herzlich tut mich verlangen," and other melodies. In fact, his settings of "Christum wir sollen loben schon" clearly preserve the Phrygian character of the melody's final cadence, even though Werckmeister claimed that it was a *tonus corruptus*, ending erroneously on the "penultima" (i.e., that it was a Dorian mode melody ending on the second degree of the scale and therefore, presumably, to be harmonized with the dominant) and even though Bach's own contemporaries and predecessors harmonized the final cadence as Aolian or as Dorian ending on the dominant (i.e., a fifth flatter than Bach's settings).

Clearly, it would have been a simple matter for Bach to have ended his settings of Werckmeister's Hypophrygian melodies with the "correct" harmonic finals. Bach's harmonizing their final cadences a fifth lower than the melodic finals, however, accords with the way that "Ach Gott, vom Himmel" was most often harmonized in the seventeenth century (ending on E in the *cantus durus*, A in the *cantus naturalis*, and D in the *cantus mollis*). And since the harmony a fifth below the Hypophrygian final sounded very much like the dominant of the mode yet another fifth below—that is, the Dorian or Hypodorian mode final—it created, as I mentioned, exactly the situation that Werckmeister objected to. Kirnberger, like Bach, sets "Ach Gott, vom Himmel sieh' darein" in a version of this mode that is melodically in B Hypophrygian but ends on an E major chord that sounds like the dominant of a. But whereas

Kirnberger sets it in the *cantus naturalis*, calling it simply Aolian and greatly favoring F over F♯ in the harmonization, Bach puts it in the *cantus durus* (i.e., the one-sharp signature), and he alternates F and F♯ phrase by phrase until the end (see the discussion of this setting in the following chapter). Wavering of this kind, the transpositional equivalent of the B♭ and B or *molle* and *quadro* degrees that identified the hexachord or system, does not belong to either the Hypophrygian or the Aolian mode, however, but it *does* belong to the Dorian and Hypodorian, in which the sixth degree of the scale was traditionally variable. Luther himself had remarked that the Hypodorian mode was analogous to the "poor weak sinner" (*peccator infirmus*) because of its wavering between "fa" and "mi"—that is, the B *quadro/molle* alternative.[49] And if we take A as the correct final of Bach's *cantus durus* setting of "Ach Gott, vom Himmel," then the mode could be described as Hypodorian ending on the dominant, if that were a permissible category (it was *not* for Werckmeister, as we have seen). Werckmeister's objection, in fact, was to the practice of harmonizing "Ach Gott, vom Himmel" and "Durch Adams Fall" as Hypodorian ending on the dominant throughout the seventeenth century.[50] To our ears, however, most such settings simply sound like the minor key ending on the dominant. Hence Lori Burns's and some eighteenth-century theorists' called it Aolian A ending on the dominant.[51]

"O grosser Gott von Macht" provides a perfect example of this kind of thinking since it was composed in the seventeenth century and the parallelism between its penultimate and final lines—the one ending on g and the other on a—reinforces the sense that the ending is on the second degree of the scale and therefore to be harmonized with the dominant (see Ex. 5.8). Bach's harmonizing it with an authentic cadence, however, suggests that he intended that D be understood as the correct final (as in the case of the setting of "Ach Gott, vom Himmel" that ends Cantata 2). At the same time, his changing its notation from the one-flat to the two-flat signature indicates that E♭ is the correct pitch, even though E♮ appears not only in the melody but also as the cadential pitch of one of its phrases. Although this gesture might be taken to indicate the mode as Hypoaolian ending on the dominant, on the basis of the final authentic cadence we might conclude that Bach intended D as the final, which would render the mode D Hypophrygian (although the melody would still be A Hypophrygian). And if D is taken to be the correct final, then the pitch content—outlining what we would call the harmonic minor scale beginning from the dominant—corresponds closely to Kircher's anomalous Hypophrygian mode.

In this light, Bach's settings do not match up exactly with any of the modes as they were normally understood. The melody identifies one mode (Hypophrygian), the final harmony another (Hypoaolian), and the way we *hear* the final harmony (i.e., as a dominant) yet another (Hypodorian or Hypoaolian ending on the dominant, depending on whether we take the key signature or the harmonic content as prescriptive of the mode). The wavering quality of the variable *molle/quadro* degree, suggestive of the Hypodorian mode, is, nonetheless, common to them all even though their final cadences can be said to represent two different types. The authentic cadences of "O grosser Gott von Macht" and the setting of "Ach Gott, vom Himmel" that ends Cantata 2 seem to lend a quasi-final quality to what would otherwise be heard entirely as dominant cadences, the penultimate A major chord "overcoming" the dominance of E♭ over E in their harmonizations (especially in the former case, where the wavering is greatest and the E♭ is "legitimated" by the key signature), while the astonishingly incomplete dominant cadences of the settings of "Ach Gott, vom Himmel" that end Cantata 77 and begin Cantata 153 "weaken" the endings by means of their leanings toward the "subdominant."

It appears, therefore, that Bach did not want the final cadences of his settings of Hypophrygian melodies to be taken simply and without question as the dominant in all situations. It is not at all impossible, therefore, that Bach viewed his settings of "Ach Gott, vom Himmel" and "O grosser Gott von Macht" as examples of pieces that wavered not only in their pitch content but also in their modal interpretation. That is, he viewed the Hypophrygian mode and the Hypodorian ending on the dominant as related in their theological associations. His settings certainly relate very closely to both Luther's remark on the Hypodorian mode and Werckmeister's on the Hypophrygian character of "Durch Adams Fall." For Bach, then, the Hypophrygian mode final would be the "weakest" of all finals in the modal spectrum, even more so than the Phrygian itself. We see this clearly in Cantata 153, in which Bach "compares" an astonishingly "weak" setting of the B Hypophrygian chorale melody "Ach Gott, vom Himmel," ending on E in the *cantus durus*, or one-sharp signature, first with an aria in E minor (Aolian), then with a setting of the Phrygian chorale "Herzlich tut mich verlangen" in E in the *cantus naturalis*, assigning all three modes different roles in the overall conception (see the following chapter). As that work and others such as Cantatas 2, 46, and 77 indicate, his settings of Hypophrygian mode chorale melodies were bound up with their tonal wavering between two transposition levels, just as was the case with Kircher's first modern version of the Hypophrygian mode. It therefore came to serve even more than the Phrygian mode as the mode of human weakness and instability, as the beginning of Cantata 153 and the ending of Cantata 77 reveal to an extraordinary degree.

Clearly, the question of modal designation is very difficult to answer in such settings; and the inconsistency of seventeenth- and eighteenth-century theorists often merely exacerbates the problem, especially since in some cases the modal designations were simply repeated from theorist to theorist. It will not do to take a purely modern harmonic-tonal approach, even though that would correspond to some of the theorists' views. One possible way of understanding the qualities just described is to imagine that certain of Bach's chorale settings demand that the listener take the final as indicative of the mode even though it sounds to varying degrees like the dominant—that is, that the listener perceive the incomplete quality of the cadential harmony (i.e., its tendency toward the mode a fifth below) as a weakening of the true modal final, as in Kuhnau's association of such a cadence with incomplete recovery from illness. During Bach's lifetime, as is well known, Germany hosted a substantial debate that concerned not only the relevance of the modes for modern composition but also the nearly related questions of the validity of solmization (i.e., the medieval-Renaissance hexachord system) and of whether consonance and dissonance should be judged on the basis of *sensus* or *ratio*—that is, on whether the ear or the mind should be allowed to answer questions that for us relate to analysis. The victory in this debate was overwhelmingly (but not unanimously) accorded to Johann Mattheson, whose aggressively polemical, even jeering, and dismissive attitude toward the traditional stance of his opponent, Johann Heinrich Buttstedt, perhaps tended to stifle opposition to Mattheson's views. Mattheson's three so-called *Orchestre* treatises, written in the first two decades of the century, form, along with the treatise *Ut, Mi, Sol, Re, Fa, La tota Musica* of Buttstedt, the center of this debate. Although these works cover much ground, Mattheson's proclamation that the traditional ideas to which Buttstedt adhered were "todte (nicht tota) Musica" and his subtitling the last of his treatises "Sensus vindicae" (the vindication of the senses) tell the story in a nutshell.[52] Mattheson was demanding, in fact, a new approach to the understanding of music, one that was based on tonal hearing alone and would therefore accord no privileged place to tradition and the past, especially to prior generations of music theorists, whose writings Mattheson was not at all shy of ridiculing when they came into conflict with his empirical outlook.

My purpose in bringing this up in relation to Bach's modal harmonizations is not, of course, to advocate either Buttstedt's or Mattheson's approaches to music as the one most relevant to our analytical needs but, rather, to indicate that Bach's stance in such matters was determined on the basis of what they offered him as a composer, and a composer, moreover, of extraordinary meditative bent. Bach's outlook was not cosmopolitan, not centered on polemic or on public self-congratulatory endeavors; still less, as Adorno argued impressively many years ago, was it mirroring the spirit of the Middle Ages in deferring to tradition and rule.[53] Bach participated to a degree in both the progressive and the traditionalist outlooks, but his unique achievement was to mold rather than to defer to tradition, to bring past and present together as if in a contrapuntal interaction whose ultimate outcome was to forecast a future that very few in his time could foresee. Bach was an extraordinarily intelligent composer, and his attitude toward the relevance of traditional aspects of music such as the modes was to draw them into a vision of far greater subtlety and complexity than can be found in the works of his German contemporaries. In holding to aspects of the seventeenth-century conception of music, therefore, Bach raised questions regarding tradition that deeply engage our own need for analysis.

Although Werckmeister does not directly address the fact that the correct final in some modes might sound like the dominant, that question is implicit throughout his discussion. Thus, when Werckmeister denies that "Durch Adams Fall" ends on the dominant and says: "Dieses Lied aber hält in A. aus" he does not mean what we might think—that A is felt as the principal tonal center for the whole melody; his citing the "In fine videbitur cujus toni" catchphrase makes that clear. Rather, he is acknowledging that the correct modal final sounds like the dominant, even though he denies that it should be understood as the dominant. For him, *ratio* and *sensus* were clearly distinguishable, with the former taking precedence over the latter. Behind his remarks, in fact, lies a clear perception of the disparity between modal and tonal perspectives on certain chorale melodies; and that quality, I would argue, was central to Bach's modal compositions, whereas strict adherence to exact modal designations was not. The disparity in question was, in fact, what the widespread acceptance of the newer modal schemes of the seventeenth century was all about. Well before the appearance of the circle of keys in the first decade of the eighteenth century, questions of modal definition had weakened under the influence of increased transposition and the newer hierarchical view of tonality, which was capable of incorporating and absorbing foreign pitches to a far greater extent than was the older polyphonic music. Above all, the phenomenon that I have called the "dominant dynamic" with respect to Monteverdi—that is, the increasing sense of the powerful role of the dominant in defining the key—led not only to the expectation that a strong dominant would be present but also to the belief that it was necessary to the definition of the final. Intensifying, often dramatizing, the arrival on the dominant became a prominent means by which the wider range of harmonies could be directed toward a single final, whereas circles of fifths and secondary dominants furthered the distinction between what we distinguish as "structural" and "nonstructural" dominant arrivals. The importance of the dominant was recognized, of course, in Renaissance music; but owing to the much narrower range of harmonies and transposition levels in relation to seventeenth-century music, its presence was seldom made the pivotal event in the forms of individual compostions that it became in Monteverdi's music, and it did not tend to require the dominant of the dominant as an extra means of bolstering the "tonic." Along with the increased perception of the defining tonal role of the dominant came, inevitably, the concept of a "subdominant" (in practice but not as yet in theory); and with it came the need for a new paradigm to replace the long-outdated gamut of medieval and Renaissance music: the circle of major and minor keys.

What all this meant for the concept of mode was devastating, as Heinichen recognized. Subtle differences that derived from the placement of the semitone no longer mattered, for all twelve semitones could be easily drawn into the key, especially when the role of the dominant in relation to the tonic was clearly defined. Kirnberger's view that a more fully chromatic harmonization was more "complete" because of its presenting greater "charm" and "variety" to the ear derives solely from this new situation.[54] The "problem" of modal music, at least for Bach, became how to differentiate it from tonal music, since it was all too easily absorbed into, or rendered subordinate to, the new tonality. And the most obvious difference was that modal music, whether purely melodic or polyphonic, often featured little or nothing of the aforementioned "dominant dynamic." The final of the Mixolydian mode tended to sound like the dominant of the mode a fifth below, a quality that Monteverdi had recognized clearly and exploited in many pieces, none more skillfully than "Cruda Amarilli," while that of the Phrygian mode tended even more in that direction. Since we are detached from any living modal tradition we are often accustomed to think that such disparities between modality and tonality are the product of modern tonal hearing; but, in fact, Kuhnau's and Werckmeister's remarks demonstrate that they were just as true in the seventeenth and eighteenth centuries (although in the eighteenth century there was, as Mattheson's attitude indicates, a much greater tendency to reject that disparity in favor of an exalting of modern tonality and sense perception over modal tradition). Werckmeister and, I would argue, Bach as well opposed the tendency of the time to reinterpret the modes in purely tonal terms, thereby eliminating the balance of *sensus* and *ratio* in favor of *sensus* alone. The latter, however, is very much our legacy, and it crops up whenever we discuss questions such as whether a particular chorale setting ends on the tonic or the dominant as if we were capable of a providing single unambiguous answer that depended on our view of analysis as an extension or validation of tonal hearing. In this light, we might conclude that the relationship between D (Dorian) and A (Hypophrygian) that Werck-

Example 4.4. Bach's setting of "Durch Adams Fall" from Cantata 18 as printed by Kirnberger and C. P. E. Bach (the original Weimar version of Cantata 18 is a tone lower)

meister perceived in "Durch Adams Fall," his denial that the A on which the melody ended was the dominant, and his claim that the melody revealed its mode (A) only at the end all express his perception of the tension between modal and tonal interpretations, one of which would tend to view the final cadence as the dominant (the tonal interpretation) and the other to take it as the correct final (but not necessarily as what we call the tonic). For Werckmeister the distinction between tonal and modal viewpoints was crucial. And as we will see, Bach plays on that distinction in highly interesting ways.

Bach's only purely cantonal setting of "Durch Adams Fall" (see Ex. 4.4) uses a different melody from that described by Werckmeister, one that was uniformly classed as Dorian in the seventeenth and eighteenth centuries, but it has in common with Werckmeister's the fact that it ends on A (albeit in the *cantus durus*) after some doubt as to whether D or A is the correct final. The melody begins on a'; the two phrases of its *Stollen* close on d' and a', respectively, and the four phrases of its *Abgesang* on f', d', g', and a'. Since it is notated entirely without accidentals in the *cantus durus*, and with an *ambitus* from d' to d" or e", it invites a D Dorian interpretation until the final cadence, whose melodic c"–b'–a' descent clearly indicates a shift to A. In Bach's settings, for example, "Durch Adams Fall" emphasizes d at the outset but ends with an authentic cadence to a (or, in one case, their transpositional equivalents a tone lower). And, in keeping with Werckmeister's remarks in general, Bach's setting makes much out of the roles of B♭ and B♮. The first phrase, for example, invokes the idea of the Dorian mode in that Bach introduces B♮ rather than B♭ into the harmony. Since the second phrase of the melody features the pitch b♮' three times and ends on an A major harmony, the sense of a D–A relationship in the *cantus durus* is strong and the A emerges naturally as the dominant of d. And since, after the repeat of these two phrases, the fifth phrase features a passing b♭' in the melody and closes on f', while the sixth phrase (which resembles the first) returns to close on d', Bach harmonizes these two phrases with B♭ rather than B, creating the sense that they, and the setting as a whole to this point, are in D minor (which can nevertheless be viewed as D Dorian because of the b♮–♭ variability of that mode). For the second half of the seventh phrase, however, the pitch b♮' returns decisively and the melody cadences on g'. Bach's harmonization of this phrase begins as if continuing in D minor (A, d, g, and F harmonies); then, with the melodic b♮' it moves toward a close in G (an authentic cadence with something of a Mixolydian sound, owing to the prominence of C in the harmony). The final phrase then moves from the G of the seventh phrase to close in a (with the *Tierce de Picardie*) after a series of three increasingly strong dominant (E and E^7) harmonies and a harmonic content that might in the preceding century have been understood as spelling out the pitch content of the harmonically interpreted C hexachord (C, d, E, F, G, and a–A). The penultimate phrase can be said to restore the B♮ after the B♭s of phrases 5 and 6 and the beginning of phrase 7, while the final phrase confirms the A of phrases 2 and 4. In that light, the final A cadence can be thought of in three ways: to end on the dominant of d (which accords with the widespread assigning of "Durch Adams Fall" to D Dorian in the eighteenth century), to modulate from d to a, or to affirm the a of the two *Stollen* endings as the true final, restored after having been weakened by the previous emphasis on d. The last of these interpretations corresponds most closely to the sense of the chorale text, which deals with the dualism of fallen and redeemed humanity simultaneously, giving precedence ultimately to the hopeful rather than the pessimistic message. Bach's setting, in fact, fits until the shift of mode at the end with Luther's description of the Hypodorian mode as analogous to the "poor weak sinner" because of its b♭–♮ variability. The ending, however, might be thought to fit with Luther's other catchphrase "In fine videbitur cujus toni" in that the mode appears at that point to be *not* D Dorian but A Hypoaolian.[55]

Werckmeister, in maintaining that the A cadence of his Hypophrygian version of "Durch Adams Fall" should be articulated by means of B♭ rather than B and interpreting the chorale text as centering exclusively on the contamination of human nature, for which the Hypophrygian mode was the appropriate musical allegory, does not allow for the possibility of a modal shift associated with the redemption of humankind from its fallen condition. Yet although "Durch Adams Fall" was traditionally classed under those chorales that deal with the "fallen" human condition ("Vom menschlichen Elend und Verderben"—"concerning human suffering and contamination"), it holds forth the promise of salvation for those who trust in God and follow His word. And that dualistic quality was mirrored, at least potentially, in the most widespread melody to which the chorale was sung in Bach's time. That melody suggests that the affirmation of A at the end corresponds to the redemption of humanity; and, in fact, the only two texted settings of this melody we have from Bach draw on two of the optimistic later verses of the chorale (verses 7 and 8). Because of the role of the pitch B♭ Werckmeister's A Hypophrygian version of "Durch Adams Fall" tends toward its "subdominant," D, whereas in part because of its replacing B♭ by B, Bach's D Dorian setting shifts to the mode of its dominant, A.

In the case of his setting of "Durch Adams Fall" in the *Orgelbüchlein*, however, Bach chose, as he had in the case of "Das alte Jahr," to bring out the pessimistic rather than optimistic aspect of the text. Presumably his decision in both cases was the outcome of a desire to project a single affect as strongly as possible in these very short untexted settings. His setting, therefore, is dominated by two pictorial devices: the many falling sevenths in the pedal part and the continual wavering between sharpened and flattened pitches in the harmony. As a result of the latter aspect this setting is just as harmonically "complete" as "Das alte Jahr," featuring all the pitches of the chromatic scale including the enharmonic equivalents E♭–D♯ and A♭–G♯. And the final A is perfectly satisfying as a tonal center. But owing to the falling sevenths and the wavering quality of the harmony throughout the setting as a whole the ending is not nearly as suggestive of the redemptive aspect of the text as is the case in Bach's other settings. Quite possibly Bach intended the fact that this setting focuses on the *fall* of humankind as a reflection of its place in the collection as a whole, since he follows it immediately by a D major setting of "Es ist das Heil," a summary of the story of the *redemption* of humankind in a pure diatonic major style.[56]

In citing Luther's phrase "In fine videbitur cujus toni" in conjunction with the mode of "Durch Adams Fall," Werckmeister means simply that the final is the principal determinant of the mode, whereas insofar as that phrase applies to Bach's settings it indicates that the final will be revealed only at the end after a period during which another pitch will have appeared appointed as the final. Bach, in other words, intends to project the idea of tonal *shift* at the cadence as an allegorical device. As mentioned earlier, the inscriptions for certain of Bach's canons likewise have this allegorical character, several of them taking up issues that Werckmeister addresses in his treatises.[57] Bach's (lost) canon on "In fine videbitur cujus toni" is also headed with another Latin motto, "Omnia tunc bona quando bona clausula est," which appears in its German form, "Ende gut macht Alles gut" (all's well that ends well), in the texts of two Bach cantatas, both of which end "higher" on the circle of keys than they begin.[58] Its meaning is not only that the ending will reveal the mode but also that a good ending justifies all that precedes it. The tonal "allegory" is that the ending represents a secure arrival in a new key (or the restoration of one that has been "weakened" by subdominant emphasis), not the kind of "weak" ending that obtains in "O grosser Gott" and "Ach Gott, vom Himmel." This idea has a tremendous resonance in Lutheranism, which is undoubtedly the reason that Bach headed his canon on "In fine videbitur cujus toni" with the word "Symbolum." There, as in the two cantatas just mentioned, it expresses the idea that dying a blessed death, in faith and according to God's will, is the goal of life. We do not know that the apparent d–a shift in the melody of "Durch Adams Fall" that Bach knew was intended to mirror the central idea in its text, that Christ, the "new man," offering life and salvation, replaces and puts in perspective the "old man," Adam, associated with death and destruction. But in the two cantatas that end with verses of "Durch Adams Fall" Bach, as we will see, draws the tonal shift within the chorale melody into the framework of larger theological allegories.[59]

Since not all musicians were as sensitive as Werckmeister and Bach to the capacity of modal melodies to mirror their texts, however, ambiguities or anomalies involving their modes caused certain chorales to exist in variant versions in which we can perceive attempts to correct or resolve the anomalies. In the case of "Jesu, nun sei gepreiset," cited previously, versions exist that end with the original shift of mode up a tone at the end, as well as ones that "correct" the disparity by returning to the mode of the opening phrases; likewise, versions exist in which the final phrases change their time signature as well as others that return to the original time signature and still others that eliminate the time signature change altogether. In the case of "O grosser Gott von Macht," the number of attempts to correct it is greater than usual. Basically, the original form of the melody, which Bach adhered to very closely, begins and ends on a' in the one-flat signature, its eight phrases cadencing on the pitches c'', a', c'', b♭', a', e', g', and a'. Its variant forms, however, end on a' in the two-flat signature, on g' in the one-flat signature, and even on b♭' in the one-flat signature (with the necessary e♭''s written in).[60]

In the following chapters I examine several cantatas that introduce chorales that Werckmeister discussed in the *Harmonologia Musica.* Bach uses verses of "Durch Adams Fall" to end Cantatas 2 and 109; of "Ach Gott, vom Himmel" to begin Cantata 153, to begin and end Cantata 2, and to end Cantata 77; of "Christum wir sollen loben schon" to begin and end Cantata 121; and a verse of "O grosser Gott von Macht" to end Cantata 46—raising questions regarding whether their final cadences modulate to the dominant, end *on* the dominant, or can be said to be poised between the two. In them Bach seizes on the qualities of modal ambiguity singled out by Werckmeister, using them for "allegorical" purposes that are not ambiguous. In chapters 7 and 8 I consider the role of "Ach Gott, vom Himmel" in Cantata 77 in relation to that of another modally anomalous chorale, "Dies sind die heil'gen zehn Gebot." Although not discussed by Werckmeister, "Dies sind die heil'gen zehn Gebot" contains a degree of modal anomaly that is comparable (but in a sense opposite, as mentioned) to that of "Das alte Jahr," in that it shifts not only its mode but also, apparently, its *cantus*—from *durus* to *mollis.* The history of the melody reveals a substantial amount of variation over the centuries that illuminates our understanding of Bach's design in Cantata 77. Finally, in chapter 9 I take up Cantata 60, "O Ewigkeit, du Donnerwort," whose final chorale, "Es ist genung," as is well known, begins with another melodic anomaly, a rising tritone. Not only is Bach's setting one of the most interesting and provocative chorale harmonizations in all his music, but also his design for the cantata as a whole derives from and leads to the final movement in ways that illuminate the interaction of modal and tonal "allegory." Examining these cantatas in light of the modal anomalies in their chorale melodies enables us to appreciate Bach's interaction with the Lutheran chorale tradition and his molding that tradition for musico-allegorical purposes of his own. In this respect Bach is capable of "delicacy" in his treatment of modal melodies of a kind that Werckmeister could never have anticipated and that Kirnberger probably did not suspect. The stimulus for this unique quality in Bach's modal settings came from his interaction with the modal melodies themselves and, just as conspicuously, with the theological content they mirrored.

FIVE

Bach's Reflection on the Past

Modal Chorales in Cantata Designs

One of the qualities we associate most with Bach's work in general is that which Theodor W. Adorno called his "genius of meditation"—that is, his ability to take something given, whether a chorale melody, a traditional form or style, or an instrumental idiom, texture, or device, and to think it through in a manner that is both mindful of tradition and transforming of its expressive capacity.[1] Nowhere is this ability to link (Bukofzer might have said to "fuse") past and present more evident than in Bach's response to the Lutheran chorale tradition.[2] Not content merely to cultivate the various chorale prelude types he inherited from his German forebears, Bach, as we know, reinterpreted those types, from the simplest chorale harmonizations to the most elaborately conceived chorale fantasias, in seemingly endless ways. With the aid of a unique harmonic sensibility—the quality Kirnberger seems to have meant in his calling Bach the "most sensitive of the newer composers"—Bach created settings of the utmost harmonic daring (such as the chorale "Es ist genung" that ends Cantata 60) as well as others in which subtlety is the key issue, especially with regard to the modal qualities of the melodies themselves.[3] And an achievement that is insufficiently recognized in this regard is the extent to which Bach was capable not just of deriving highly individual harmonic qualities from the traditional chorale melodies but also of extending the tonal qualities of the melodies to the movement sequences of entire cantatas. The latter quality almost always involves his perceiving a link between the tonal characteristics of a given melody and the theological intent of its text and then elaborating that link in terms of the musico-allegorical design of the work as a whole. Although there are many chorales in which the matchup of text and melody offers little of interest, especially in the area of modal-tonal qualities, there are also many in which it offers a great deal to anyone with Bach's sensitivity to detail. In most cases, therefore, the meditative quality in question involves as its starting point Bach's probing the pitch content of the melodies for their "expressive" qualities, actual or potential, and—

just as important—for the ways in which those qualities relate to the theological content of the texts to which they are matched.

"Durch Adams Fall ist ganz verderbt" in Cantatas 18 and 109

Cantata 18, "Gleichwie der Regen und Schnee"

Cantata 18, "Gleichwie der Regen und Schnee vom Himmel fällt," written around 1711–15 in Weimar to a text of Erdmann Neumeister, ends with the eighth verse of "Durch Adams Fall," which is thereby drawn into the theme of Sexagesima Sunday, for which the cantata was composed (see Table 5.1).[4] That theme, the power of God's word in the process of faith, is articulated by the Gospel for the day (Luke 8: 4–15) by means of the parable of the seed and the sower: as the seed falls on fertile or unfertile ground, so the word of God is received by some and rejected by others. Jesus' parable seems to hark back to another, from Isaiah (55:10–11), in which God proclaims that His word is like the rain and snow that fall from heaven and fertilize the earth so that it gives forth seeds to sow and bread to eat:

> Gleichwie der Regen und Schnee vom Himmel fällt und nicht wieder dahin kommet, sondern feuchtet die Erde und macht sie fruchtbar und wachsend, daß sie gibt Samen zu säen und Brot zu essen;
> Also soll das Wort, so aus meinem Munde gehet, auch sein; es soll nicht wieder zu mir leer kommen, sondern tun, das mir gefället, und soll ihm gelingen, dazu ichs sende.
>
> (For as the rain cometh down and the snow from heaven and returneth not thither, but watereth the earth and maketh it bring forth and bud, that it may give seed to the sower and bread to the eater;
> So shall My word be that goeth forth out of My mouth; it shall not return unto Me void, but it shall accomplish that which I please, and it shall prosper in the thing whereto I sent it.)

Neumeister must have been particularly drawn to this subject, since it articulates the very goal of hermeneutics: the believer's understanding and internalizing God's word. Once again, therefore, he drew upon the patterns and devices of traditional hermeneutics to represent stages in that understanding, citing the passage from Isaiah as the introductory *dictum* to a four-movement design whose next movement draws a very free paraphrase and expansion of the Gospel parable into the recitative portions of a fourfold recitative-cum-litany complex. Behind Neumeister's text lies the dualism of falling and rising as a two-stage process that leads from God to humankind and back to God. In the passage from Isaiah falling is a necessary part of the process of growth: the falling snow and rain bring about new growth and new seeds, and the falling seeds themselves renew the cycle as well as providing bread to eat; analogously, God's word provides spiritual nourishment for the faithful, who return the word to Him through prayer. The Gospel-based recitatives then bring out the analogy of the faithful to the fertile ground on which the seeds fall and of those who have given themselves over to "the world" to the infertile ground. Thus, they ex-

Table 5.1 Cantata 18, "Gleichwie der Regen und Schnee vom Himmel fällt" Weimar, 1711–15. Sexagesima Sunday. Text by Erdmann Neumeister, 1711.

Movement	Genre	Instrumentation	Text incipit	Key
1	Sinfonia	Recorders, str., b.c.	Untexted	g
2	Recitative	Bass, b.c.	Gleichwie der Regen und Schnee vom Himmel fällt	g
3	Recitative plus litany	SATB soloists and chorus, str., b.c.	Mein Gott, hier wird mein Herze sein . . . Erhör uns, lieber Herre Gott!	E♭–c
4	Aria	Sop., str., b.c.	Mein Seelenschatz ist Gottes Wort	E♭
5	Chorale	SATB chorus, b.c.	Ich bitt, o Herr, aus Herzens Grund	g

tend the idea of falling to all who, like rotten fruit falling from a tree, reenact the fall of humankind in their devotion to the world, falling away from God's word and bringing about their own destruction. In contrast, the four chantlike litany passages represent the prayers of the faithful—that is, the process by which the "word" returns to God. With the culmination of each of the four recitatives in one of these passages (set by Bach for soprano solo answered by chorus), Neumeister creates a sequence representing the viewpoints of the Old Testament (Isaiah), the New Testament, and the church (the recitative and litany passages), following that by the perspective of the individual believer (the aria "Mein Seelenschatz ist Gottes Wort": God's word is the treasure of my soul). The eighth verse of "Durch Adams Fall" then affirms the centrality of God's word to the believer's hopes of salvation.

The role of "Durch Adams Fall" in this sequence involves our understanding its overall message of the redemption of a contaminated human nature and of the word of God as the source of that message. In five of its nine verses "Durch Adams Fall" speaks directly of God's word, first as the word that Adam and Eve ignored in Eden, causing the fall of humanity, then as the promise of redemption through Jesus, the object of faith, and the light that leads the believer forward from original sin to hope. In verse 8 the believer prays that God will not take His holy word from the believer's mouth, leaving him "shamed" by his sin and guilt. Through prayer the believer acknowledges his sins and is freed from death, the punishment for original sin. Thus, in linking the passage from Isaiah with "Durch Adams Fall," Neumeister's text makes the point that as the catalyst to faith and salvation God's word does not return to Him "empty." Behind the idea that the word which went forth from God's mouth is now in the believer's mouth lies an indirect reference to bread in the passage from Isaiah, which itself recalls the widespread interpretation of God's word as spiritual manna from heaven. The principal "content" of that word is the substance of the third verse of "Durch Adams Fall"—namely, that Jesus is God's response to Adam: as Adam's fall brought death, through Jesus' death and resurrection what was contaminated was renewed.

"Durch Adams Fall" juxtaposes Adam to Jesus, the world below to heaven above, death to eternal life, and fallen humanity to the faithful in hope of salvation. It therefore articulates what Luther called the "summary" of scripture and the only basis for allegorical interpretation: the dialectic of destruction and restoration.[5] The dualism in question, since it is central to the message of redemption, is one that underlies countless of Bach's sacred texts. In the *St. Matthew Passion*, for example, the arioso "Der Heiland fällt vor seinem Vater nieder" (The Savior falls low before His Father), representing Jesus' prostration before God in Gethsemane, His submission to the necessity of a human death, takes up the dualism not only in its text—which continues: "dadurch erhebt er mich und alle von unserm Falle hinauf zu Gottes Gnade wieder" (through which He raises me and all from our fall back up to God's grace)—but also in the contrary motion between the continually descending arpeggio figures of the strings and the scalar ascent of the bass line. Later in the passion, after the crucifixion and the narrative of Jesus' burial, another arioso, "Am Abend, da es kühle war, ward Adams Fallen offenbar" (In the evening, when it was cool, was Adam's fall made manifest), refers back to Jesus' "fall" in Gethsemane as His suppression of Adam (the flesh)—"Am Abend drücket ihn der Heiland nieder" (In the evening the Savior brought him [Adam] down)—and to explain His death as the restoration of humanity to God's grace: "Der Friedensschluß ist nun mit Gott gemacht, denn Jesus hat sein Kreuz vollbracht" (The reconciliation with God is now accomplished, for Jesus has completed His cross). As is well known, the arioso in question also compares Jesus' fall and act of restoration to the story of Noah and the flood, which also came to a conclusion in the evening, in keeping with the underlying "purpose" of representing the story of redemption (destruction followed by restoration) as the subject matter of the entire scriptures.[6]

Bach must have been closely attuned to the underlying descent–ascent dynamic of Neumeister's text, for he begins "Gleichwie der Regen und Schnee" with an introductory sinfonia, whose principal theme represents the dualism of falling and rising, by means of both its rising sequences of falling fifths and its falling and rising eighth-note patterns. Immediately following the Sinfonia, the bass soloist (traditionally used by Bach to represent the voice of God) enters with God's words as given in Isaiah, making clear the meaning of the falling and rising patterns in the Sinfonia by means of its division into two halves, the first taking up the literal image of the falling rain and snow, then the growth of seeds to sow, and the second the allegorical interpretation in terms of God's word (mm. 1–7 and 8–15). Bach respects the division of the text into literal and figurative meanings by setting up musical parallels between the two halves; thus the first words in each half, "Gleich wie der Regen" and "also soll das Wort," are motivically alike, as are the lines "und nicht wieder dahin kommet" and "so aus meinem Munde gehet." Each "half" features a shift from recitative to andante arioso style toward the end as the text turns to the fruitful outcome of the snow and rain, on the one hand, and the word of God, on the other.

After these two movements, both in G minor, the beginning of the recitative-litany complex bridges between the Old Testament *dictum* and the first of the four litany passages. Turning to E♭, the tenor compares the believer's open heart to the tilled ground awaiting the seed of God's word and hoping to bring forth its fruit in hundredfolds; its final line intensifies and becomes more anguished as it turns to C minor in prayer: "O Herr, Herr, hilf! O Herr, lass wohl gelingen" (O Lord, Lord, help! O Lord, let things turn out well). Now the soprano enters, continuing the prayer with the first recitation—"du wollest deinen Geist und Kraft zum Worte geben" (We pray Thou wouldst give Your Spirit and power to Your word)—and leading the reiterated d"s to a B♭ cadence, after which the choral response, "Erhör' uns, lieber Herre Gott!" (Hear us, dear Lord God!), returns to close in C minor (Ex. 5.1). In this sequence both Neumeister's text and Bach's setting are very skillfully arranged so as to articulate the sense of continuity from the Old Testament to the New. The phrase "lass wohl gelingen" echoes the ending of the passage from Isaiah, "und soll ihm gelingen, dazu ichs sende," while the soprano incantation seems to link up with the Epistle for the day (2 Corinthians 11:19–12:9), which culminates with God's words to St. Paul that His strength is made perfect in weakness. The almost casual reminiscences of the principal motive of the bass solo in passages from the tenor recitative (such as "so ströme deinen Saamen, als in ein gutes Land hinein": thus your seeds pour forth as in a fertile land) convey the equivalence of the Old and New Testament passages in a subtle, unforced manner. Most of all, however, the tonal motion from the g of the Old Testament recitative through the tenor's E♭ and c provides a palpable sense of descent to the "subdominant" as the tenor cries out in prayer. The choral response, in returning to c after the soprano's B♭ cadence, confirms prayer as the outcome of the falling of the seed of God's word into the hearts of the faithful—that is, the g–E♭–c descent. C minor thus becomes a symbol of human weakness and the point from which the return of the word to God begins.

The idea of falling in the remainder of this movement centers, however, on the falling away of the rest of humankind from the reception of God's word. The second tenor recitative expresses this clearly: "Ach! viel verleugnen Wort und Glauben und fallen ab wie faules Obst" (Ah! many deny word and faith and fall like rotten fruit). The idea behind Adam's "fall" therefore dominates the recitative narratives of human failings, all of which then conclude with the litany passages (mm. 12–19, 32–38, and 50–59 and the final measures, 82–88). Although all four litanies exhibit the same tonal design (a soprano recitation closing in B♭ followed by a C minor choral response), the second, third, and fourth recitatives modulate increasingly widely, mostly in analogy to the ideas of deception and temptation by means of which the devil and the world seek the downfall of the faithful. This modulatory quality is especially pronounced in the last of the four recitatives, which moves rapidly through A♭, f, b♭, c, E♭, d, and g as the text narrates how God's word loses its power among those who are led astray by their too-great involvement in the world. Bach emphasizes the "errors" of the unfaithful by means of dissonant clashes and continual deviation from any central key. In this context the fourfold recurrence of the litany serves to articulate the key of C minor as tonic almost by default; and the fact that each soprano incantation cadences in B♭ after the G minor underpinning of its recitational tones, while the choral responses all close in C minor, causes each successive return to c to project an "allegorical" quality. That is, the C minor cadences do not follow from the tonal sequences within the solos to nearly the same degree as the first one did after the tenor's E♭ and c. Instead, each of the reappearances of c has the effect of returning to a tonal framework that can serve as the "tonic" key of the movement only by virtue of the reference back to its first appearance. In terms of the relationships among the various keys, G minor, the key of the cantata as a whole, is equally or more prominent (by virtue of the several articulations of its domi-

Example 5.1. Cantata 18: Third Movement, mm. 12–19

nant). And the fact that the long final recitative makes a conspicuous return to g as it describes the straying of humanity from heaven is a very telling occurrence. When the last of the litanies prays for God to bring back all those who have fallen into error and temptation, cadencing not in g but on B♭ and c as usual, the C minor cadence seems not only to weaken the tonic but also to link up with the association of that key to the deception of the world in the final recitative. By such means Bach conveys a sense that the affective quality of the litanies was intended as a representation of human weakness, a cry for mercy like the "Kyrie eleison" that ends many

Lutheran chorales. At the same time, the faithful, in returning repeatedly to c after the tonal digressions of the recitatives, can be said to hold onto God's word in the midst of worldly deceptions. In this context we are not far from Werckmeister's interpretation of tempered music as a representation of human weakness, from Johann Kuhnau's description of constant modulation as a "deception of the ear" or from Kuhnau's assertion that emphasis on the subdominant toward the end of a movement has an effect of weakening the tonic that is analogous to incomplete recovery from illness.[7]

The central recitative-litany complex, since it is based on Jesus' parable in the Gospel for the day, occupies a pivotal role in the design of Cantata 18, its subdominant tonal framework and wide-ranging flat modulations expressing the believer's faith struggles in the world. In this respect it can be said to represent the "nadir" of a descent–ascent design from the initial g (movements 1 and 2) to the E♭ beginning of the first recitative and the reiterated subdominant cadences of the litanies, and back to g through the E♭ aria that follows. That aria, "Mein Seelenschatz ist Gottes Wort," the only major-key movement in the cantata, describes the believer's adherence to God's word as the source of his spiritual riches and his rejection of all the worldly delights that are really "nets" to ensnare iniquitous souls. In relation to the preceding movement, its quasi-symmetrical sequence of stable tonal regions—E♭–B♭–g–c–B♭–E♭—seems to overcome the temptations and deceptions of the world, to return to the key with which the optimistic first recitative of the third movement began. Its surface figuration intermingles descending and ascending patterns into what seems like a higher union than that of the "allegorical" descent–ascent patterns that have hitherto held sway.

Against this optimistic background, the final chorale returns to g, "weakening" that g, as already described, by the subdominant emphasis in its first, third, fifth, and sixth phrases, but restoring it provisionally in the second and fourth phrases and decisively in the eighth.[8] The restoration itself might suggest the idea expressed in the initial *dictum*, that through prayer the word does not return "empty" to God—that is, that prayer, now interpreted as the believer's acknowledgment of his sin and guilt, his cry of weakness to God, is the seed that brings about the fruit of eternal life: "Ich bitt', o Herr, aus Herzens Grund, du wollst nicht von mir nehmen dein heil'ges Wort aus meinem Mund; so wird mich nicht beschämen mein Sünd und Schuld, denn in dein' Huld setz ich all mein Vertrauen. Wer sich nur fest darauf verlässt, der wird den Tod nicht schauen" (I pray, O Lord, from the depths of the heart, that You will not take Your holy word from my mouth; then my sin and guilt will not shame me, for in Your favor I place all my trust. Whoever entrusts himself firmly to that will not look upon death).

Cantata 109, "Ich glaube, lieber Herr, hilf' meinem Unglauben!"

The one other cantata in which Bach introduces a verse from "Durch Adams Fall"—once again as the final movement—centers on the antithesis of doubt versus faith. Cantata 109, "Ich glaube, lieber Herr, hilf' meinem Unglauben!" (I believe, dear Lord, help my unbelief!), written for the twenty-first Sunday after Trinity, 1723, draws the biblical motto of its opening chorus not from the Gospel for the day (John 4:47–54), but from a similar miracle story (Mark 9:24), where it is spoken by the father of a possessed child in response to Jesus' "all things are possible to him that believeth." The borrowed text enabled Bach to emphasize the conflict experienced by those whose faith is not self-sufficient and to bring out the point that Jesus still works miracles in those who struggle with faith and hold to His promises.

"Ich glaube, lieber Herr" (see Table 5.2) can be divided into two parts, the first of which (movements 1–3) emphasizes the conflicts of faith and doubt (opening cho-

Table 5.2 Cantata 109, "Ich glaube, lieber Herr, hilf' meinem Unglauben!" Leipzig, 1723. Twenty-first Sunday after Trinity.

Movement	Genre	Instrumentation	Text incipit	Key
1	Chorus	SATB chorus, hrn., ob. 1, 2, str., b.c.	Ich glaube, lieber Herr, hilf' meinem Unglauben!	d
2	Recitative	Tenor, b.c.	Des Herren Hand ist ja noch nicht verkürzt, mir kann geholfen werden.	B♭–e
3	Aria	Tenor, str., b.c.	Wie zweifelhaftig ist mein Hoffen	e
4	Recitative	Alto, b.c.	O fasse dich, du zweifelhafter Mut, weil Jesus itzt noch Wunder tut!	C–d
5	Aria	Alto, ob. 1, 2, b.c.	Der Heiland kennet ja die Seinen, wenn ihre Hoffnung hilflos liegt.	F
6	Chorale	SATB chorus, hrn., ob. 1, 2, str., b.c.	Wer hofft in Gott und dem vertraut	a

rus) and fear and hope (first recitative and aria), while the second (movements 4–6) urges building on God's promises (second recitative), affirming God's presence in times of conflict and tribulation and the ultimate victory of faith (second aria and final chorale). The closed movements are in d (no. 1), e (no. 3), F (no. 5), and a (no. 6), while the first recitative (no. 2) represents the conflict between the believer's faith and doubt by means of alternating forte and piano dynamics and a sequence of keys that tends to reverse the tonal direction from phrase to phrase, making an overall shift of a tritone from beginning to end: B♭ (forte, faith), c (piano, doubt), F (forte, faith), E♭ (piano, doubt), d (forte, faith), e (first half piano, associated with doubt; second half forte, changing to adagio arioso style for the believer's cry to God: "Ach Herr, wie lange?"). There is a marked tendency for the forte phrases to shift in the sharp direction and to utilize rising lines, while certain of the piano phrases do just the opposite. The d and e of the ending phrases seem to summarize the uncertain tonal relationship of the first two closed movements in terms of the believer's longing for resolution of his doubts.

As yet, however, that resolution is not forthcoming. The E minor aria utilizes a passionate Italian concerto style that features frequent conflict of triple and quadruple subdivision of the beat to intensify the believer's cry of inner tribulation: "Wie zweifelhaftig ist mein Hoffen, wie wanket mein geängstigt Herz. Des Glaubens Docht glimmt kaum hervor, es bricht dies fast zerstoßne Rohr, die Furcht macht stetig neuen Schmerz" (How doubtful is my hope, how my tormented heart wavers. The wick of faith hardly glimmers forth, this almost crushed reed breaks, fear continually brings on new pain).

To this point the sequence of movement keys leaves the overall tonal design itself in some doubt. As the key of the opening chorus, D minor is the likeliest candidate for the tonal center to which the others will relate; and after the E minor aria the second recitative returns to d as it urges the believer to trust in God's promises when the fulfillment of the expectations of faith seems too distant: "Die Glaubens-Augen werden schauen das Heil des Herrn; scheint die Erfüllung allzu fern, so kannst du doch auf die Verheißung bauen" (The eyes of faith will see the salvation of the Lord; if the fulfillment appears all too distant, then you can build on His promise). Throughout the cantata to this point the theme of delayed hopes has run like a thread: "Ach Herr, wie lange?" (no. 2), "Des Glaubens Docht glimmt kaum hervor" (no. 3), and "scheint die Erfüllung allzu fern" (no. 4). Now Bach introduces a second aria, in F major, in French dance style (*Passepied*) and homophonic texture—an aria, that is, that might be taken as the opposite type to the E minor aria—in order to underscore the inner change that God's presence through faith works in the believer: "Der Heiland kennet ja die Seinen, wenn ihre Hoffnung hilflos liegt. Wenn Fleisch und Geist in ihnen streiten, so steht er ihnen selbst zur Seiten, damit zuletzt die Glaube siegt" (The Savior certainly knows His own, when their hope lies helpless. When flesh and spirit struggle in them, then He stands by their side, so that faith wins out in the end). Although cast in a da capo mold, this piece takes care to suggest that the meaning of its closing line, the ultimate victory of faith ("damit zuletzt die Glaube siegt," ending the "B" section), represents the miraculous character of God's intervention. This Bach accomplishes by setting the first forty measures of the "B" section in flat tonalities (mostly g, with some c and B♭), then shifting to A minor for the final "damit zuletzt die Glaube siegt." Following a very active passage for "wenn Fleisch und Geist in ihnen streiten," Bach drops out the *basso continuo*, returning to g from B♭, for "so steht er ihnen selbst zur Seiten"; on "Seiten" the *basso continuo* returns, presumably as an allegory of God's presence, and the key shifts abruptly to A minor for "damit zuletzt die Glaube siegt." Bach marks the final A minor cadence adagio, duplicating the absence and return of the *basso continuo* as before.

The gesture just described hints that A minor, representing the final victory of faith over unbelief, is the key to which all the preceding ones relate; and that, of course, is what Bach's setting of the seventh verse of "Durch Adams Fall" confirms, in its overall shift from D minor to A minor. The message is that of hope in God, for God will help the faithful who put their trust in Him:

Wer hofft in Gott und dem vertraut,	Whoever hopes and trusts in God,
Der wird nimmer zuschanden;	Will never come to ruin;
Denn wer auf diesen Felsen baut,	For whoever builds on this rock,
Ob ihm gleich geht zuhanden	Even if much misfortune
Viel Unfalls hie, hab ich doch nie	Happens to him now, never yet have I
Den Menschen sehen fallen,	Seen that person fall,
Der sich verläßt auf Gottes Trost;	Who consigned himself to God's comfort;
Er hilft sein'n Gläub'gen allen.	He helps all His faithful ones.

Bach's setting is strongly tonal, and Bach clarifies the tonal levels of the piece by means of a ritornellolike instrumental passage that introduces the movement, sounds in full between the two *Stollen* and the *Abgesang* and at the end, and serves, in abbreviated forms, as interlude between the chorale lines. The principal recurrent element in this ritornello is a circle-of-fifths harmonic progression that outlines the basic harmonies of the key in a descending sequence: A, d, g, C, F^7, B♭, e°, and A, in the case of D minor. It thus functions as such circle-of-fifths patterns often do in the music of Monteverdi: to spell out the harmonic spectrum of a discrete hexachordal or tonal level that may then be transposed for the purpose of clarifying the tonal structure.[9] The predominance of descending patterns in the instrumental lines suggests a representation of the "fallen" nature of humankind. After the close of the two *Stollen* in A minor, the ritornello transposes up a fifth for the beginning of the *Abgesang*, then back down for the instrumental music associated with the first two chorale phrases of the *Abgesang* (phrases 5 and 6). Those two phrases, the second of which is identical to the first (and the third) phrase of the *Stollen*, thus return to the flat sphere of the beginning of the movement (closing on F and d respectively). The four phrases of the *Abgesang*, therefore, confirm the d–a shift that occurs in the two *Stollen*.

To highlight it still further Bach departs from his usual harmonization of the penultimate (seventh) phrase, leading it to a close in E minor. This detail is very significant, for in Bach's other settings of "Durch Adams Fall" this line ends on G (or its transpositional equivalent). The E minor ending enables Bach to transpose the ritornello that follows up *two* fifth levels from the original (i.e., B, e, a, D, G^7, and C), to encompass the harmonic spectrum associated in the seventeenth century with the one-sharp hexachord (triads or seventh chords on G, A, B, C, D, and E). Bach's transposition solidifies the shift to A minor for the final phrase ("er hilft sein'n Gläub'gen allen"), after which the entire ritornello returns in A minor, further confirming the shift of key in the setting as a whole. The d–e shift between the antepenultimate and penultimate phrases recalls, of course, the keys of the opening chorus and first aria as well as of the final phrases of the recitative that comes between them. In "Durch Adams Fall," however, they appear successively in the context of a (i.e., as subdominant and dominant) for the first time. Since, in terms contemporary with Bach, all three keys of d, a, and e appear within the *ambitus* of C and a (F, d, C, a, G, and e) but not in that of d (B♭, g, F, d, C, and a), the effect in toto is that A minor seems to put all the foregoing keys in perspective, an analogue of how faith eventually overcomes doubt and tribulation and an exact equivalent of Luther's (and Werckmeister's) catchphrase "In fine videbitur cujus toni."[10]

"Ach Gott, vom Himmel sieh' darein" in Cantatas 153 and 2

Cantata 153, "Schau, lieber Gott, wie meine Feind"

Even though the first Sunday in the new year occurred generally before rather than after Epiphany, its Gospel story, of the flight of the holy family to Egypt (Matthew 2:13–23), belongs chronologically later in the liturgical sequence. Among Bach's works for those two occasions, only the *Christmas Oratorio*, since it is a cycle, preserves the correct chronology. But since the flight of the holy family was traditionally interpreted as a reenactment of the Old Testament narrative of the captivity of Israel in Egypt, as well as a prefiguring of the contemporary believer's longing for eternity as a release from worldly persecution and tribulation, it is appropriate that

Table 5.3 Cantata 153, "Schau, lieber Gott, wie meine Feind." Leipzig, 1724. Sunday after New Year.

Movement	Genre	Instrumentation	Text incipit	Key
1	Chorale	SATB chorus, str., b.c.	Schau, lieber Gott, wie meine Feind	♯/E modal
2	Recitative	Alto, b.c.	Mein liebster Gott, ach lass dichs doch erbarmen	a–b
3	Arioso	Bass, b.c.	Fürchte dich nicht, ich bin mit dir	e
4	Recitative	Tenor, b.c.	Du sprichst zwar, lieber Gott, zu meiner Seelen Ruh' mir einen Trost in meinem Leiden zu	G–d
5	Chorale	SATB chorus, str., b.c.	Und obgleich alle Teufel	E Phryg.
6	Aria	Tenor, str., b.c.	Stürmt nur, stürmt, ihr Trübsalwetter	a
7	Recitative	Bass, b.c.	Getrost! Mein Herz, erdulde deinen Schmerz,	F–C
8	Aria	Alto, str., b.c.	Soll ich meinen Lebenslauf unter Kreuz und Trübsal führen	G
9	Chorale	SATB chorus, str., b.c.	St. 1) Drum will ich, weil ich lebe noch St. 2) Hilf mir mein Sach recht greifen an St. 3) Erhalt mein Herz im Glauben rein	C

it come as early as possible in the new year. Its theme, that is, articulates the metaphor of the old year as the time of Israel, the new as the time of Christ and the church, thereby encouraging the believer to draw parallels between the turning of the year, the changing eras of salvation history, and his own faith experience.

The typical character, or "dynamic," of that faith experience was, of course, that of Luther's "analogy of faith"—that is, destruction followed by restoration. Countless Bible stories—the flood, Daniel in the lions' den, the three men in the fiery furnace, the destruction of Jerusalem and of Sodom and Gomorrah, Israel in Egypt, and others—exhibited this dynamic, and a considerable number of Bach's cantata texts cited such stories in order to draw analogies to the believer's situation.[11] In fact, as we have seen (Chapter 1), in Bach's 1723–24 cycle the cantata for the final Sunday of the liturgical year (Cantata 70, "Wachet! betet! betet! wachet!" for the twenty-sixth Sunday after Trinity) had used the metaphor of the world as Egypt in order to aid in developing the theme of destruction and restoration, interpreting the ending of the liturgical year as the "letzte Zeit" before the end of the world and the beginning of the new as the "Anfang wahrer Freude" of God's restoration of the faithful to the "himmlische Eden."

Cantata 153 articulates the metaphoric layers just described by means of a three-stage design, each stage involving three movements: an aria, a recitative, and a chorale (see Table 5.3). Bach rotates the ordering of the movement types within each segment, however, so that the three chorales constitute the beginning, middle, and ending movements of the cantata (nos. 1, 5, and 9) as well as of the three segments in turn: chorale, recitative, aria (segment 1); recitative, chorale, aria (segment 2); and recitative, aria, chorale (segment 3). The harmonizations and placement of the three chorale settings provide, in fact, an important key to understanding Bach's intentions in this cantata. The melodies of the first and second chorales—that of "Ach Gott, vom Himmel sieh' darein" for "Schau, lieber Gott, wie meine Feind" (Look, dear God, how my enemy) and that of "Herzlich tut mich verlangen" for "Und obgleich alle Teufel" (And although all demons)—belong to a group including such other melodies as "Aus tiefer Not," "Erbarm dich mein, o Herre Gott," and "Christus, der uns selig Macht," which are generally identified as Phrygian or Hypophrygian. The distinction drawn in the preceding chapter between Bach's treatment of melodies in those two modes comes very much into play in Cantata 153. The third melody, however—that associated principally with "O Jesu Christ, meins Lebens Licht" and secondarily with "Ach Gott, wie manches Herzeleid"—is a pure Hypoionian (C major) setting that creates an entirely different effect at the end of the work. While Bach's harmonizations of the first and second chorales are complex and their final cadences sound like dominant endings, the third is one of the most straightforward "tonal" settings in Bach's work, its four phrases, in note-against-note style, cadencing to D (half close on V of V), G (tonicized), G (V of C), and C (I) in turn. Bach's indicating that three successive verses of the hymn be sung to this harmonization ensures that the ending of the cantata creates the effect of laying all earlier conflicts and ambiguities to rest.

In addition, the first six movements are in either modal or minor-key settings, while the final recitative (no. 7) turns to C for the last of its three sections and the final aria and chorale are in G and C, respectively. Within this scheme the three arias unfold a progression forward from the word of God, cited from Isaiah (no. 3), and set for bass and *basso continuo* only, through a representation of the believer, beset by "storms" of tribulation but clinging to God's promise (no. 6), to an expression of the believer's confidence in the certainty of eternal life (no. 8). All three arias are through-composed, the last one comprising three sections of increasingly jubilant character. The three recitatives (nos. 2, 4, and 7) are all of highly modulatory character, but with quite different tonal characters and roles in the overall design, the first articulating a sharpward motion that bridges from the sphere of the believer in extreme torment (no. 1) to God's promise (no. 3), the second moving in the flat direction to set up the effect of God's promise on the believer, and the third effecting the shift from the minor keys of the preceding movements to the concluding major-key movements of the cantata. The third recitative, like the third aria and the third chorale, presents us with a three-stage design that mirrors that of the cantata as a whole.

Bach's confronting minor/major keys and modal/tonal styles in "Schau, lieber Gott" reflect the way that the affective character and overall design of the work derive from familiar hermeneutic principles. The pivotal moment in the inner dynamic of the cantata coincides with the believer's recognizing the meaning of the flight to Egypt for him personally—that is, in the tropological sense. While the first and second segments center on his feelings of persecution, drawing heavily, like the first part of Cantata 21, on expressions from the most tormented of the Psalms, both featuring modal chorales that cadence on E and both ending with minor-key arias that contain promises of God, the recitative that begins the third segment introduces a reference to Jesus' flight from Herod's persecution, turning to C at the end, as it presents Jesus' sufferings as the source of comfort for the believer: "Wohlan, mit Jesu tröste dich und glaube festiglich: Denjenigen, die hier mit Christo leiden, will er das Himmelreich bescheiden" (So then, comfort yourself with Jesus and believe firmly: that those who suffer with Christ here, to them He will grant the Kingdom of Heaven). After the dominance of Old Testament–derived texts, the reference to the Gospel for the day marks a turning point. The modern minuetlike style of the G major aria and the uncomplicated tonal character of the C major chorale then effect a shift to the joyful affective sphere of the contemporary believer and his hopes for salvation. The three concluding chorale verses then seem to place the three stages in the believer's understanding within the perspective of his hopes for eternal life (i.e., the eschatological perspective).

Within this basic design the first six movements focus on the opposition of the believer's weakness and God's promises of support and redemption, which Bach establishes in the first segment by means of a progression from the opening chorale, associated with the believer's feelings of persecution, to the first aria (no. 3), God's words of support, drawn from Isaiah 41:10.

The cantata begins with a striking representation of the believer's awareness of the forces that threaten his destruction in the world: the first verse of David Denicke's "Schau, lieber Gott, wie meine Feind" (1646), set to the melody of "Ach Gott, vom Himmel sieh' darein," an appropriate association, since both chorale texts emphasize human weakness and the necessity of calling out for God's intervention, "Schau, lieber Gott" even more, perhaps, than "Ach Gott, vom Himmel," since it dwells on how easily the believer's enemies overcome him (Ex. 5.2).

Alfred Dürr speculates that Bach's choice of a four-part cantional setting for this chorale was motivated by external circumstances—namely, Bach's already having produced a large number of cantatas with elaborate opening choruses in the preceding weeks of the season.[12] While that may be true, it is clear that Bach was also stimulated very much by internal concerns—namely, the prominence of human weakness in the theological message of Cantata 153. His setting of "Schau, lieber Gott" has close affinities, especially in its final cadence, with the setting of "Ach Gott, vom Himmel" that ended Cantata 77 the preceding summer (on the thirteenth Sunday after Trinity, August 22). In that work, which is the subject of chapters 7 and 8 of the present study, the final chorale culminates a shift from the *cantus durus* of the opening movement (in which extensive flat modulations undermine its stability) to the final *cantus mollis* setting of "Ach Gott, vom Himmel," in which, as we will see, Bach created an astonishing aural image of the inability of humankind to live up to God's demands (see Ex. 8.8). Seeming almost to reflect back on the ending of that work, Cantata 153 takes the undermining or weakening of the believer by his enemies as its starting point, after which the design centers on the opposition between the threat of destruction and the supportive power of God's promises.

Bach's chief means of representing that opposition involves the disparity between "weak" and "strong" tonic keys, principally the disparity of stable and unstable E cadences throughout much of the first two segments. Bach indicates the nature of the dichotomies involved in the first segment by notating it and the modulatory

Example 5.2. Cantata 153: Opening chorale

recitative that follows (no. 4) entirely in the one-sharp key signature even though only the aria (no. 3) can be said to be in e.

At this transposition level the melody of "Schau, lieber Gott" ("Ach Gott, vom Himmel") is in what Werckmeister considered to be (B) Hypophrygian in the *cantus durus*, containing an f♯' in phrase 5, but no f♮s at all. Kirnberger, who published a setting at the same pitch level, and also ending on an E major chord, notated the melody without a sharp in the signature (even though he compared his Aolian setting with a G major setting at the same pitch that he notated in the one-sharp signature). And except for phrase 5, which has the melodic f♯' and which Kirnberger ended with a Phrygian cadence to B, he harmonized it with f♮s throughout. Hence the fact that his harmonization, designated clearly as Aolian, has been interpreted as (E) Phrygian and as Aolian ending on the dominant, the latter interpretation implying that the true final (A) is *two* fifths lower than the melodic final. In the latter interpretation the B Hypophrygian melody is simply absorbed into the key of a, ending on the dominant of that key.[13]

In fact, most settings of "Ach Gott, vom Himmel," including Bach's, create exactly this impression—of ending on a dominant harmony that is a fifth below the melodic final—which, as we saw, Werckmeister rejected. Bach's one-sharp key signature, however, might have indicated his awareness of a "problem." He might, that is, have perceived the disparity between the B Hypophrygian mode of the melody and the fact that its sevenfold alternation of phrases ending on b' and a' invited interpretation in terms of A minor. His setting, which is considerably more complex and subtle than Kirnberger's, reflects the alternating phrase endings by alternating the pitches F♯ and F phrase by phrase. Phrases 1, 3, and 5 (with cadences to E, E, and B) all feature the pitch F♯ without F♮ in the harmony (a striking difference from Kirnberger's emphasis on F♮ in phrases 1 and 3), while phrases 2, 4, and 6 (all cadencing on A) feature F with no F♯s. In the two (repeated) phrases of the *Stollen* this difference is insignificant, since the single f♯' of the first phrase is merely a passing tone, and the relationship of the two phrases creates the sense of an antecedent/consequent pairing in A minor. Nevertheless, Bach took pains to give the change from f♯' to f' an "expressive" character on the first chord of phrase 2, where the tenor f' "contradicts" the alto f♯' of the preceding phrase ending, then to draw attention to the f' on the fifth chord, where it is dissonant against the bass e. And in phrases 5 through 7 the f♯–f difference mirrors the meaning of the single sentence that spans those phrases: "Herr, wo mich deine Gnad' nicht hält / so kann der Teufel, Fleisch und Welt / mich leicht in Unglück stürzen" (Lord, if Your grace does not sustain me / then the devil, the flesh and the world / can easily cast me into misfortune). In these three phrases Bach matches the reference to what will happen to the believer if God and His grace are not present by setting phrase 5 entirely within the framework represented by the one-sharp signature, then undermining that framework over the next two phrases in analogy with the progressive "weakening" of the believer by his enemies. Phrase 5 matches Werckmeister's requirements for the Hypophrygian mode exactly. It not only ends with the Phrygian cadence to B but also features f♯ throughout the phrase; at the outset the bass line even presents the pitches of the first phrase of the chorale melody one degree sharper than at the beginning of the setting (i.e., beginning from f♯, rather than b, but accented differently, of course), and at the end it introduces the last four pitches of the first phrase (down two octaves). This phrase therefore sounds like a variant of the first phrase, but solidly in the one-sharp framework for the first time in the entire setting. In other words, although we may draw this phrase into the key of a (as V of V), we lose something important in Bach's setting if we do not recognize that it represents a sharper region than the preceding phrases—that is, if we discount its "hexachordal" aspect.

After the six f♯s of phrase 5, the shift to an F major root-position triad on the second chord of phrase 6 represents another very expressive gesture, turning the cadence of that phrase back to a. The seventh and last phrase of Bach's setting, however, is the most telling of his intentions, since not only does it break the pattern of phrase-by-phrase F–F♯ alternation, beginning with F and ending with F♯, but directly before the final E cadence it moves to the furthest point in the flat direction of this entire setting. Bach begins the seventh phrase as if A minor were the tonic key, even moving to harmonies that suggest to our ears the *subdominant* of a in the penultimate measure: D minor and C♯ diminished-seventh chords. The tenor b♭ of the C♯ diminished-seventh chord extends the pitch spectrum of the movement one step in the flat direction beyond F, its flat limit to this point, and the a-b♭-a of the tenor line points unmistakably toward D minor. However, Bach changes the D minor to D major on the next chord and follows it by a diminished-seventh chord on d♯, then the final E major chord (i.e., transposition of the C♯ diminished-seventh and D major chords up a tone in sequence). Thus, instead of either a plagal or an authentic cadence to E, by far the preferred cadences in the harmonizations of other composers, Bach approaches the final bass note e by means of a chromatic ascent from c♯ and d through d♯. Although the D major chord has a strikingly "fresh" and relatively sharp sound at the point where the alto f♯' replaces its earlier f', Bach's sequence emphasizes the flat/sharp, whole-tone relationship that normally exists between the subdominant and the dominant, especially in minor keys, unmistakably causing the E to sound like the dominant of a. After the weakening effect of the shift toward D minor, the reappearance of f♯' in the antepenultimate D major chord has the quality of hope against hope, so to speak—that is, it represents a local brightening of the harmony that, although very expressive, still functions like the subdominant of a. After the dominant (sharp) character of phrase 5, the F major harmony near the beginning of phrase 6 and the replacement of F♯ by F♮ throughout that phrase seem to mirror the believer's envisioning the absence of God's grace, to make the point that in order for the E ending to sound secure F♯ must constitute a fundamental pitch —that is, a component of the basic scale and the fifth of the B major chord. It does not seem far-fetched, therefore, to interpret the progressive flattening of the tonality through phrases 5 to 7 as an analogue of the believer's fears and the final cadence to E as representing a level he cannot sustain (the sharp system of Bach's key signature).

And the opposition of stable and unstable tonal regions continues throughout the first seven movements of the cantata, the sharp region generally undermined by the flat until the final aria and chorale. Directly following the opening chorale, the first recitative amplifies the believer's cries of persecution: "Mein liebster Gott, ach laß dichs doch erbarmen, ach hilf doch, hilf mir Armen! Ich wohne hier bei lauter Löwen und bei Drachen, und diese wollen mir durch Wut und Grimmigkeit in kurzer Zeit den Garaus völlig machen" (My dearest God, ah, permit Yourself to have mercy, ah, help, help this poor weak one! I dwell here among lions and dragons, and they want through rage and fury to do me in completely). And it confirms the "weak" ending of the chorale by moving immediately to a, in association with the believer's cry for God's mercy. Its tonal direction, however, is markedly toward the sharpest region of the cantata, reaching the dominant of F♯ in its sixth measure and closing in b two measures after that. It appears that after the "subdominant" threat of the believer's destruction at the end of the opening chorale the unremitting motion in the sharp direction represents the violence of his enemies—that is, it was intended to project a *durus* quality. Bach's response is the E minor of the ariosolike aria for bass and *continuo*, drawn, as in the biblical *dictum* of Cantata 18, from Isaiah (41:10): "Fürchte dich nicht, ich bin mit dir. Weiche nicht, ich bin dein Gott; ich stärke dich, ich helfe dir auch durch die rechte Hand meiner Gerechtigkeit" (Fear thou not, for I am with thee. Be not dismayed, for I am thy God; I will strengthen thee, I will help thee also with the right hand of My righteousness). This solo marks a point of culmination in the cantata, since of the first three movements, all of which Bach notated with the one-sharp key signature, this is the only one to offer a positive message and the only one to settle solidly and unambiguously on e. And this E minor—the first point of real tonal stability in the cantata—not only projects an entirely different tonal character from the weak E of the opening chorale but also mirrors the text of the aria. The lines "Weiche nicht, ich bin dein Gott; ich stärke dich, ich helfe dir auch durch die rechte Hand meiner Gerechtigkeit," urge the believer not to yield to his foes, for God gives strength and assistance. In this passage the words "weiche nicht" ("do not yield"—literally, "do not *soften*") may well bring up musical associations for anyone familiar with the common usage of the terms *hart* and *weich* as synonyms for *dur* (sharp, major) and *moll* (flat, minor) in seventeenth- and eighteenth-century Germany. That is, this representation of the voice of God urges the believer (metaphorically) not to allow the flat, or subdominant, tonal region to weaken or undermine his faith, as it had threatened to in the opening chorale.

In the first segment of the cantata the two very different E modes attest to Bach's awareness of the issues involved in modal composition within a basically tonal framework. They correspond closely, in fact, to the two viewpoints on the Hypophrygian mode that Athanasius Kircher set forth in 1650, the one mode undermining its final E by means of flat elements in the pitch spectrum and the other strengthening it by drawing on the one-sharp system to provide its dominant.[14] In this light, Bach's setting of "Schau, lieber Gott" confronts both views of the mode, since it proclaims f♯ as a fundamental pitch in both its key signature and the setting of its fifth phrase even while it tends toward the subdominant of a just before the end. The E minor aria then provides a model for the strong sense of key that the believer must (metaphorically) attempt to sustain.

Although the fourth movement, a tenor recitative, carries forward the one-sharp signature of the preceding movements, its validity is contradicted by the modulatory course of events after the first six of its nineteen measures. After beginning in G and cadencing in b for the believer's response to God's words of *Trost*—"Du sprichst zwar, lieber Gott, zu meiner Seelen Ruh' mir einen Trost in meinem Leiden zu" (Thou speakest to be sure, dear God, for my soul's rest a comfort to me in my sufferings)—Bach shifts the modulatory direction toward a and e, closing in the latter key: "Ach, aber meine Plage vergrössert sich von Tag zu Tage" (Ah, but my torment increases from day to day), so as to initiate the next stage in the undermining of the believer by his enemies. With the next phrase, Bach reintroduces the pitch b♭ for the first time since the ending of the opening chorale, and with obviously related associations: entering on the word "Feinde" ("denn meiner Feinde sind so viel": for my enemies are so many), it converts the E minor cadence into a motion toward d that leads ultimately to g and even c, as the believer voices his fears and cries out for God's aid. It appears that the flat region continues to symbolize the believer's weakness by invoking the affective sphere associated with the term *mollis*: "denn meiner Feinde sind so viel, mein Leben ist ihr Ziel, ihr Bogen wird auf mich gespannt, sie richten ihre Pfeile zum Verderben, ich soll von ihren Händen sterben; Gott! meine Noth ist dir bekannt, die ganze Welt wird mir zur Marterhöhle; hilf, Helfer, hilf! errette meine Seele!" (For my enemies are so many, my life is their goal, their bow is drawn toward me, they direct their arrows toward my destruction, I will die from their hands; God! my need is known to You, the entire world is become a pit of martyrdom to me; help, helper, help! rescue my soul!) (Ex. 5.3).

Since the "goal" (*Ziel*) of the believer's enemies in the world is depicted in this recitative as the key of d, which appears first on the word "Ziel," then serves as the key of the final cadence, it is evident that the "weakening" or "softening" warned against in the E minor aria has taken place. In contrast to the sharpward motion of the first recitative and its culmination in the E minor aria, the flat motion of the second

Example 5.3. Cantata 153: Second recitative (no. 4)

Example 5.4. Cantata 153: Second chorale setting (no. 5)

one leads to a second E mode chorale verse, ending now with a reference to *God's* "Ziel" (Ex. 5.4):

Und obgleich alle Teufel	And although all the demons
Dir wollten widerstehn,	Want to oppose you,
So wird doch ohne Zweifel	Nevertheless without doubt
Gott nicht zurücke gehn;	God will not desert you;
Was er ihm fürgenommen	What He has undertaken
Und was er haben will,	And what He wants to happen,
Das muss doch endlich kommen	That must come in the end
Zu seinem Zweck und Ziel!	To His purpose and goal!

Bach's setting, sung to the Phrygian melody "Herzlich tut mich verlangen," appears in the "natural" instead of the one-sharp key signature (the first key-signature shift in the work). The only Phrygian cadences of this setting, however, on phrases 1 and 3 of the *Stollen*, are to the one-flat hexachord (i.e., to A, sounding like the dominant of d), after which the second and fourth phrases close solidly in a with the aid of diminished- and dominant-seventh chords functioning as V of V. In other words, the chorale begins in the flat region of the recitative ending but moves sharpward. Likewise, in the *Abgesang*, half closes in F and d (phrases 5 and 6) give way to a full close to G (phrase 7) and the final plagal cadence to E. The flat–sharp motion of both the *Stollen* and the *Abgesang* mirrors the overall sense of the chorale verse, which begins with reference to the devil's opposition to the faithful and ends with an affirmation of God's help in leading things to His "Zweck und Ziel." In relation to the opening complex (movements 1–3) this second modal chorale to end on E is much more affected than the first one by the emphasis on d at the beginnings of the *Stollen* and the *Abgesang* (rather than at the end, as in "Schau, lieber Gott"). This quality suggests at first that the believer's difficulty in holding onto E has increased under the undermining effect of his enemies as narrated in the foregoing recitative. The tonal motion that follows in both cases, however, seems to "overcome" the flat emphasis. In the final phrase Bach reaches the penultimate A minor harmony by introducing a secondary-dominant sequence above the chromatic f♯–g–g♯–a ascent that precedes the final e in the bass (thus ending the chorale with the harmonic sequence D^6_5–G–E^6_5–a–E). The first two of these harmonies seem to be preparing a final cadence on C beneath the final g♮'–e' descent of the melody, as, in fact, other Bach settings of this chorale end, but at the last moment Bach leads the lower parts upward to a plagal a–E cadence instead. The effect is to render the "fresh"-sounding antepenultimate E^6 chord part of a logical process that seems to continue the cadence further than expected. Owing partly to the metrical placement of the final chords, we have no difficulty in accepting the plagal E cadence as a Phrygian final despite its dominant sound. This dualistic quality is subtly suggestive of the distinction between God's goal and the believer's tormented condition. The E cadence is, in fact, far less "weak" than the final E of the opening chorale, since its *cantus naturalis* tonal context does not proclaim the disparity between modal and tonal interpretations (i.e., the failure of the final E to serve as a "tonic") so intensely.[15] In other words, there is more of a balance between the Phrygian E ending and the dominant of A minor, analogous to the believer's accepting his own weakness and placing his trust in God's aid.

After this second chorale Bach confirms A minor, as he had directly following the ending of the first chorale. The tenor aria "Stürmt nur, stürmt, ihr Trübsalswetter" juxtaposes the "storms" of tribulation, the "flames" of misfortune, and the hostility of the believer's enemies to God's words of comfort: "ich bin dein Hort und Erretter." But now the believer, secure in God's promise, defies the world to do its worst:

Stürmt nur, stürmt, ihr Trübsalswetter,	Rage away, you storm of tribulation,
Wallt, ihr Fluten, auf mich los!	Seethe, you floods, right at me!
Schlagt, ihr Unglücksflammen,	Beat, you flames of misfortune,
Über mich zusammen,	Over me entirely,
Stört, ihr Feinde, meine Ruh,	Disrupt, you enemies, my rest,
Spricht mir doch Gott tröstlich zu:	Since God speaks comfortingly to me:
Ich bin dein Hort und Erretter.	I am thy refuge and rescuer.

The aria is, of course, through-composed, featuring sections in a–e (lines 1–2; mm. 1–18), d (lines 3–5, mm. 18–24), and d–a (lines 6–7, mm. 24–35). Not unexpectedly, God's words in the final line bring about the return to the original A minor tonality after a middle section that once again introduces the subdominant tonal sphere. While the opening section closes solidly in the dominant, e, suggesting, when taken along with the text, the necessary combination of violent energy (the storms of tribulation) and structural solidity (the believer's confidence), the second section uses the subdominant region to bring about a weakening effect once again. The first b♭ enters, as it did at the end of the first chorale ("mich leicht in *Unglück* stürzen"), with a reference to the believer's misfortune, on the word "Unglücksflammen" ("Schlagt, ihr Unglücksflammen, über mich zusammen, stört, ihr Feinde, meine Ruh'"); now the b♭ converts an E minor cadence to the diminished-seventh chord on c♯, turning the tonality toward d, just as it did in the second recitative ("denn meiner *Feinde* sind so viel"). And the ending phrase, "stört, ihr Feinde, meine Ruh'," introduces the subdominant of d, leading to a sustained b♭ on "Ruh'" that pauses on the same c♯ diminished-seventh chord again. All these places have in common their association of the subdominant region with the undermining or weakening of the faithful by their enemies.

After the pause on "Ruh'" the tenor continues with the introduction of God's words of comfort, "spricht mir doch Gott tröstlich zu: Ich bin dein Hort und Erretter," cadencing in d on "zu." For God's words, however, Bach moves rapidly away from d and back to a, a gesture that creates the effect of overcoming the subdominant weakening; the final vocal flourish on "Erretter" underscores that quality. In this aria Bach confirms the key toward which the opening chorale had tended, where it represented the reality behind the believer's unsuccessful attempt to cadence solidly in E. In the first aria God's promise had introduced a secure E minor in response to the narrative of the believer's persecution by his enemies; and in the E Phrygian ending of the second chorale the reference to God's "Ziel" had set up the A minor of the second aria, in which the believer comes to accept God's promise as the means by which he can overcome both tribulation and persecution.

If these events were intended by Bach in terms of the kind of tonal "narrative" I have described, then the final outcome of the cantata ought to be in major (i.e., not *weich* or *moll*, and not, of course, in a flat key). In this context the recitative that follows the A minor aria occupies, as mentioned earlier, a pivotal place in the design, since, beginning and ending on C, it sets up the G and C of the final aria and chorale. Bach divides the recitative into three distinct segments, of which the first and third deal with the contemporary believer and his hopes for salvation; they are in major (ending in G and C, respectively), while the second segment, summarizing the Gospel narrative of the flight to Egypt, is in E minor. The keynotes thus outline the C major triad. Once again Bach seems to have designed the tonal aspects of the movement with a view for the differentiation of flat and sharp areas. Beginning on a C^6 chord and a C arpeggio in the voice ("Getrost! Mein Herz": Be comforted! My heart), Bach has the bass solo leap a seventh to b♭ as the text reminds us of the necessity of patient suffering: "erdulde deinen Schmerz, lass dich dein Kreuz nicht unterdrücken!" (endure your pain, do not let your cross overwhelm you!). The *basso continuo* e then shifts to e♭ and leaps from there down a diminished sixth to G♯ on "Kreuz" as the bass leaps up a tritone to b♮. These provocatively audible rhetorical devices form, however, only part of a broader sequence of events. After this phrase cadences to a, the final phrase of this first segment turns to G as the bass anticipates the positive outcome of the believer's suffering: "Gott wird dich schon zu rechter Zeit erquicken" (God will certainly revive you at the appropriate time).

Then the second segment of the recitative, entirely and solidly in e, explains Herod's persecution and the flight to Egypt as an example of how Jesus became a fugitive immediately after His birth. The return to e might well have been conceived by Bach as the fulfillment of God's promise in the E minor arioso: that is, God's standing by and strengthening the believer come to pass in Jesus' sufferings on his behalf. Immediately following the e cadence, Bach once again reintroduces the pitch b♭ in the voice, this time, however, not with the c♯ diminished-seventh chord, but with the dominant of F, which resolves to F, then shifts to C as the character of the recitative turns from Jesus' persecution by Herod to its benefit for the believer: "Wohlan, mit Jesu tröste dich, und glaube festiglich: denjenigen, die hier mit Christo leiden, will er das Himmelreich bescheiden" (Now then, comfort yourself with Jesus, and believe firmly: that to all those who suffer with Christ here He will grant the Kingdom of Heaven). Within this final C major arioso passage Bach sounds the b♭ twice more—first as a sustained tone on "leiden" that gives way almost immediately to a b♮–b♭–b♮ succession within the phrase "will *er* [b♮] das Himmelreich [b♭] bescheiden [b♮]." The ease of this last shift makes clear that the two pitches are no longer representative of polarized tonal regions but simply part of the final articulation of C.

In fact, this recitative touches on all the keys of the C–a *ambitus* except the one that has served throughout the cantata to represent the "undermining" of the believer, D minor. In this light, it suggests that behind Bach's tonal design for the work as a whole lies an allegorical perception of the dominant or one-sharp region (e–G) as strengthening the "natural" or a–C region, while the subdominant or flat region (principally d with elements of g and c in the second recitative) weakens it. The believer is located midway between two worlds, one of which represents the goal of his hopes and trust in God while the other represents all that threatens his stability in the world. With the turn to G and C for the final aria and chorale there are no more flat accidentals of any kind in the cantata.

When, just six weeks before the first performance of "Schau, lieber Gott," Bach had represented the world by analogy with Egypt in the aria "Wenn kömmt der Tag, an dem wir ziehen aus dem Ägypten dieser Welt?" of Cantata 70, he had anticipated the believer's escape from the world by means of a "rising" tonal progression through two arias in a and e that had culminated in the triple-meter chorale in G that ended part 1.[16] That chorale voiced the believer's anticipation of eternity in terms of Jesus' calling him from the "vale of tears" to the jubilation and triumph of eternity. The final aria of Cantata 153 expresses virtually the identical sentiments, turning to G major and triple meter:

Soll ich meinen Lebenslauf	If I must lead my life's course
Unter Kreuz und Trübsal führen,	Under cross and tribulation,
Hört es doch im Himmel auf.	It will however cease in heaven.
Da ist lauter Jubilieren,	There is pure jubilation,
Daselbsten verwechselt mein Jesus das Leiden	There my Jesus will exchange my suffering
Mit seliger Wonne, mit ewigen Freuden.	For holy bliss, eternal joy.

Example 5.5. Cantata 153: Final chorale (no. 9)

As mentioned earlier, this aria adopts the style of the minuet, dominated by a flowing melodic style. It unfolds in three stages, the last one marked allegro and introducing the believer's anticipation of Jesus' changing his sufferings into joy. After this aria the four phrases of the final chorale—also in triple meter—strengthen the C by means of the aforementioned succession of cadences on D (half close), G, G, and C. Its text draws on the last three verses of "Ach Gott, wie manches Herzeleid" (16 through 18), sung in immediate succession, to summarize the progression from acceptance of worldly persecution (verse 16) to readiness for death (v. 17) and the anticipation of eternity (v. 18), ending with the believer's cry of longing to be with God: "O mein Heiland, wär ich bei dir!" (Ex. 5.5). In the third segment of the cantata the initial sections of the recitative, aria, and chorale all take up the believer's *Kreuz*, a symbol, of course, of his enduring worldly persecution, after which the subsequent progression of ideas in each movement leads to the anticipation of eternity, thus mirroring the dynamic of the cantata as a whole. Eternity is, of course, the "promised land" of the Old Testament exodus, reinterpreted eschatologically:

Drum will ich, weil ich lebe noch, Das Kreuz dir fröhlich tragen nach; Mein Gott, mach mich darzu bereit, Es dient zum Besten allezeit!	Therefore I will, while I yet live, Bear the cross joyfully after You; My God, make me ready for that, It is for the best always!
Hilf mir mein Sach recht greifen an, Da ich mein' Lauf vollenden kann, Hilf mir auch zwingen Fleisch und Blut, Für Sünd und Schanden mich behüt!	Help me to take up my affairs now, So that I may finish my course, Help me to compel the flesh and blood, Guard me from sin and shame!
Erhalt mein Herz im Glauben rein, So leb und sterb ich dir allein; Jesu, mein Trost, hör mein Begier, O mein Heiland, wär ich bei dir!	Keep my heart pure in faith, That I live and die for You alone; Jesu, my comfort, hear my desire, O my Savior, were I with You!

From this perspective, Bach's beginning Cantata 153 with a simple setting of the melody of "Ach Gott, vom Himmel sieh' darein" enabled him to bring the modal quality of that setting into the foreground, to draw it into a larger framework in which the subdominant coloring of its final cadence would fit with recurrences of the subdominant or flat side of the *ambitus* throughout the cantata as an allegory of the undermining of the believer's faith by his enemies in the world. In the first two movements (chorale and recitative) there is a disparity between the tonal region represented by the one-sharp key signature of the opening chorale and the much flatter harmonization of the movement as well as between the believer's A minor cry for mercy and the increasing sharpness of his persecutors in the first recitative. God's response (the E minor aria) puts these tonal disparities in perspective, after which the introduction of flat tonal regions in the second recitative mirrors the continuing narrative of the believer's persecution. The believer has to resist such undermining, to suffer patiently, trusting in God's intervening on his behalf, which the second chorale and aria reaffirm, now in the *cantus naturalis.* The third and final recitative resolves the believer's doubts by articulating the role of suffering and persecution as his "cross," to be endured in faith until such time as he inherits the benefits of Jesus' sufferings on his behalf (the closing lines, as cited previously). The texts that Bach sets with the solid G and C major tonalities that end the first and third segments of this recitative ("Gott wird dich schon zu rechter Zeit erquicken": G; "will er das Himmelreich bescheiden": C) suggest that the emergence of those keys is associated with God's "goal" for the believer as forecast in the penultimate G major phrase and the averted C major cadence of the second chorale. They enable the third segment of the cantata to articulate a secure dominant–tonic relationship centered on C major, in which key the final chorale proclaims, once again in three stages, the full confidence of the believer's faith and its eschatological goal.

In what I have just outlined for Cantata 153 there are, inevitably, many interpretative uncertainties regarding Bach's precise intent for the numerous details that make up such an elaborate design. Absolute proof of such intent will never, of course, be forthcoming, and the balancing of musical and theological features of his works remains a subtle process that involves two quite different kinds of analytical procedures. Usually, however, there are certain very broad aspects of any cantata design that provide us with very strong indications of overall musico-theological intent. In the case of Cantata 153 the changes from modal to tonal chorale settings and from minor to major movement keys at the end go hand in hand with the obvious differences in style that emerge in the final aria and chorale to make clear the role of the third recitative in effecting a shift from the pejorative tone of the opening movement to the affirmational tone of the ending. The shifting tonalities finally settle on a clear C major framework at the end, just at the point where the believer comes to full understanding of the role of worldly persecution in his hopes for salvation. On a large scale the affective "dynamic" of the work is increasingly hopeful, whereas the individual details cannot be so unambiguously defined. The paradoxical aspect of the theological message—that worldly tribulation and persecution, while destructive in themselves, have ultimately positive value—can probably only be mirrored in music with the aid of a text to point the way (as Kuhnau asserted). The technique of thematic transformation, were it a part of Bach's style, might offer means of indicating such gradual and "internal" processes as the growth of faith, understanding, and confidence. Within Bach's compositional framework one of the closest equivalents is provided by sequences of changing styles and, in many cases, *tonal* styles and key successions. The subtlety of Bach's tonal devices, especially when the church modes are involved, raises questions that can never be unambiguously answered—as can those of the poetic texts—but whose very existence is a compelling stimulus to the analysis of music and "word" together as signposts to a unified reality.

Another cantata that features some very similar tonal-allegorical features to Cantata 153 and that therefore makes a good point of comparison is Cantata 25, "Es ist nichts Gesundes an meinem Leibe" (There is nothing healthy in my body), composed for the fourteenth Sunday after Trinity, 1723. "Es ist nichts Gesundes" begins with an E Phrygian chorale setting—based on the melody "Herzlich tut mich verlangen"—and ends with securely tonal C major/Ionian settings (aria and chorale). Once again, Bach reserves the appearance of triple meter for the last aria, whose expression of the believer's eschatological hopes in terms of music might even have had personal associations: "Öffne meinen schlechten Liedern, Jesu, dein Genaden Ohr! Wenn ich dort im höhern Chor werde mit den Engeln singen, soll mein Danklied besser klingen" (Open Your ear of grace, Jesu, to my poor songs! When I sing in the choir above with the angels, my hymn of thanks will sound better). And the final chorale, likewise, ends with the anticipation of eternity, so that the turn to major for the final movements seems to have been associated with the believer's anticipation of release from worldly tribulation, symbolized in the famous comparision of sin to disease and the world to a hospital for the deathly ill. The chorale, although not in triple meter, is sung to the melody of "Freu' dich sehr, o meine Seele" (Rejoice greatly, O my soul), which Bach had associated with the joyful anticipation of eternity as release from the world in Cantata 70 (see "Aspects of the Liturgical Year" in chapter 1).

In Cantata 25, as in other cantatas that center on Phrygian modal settings, such as Cantatas 135 and 38, Bach causes the weakening aspect of the Phrygian tonality—its tendency toward the tonality of which its final cadence sounds like the dominant—to precipitate modulation in the subdominant (flat) direction. In the opening chorus and in the two recitatives that surround the first aria, in d, substantial modulations in the flat direction (to c in the first instance, g in the second) weaken the key in analogy with the believer's characterization of the world as ridden by sin. In the opening movement, above all, Bach introduces tortured-sounding flat accidentals into the first appearance of the second theme, a variant of the first chorale phrase, projecting a quality of unrest that exactly matches the text: "und ist kein Friede in meinen Gebeinen vor meiner Sünde" (and there is no rest in my bones because of my sins) (Ex. 5.6). And again, toward the end of the movement, Bach colors the harmony with flat modulations that cause another substantial weakening effect. When the turn to C occurs, at the close of the second recitative, its positive tone contrasts strikingly with the tone of the ending of the first recitative, a cry of torment from the soul in dire distress: "Ach! dieses Gift durchwühlt auch meine Glieder. Wo find' ich Armer Arzenei? Wer stehet mir in meinem Elend bei? Wer ist mein Arzt, wer hilft mir wieder?" (Ah! this poison even bores through my limbs. Where will I, poor wretch, find healing? Who will stand by me in my suffering? Who is my physician, who will

Example. 5.6. Cantata 25: Excerpt from opening movement, mm. 41–45

help me further?) The earlier recitative is one of the most harmonically complex in the Bach cantatas, modulating first from its initial a/d/g tonalities into sharp regions and back. From a suddenly introduced E$\sharp^{6}_{5}$ chord, its ending phrases, whose text I have just cited, move toward b and e, before settling on the final Phrygian cadence to A. Behind the tonal juxtapositions lies a circle-of-fifths tonal motion that sets up the D minor of the central aria "Ach, wo hol' ich Armer Rath?" (Ah, where will I, poor wretch, obtain counsel?), whose reduction in scoring to bass and *basso continuo* alone seems to express the patient/believer's need for spiritual healing. After the second recitative the shift to C and the return of recorders, oboes, and strings for the soprano aria both aid in projecting the believer's hopes for the metaphoric healing and recovery of eternal life. Throughout the first half of this cantata the metaphor of deathly illness for sin prompted Bach to introduce tonal qualities of the kind that

Werckmeister associated with the imperfection and mortality of human life (chromaticism) and that Kuhnau described as an incomplete recovery from illness (a strong tendency toward the subdominant). After the "patient's" cries of need and trust for his "physician" in the centralized subdominant aria, the second half of the work takes up the other side of the metaphor: diatonic, strongly tonal, major-key music as the mirror of the believer's hopes for salvation.

Cantata 2, "Ach Gott, vom Himmel sieh' darein"

The "weak" modal character of "Ach Gott, vom Himmel sieh' darein" expresses the tortured cry to God from one in great need. Bach's first texted harmonization of the melody appears as the final movement of Cantata 77, to be taken up in chapters 7 and 8 of this study, and his second in Cantata 153. His third, and last, so far as we know, is in his chorale cantata based on "Ach Gott, vom Himmel" (BWV 2, for the second Sunday after Trinity, 1725; see Table 5.4). Bach set that work in the *cantus mollis* or one-flat signature so that, in Werckmeister's terms, the melody is in A Hypophrygian. This time, however, the chorale settings that serve as the first and last movements end with authentic A–D cadences even though the verses are pessimistic in tone (the first verse ends "der Glaub' ist auch verloschen gar bei allen Menschenkindern": faith is completely extinguished among all the children of humanity, and the last "der gottlos' Hauf' sich umher find't, wo solche Leute sind in deinem Volk erhaben": the godless multitude are found all around where such people are prominent among your own). The overall context, however, is not pessimistic, since the thrust of "Ach Gott, vom Himmel," as of "Schau, lieber Gott," is as a prayer for God's intervention to aid the faithful against their enemies in the world. Rather, the pessimism is the "surface" that conceals God's aid. The message of Cantata 2, therefore, is pure *theologia crucis*, the only true theology according to Luther. The believer must suffer patiently in the world, trusting in God's word and awaiting the promised salvation. This is the message of the penultimate movement of the cantata, the tenor aria "Durch's Feuer wird das Silber rein."

Durch's Feuer wird das Silber rein,	Through fire the silver is purified,
Durch's Kreuz das Wort bewährt erfunden.	Through the cross the word is preserved.
Drum soll ein Christ zu allen Stunden	Therefore a Christian should at all times
In Kreuz und Noth geduldig sein.	Be patient in cross and need.

The message of the theology of the cross is thus an inverted one: the cross is the only true revelation of the deity; and the life of the faithful duplicates Jesus' patient acceptance of suffering as told in the scriptures. Suffering becomes, paradoxically, of positive value.

And once again Bach represents the believer's life of tribulation and persecution in the world by means of modulation into flat-minor tonal regions, associating the flat-minor area with the "subdominant" quality of the modal melody of "Ach Gott, vom Himmel." Within the opening chorale-motet setting Bach evokes an archaic atmosphere appropriate to a chorale that is based on a paraphrase of the twelfth

Table 5.4 Cantata 2, "Ach Gott, vom Himmel sieh' darein." Leipzig, 1724. Second Sunday after Trinity.

Movement	Genre	Instrumentation	Text incipit	Key
1	Chorus	SATB chorus, tbne. 1–4, ob. 1, 2, str., b.c.	Ach Gott, vom Himmel sieh' darein	♭/D modal
2	Recitative	Tenor, b.c.	Sie lehren eitel falsche List	c–d
3	Aria	Alto, vln. 1, b.c.	Tilg, o Gott, die Lehren, so dein Wort verkehren!	B♭
4	Recitative	Bass, str., b.c.	Die Armen sind verstört	E♭–g
5	Aria	Tenor, vln. 1, 2, ob. 1, 2, vla., b.c.	Durch's Feuer wird das Silber rein,	g
6	Chorale	SATB chorus, plus all instruments, b.c.	Das wollst du, Gott, bewahren rein	♭/D modal

psalm, a pure lament, by means of the somber *colla parte* instrumentation of the trombone and cornetto choir. In the first movement of Cantata 25 he had used this sonority, with the addition of two recorders, for the instrumental choir that plays the Phrygian chorale melody, while the rest of the movement was accompanied by strings and oboes. He had then dropped out the cornetti and trombones to achieve a brighter sound for the C major aria and reintroduced the full instrumental complement to double the final chorale. In the opening movement of Cantata 2 the successive chorale lines, presented as a *cantus firmus* in the alto, are anticipated in the remaining voices; and although Bach introduces three pitch levels for these imitative entries, corresponding to the tonic, subdominant, and dominant levels, the subdominant greatly predominates, as it does in the melody itself. Toward the end of the movement Bach amplifies this quality by continuing the G minor tonality of the penultimate phrase (g cadence in m. 147) on to c just seven measures before the final A–D cadence.

This gesture, which coincides with the antepenultimate tone, c", of the chorale melody at the point where all the voices sing the final word, "Menschenkinder" (i.e., a reference to the human condition in the final lines, "der Glaub ist auch verloschen gar bei allen Menschenkindern"), goes beyond anything suggested by the melody itself. The resultant sense that despite its final A–D cadence the ending sounds like the dominant of g then leads Bach to begin the recitative that follows with a transposition of the opening phrase of "Ach Gott, vom Himmel" down a fifth (i.e., beginning from d'–e♭'–d') and, furthermore, to answer it in the continuo in quasi-canonic imitation at the same pitch, but to lead the answer to a low A♭. This gesture has the effect of initiating a continuing flat motion that moves toward B♭ minor without, however, ever arriving at a cadence. Instead, Bach uses the multidirectional quality of the diminished-seventh chord to lead toward phrase 5 of the chorale melody, normally the sharpest phrase, but now transposed *two* fifths below its original pitch; this point coincides with the idea that humankind is split into individual factions—"Der Eine wählet dies, der Andre das" (the one chooses this, the other that)—whose reliance on reason leads them astray: "die thörichte Vernunft ist ihr

Compass" (foolish reason is their compass). Tonally, the impact of all these devices, of course, is to embed the final D minor tonality entirely in a subdominant context.

The B♭ aria that follows, "Tilg' o Gott, die Lehren, so dein Wort verkehren" (Strike out, O God, the teachings that twist Your word), mixes triplet and duplet subdivisions of the beat, including many simultaneous three-against-two passages, presumably to depict those who set themselves in opposition to God and His word. The aria has a strutting quality owing to its principal motive and its insistent sequential repetition above a staccato bass. In the middle section the reiterated cries, "Trotz dem, Trotz dem, Trotz dem, Trotz, der uns will meistern" (Defiance to those who oppose us), give direct voice to the obstinacy of God's and the believer's enemies. After the g of the preceding twenty measures, Bach moves suddenly to d to end the "B" section with this passage, perhaps intending to further an association throughout this cantata of the d/D modes with all that the believer has to endure in the world. At first the very punctuated, emphatic character of the reiterations of "Trotz dem" projects an arrogant character. Then, for the penultimate phrase, Bach sets the line with the final phrase of the chorale melody transposed up a fifth—that is, in the sharp direction—for the only time in the cantata. Ending on e', this phrase, which Werckmeister would consider to be in E Hypophrygian, leads to d; and Bach follows it by a sudden leap up a diminished fifth on the second beat ("Trotz") and a descent to the d cadence beneath the final measures of the ritornello transposed up a third. These gestures seem to encapsulate the meaning of the aria: both the sharp transposition and the violin's upward striving to the high d''', followed by a plummeting two-octave descent to the cadential d', suggest the believer's hope that God will overthrow the arrogant opponents of the faith. The immediate return to B♭ from its mediant duplicates the d–B♭ shift with which the aria began, summarizing the descent character of the keys of the closed movements to this point.

This aria, the only major-key movement in the cantata, stands apart as a representation of worldliness, against which the modulatory character of the recitatives and the gravity of the two chorale settings paint a far more seriously tormented character. Indeed, the second recitative, set now as a bass solo with string *accompagnato* (since it contains God's answer to the faithful), seems to pick up on the incomplete motion toward B♭ *minor* of the first recitative, cadencing in that key as it describes the effect of the enemies on the faithful: "Die Armen sind verstört, ihr seufzend Ach, ihr ängstlich Klagen bei so viel Kreuz und Noth" (The weak are distraught, their sighing cries, their anxious laments, in so much cross and need). With the narrative of God's hearing the tormented cries of the pious—"wodurch die Feinde fromme Seelen plagen, dringt in das Gnadenohr des Allerhöchsten ein" (through which the enemies torment pious souls, penetrate the Almighty's ear of grace)—the tonality moves from b♭ to c, cadencing in the latter key in preparation for God's response: "Darum spricht Gott: ich muss ihr Helfer sein, ich hab' ihr Fleh'n erhört, der Hilfe Morgenroth, der reinen Wahrheit heller Sonnenschein soll sie mit neuer Kraft, die Trost und Leben schafft erquicken und erfreu'n" (Therefore God speaks: I must be their helper, I have heard their weeping, the sunrise of My help, the sunshine of pure truth shall revive and rejoice them with the new strength that comfort and life provide). Bach matches this remarkable change in tone with an equally striking shift in the tonal and figurational character of the music, which now introduces rising scalar patterns in imitation and steady eighth-note rhythm between the voice and *basso continuo* as it moves toward a secure F major cadence. After this, the final two phrases move from F to g as God describes His word as the manifestation of His compassion for the suffering of the faithful, giving strength to their weakness: "Ich will mich ihrer Noth erbarmen, mein heilsam Wort soll sein die Kraft der Armen" (I will have mercy on their need, My healing word shall be the strength of the weak).

This last passage now sets up the G minor aria whose text was cited earlier. Its constant contrary-motion ascent–descent figures are a well-known representation of the cross, depicting at the same time the process of purification of the silver—down into the fire and out again—a descent–ascent pattern manifested in many scriptural passages that were subjected to allegorical interpretation from time immemorial, as well as in the act of Baptism, which Luther interpreted as a prefiguring of death and resurrection. "Durch's Feuer wird das Silber rein" perfectly represents the descent–ascent dynamic of Luther's "analogy of faith"—the shape of the cantata as a whole and the opposite of the ending measures of the first aria's ritornello—not only in its figurational character but also in its tonal dynamic, which modulates into deeper flat regions in the middle section—principally c and E♭, the latter inflected with the minor mode—before returning to d in preparation for the da capo. That d, although it underscores the necessity of tribulation—"drum soll ein Christ zu allen Stunden in Kreuz und Noth geduldig sein"—and serves, of course, as the dominant of g, now points to a positive context for suffering and worldly persecution. Throughout the cantata d/D always appears in flat contexts that lend it a dominant or mediant character and provide a frame of reference for the dynamic of the work as a whole. We can, therefore, separate the tonal design that is exhibited in the closed movements—D–B♭–g minor–D, representing a form of descent–ascent scheme—from the more extravagant devices of the recitatives, the first of which delineates a form of descent–ascent pattern in its motion toward b♭ and back to d, while the second outlines a progression from b♭ and c to g and F, then back to g.

In the design of "Ach Gott, vom Himmel" as a whole, the triadic descent pattern of the keys of the closed movements to the "subdominant," g, leads to the central message of the theology of the cross in the second aria. The final chorale verse then restores the d/D final after the various modulatory excursions of the preceding movements, all of which have been on the flat side of the *ambitus*. The first two movements had ended on D and d, respectively, after flat modulatory coloring; the third had associated d with its point of greatest dramatic intensity, an expression of worldly opposition to the faithful; the fourth had returned to g after progressing from b♭ to F, as I have described; and the fifth had returned to d/D at the close of the middle section, in preparation for the return of its principal key, g. In this context, the modal D harmonization of the final verse of "Ach Gott, vom Himmel" can be described as Bach's representing a perspective on the balance between the torment and weakness of the faithful and their holding onto God's promise by means of the relationship between the correct modal final of the chorale, D, and all the tonal tendencies toward the flat or subdominant side that threaten its integrity. In contrast to the setting of this melody that begins Cantata 153, the final cadence must now be taken as the "tonic" key. Although the two repeated phrases of the *Stollen* describe the key of g, with cadences to the dominant, D (phrase 1), and tonic (phrase 2), the final phrase of the setting ends with an authentic cadence to D (Ex. 5.7). The last three phrases end, respectively, with the Phrygian cadence to A, an authentic cadence to g, and the aforementioned authentic D cadence (the first two phrase endings are transpositional equivalents of the corresponding points in "Schau, lieber Gott," while the third is not, even though the descending bass patterns of phrases 5 and 7 duplicate those of the earlier setting). As in "Schau, lieber Gott," phrase 5, which articulates the "dominant" region most clearly of all the phrases, certainly fits well with the notion of D as the final. But the g of phrase 6, even more than that of phrases 2 and 4, is clearly in a subdominant context. Also, phrase 7, until the last moment before the A–D cadence, gives prominence to the subdominant of g, with two C minor chords, the second one preceded by its dominant and sounding immediately before the final g, A, and D harmonies. In this respect, the final chorale presents the same tonal quality as the opening movement, now in microcosm. The net effect of all this is to weaken the D cadence substantially in a manner that seems to symbolize the believer's struggles with the forces of spiritual destruction that surround him in the world.

"O grosser Gott von Macht" in Cantata 46

Cantata 46, "Schauet doch und sehet, ob irgend ein Schmerz sei" (Look and see if there be any suffering like my suffering), for the tenth Sunday after Trinity, 1723, ends with another chorale verse that Werckmeister had described as Hypophrygian. And the keys of its closed movements are virtually identical to those of "Ach Gott, vom Himmel"—d, B♭, g, d and D—the only difference being that the opening chorus is not based on a chorale and is therefore a straight D minor rather than a modal D setting. Once again, the "triadic" descent of the key sequence leads to the subdominant, g, of the penultimate movement as the point at which the theological "goal" and turning point of the cantata comes. And, once again, the final chorale ends with an authentic A–D cadence that is greatly weakened by the striking emphasis on the subdominant that precedes it and even, in this case, sounds simultaneously with it. Cantata 46 is to a very considerable degree "paired" with Cantata 105 of the week before, in both its musical and its theological character.[17] I will, therefore, set forth here only those aspects of the work that are most directly relevant to the question of how the modal character of its final chorale relates to the work as a whole and the other works discussed in this chapter.

The subject matter of Cantata 46 centers around the destruction of Jerusalem in A.D. 70, as predicted by Jesus in the Gospel for the day (Luke 19:41–48). And since, as we have seen (chapter 1), the destruction and restoration of Jerusalem in the time of Jeremiah was discussed by Luther as a model for the "analogy of faith," the basic principle in his hermeneutics, it is not surprising that the author of the text of Bach's cantata used a passage from the Old Testament narrative (Jeremiah 1:12) as the text of the opening movement. Jerusalem was, in fact, one of the most common examples in the medieval hermeneutic tradition of the four senses, since it was widely interpreted allegorically as the church, tropologically as the soul, and eschatologically

Example 5.7. Cantata 2: Final chorale

as the Kingdom of Heaven.[18] In fact, one of the widespread traditions in Lutheran Germany from the sixteenth century until Bach's time was the reading at the Vesper service on the tenth Sunday after Trinity of a version of Josephus's account of the first-century destruction of Jerusalem. This tradition, which originated with the man who has been called "Luther's pastoral organizer," Johann Bugenhagen, because of his translating Luther's ideas into "practical form," is documented for Bach's early Leipzig years by its inclusion in a hymnbook of that time.[19] As Robin A. Leaver has explained, Bugenhagen's 1530 harmony of the Gospel accounts of the Passion, *Historia des leidens und Aufferstehung unsers herrn Jhesu Christi aus den vier Evangelisten durch Joh. Bugenhagen Pomer auffs new vleissig zusamen bracht*, was issued in many sixteenth-century editions that were expanded by the addition of Psalm 22 and Isaiah 53, two of the principal Old Testament texts that were understood as prefigurings of the Passion and that formed the alternate "preaching texts" for Good Friday in the Leipzig churches, as well as by Bugenhagen's edited account of Josephus's history of the destruction of Jerusalem in A.D. 70.[20] Leaver points out that a Leipzig chorale collection of Bach's time included as an appendix the Passion texts of Matthew and John along with Bugenhagen's harmony of the Passion from all four Gospels and his version of Josephus's account of the destruction of Jerusalem. From all this it is clear not only that the destruction of Jerusalem was closely associated with the Passion in Leipzig, as elsewhere, and that the tenth Sunday after Trinity was uniquely set apart in the year on that account but also that this particular story had an almost unique potential for spanning enormously separated historical eras and relating them to the faith experience of the modern believer.[21] The times of Jeremiah, Jesus, and Josephus relate to the believer through the dynamic of destruction and restoration, God's wrath and His mercy; that dynamic underlies the stories of Jerusalem, Jesus' Passion and resurrection, and the inner experience of faith.

Cantata 46 begins with a comparison of the believer to the city of Jerusalem lamenting its destruction by God, using that comparison to lead the believer toward the only solution: recognition of Jesus' love and intervention on his behalf, the subject of the penultimate movement. Thus, Cantata 46 describes a motion from God's wrathful side as manifested in the Old Testament narrative of destruction to His merciful side as manifested in Jesus and the message of the Gospel. The two arias stand in a virtually antithetical relationship to each other, the first, scored for trumpet and *stile concitato* strings, representing images of destruction, and the second, scored for two recorders and a *bassetchen* part for oboes *da caccia*, countering the believer's fears with the promise of redemption. Between them a recitative sets forth explicitly the meaning of the shift in terms of the tropological sense—that is, the interpretation of the fate of Jerusalem as a figure of the believer's spiritual destruction: "Doch bildet euch, o Sünder, ja nicht ein, es sei Jerusalem allein von andern Sündern voll gewesen. Man kann bereits von euch dies Urteil lesen: weil ihr euch nicht bessert, und täglich die Sünden vergrößert, so müsset ihr alle so schrecklich umkommen" (But do not convince yourself, O sinner, that it is Jerusalem alone that is full of other sinners. One can readily draw this conclusion from you: because you do not better yourselves, and daily increase your sins, you must all die just as horribly). Modulating to C minor through its subdominant, f, this recitative sets up the G minor aria as the tonal "nadir" of a descent–ascent design once again.

And after the turnaround that comes with that aria, the concluding chorale verse returns to close in D, as had that of Cantata 2 after its G minor aria (Ex. 5.8). Its text relates to the preceding movements in that it tells of Jesus' "calming" God's anger through His sufferings, concluding with a prayer that God will protect the faithful on that account rather than judging them for their sins: "Um seinetwillen schone, und nicht nach Sünden lohne" (For His sake protect [us], and do not pay us for our sins). In order to make the point that this chorale represents the unity of God's wrathful and merciful sides and not simply the replacing of the one by the other, Bach combines both the trumpet/strings and the recorder instrumental groups in a very telling manner. The trumpet and strings double the chorus, while the recorders play freely composed lines, including duet interludes without *basso continuo*, between the phrases of the chorale. Thus, the texture and style of the G minor aria reappear between the lines of the chorale, their sixteenth-note runs contrasting with the slower motion of all parts when the chorale sounds. And, even more telling, the interludes are set more markedly in the subdominant region than the chorale phrases themselves. The pitches e♭' and e' are exchanged frequently throughout the setting. Bach, in fact, originally set this movement in the one-flat key signature, perhaps because not only does the melody contain one e♮' and no e♭' (as did "Ach Gott, vom Himmel"), but also its antepenultimate phrase cadences on the e♮'. He subsequently changed his mind, however, and set the movement in the two-flat signature, undoubtedly because several of the interludes and the harmonization of certain phrases are so strongly oriented toward the subdominant. The final pair of phrases

Example 5.8. Cantata 46: Final chorale, mm. 1–6

—*continued*

Example 5.8. (*continued*)

Example 5.8. (*continued*)

—*continued*

Example 5.8. (*continued*)

brings out this quality to the utmost, since their melodies are nearly identical, except that the first of the pair descends a fourth to its cadence on g', while the second makes the same descent but stops on the a' and repeats it as the final tone. The effect of the melody is distinctly to suggest an ending one tone above the final. But Bach harmonizes the final tones with the A–D authentic cadence, as he had the ending of "Ach Gott, vom Himmel" in Cantata 2. On the final phrase all the instruments sound together and, for the first time in the setting, the recorders play their sixteenth-note runs above the *basso continuo*, which holds the cadential D for two measures. The recorders begin the measure playing the G minor scale, however, and shift from e♭' to e♮' only on the final beat, thereby raising the question of whether the final chord is the dominant or the tonic to an extraordinary degree. This quality was surely Bach's means of suggesting both that the ending of the cantata returns to the harmony on which its first movement had ended and that the final D represents the hope of the believer for God's mercy, an acknowledgment of weakness, not a solid statement of fact. The spirit of the ending is very much that of a cry from Luther's *peccator infirmus.* In that the Lutheranism of Bach's time taught that God would indeed be merciful to the faithful, we are perhaps obliged to conclude that Bach intended the D to be taken as the tonic rather than the dominant, even though he weakened it to a very considerable degree.

SIX

Two Chorale Cantatas

Cantata 121, "Christum wir sollen loben schon"

The question of how the mode of a chorale melody may affect the musico-theological design of an entire cantata of several movements has seldom been addressed in the Bach literature, one of the main reasons for that being the generally tenuous connections between the theological content of most chorale verses and the modes of their melodies. There are, nevertheless, cases where such connections *do* exist and others where, even if they do *not*, Bach's treatment of the melodies indicates that he either perceived them to exist or introduced them by various means. Such is the case with the chorales that form the basis of the two cantatas to be examined in this chapter, "Christum wir sollen loben schon" (Cantata 121) and "Es ist das Heil uns kommen hier" (Cantata 9).[1] In them Bach seized on details in the melodies that proved to be of enormous potential in his articulating a bond between music and theology over the course of their multimovement sequences.

Luther's chorale "Christum wir sollen loben schon" had ancient roots, in that not only does the poem paraphrase the first seven strophes of the medieval hymn "A solis ortus cardine," written by Caelius Sedulius in the fifth century, but also the melody derives from the Gregorian melody associated with the Latin hymn. Sedulius was of considerable influence on later Latin poetry because of a five-book collection of poetry titled *Paschale Carmen* that treated of the miracles of the Old Testament in its first book, then those of Jesus from the incarnation up to the Passion and resurrection in the remaining four.[2] "A solis ortus cardine," although it is a separate and much shorter poem, follows a similar design for the life of Jesus. That is, it begins with the incarnation, treating it in what has been called a "cosmic" manner, and covers many of the events of Jesus' life as told in the four Gospels, ending with His victory over Satan and His ascension. The incarnation and the ascension circumscribe the beginning and completion of Jesus' work on earth. And the layout of the poem as a whole is related to this aim: its twenty-three verses form an alphabetical acrostic (i.e., an "abecedarius"), in that each strophe begins with one of the letters of the Latin alphabet (i.e., the twenty-six letters of the English alphabet minus *j*, *u*, and *w*). This detail was certainly intended to symbolize the idea of completeness in association with Jesus' life and work. Behind it lies, of course, the idea of Jesus as Alpha and Omega. Additionally, its first line appears to be indebted to the beginning of Psalm 112, "A solis ortu usque ad occasum laudabili nomen Domini," which describes the praise of God in terms of the eastern and western horizons or, as Sedulius's hymn puts it, from the point of the rising sun to the ends of the earth ("ad usque terrae limitem"). Since the word "cardine" ("cardo") meant a pivot or hinge, it became associated with the axis or rotation of the earth as well as with a point of the compass.[3] And this association undoubtedly underlay the fact that the first seven verses of the hymn, dealing with the incarnation, were traditionally associated with Christmas, while several of the following verses were linked with Epiphany. Christmas, that is, celebrated the coming of God's light into the world, associating that light since ancient times with the turning of the sun at the winter solstice, while Epiphany also celebrated an east–west cosmological motion, that of the star of Bethlehem, associated not only with the incarnation but also with the manifestation of Jesus to the Gentiles—that is, to the entire world. In this way "A solis ortus cardine" represented the incarnation as the turning point of history, as Christmas and Epiphany were associated with the turning of the liturgical, geophysical, and civil new years.

And, whether accidental or not, the melody of "A solis ortus cardine" can be considered to mirror the idea of a new beginning such as that of the rising sun: its melody shifts up a tone from its D Dorian beginning to an ending in E Phrygian. In the four-phrase Gregorian melody both the first and the last phrase begin on d and end on e, while the second and third close on b and a, respectively. And the chorale version follows the same basic pattern, sticking close to the outline of the Gregorian melody but simplifying its contours and altering the cadential tone of the second phrase from b to c'. Likewise, Luther's text sticks very closely to the first seven verses of Sedulius's poem, except that it adds, as its eighth verse, a doxology not in the original. The most common harmonization pattern of the melody in the Lutheran chorale books, however, did not generally confirm its Phrygian mode interpretation but tended rather to treat the final e as the second degree of the scale, harmonizing it, therefore, as the dominant of D. Even Werckmeister, who tended very much to argue for the correct modal finals, did not in this case. Instead, his interpretation of the tonal shift in "Christum wir sollen loben schon" in the *Harmonologia Musica* was a pragmatic one: antiphonal singing practices in ancient times had caused the final line to end on the second degree of the mode, e, rather than the first, d. Since that shift indicated for Werckmeister that the melody had an incomplete ending and should, therefore, be harmonized with the dominant—that is, as a half close—he classed it, along with "Der du bist drey in Einigkeit" (which began in d and ended on g), as a *tonus corruptus*.[4] All Bach's settings of "Christum wir sollen loben schon," however, end with a plagal cadence to the harmony whose root is the second degree of the mode—that is, they shift from D Dorian to E Phrygian (or, in Cantata 121, from E Dorian to Phrygian F♯)—creating the impression of ending, in modern terms, on the dominant of the dominant. This difference had great significance for

Table 6.1 Cantata 121, "Christum wir sollen loben schon." Leipzig, 1724. Second day of Christmas.

Movement	Genre	Instrumentation	Text incipit	Key
1	Chorus	SATB chorus, ctto., ctto., tbnes. 1-3, ob. d'am., str., b.c.	Christum wir sollen loben schon	E Dor.–F♯ Phryg.
2	Aria	Tenor, ob. d'am., b.c.	O du von Gott erhöhte Kreatur	b
3	Recitative	Alto, b.c.	Der Gnade unermeßlich's Wesen	D–C
4	Aria	Bass, str., b.c.	Johannis freudenvolles Springen erkannte dich, mein Jesu, schon.	C
5	Recitative	Sop., b.c.	Doch wie erblickt es dich in deiner Krippe?	G–b
6	Chorale	SATB chorus, plus all instruments, b.c.	Lob, Ehr und Dank sei dir gesagt	E Dor.–F♯ Phryg.

Bach, whose interpretation of the mode can therefore be said to be closer to that of the Gregorian melody than Werckmeister's.

Before taking up the tonal design of Cantata 121, we must note that the text of Bach's cantata amplifies certain features of both Luther's chorale and the Latin hymn, such as the idea of the elevation of the flesh through Jesus' incarnation, the miraculous nature of the incarnation, and, most particularly, the necessity of abandoning any attempt to "understand" the incarnation. This set of ideas emerges in what has been viewed as the first "half" of the cantata (movements 1 through 3), while the second "half" (movements 4 through 6) emphasizes the believer's response to the wondrous nature of the incarnation, his acceptance of the union of the divine and the human in the infant Jesus as the foundation of his hopes for eternal life (see Table 6.1).[5] While Sedulius's poem uses the incarnation and ascension of Jesus to circumscribe His work, Bach's text describes, as we will see, a descent–ascent tonal dynamic that mirrors the meaning of that work on several levels. And the turning point in question adds a dimension to the work that reflects the organization of its doctrinal-theological message according to the tropological and eschatological "senses" of hermeneutics.

The first and last (eighth) verses of "Christum wir sollen loben schon" are parallel in that they both begin with praise of Christ, tell that He was born of a pure virgin, and end with expressions of His all-encompassing rule. The first strophe, making the traditional comparison between Jesus (*Sohn*) and the rising sun (*Sonne*), describes Jesus' rule in geographical terms—"so weit die liebe Sonne leucht't / und an aller Welt Ende reicht" (as far as the beloved Son shines / and reaching to the ends of the earth)—while the last views it in temporal terms, "samt Vater und dem heil'gen Geist, / von nun an bis in Ewigkeit" (with the Father and the Holy Spirit / from now until eternity).[6] The progression from the point at which the sun rises to the boundary of the world becomes analogous to that from the incarnation to eternity. In this sequence the believer and his time (the "nun" of the final line) are centrally located between the historical incarnation and the future "elevation" of humanity. Thus, the cantata as a whole articulates a progression from the physical to the spiritual realm that is analogous to the widespread description of the incarnation as "elevating" humanity to the status of God's children. In this scheme the incarnation, the meeting of the divine and human in Jesus, is the pivot between the two, marking the division between the "eras" of Israel and of Christ.

And Bach's overall design for the cantata mirrors these dualisms in several ways. One of these involves the sense that the outermost movements (the chorale settings) represent a traditional or fundamental layer of meaning, not only in style and modal character, but in their scoring for *colla parte* cornetto and trombones, an instrumentation that Bach utilizes principally in conjunction with the evoking of an archaic atmosphere.[7] The first movement is basically a traditional chorale-motet setting in somewhat archaic style in which Bach introduces the idea of forward progression by beginning each of the successive lines of the chorale in the lower voices (the soprano has the *cantus firmus*) in long note values (half or whole notes depending on the line in question), then speeding up the motion to quarter and finally eighth notes. The increasing activity goes hand in hand with long ascending and descending lines and the change of tonal center in the final line to suggest an eschatological (i.e., temporal and spiritual) as well as geographical (physical) meaning for the "Welt Ende" of its text. Bach likewise adds running eighth notes to the last phrase of the final chorale, thus prolonging the word "Ewigkeit" (eternity) for five measures (see Ex. 6.3).

In striking contrast to the archaic dimension of the two chorale settings, the two arias (movements 2 and 4) are modern in style, especially the second, whose ritornello features a periodic phrase construction with piano/forte echo devices, sequential features, and a tonal design that modulates to the dominant at the midpoint and returns to the tonic over the second half. The figural surface of the first aria, "O du von Gott erhöhte Kreatur" (O you creature raised by God), seems to mirror the idea of the dualism of the divine and human, while its B minor tonality can be viewed as the outcome of the shift from e to F♯ (by hindsight from the subdominant to the dominant of b) in the last phrase of the preceding movement, an analogue, perhaps, of the elevation of humanity through the incarnation.[8]

The text of the first aria also emphasizes that human nature cannot "understand" God's redemption of humanity through the incarnation and should therefore respond only with wonder: "Begreife nicht, nein, nein, bewund're nur: Gott will durch Fleisch des Fleisches Heil erwerben" (Do not comprehend, no, no, only be amazed: God wants to earn the salvation of the flesh through the flesh). The recitative that bridges the two arias centers on that idea, expanding the subdominant/dominant dualism of the ending of the chorale to the level of what Werckmeister called a "grosse Metamorphosis in der Harmonie"[9] (Ex. 6.1) In it Bach modulates from the initial D major chord to A major, then C♯ minor for the following text: "Der Gnade unermeßlich's Wesen hat sich den Himmel nicht zur Wohnstatt auserlesen, weil keine Grenze sie umschliesst [A major cadence]. Was Wunder, daß allhier Verstand und Witz gebricht? ein solch' Geheimnis zu ergründen, wenn sie sich in ein keusches Herze giesst [C♯ minor cadence]" (The being of immeasurable grace did not choose the heavens for His dwelling place, because no boundaries circumscribed it. What a wonder, that at this the understanding and intellect fail to fathom such a mystery,

Example 6.1. Cantata 121: Third movement

when it flows into a chaste heart). The progressively sharpward motion of these opening phrases has, as we might expect, a particular purpose that is revealed in the phrases that follow: "Gott wählet sich den reinen Leib zu einem Tempel seiner Ehren, um zu den Menschen sich mit wundervoller Art zu kehren" (God chose the pure body for a temple to His honor, in order to turn to humankind in a wondrous manner). After the reference to the eastern and western boundaries of the earth in the opening chorus, the remark that God chose the human form as His dwelling place over the heavens, *because the latter had no boundaries*, makes clear the centrality of the incarnation to the salvation of humanity. The "wundervolle Art" in question is, of course, the enharmonic shift that takes place at the final cadence of the recitative, where the e♯–b tritone between the *basso continuo* and the voice, instead of contracting inward to an F sharp harmony, expands outward to C major. The tritone shift in the harmony is an analogue or "allegory" of the descent of God into human form, while the enharmonic modulation represents the miraculous (i.e., instantaneous) means ("wundervolle Art") by which God effects the descent.[10] Bach expands the idea of the tonal shift in the chorale melody to that of a transformation, not only representing the miraculous nature of the incarnation but also introducing a tonal device that most likely would have been felt but not rationally understood by the listener in Bach's congregation.[11] In this respect it prepares the C major aria that follows. It seems clear, therefore, that the sharpward motion at the beginning of the recitative points to the sphere of God, while the sudden reversal of the tonal direction represents the shift to the human perspective. The verb "kehren" (to turn, reverse direction, etc.) extends the meaning behind the word "cardine" in the Latin poem to that of a turning point, which now bears the association of a new era for humankind, indicated by its immediate response to the incarnation. Thus, the ending of the third movement and the beginning of the fourth can be said to pivot between God's miraculous work and humanity's response—that is, the two "halves" of the cantata—in a manner that fulfills the "cosmic" implications of Sedulius's poem.

In order to bring out the quality of unmediated awareness called for in the preceding two movements—that is, of an understanding that goes beyond the "Verstand und Witz" (understanding and intellect) mentioned in the recitative—the text of the aria turns to the narrative of the Visitation of Mary to her cousin Elisabeth, whose conception of a child in old age was told to Mary by the angel of the annunciation (Luke 1:36). Mary's subsequent visit to her cousin in the sixth month of Elisabeth's pregnancy then brought forth the response of the child, John the Baptist, who leaped in Elisabeth's womb as she heard Mary's greeting. Elisabeth was immediately filled with the Holy Spirit and thereby empowered to interpret that event as John's leaping for joy (Luke 1:44). Traditionally, the entire narrative of the Visitation and the subsequent one of John's birth were interpreted as initiating a new era in salvation history. John's was the first response to the news of the conception of Jesus, and it came before his birth. As such it represented the quality of simple unquestioning faith. And John's role as Baptist and precursor of Jesus reinforced the interpretation of the story as a turning point in history, a quality that was further underlined by the six months that separated his birth from that of Jesus. The celebration of the feast day of John the Baptist on June 24 brought out the parallel between the

Example 6.2. Cantata 121: Beginning of fourth movement

beginnings of the two halves of the liturgical year, the one, Christmas, aligned with the winter solstice and representing symbolically the onset of the new era, the other coming soon after Pentecost, aligned with the summer solstice, and closely paralleling the beginning of the Trinity season—that is, with the part of the year that represents both the time of the church and the time of Israel awaiting the Messiah.[12]

The melodic gestures at the beginning of the aria—the bass shooting downward through the C major arpeggio to the lowest note in the pitch spectrum and the violin leaping upward immediately afterward as if to depict John's response—foretell the outcome of the cantata, the elevation of humankind to God's children, as we are told in several other Bach cantatas (Ex. 6.2). The key of C, highlighted in the enharmonic modulation and the beginning gestures of the aria, can be thought of here as representing simultaneously the depths of human nature to which God has descended and the turning point for humanity that began with John the Baptist's recognition, while still within his mother's womb, of Jesus as the Messiah. It might well have been chosen because of its association as "the easiest key in music"—that is, as a representation of the unmediated (unintellectual) awareness of Jesus' identity by the child in the womb.[13] The affect that accompanies that recognition is joy. Bach's very modern tonal design and phrase structure in the ritornello set that tone for the aria as a whole. The middle section then utilizes a tripartite tonal scheme, featuring the keys of a, e, and G to present its text three times, the first suggesting (by virtue of the shift to the submediant or relative minor, the change to a *piano* dynamic level, and new figurational detail) the believer's symbolic approach through faith to the crib of Christ: "Nun da ein Glaubensarm dich hält, so will mein Herze von der Welt zu deiner Krippe brünstig dringen" (Now that the arm of faith holds You, my heart will passionately hasten from the world to Your crib). The sharpward direction of the key sequence, however, perhaps indicates something of the outcome of the believer's holding Jesus with the "arm" of faith and his heart's eagerly abandoning the world for the crib of the nativity.

The second recitative—beginning "Doch wie erblickt es dich in deiner Krippe?" (Yet how does it [the heart] look upon You in Your crib?)—analyzes the effect of the believer's approach to the crib of Christ as a sequence that progresses from the sighing of the heart as the believer's "trembling and almost closed lips" attempt to offer thanks (A minor cadence), through recognition of God's immeasurable nature in the lowliness of Jesus' human condition (E minor cadence), to the ultimate benefit of the incarnation for humanity, participation in the heavenly choir (B minor cadence, perhaps alluding to the key of "O du von Gott erhöhte Kreatur"). This sequence of ideas is an addition to the ideas conveyed in the chorale text, an amplification of its poetic imagery in more "theological" terms. To the extent that it's a–e–b key sequence can be thought of as related to that in the middle section of the aria (a–e–G), as its text is an extension of that of the aria, we may conclude that the pattern is an "ascending" one—that is, the dualism of God's miraculously becoming human in the incarnation (mirrored in the f♯–C enharmonic shift of the first recitative), and of John's recognition of the dual natures of Christ (the descending and ascending C major arpeggios that begin and run throughout the second aria) leads to the believer's recognition of Jesus' divinity through faith and the hastening of his (the believer's) heart away from "the world." The recitative articulates the final stage of the believer's leaving the world in terms of his anticipation of participating in the heavenly choir. The chorale that follows then affirms the eschatological vision in the e–F♯ modal shift of its final line ("von nun an bis in Ewigkeit"—from now until eternity). And to underscore the shift all the more Bach carries forward the pitch C *natural*, heard for the first time in the Phrygian cadence to B (i.e., V of e) that ends phrase 3, allowing it to permeate the harmony in all registers for the first two measures of the final phrase. The flattening of the harmony even brings about a passing C major harmony as the outermost voices expand by scalar motion to their point of widest separation on the beginning of the final word, "Ewigkeit." Then, suddenly, the entrance of the F♯ major harmony on the first completion of that word in the alto and soprano four measures before the end reintroduces the C♯ along with the first appearance of A♯ in the movement. From this point on the harmonies alternate between B minor and F♯ almost exclusively, settling ultimately on F♯ major, at least in part to recall the realm from which Jesus' descent to the sphere of humanity (C) was "described" tonally in the first recitative[14] (Ex. 6.3). It can, of course, be taken as an incomplete ending—that is, as the dominant of B minor—indicating the future character of the "Ewigkeit" of the final cadence and perhaps linking up with the B minor of the first aria (the elevation of the flesh by God) and the second recitative (the believer's anticipation of eternity). In that view the F♯ major harmony would represent a still more elevated sphere present only in the believer's hopes. At the same time, however, the final f♯' is, despite the common practice of harmonizing it as the dominant of e (or the transpositional equivalent) in Bach's time, a perfectly

Example 6.3. Cantata 121: Final movement

—continued

Example 6.3. (*continued*)

legitimate Phrygian final, approached through a plagal cadence. If we accept it as such, then we must understand Bach's intention as affirming the certainty of salvation for those who accept the incarnation.

Without wishing to generalize too far beyond the musico-allegorical frame of reference provided in Cantata 121, we may nevertheless speak of potentially general principles that mirror elemental directional qualities in the text. That the incarnation was viewed as the *descent* of God into human form is, I hope, unnecessary to document; likewise, that its principal goal was the elevation of humanity (to the status of God's children, as the texts of Cantatas 40, 64, and 173 and other Bach cantatas tell us) is far too well known to require "evidence." What I have described in terms of the relative sharpness and flatness of certain keys in this cantata (particularly the subdominant and dominant qualities of e and F♯ in the chorale and the A–c♯–f♯ succession versus the sudden shift to C in the central recitative) goes hand in hand with the directional qualities that lie behind the text, qualities that are mirrored rather obviously in the melodic dualisms of the two arias. The rising imagery in the cantata text is expressed in the analogy of Jesus and the rising sun, in the description of humanity as "erhöhte Kreatur," in John's leaping in his mother's womb, and in the anticipation of eternity in the penultimate recitative and final chorale. That of descent is embodied in the incarnation and the turning of the believer to the crib of Christ, both of which symbolize turning points, the former that of history and the latter that of faith. The change from descent to ascent occurs precisely with the following of the enharmonic cadence by the melodic dualism with which the C major aria begins. It can also be thought of in terms of the turning of the sun at the winter solstice. In this sense the turning point of the cantata can be described as descent followed by ascent, mirroring the change from darkness to light that belongs to its place in the liturgical and geophysical years, as well as the turning point to faith unmediated by intellectual understanding. The descent–ascent "shape" describes the incarnation of Jesus and the subsequent elevation of humanity through faith in the incarnation (i.e., the acceptance of Jesus' human lowliness in the crib as the foundation of the hope of eternity).

The pattern—common to countless Bach cantatas—of the duplication of the dynamic quality of an event within the human heart is the cornerstone of Lutheran hermeneutics and an expression of its purpose: to bridge the gap between "history" (in the broadest sense, which includes the notion of human finiteness) and its goal, the fulfillment of faith in eternity. History, beginning with literal, "finite" interpretation, yields to the faith experience and ends with the eschatological perspective. That sequence is an ascending one, progressing from the earthbound experience, centered in the reality of the physical, or what Lutheranism viewed as "flesh" (including purely intellectual understanding, which the first aria and recitative urge the believer to overcome), to the spiritual experience and the higher reality to which it tends. In the language of traditional hermeneutics, such sequences articulate a progression from the literal-historical, through the tropological, to the eschatological sense.[15] The cantata text adds this dimension to the movement sequence of the hymn. In Cantata 121 Bach seized on a tonal anomaly of the melody of "Christum wir sollen loben schon" and expanded it into a design that can be said to mirror the dichotomies of the historical and the spiritual, human and divine, in several important respects: the differentiation of relatively archaic and modern styles, of "subdominant" (relatively flat) and "dominant" (relatively sharp) tonal areas and directions, and of melodic descent and ascent shapes. The keys of the two arias, B minor and C major, might be thought of as the "mi" and "fa" degrees of the *ambitus* of E minor or E Dorian, while the F♯ cadences of the outermost movements extend beyond those limits, making what Bach perhaps viewed as a *mutatio* of both mode and *cantus.* The enharmonic change in the first recitative centers and gives a sharper focus to the tonal "allegory" of the chorale by amplifying its dualism to the level of a transformational opposition of tritone-related keys—a "mi" contra "fa."

"Es ist das Heil uns kommen hier" (Cantata 9)

As described in chapter 1, the Bach cantata that most clearly exemplifies both the basic Lutheran doctrine of justification and the musical equivalent of Luther's "analogy of faith" is Cantata 9, "Es ist das Heil uns kommen hier," based on one of the best-known hymns of the early Reformation period (Table 6.2). The design of Cantata 9, as we saw, pivots around the core ideas of the chorale text—Law, Gospel, and faith—whose affective characteristics are mirrored in the descent–ascent shape of its tonal plan. And this latter aspect of the work derives from Bach's understanding of the matchup of text and melody in the chorale itself. In this respect Cantata 9 serves as a model for how a subtle matching of text and theology in a chorale melody may lead to the most elaborately conceived results in the design of an entire cantata.

The melody of "Es ist das Heil uns kommen hier" contains a slight modal anomaly in its opening phrase, in that after four reiterations of the dominant on the words "Es ist das Heil," the line moves upward to the flat seventh degree of the scale for "uns," then down by step to the "subdominant" (i.e., the fourth degree of the scale) for "kommen hier." (See Ex. 6.6.) The effect is to suggest the Mixolydian rather than Ionian mode for the first phrase, although the remainder of the chorale is un-

Table 6.2 Cantata 9, "Es ist das Heil uns kommen hier." Leipzig, 1732–35. Sixth Sunday after Trinity.

Movement	Genre	Instrumentation	Text incipit	Key
1	Chorus	SATB chorus, fl., ob. d'am., str., b.c.	Es ist das Heil uns kommen hier	E
2	Recitative	Bass, b.c.	Gott gab uns ein Gesetz	c♯–b
3	Aria	Tenor, vln. 1, b.c.	Wir waren schon zu tief gesunken	e
4	Recitative	Bass, b.c.	Doch musste das Gesetz erfüllet werden	b–A
5	Duet aria	Sop., alto, fl., ob. d'am., b.c.	Herr, du siehst statt guter Werke auf des Herzens Glaubensstärke	A
6	Recitative	Bass, b.c.	Wenn wir die Sünd' aus dem Gesetz erkennen	f♯–E
7	Chorale	SATB chorus, fl., ob. d'am., str., b.c.	Ob sich's anliess als wollt er nicht	E

ambiguously Ionian. But, in fact, "Es ist das Heil" began life as a pure Mixolydian melody; and it was almost universally designated Mixolydian in the seventeenth and eighteenth centuries, despite the fact that by Bach's time the flat seventh degree appeared only in the first phrase and the raised leading tone to the dominant had also been introduced in phrase 2.[16] The Mixolydian classification perhaps acknowledged that in harmonically oriented modal theory and composition the raising of leading tones was commonly viewed as a permissible device that did not affect the *basic* pitch content of the mode. That is, under the rubric of the *subsemitonium modi* the raised leading tone was considered a device for the cadence only, whereas the *flat* seventh degree remained the basic pitch of the scale. The raised seventh degree of the scale in Bach's version of "Es ist das Heil" does not always occur at cadences, however, and Bach's key signatures always confirm the Ionian rather than the Mixolydian interpretation. Also, in Bach's and other settings the very solid close on the dominant in the second phrase clears up the ambiguity right at the outset. The tonal quality of the melody, therefore, is unequivocally that of the modern major scale, whose very solid dominant–tonic cadences lend it a positive character that suits its subject, a summary of the Lutheran doctrine of salvation ("Heil"). Nevertheless, the subdominant quality of the first phrase, slight as it is, mirrors the quality of humility that Bach associates with the word "uns" in other works, as well as the idea of descent from the sphere of God to that of humankind for "kommen hier," after which the strong assertion of the dominant matches the quality of "von Gnad' und lauter Güte."[17] The underlying antithesis of God and humankind as suggested in the opening phrases of the chorale was of enormous stimulation to Bach in the creation of his design for Cantata 9.

From this standpoint, therefore, Cantata 9 shares with Cantata 121 its incarnational perspective. In fact, Cantata 9 can be said also to "center" on that theme, in that, as we have seen (chapter 1), it features three bass recitatives—movements 2, 4, and 6—that narrate the history of salvation, from the time of the Law (no. 2), through the time of Jesus (no. 4), and ending with the era of the church and the contemporary believer (no. 6). And in this sequence the second recitative (no. 4), the central movement of the cantata, deals with Jesus' incarnation and fulfilling of the Law, the message of the Gospel.[18] It is perhaps significant, therefore, that the chorale "Es ist das Heil uns kommen hier," whose first line announces its theme as the story of the coming of salvation to humankind, is, like "Christum wir sollen loben schon," a form of alphabetical representation of Jesus' work, although it is not an acrostic. As mentioned in chapter 1, the chorale tells the story of Jesus' work of redemption in fourteen verses followed by fourteen paragraphs headed respectively with the letters of the Latin alphabet from *A* to *O* (minus *j*, of course). The *A* and *O* represent the first and last letters of the Greek alphabet, Alpha and Omega, as Jesus is described in the book of Revelation and in countless theological writings and hymn texts throughout the centuries. As is explained in the original print of the chorale, the fourteen paragraphs contain the basic scriptural passages on which the theological content of the chorale is based. "Es ist das Heil," therefore, purports to be a summary of the basic doctrine of scripture from the Lutheran perspective—above all, the roles of Law and Gospel, the doctrine of justification by faith, the incarnation and work of Jesus, and the three stages of salvation history, in which Jesus, occupies the central position. The reduction of the fourteen strophes to seven for the chorale text may have been motivated by more than mere expediency, since the number seven, as I suggested in the case of the last movement of Cantata 21 (see chapter 3), was associated with Jesus in the book of Revelation.

And in another respect Cantata 9 may be compared with Cantata 121: its E major tonality represents the sharpest tonal region in the Bach cantatas. While the sharpness of the F♯ major on which Cantata 121 ends may legitimately be debated, since it is a Phrygian final and therefore represents the two-sharp key signature or system, the E of Cantata 9 represents the true four-sharp system, the sharpest tonal region in Bach's cantata oeuvre. There are no closed movements in any of the Bach cantatas in key signatures of more than four sharps, and there are no cantatas in C♯ minor. E major, therefore, represents a special choice of key for Bach, one made in full knowledge that the other movements of a cantata in that key will be on the subdominant side of the key. Even the dominant, B, will not be present as the key of a closed movement. Likewise, in the almost panoramic key spectrum of the *St. Matthew Passion*, E major is the sharpest movement key, the "goal" of two extended progressions from "deep" flats (principally F minor) to "deep" sharps (E) in part 1. And as those lengthy tonal "anabases" make clear, E major has positive associations that accrue to it from Bach's aligning it with pivotal points in the salvific or soteriological message of the passion. In the passion Bach introduces E major in part as a counterfoil to E minor, the first and most prominent key of the work; and at the end of part 1, where two large choral movements in E minor and E major appear at close quarters, their associations are comparable to those of the E minor and major movements in Cantata 9.[19]

And since E major is the sharpest key of any closed movements in all Bach's vocal music, whenever we are dealing with an E major cantata, of necessity, the other movements will be flatter, a feature that encourages the idea of descent (flatward motion) followed by ascent (the return to the original key). Cantata 8, "Liebster Gott, wann werd' ich sterben," for example, "descends" from E through C♯ minor to

A major before returning to E. And Cantata 9 descends from its original E to E minor, then returns through A major to E. When Bach chooses E as the key of a cantata, one factor in that choice is that the cantata will exhibit some form of descent–ascent tonal design. And if the chorale in question is Mixolydian, an additional factor that encourages the idea of tonal "descent" will be the tendency of that mode toward the subdominant direction. The same is true of Phrygian chorales, since within the diatonic system of the modes (whether transposed or not) the Phrygian and Hypophrygian are the sharpest in the sense that they borrow from the next adjacent system or *ambitus* in the sharp direction; otherwise they tend toward the subdominant.[20] Bach cantatas that begin with or are centered on Phrygian, Hypophrygian, and Mixolydian chorales (such as Cantatas 2, 9, 38, 77, 121, 135, and 177, discussed to varying degrees in this book) all exhibit this quality of motion in the subdominant direction and back. In this sense E major represents the sharp end of the practical spectrum of major and minor keys in Bach's vocal work as the Phrygian and Mixolydian modes do the sharp end of the diatonic modal framework.

In Cantata 9 the opening movement is solidly in E major (Ionian), as befits its very positive theological message of salvation. From there on, however, the difference between the two pitches D and D♯ plays a vital role in the tonal design of the cantata, and one that is readily susceptible to analysis. Immediately following the opening chorus, the pitch D in the first recitative—the flat seventh in the tonic key of E major—precipitates a series of modulations in the subdominant direction that lead it to a close in B minor in preparation for the E minor aria that follows. But the sequence of modulatory events is considerably more complicated and vastly more interesting than that simple statement suggests. The recitative begins in C♯ minor and makes its first major internal cadence in b, after a passing cadence to F♯ minor (Ex. 6.4). This passage narrates the "fallen" condition of humanity under the Law ("Gott gab uns ein Gesetz doch waren wir zu schwach, daß wir es hätten halten können; wir gingen nur den Sünden nach, kein Mensch war fromm zu nennen (f♯); der Geist blieb an dem Fleische kleben und wagte nicht zu widerstreben (b)."[21] The first hint of a shift comes with the d' on the word "Sünden" (indicating the direction followed by humanity); its initial outcome is the f♯ of "kein Mensch war fromm zu nennen." Then, for "der Geist blieb an dem Fleische kleben," the vocal line plummets downward more than an octave, its low B dipping below the d of the *basso continuo* at "Fleische kleben"; after this the root-position B minor cadence at "wiederstreben" confirms the shift, the voice completing an overall third descent from the initial d' to the b of the cadence in analogy to the inability of humankind to resist the downward motion.

After this point, however, the recitative narrates that humanity *should have* used the Law to provide a mirror of its (humanity's) sinful nature: "Wir sollten in Gesetze gehn, und dort als wie in einem Spiegel sehn, wie unsere Natur unartig sei." As the third recitative will make clear, (see the following discussion), the role of the Law was to strike down the human conscience because of its inability to escape sin and satisfy God's demands. For the narrative of how the Law should have worked on humankind (but of course did not), Bach returns to the low B in the voice, reintroducing the pitch d♯ immediately as it moves upward ("Wir sollten in Gesetze gehn"), then leaping up to d♮' again ("und *dort* [i.e., in the Law] als wie in einem Spiegel

Example 6.4. Cantata 9: First recitative

sehn"). Avoiding both f♯ and b, however, Bach moves instead to G♯ minor, then to an E major cadence, as the text describes humanity's unruly nature and its failure to comprehend the true purpose of the Law. The "back where we started" quality of this passage has the effect of canceling out the subdominant effect of the pitch D and its association with sin and the humiliating nature of the Law. Humankind, in other words, refused to accept what Luther called God's "alien work," the necessity that the conscience be stricken by the Law and awareness of sin before receiving the message of salvation through the Gospel (God's "proper work"). The premature return to E therefore comes to represent humanity's resistance to God's purposes, its attempts to seek salvation through its own efforts, whereas, as the unfolding design of the cantata will reveal, Jesus' work and the believer's faith in the message of the Gospel (the content of the second recitative) are the means by which humankind is set on the path of salvation, *after* the Law has done its work; only then will E major return in association with salvation.

After the E cadence of the first recitative, the text continues to describe humanity's weakness and inability to escape sin: "Aus eigner Kraft war Niemand fähig, der Sünden Unart zu verlassen, er möcht' auch alle Kraft zusammenfassen." And for this concluding segment of the recitative Bach makes strikingly clear the role of D in the musico-allegorical design of the movement—first by undermining the upward-shooting E major arpeggio on "aus eigner Kraft" with the *basso continuo*'s d ("Kraft"), then by leading the voice to cadence on the pitch d as B minor is reached once again ("war Niemand fähig, der Sünden Unart zu verlassen"), and, finally, by leading the voice upward to a high d' on the word "Kraft" ("er möcht' auch alle Kraft zusammenfassen") as the recitative closes in b. The association of the third degree of the B minor scale with human weakness (so that the "Kraft" of the second half of the recitative is ironically equivalent to the "schwach" of the first) is very pronounced throughout the entire passage. What is most interesting in Bach's conception is that the role of the Law to bring humanity down takes place despite human misunderstanding of that purpose and efforts to the contrary. The prominent placing of the pitch D throughout the recitative makes clear that the flattening of the harmony is a representation of human weakness.

And this articulation of the minor rather than the major dominant of E sets up in turn the tonic minor (e) for the first aria, which speaks, as we know, of the depths to which humanity had sunk under the Law: "Wir waren schon zu tief gesunken, der Abgrund schluckt uns völlig ein." One of the most noteworthy details in its principal theme is the dualism of melodic directions between the long syncopated descent of the uppermost line and the slow on-the-beat ascent of the bass, a depiction, one would think, of the opposition between God's "alien" and His "proper" work—that is, the idea that the downward or "mortifying" tendency of the Law is a means by which God effects His true purpose: the salvation of humanity.[22] When understood correctly—that is, as the impetus to *Sündenerkenntnis* (acknowledgment of sin)—the Law has a directly positive side as well, although that fact will not become clear until the following sequence of movements is complete. From this point on, however, the sequence of movement keys moves back by stages toward E major.

Initiating this upward tonal motion, the second recitative makes a partial reversal of the key sequence of the first, leading from b through f♯ to A as it narrates Jesus' death as fulfilling the Law and "stilling" God's wrath (b), proclaims salvation for all who put their trust in Jesus' sufferings (f♯), and affirms that heaven is chosen for those who embrace Jesus through faith (A). In the sequence the pitch D is very prominent once again, now as a signpost to the positive outcome of faith.

The canonic A major duet aria that follows affirms the basic Lutheran doctrine of justification by faith alone as the key to salvation by means of a double canon between flute and oboe d'amore on the one hand and the soprano and alto voices on the other. But what is most interesting in this movement is that the very attractive melodic surface of the canon belies its dogmatic message by offering a moving simplicity of tone to indicate the comfort that particular doctrine provides for the believer. Canonic devices often bear the association of strictness and the Law in Bach's work; the opening movement of Cantata 77 is a striking instance, as we will see. In this case, however, the covering up of the learnedness with an unusually appealing intertwining of the melodic lines is the foremost "message" of the movement, breathing life and warmth into what might otherwise appear as an abstract theological dogma.

After the return to A major in the second recitative and aria, the final recitative and chorale will, of course, restore the raised leading tone, D♯, in conjunction with the return to E that completes the "ascent" part of the cantata. In fact, the tonal motion through these two movements—B minor to E major—reverses that of the first two in a manner that allies the restoration of D♯ to the idea of tonal ascent in association with God's design for human salvation. At the outset, therefore, this third recitative doubles back as if to summarize the message of the cantata to this point, to place the affective quality of the duet in its theological context. The opening phrases juxtapose Law and Gospel strikingly, the first one accompanying the narrative of the Law's striking down the human conscience with a modulation from the f♯ in which it begins to the B minor cadence with which it ends: "Wenn wir die Sünd' aus dem Gesetz erkennen, so schlägt es das Gewissen nieder" (Ex. 6.5). Immediately, however, the juxtaposed answering phrase, entering from a D–D♯ shift in the *basso continuo*, reverses the affect and the melodic direction, modulating to A as it tells of the comforting antidotal effect of the Gospel on the conscience: "Doch ist das unser Trost zu nennen, daß wir im Evangelio gleich wieder froh und freudig werden: dies nur stärket unsern Glauben wieder." The two phrases thus recall the overall modulatory goals of the first and second recitatives in preparation for the return to E. To make the point all the clearer, Bach brings back the rising E major arpeggio that had been undermined by the bass tone d in the first recitative, now leading it directly to A: "Gleich wieder froh und freudig werden." And instead of emphasizing the pitch d' as an expression of human weakness (ironically on the word "Kraft"), it tells how the Gospel strengthens our faith: "Dies nun stärket unsern Glauben wieder."

The full reestablishment of the pitch D♯, however, comes with the subsequent phrase, which cadences in G♯ minor as it tells how on the basis of the Gospel humanity hopes for the eternal life promised by God's beneficence, but the exact time of which God has hidden from us "aus weisem Rath" ("Drauf hoffen wir der Zeit, die Gottes Gütigkeit uns zugesaget hat, doch aber aus weisem Rath die Stunde uns verschwiegen"). More even than a move to the dominant of E, this tonal event signals the return to E by moving one step further in the sharp direction (an analogy, one would think, to the hoped-for "Zeit," which has not yet arrived).[23]

Example 6.5. Cantata 9: Third recitative

The allegorical role of G♯ minor in this recitative is, thus, entirely in keeping with its association in the first recitative, in which it countered the downward tonal motion to B minor. There it was associated with humanity's misunderstanding the purpose of the Law; here it accompanies a reference to the "hiddenness" of God's plan of salvation—that is, the Lutheran view that the Law represents God's "alien work" and the Gospel His "proper work."[24] Modulation to the sharpest region of the tonal spectrum represents, of course, the direction associated with salvation (i.e., an "ascent"); but within the tonal-allegorical framework of Cantata 9 it represents God's work, not humanity's. Thus, in the first recitative G♯ minor counteracted the descending modulatory direction in association with humanity's contrary nature in resisting the true purpose of the Law, while in this one it strengthens the return to E in association with humanity's acceptance of God's "weisem Rath": "Jedoch, wir lassen uns begnügen: er weiss es, wenn es nötig ist." The recitative then closes securely in E, after referring back to the subdominant quality of D solely for the purpose of affirming that God uses no deception in his dealings with humanity ("und brauchet keine *List* an uns") and following it by an association of D♯ with the dominant for the quality of building on God's promises ("wir dürfen auf ihn *bauen* und ihm allein vertrauen").

The events just described complete the restoration of the key of E and the pitch D♯ in the cantata. But Bach saves his coup de grâce for the final chorale setting, whose opening phrases echo the "hiddenness" of God's plan for human salvation once again: "Ob sich's anliess, als wollt er nicht, / lass dich es nicht erschrecken, / denn wo er ist am besten mit, / da will er's nicht entdecken."[25] These phrases mirror, in fact, what Bach probably perceived as the basic impulse behind the "Mixolydian" flat seventh degree (D♮) in the opening phrase of the chorale melody—that is, they deal with a basic antithesis between God's ways and those of human expectations. In the opening strophe the antithesis is implied—between God's salvation itself and its unworthy human recipients, the "uns" of the first line. The subdominant/dominant tonal-directional dualism of its first two phrases is, as I have suggested, a key to the descent–ascent tonal design of the cantata as a whole. And for the final chorale Bach draws out the implications of the D in a striking manner by leading the first phrase to a plagal cadence to D just as the text describes how God's positive purpose appears as a negative to humankind (Ex. 6.6). The effect of this cadence to the subdominant of the subdominant is further increased by the fact that in itself it is a subdominant (i.e., plagal) cadence. Within the first phrase, therefore, we hear a continuously flattening quality—triads or seventh chords on B, E, A, D, and G—in analogy to the human perspective on God's "alien" work, then a restoration of E via its dominant in the directly positive message of the second phrase. And once again the D–D♯ shift appears in a direct juxtaposition of those two pitches in the *basso continuo* at the phrase juncture.

What I have just described for Cantata 9—the derivation of an overall tonal design of several movements, and of many individual details as well, from a small detail in the chorale melody—is not at all uncommon or unusual for Bach. Nor is it uncommon for chorale melodies to mirror their theological content by special tonal means.[26] We have already considered several examples. One additional one may be adduced here since, like Cantatas 121 and 9, it derives its overall design from qualities

Example 6.6. Cantata 9: Final chorale

in the chorale melody and theology together that were not at all self-evident and may never have been intended by the chorale's composer. Cantata 127, "Herr Jesu Christ, wahr'r Mensch und Gott," whose theological character has been thoroughly investigated by Lothar and Renate Steiger, centers on a chorale that shifts to the dominant on its final phrase—that is, from F to C.[27] But since in the final verse of the chorale that line ("bis wir einschlafen seliglich") refers to the concept of the "sleep of death," Bach colors the tonality substantially with harmonies from the minor mode—that is, C minor. And he extends the C minor/major dualism to the juxtaposition of the cantata's only two arias, the first, "Die Seele ruht in Jesu Händen," in C minor and the second, "Wenn einstens die Posaunen Schallen," ending in C major, a tonal juxtaposition that mirrors the opposition of death and resurrection.

But striking as these dualisms are, it is in the opening movement of Cantata 127 that Bach makes his most detailed statement regarding the complex of ideas in the work as a whole and their relationship to the incarnation—that is, the dual natures of Jesus as "wahr'r Mensch und Gott." In that movement Bach, for the only time in his cantatas, combines two complete chorale melodies simultaneously, "Herr Jesu Christ, wahr'r Mensch und Gott," texted in the chorus, and "Christe, du Lamm Gottes," untexted in the various instrumental groups (strings first, then oboes, later flutes, and, finally, strings again). Although "Christe, du Lamm Gottes" enters at the beginning of the ritornello, it is "Herr Jesu Christ" that provides the motivic material for the movement. The presence of two chorales relates, of course, to the fact that the Gospel for Quinquagesima Sunday not only anticipated the Passion, to which the German Agnus Dei, "Christe, du Lamm Gottes," relates, but also described Jesus' healing a blind man along the way to Jerusalem. Recognizing Jesus' divinity, the blind man addressed Him as "true man and God"; hence the chorale that meditates on that event. The blind man also recognized his own sinfulness, however, and to bring that quality out all the more Bach introduced the first phrase of yet a third chorale melody—that of "Herzlich tut mich verlangen"—at six points in the *basso continuo*. Although that phrase is untexted, Bach must have associated the melody in this instance not with "Herzlich tut mich verlangen," but with "Ach Herr, mich armen Sünder," whose first, fifth, and sixth lines ("Ach Herr, mich armen Sünder, . . . du wolltest mir vergeben mein Sünd' und gnädig sein") correspond to the final line of "Herr Jesu Christ" ("du wollst mir Sünder gnädig sein"). In keeping with the anticipation of the Passion, however, it is distinctly possible that Bach intended more than one association, since, as we know, the passion chorale "O Haupt voll Blut und Wunden" was also sung to the same melody.

The most important *musical* point regarding Bach's bringing together references to three different chorales in this movement, however, is a tonal one. "Herr Jesu Christ" is in F major ending in C, as we saw; and its several phrases cadence mostly on either F or C. "Christe, du Lamm Gottes," however, begins as if in F and ends in G Dorian—that is, it is in a minor mode. And Bach presents the first two of its three phrases at two transposition levels each, corresponding to the F and C systems. The first phrase of "Ach Herr, mich armen Sünder" is Phrygian, although it sounds as though it ends on the dominant, and Bach transposes it to four different pitch levels throughout its six occurrences in the movement, the first and last two in G and C Phrygian, respectively (i.e., C minor and F minor) and the third and fourth in E and A Phrygian. The intricate details that surround Bach's building a unique tonal design from the interaction of these three chorale elements go beyond the scope of the present discussion. Suffice it to say that when the ordinarily "sharp" Phrygian mode is transposed to the level of the Ionian mode with the same final, it is necessarily flattened considerably (i.e., C Phrygian sounding like the dominant of F minor). The first, second, fifth, and sixth appearances of this phrase, therefore, introduce a very substantial flat coloring into the movement. In this and many other subtle details Bach's design is very evocative of the interaction of both tonic major/minor and relative major/minor modes, suggesting an allegory of the interaction of the divine and the human in Jesus ("wahr'r Mensch und Gott") as well as the disparity between Jesus and the sinner whose cry of penitence underlies the chorus. The dominance of flat tonal regions in the first half of the cantata—the ending of the opening movement is heavily colored by F minor, the first recitative cadences in f, and the first aria is in c—gives way to C major in the second aria (which shifts from F to C with a corresponding shift of key signature after its first twenty measures). After that, the shift from F to C for ending of the final chorale and the intermingling of C major and C minor on its final phrase represent the believer's anticipation of death and resurrection simultaneously.

Perhaps the most striking of all such derivations of an entire cantata design from a chorale melody, however, comes not in a chorale cantata but in the cantata that is most famous for its numerological element, "Du sollt Gott, deinen Herren, lieben,"

BWV 77, for the thirteenth Sunday after Trinity, 1723. In that work, the subject of the next two chapters, the Law is represented in the opening movement in the various canonic devices surrounding Luther's Ten Commandments chorale and its Mixolydian melody, while the so-called great commandment to love God and one's neighbor constitutes the sung text of the movement and its "free" treatment of the chorale melody. The G Mixolydian melody contains an anomaly, in that it introduces the pitch B♭ in its final phrase, effecting, in fact, a shift from the *cantus durus* to the *cantus mollis* that Bach extends in his opening movement to a tremendous tonal motion to C minor for the juxtaposition of God and humanity (i.e., one's neighbor). The net effect of this flat motion within the movement is that the return to G at the end is greatly weakened—to the point that Alfred Dürr, for example, pronounces the key of the movement as not G but C major.[28] And the flat motion just described continues throughout the cantata, the final movements dealing with human weakness to an extraordinary degree. The final chorale, a setting of the melody "Ach Gott, vom Himmel sieh' darein," shifts openly to the *cantus mollis*—that is, to the one-flat key signature—and its ending is on the dominant, the most striking such occurrence in all Bach's music.

SEVEN

Cantata 77

The Theological Background

"Dies sind die heil'gen zehn Gebot": The Chorale and Its History

The first movement of Cantata 77, "Du sollt Gott, deinen Herren, lieben," the cantata that will serve as the focus of interest for this and the following chapter (see Table 7.1), centers on Luther's chorale "Dies sind die heil'gen zehn Gebot," which summarizes the Ten Commandments in poetic form. This chorale, which was apparently written in early 1524 and first appeared in Lutheran chorale books in that year, set to the melody of a medieval pilgrimage hymn, "In Gottes Namen fahren wir," was from the time of its publication one of the core chorales of the Lutheran catechism. Luther, in fact, wrote chorales for all six principal parts of the catechism: the three basic summaries of the word of God—the Ten Commandments, the Apostles' Creed, and the Lord's Prayer—along with the sacraments of Baptism and the Lord's Supper, with penitence (confession and absolution) included as a preparation for the Lord's Supper.[1] Luther viewed not only the creeds (the three so-called *Symbola* of the church) but also the Ten Commandments, the first commandment alone and the catechism as a whole as comprising the meaning of scripture in summary forms. As he remarked in his introduction to the Large Catechism, "This much is certain: anyone who knows the Ten Commandments perfectly knows the entire Scriptures. . . . What is the whole Psalter but meditations and exercises based on the First Commandment? . . . the Catechism . . . is a brief compend and summary of all the Holy Scriptures."[2] As a result, certain of the oldest chorale books were organized according to the catechism, beginning with "Dies sind die heil'gen zehn Gebot," while others that followed the order of the liturgical year tended, as mentioned previously, to associate the catechism with the beginning of the Trinity season.[3]

When Luther came to write his chorale on the Ten Commandments, "Dies sind die heil'gen zehn Gebot," he did so with the intent of expressing how the Ten Com-

Table 7.1 Cantata 77, "Du sollt Gott, deinen Herren, lieben." Leipzig, 1723. Thirteenth Sunday after Trinity.

Movement	Genre	Instrumentation	Text incipit	Key
1	Chorus	SATB chorus, trba. da tir., str., b.c.	Du sollt Gott, deinen Herren, lieben	G Mix.
2	Recitative	Bass, b.c.	So muss es sein! Gott will das Herz vor sich alleine haben.	C
3	Aria	Sop., ob. 1, 2, b.c.	Mein Gott, ich liebe dich von Herzen	a
4	Recitative	Ten., str., b.c.	Gib mir dabei, mein Gott! Ein Samariterherz	e–G
5	Aria	Alto, trba. da tir., b.c.	Ach, es bleibt in meiner Liebe lauter Unvollkommenheit!	d
6	Chorale	SATB chorus, plus all instruments, b.c.	Left untexted by Bach (melody of "Ach Gott, vom Himmel sieh' darein")	♭/D modal

mandments embodied the core meaning of scripture as a whole. As a result the text of "Dies sind die heil'gen zehn Gebot" is a twelve-strophe paraphrase of the Ten Commandments that is imbued with the spirit of Luther's view of the roles of Law and Gospel in justification. After an introductory first strophe, Luther summarizes the commandments in nine, rather than ten, strophes; the first two commandments are telescoped into a single strophe in a manner that eliminates the main body of the second commandment (the prohibition of graven images). Since, however, the second commandment ends with God's promise of mercy toward those who love Him and keep His commandments, Luther supplies the commandment to love God—"von Herzensgrund auch lieben mich"—that derives from the "great commandment" to love God and one's neighbor that Jesus gave as the summary of the Law in the New Testament.[4] Although, therefore, Luther omits the expression of God's wrathful side that lends the second commandment its severe character, each of the twelve strophes of his paraphrase ends with the word *Kyrieleis*, the appeal for mercy that expresses humanity's need for the abatement of God's wrath. After the nine summary strophes, the final two strophes explain the purpose of the Law according to Luther's Pauline interpretation: the Ten Commandments were given to humanity for the purpose of teaching recognition of sin (*Sündenerkenntnis*) as the way to "live before" God (strophe 11). In that endeavor aid from Jesus Christ, the mediator, is necessary; otherwise human actions come to nothing and earn only God's wrath (strophe 12). The final strophe therefore ends with a juxtaposition of God's wrath (*Zorn*) to the appeal from an undeserving humanity for His mercy.[5]

Dies sind die heil'gen zehn Gebot,	These are the holy ten commandments,
Die uns gab unser Herre Gott	Which our Lord God gave us
Durch Mosen, seinen Diener treu,	Through Moses, His faithful servant,
Hoch auf dem Berg Sinai,	High on Mount Sinai,
Kyrieleis.	Kyrie eleison (Lord, have mercy).

Ich bin allein dein Gott und Herr,
Kein Götter sollt du haben mehr
Du sollt mir ganz vertrauen dich,
Von Herzensgrund auch lieben mich.
Kyrieleis.

I alone am thy God and Lord,
You shall have no other Gods
You shall completely entrust yourself to me,
And love me with all your heart.
Kyrie eleison.

Du sollt nicht führen zu Unehr,
Den Namen Gottes, deines Herrn:
Du sollt nicht preisen recht noch gut,
Ohn was Gott selber redt und tut.
Kyrieleis.

You shall not bring to dishonor
The name of God, your Lord:
You shall not prize as right and good,
Except what God Himself says and does.
Kyrie eleison.

Du sollt heilgen den Sabbattag,
Daß du und dein Haus ruhen mag:
Du sollt von deinem Tun lassen ab,
Daß Gott sein Werk auch in dir hab.
Kyrieleis.

You shall keep the Sabbath Day holy,
So that you and your house may rest:
You shall leave off from your work,
So that God has His work in you also.
Kyrie eleison.

Du sollt ehren und gehorsam sein
Dem Vater und der Mutter dein,
Und wo dein Hand ihn' dienen kann,
So wirst du langes Leben han,
Kyrieleis.

You shall honor and obey
Your father and your mother,
And serve them where you can,
Thus you will have a long life,
Kyrie eleison.

Du sollt nicht töten zorniglich,
Nicht hassen, noch selbst rächen dich.
Geduld haben und sanften Mut
Und auch dem Feinde tun das Gut.
Kyrieleis.

You shall not angrily kill anyone,
Not hate, nor take revenge.
Have patience and a soft manner
And do good even to your enemy.
Kyrie eleison.

Deine Ehe sollst du bewahren rein,
Daß auch dein Herz kein anders
mein
Und halten keusch das Leben dein
Mit Zucht und Mäßigkeit gar fein.
Kyrieleis.

You shall keep your marriage pure,
So that even your heart intends nothing
else
And keep your life chaste
With good breeding and moderation.
Kyrie eleison.

Du sollt nicht stehlen Geld noch Gut,
Nicht wuchern jemands Schweiss
und Blut;
Du sollt auftun dein milde Hand
Dem armen Volk in deinem Land.
Kyrieleis.

You shall not steal money or goods,
Not exploit anyone's sweat and
blood;
You shall open wide your gentle hand
To the poor people in your land.
Kyrie eleison.

Du sollt kein falscher Zeuge sein,
Nicht lügen auf den Nächsten dein:
Sein Unschuld sollt auch retten du
Und seine Schand decken zu.
Kyrieleis.

You shall not bear false witness,
Not lie about your neighbor:
You shall also protect his innocence
And cover up his shame.
Kyrie eleison.

Du sollt deines Nächsten Weib
und Haus
Begehren nicht, noch etwas draus;

You shall your neighbor's wife and
house
Not covet, nor anything of his;

Du sollt ihm wünschen alles Gut, Wie dir dein Herz auch selber tut. Kyrieleis.	You shall wish him everything good, As your heart does unto itself. Kyrie eleison.
Die Gebot all uns gegeben sind, Daß du dein Sünd, o Menschenkind Erkennen sollt und lernen wohl Wie man vor Gott recht leben soll. Kyrieleis.	The commandments are all given unto us, So that you, O child of man Recognize your sin and learn well How one should rightly live before God. Kyrie eleison.
Das helf uns der Herr Jesu Christ, Der unser Mittler worden ist: Es ist mit unserm Tun verlorn, Verdienen doch nur eitel Zorn. Kyrieleis.	The Lord Jesus Christ helps us with that, Who is become our mediator: Everything is lost with our own doing, It earns only futile anger. Kyrie eleison.

In proclaiming the purpose of the Law as that of leading the believer to recognition of sin, in emphasizing that on its own humanity can only merit God's wrath, and in outlining a progression from Moses the lawgiver in the first strophe to Jesus the mediator and redeemer in the last strophe, "Dies sind die heil'gen zehn Gebot" expresses much of the central core of Luther's theology. Placing the second commandment within the context of the first causes it to mirror Luther's view of the first commandment, which demands faith as the primary means by which humanity honors God. Since the "work" of the first commandment was faith, fulfilling the first commandment included fulfilling all the others.[6] All other works were directed toward one's neighbor and were expressions of the love of God manifested in love of the neighbor (the last two commandments speak directly of the neighbor). This meant that the believer followed the pattern of Christ, Who in "taking upon himself the human form of a servant . . . wished to take our love which is falsely directed up toward heaven and turn it completely downward in love to our neighbor."[7] In this way the downward dynamic of the Law was fulfilled in both faith and love, the latter associated with Jesus' humanity and directed toward humanity as represented by the concept of the neighbor; as Paul Althaus expresses it, "Luther's understanding of love is completely dominated by his faith in the incarnation."[8]

It is not known exactly how Luther's chorale first became associated with the melody of the medieval pilgrimage hymn "In Gottes Namen fahren wir," but it is often presumed that, because of the metrical parallels between the two poems, Luther intended his chorale to be sung to the old melody. Nevertheless, "Dies sind die heil'gen zehn Gebot" was sung to at least one other melody, although that combination was not nearly as widespread as the one we know. Less certain are whether Luther (or whoever set Luther's poem to the melody of "In Gottes Namen") intended a religious connection between the two hymn texts and exactly what the original form of the melody of "In Gottes Namen" was. As it was first published, the melody was in the transposed Dorian mode—that is, in *cantus mollis* g—but very early in its history it appeared in Mixolydian G, sometimes with and sometimes without the pitch B♭ substituting for B in its final phrase (in some cases in the penultimate phrase). It has been suggested that the connection between the two hymns underscores the fact that the believer's justification is a "pilgrimage," that the physical journey to Jerusalem paralleled the spiritual journey of the believer to the Jerusalem that was a metaphor for God's Kingdom.[9] And, indeed, one early chorale book that contains both "In Gottes Namen fahren wir" and "Dies sind die heil'gen zehn Gebot" (which is decidedly not the norm) illustrates them both with woodcuts depicting processions.[10] Certainly, the fact that "In Gottes Namen" was basically an appeal to God for protection, ending in its various versions with either an invocation of the Trinity or simply a final *Kyrieleis*—that is, it belonged to the genre known as *Leisen*—must have resonated with Luther's conception of the role of the Ten Commandments and the Law in justification.

The text of "In Gottes Namen" was presumably widely known by the early thirteenth century, since the earliest reference to its first line appears in Gottfried von Strassburg's *Tristan und Isolde*; in that poem it was sung at the start of the ocean voyage from Ireland to Cornwall. And the association of "In Gottes Namen" with a ship voyage, in which Christ was the captain or pilot, was a thread, albeit a slender one, that ran throughout its history.[11] Although older forms of the text of "In Gottes Namen" exist, the earliest appearances of the text and melody together were in the second third of the fifteenth century, in two virtually identical sources that preserve the chorale within an anonymous eight-part composition.[12] This composition is a setting of two texts simultaneously, the other being the Latin Marian hymn "Ave mundi spes, Maria," which is the only text for the two uppermost voices and is heard in part in four of the lower voices as well. "In Gottes Namen" enters first in measure 19 of the 46-measure piece, in the *Contra altus tertius* part immediately following the third phrase of the Marian hymn. After that point it spreads through the six lower voices (*Tenor primus* and *secundus*, *Contra altus primus*, *secundus* and *tertius*, and *Contrabassus*), generally dominating them after about measure 25, although parts of the Marian text appear in the *Tenor primus* and *Contra altus tertius* toward the end. This version of "In Gottes Namen" has five phrases plus the final *Kyrieleis*:

In Gotes namen faren wir,	We journey in God's name,
Seiner genaden geren wir,	We long for His grace,
Des helf uns die Goteskraft	In this God's power helps us
Und das heilige Grab,	And the holy Grave,
Do Got selber inne lag.	Since God Himself lay in it.
Kyrieleis.	Kyrie eleison.

In the polyphonic setting just described, the melody of "In Gottes Namen" appears in complete form only in the *Tenor secundus*, beginning in measure 29 and continuing to the end of the movement (the *Tenor secundus* is the last part to enter, it has no music before this point, and only it and the *Contrabassus*, which enters first in measure 25, contain no reference to the Marian hymn). One other part, the *Contra altus secundus*, contains a virtually complete version of the melody of "In Gottes Namen," from measure 31 to the end, the principal differences being that it transposes the first two phrases up a tone, to a instead of g, then returns to g for the remainder of the tune, and its version of the concluding *Kyrieleis* is not the ending of the tune itself but a slightly elaborated version of the ending that serves in part as a contrapuntal filler for the cadence.

Interestingly, in light of what we will discover concerning the mode and tonal character of the chorale, the *Tenor secundus, Contra altus primus,* and *Contra altus secundus* are notated in the *cantus durus* and all the remaining parts in the *cantus mollis.* Thus, the two parts that present "In Gottes Namen" in their most complete forms are in the *cantus durus.* Owing to the predominance of the *cantus mollis* in the other parts, however, they are forced to accommodate by introducing the pitch b♭ at various points. There is a loosely canonic relationship between these two parts; the transposition of the first two phrases of the tune up a tone in the *Contra altus secundus* perhaps arose from that fact as well as from the fact that, beginning from a instead of g, the melody skips both b and b♭ in the first two phrases, thereby avoiding the question of which of those pitches is "correct."

In light of the fact that the melody of "Dies sind die heil'gen zehn Gebot" exists in three distinct forms, one of which features b♭ and another b♮ throughout, while a third one—ultimately its most common form—features a b–b♭ shift in its final line, we might imagine that the melody became altered as a result of ♭/♮ variability in the earliest polyphonic settings of "In Gottes Namen." Since, in the setting just described the uppermost parts, which are confined to the Marian hymn, are entirely in the *cantus mollis,* while the parts that center most on "In Gottes Namen" are in the *cantus durus,* we might speculate that the combination of these two hymns was related to their original tonal qualities (which are no longer known). That is, the appeal to the virgin Mary, described in the hymn text as "Imperatrix miserorum consolare peccatorem in peccatis nunc sedentem," might have been associated with the *cantus mollis,* thereby lending a quality of "softening"—that is, mercy—to the setting as a whole.

The next settings of "In Gottes Namen" to survive are all from around the turn of the sixteenth century, by well-known composers such as Heinrich Isaac, Paul Hofhaimer, and Heinrich Finck.[13] And some of these are also suggestive with respect to the mode of the melody. Isaac's setting, for example, places the tune in the *altus* and *bassus* of a four-part composition. The piece ends on G with an authentic cadence, but the melody of "In Gottes Namen" is pitched in D; and its first complete statement brings about a prominent melodic cadence to D just after the midpoint of the piece. For the first half the *altus* part states the melody in full, while the *bassus,* which introduces the first phrase, presents phrases 1 to 3 with free interludes. In the second half this procedure is reversed, the *bassus* now serving as the principal bearer of the *cantus firmus* (but ending on G rather than the final of the melody, D). What is particularly interesting about this setting is that the opening phrases of the melody introduce the pitch f♯' (or f♯) via *musica ficta* (the raised leading tone or *subsemitonium*) as the lines ascend from d' to g' for the phrase cadences. Coupled with the fact that several of the lines that serve as contrapuntal answering voices in the remaining parts descend from d'' to g', this feature creates a strong sense of a G tonality at the beginning of the piece. With the third phrase, however, the tonality shifts in the direction of C, and the overlap between that phrase (in the *bassus*) and the fourth phrase (in the *altus*) leads the first major division of the piece to a D cadence for the phrase "do Gott selber inne lag"; it then continues on to G for the completion of the *Kyrieleis.*

Isaac's text is a longer form of "In Gottes Namen" than the one cited previously, the final *Kyrieleis* extending the piece as follows:[14]

Kyrieleys. Cristeleys,	Kyrie eleison. Christe eleison.
Das helff uns der heylig geyst	May the Holy Spirit help us
Und die war Gottes stym,	And the true voice of God,
Das wir frölich farn von hyn.	So that we joyfully travel from here.
Kyrieleys.	Kyrie eleison.

In this version the extension of the final *Kyrieleis* picks up the basic d–g ascent idea of the first phrase (without the initial repeated tones), after which the melody repeats from phrase 3 to the end. This time the final tone, d, of the bass *cantus firmus* drops to G for the final cadence. The overall tonal character of the melody of "In Gottes Namen" in this piece is that it is in G with prominent f♯s at the beginning that are introduced via raised leading tones in melodic and harmonic cadence patterns but that give way to f♮s in the latter phrases (from phrase 3 on). The final cadence would reintroduce the leading tone f♯' once again, of course; but the effect is that of a G Mixolydian setting. If the melody were abstracted from this setting, however, and transposed to G, it would feature prominent b♮s at the beginning and b♭s toward the end. In our terms Isaac's melody is in D Dorian with some fs raised to f♯ as a result of harmonic exigencies; f♮ would remain the basic pitch, and the setting would have a "subdominant" character that is reflected in the G tonality, which would probably be judged Mixolydian.

I have given this much attention to Isaac's setting because it suggests that in polyphonic settings, at least, "In Gottes Namen fahren wir" might have raised questions regarding its mode that conditioned its later history. Paul Hofhaimer's setting likewise raises questions of this kind, although its modal treatment is different from Isaac's. Hofhaimer's four-part setting, which is in G, places the melody of "In Gottes Namen" in the two inner parts, in canon at the fifth below at the distance of a half note, beginning from d' in the alto and g in the tenor, while the soprano and bass lines (presumably instrumental parts, since they are untexted and often rapid and figurational in nature) move at a considerably faster rate of speed and are not derived from the chorale tune. What is most interesting about this setting from the modal standpoint is that while all parts are notated in the *cantus durus*, the canonic imitation necessitates the introduction of b♭s in order to avoid tritones between adjacent harmonies as well as between the ending of phrase 3 in the alto (on f) and the beginning of phrase 4 in the tenor part. The b♭s are notated in the tenor part at the beginning of the fourth phrase, and they suggest a flattening at that point in the piece that is confirmed by the appearance of b♭s in the "free" parts as well. At the beginning of the piece, however, there are no b♭s in the tenor, so that the effect is that of a minor (Dorian mode) version of the tune in the alto that is answered immediately by a major (Mixolydian) version in the tenor. Whereas in Isaac's setting the application of *musica ficta* caused a raising of the minor third, f, to f♯ of the Dorian d mode in the first two phrases, in Hofhaimer's it caused a flattening of the major third, b to b♭, of the Mixolydian G mode in the final phrases. As was the case in Isaac's setting, the tonality of Hofhaimer's is G, so the b/b♭ anomaly, if there truly is one, is overcome by the introduction of b♭ toward the latter part of the setting. That is, the "conflict" between D Dorian and G Mixolydian is resolved by an ending that suggests G transposed Dorian—the flattening of the original mode as a result of its transposition a fifth down in the answering voice. The exact application of accidentals in this setting, however, is sufficiently uncertain for Hans Joachim Moser, the editor of the piece, to raise the possibility that the entire piece should be notated in the *cantus mollis*, even though its two sources are unequivocally notated in the *cantus durus* (and to change the b's to b♭s at the beginning of the setting would raise tritone problems).[15] Another possibility that might be considered is that the *tonal* aspect of Hofhaimer's setting, manifested in the G tonality and the transpositional relationship of the two canonic voices—that is, the sense of shift from a relatively *durus* to a relatively *mollis* region—takes precedence over the idea of modal integrity. And that tonal variability (which appears in all the settings described to this point) was perhaps related to the idea of pilgrimage in the text, as a form of *peregrinatio*, analogous to the final line ("do wir frölich farn von hyn"). In any case, if the melody of "In Gottes Namen" were extracted from the alto part of this setting we would have a D Dorian piece, whereas if it were extracted from the tenor part we would have a piece that began in G Mixolydian and ended (presumably) in G transposed Dorian. The latter would be essentially the same as the melody we would extract from Isaac's setting, and it would be virtually identical to the form of the tune that would ultimately be associated most closely with "Dies sind die heil'gen zehn Gebot."

In fact, the continuing history of "In Gottes Namen" and "Dies sind die heil'gen zehn Gebot" exhibits exactly this quality of uncertainty (or dualism) regarding the pitches b♭ and b. The first appearances of "Dies sind die heil'gen zehn Gebot," as a melody only in the Erfurt *Enchiridion* of 1524 and as a tenor *cantus firmus* in Johann Walther's polyphonic setting of 1524, are in transposed Dorian—that is, in g in the *cantus mollis.*[16] But, as Zahn points out, the most common later form of the melody was that in which b♮ appeared in the first two phrases and was replaced by b♭ for the final phrase.[17] According to Zahn, this version appeared as early as the Erfurt *Enchirdion* of 1527 and was carried over into *Das Klug'sche Gesangbuch* from 1533 on (Ex. 7.1). In 1544 it appeared as the tenor of a polyphonic setting by Balthasar Resinarius in Georg Rhau's *Neue deutsche geistliche Gesänge*, and in 1545 the melody alone was printed in Leipzig in *Das Babstsche Gesangbuch.* Also, a version that was far less widespread—in G Mixolydian with no b♭s whatsoever—emerged as early as 1536 and was printed, in a setting by Johann Hermann Schein, in the *Neu Leipziger Gesangbuch* of Gottfried Vopelius in 1682. Throughout the seventeenth century the tune appeared in all three forms, but the clearly favored form was the one that introduced b♭ only at the end, thereby suggesting a shift of mode or of *cantus*, even though the melody was often classed simply as Mixolydian.[18] Praetorius provides us with no fewer than eight settings in the two Mixolydian versions, but with a clear predominance (seven) of the one that introduced the b♭ at the end; he further identifies the version without b♭ as the way the tune was sung in Thuringia, the version with b♭ as the way it was sung in Prussia, and the latter melody with a different text as an old Bavarian version.[19] In a setting by Johann Michael Bach that J. S. Bach surely knew, the melody is transposed to F in the *cantus mollis* (i.e., F major or F Mixolydian), its third phrase ends on e♭', the transpositional equivalent of the f♮' in a G Mixolydian setting, but its final phrases do not introduce the minor third, a♭'.[20]

Example 7.1. "Dies sind die heil'gen zehn Gebot": oldest appearance of melody in its *cantus mollis* (Dorian) and *cantus durus* (Mixolydian) versions. (a) From the Erfurt *Enchiridion* of 1524; (b) From *Das Klug'sche Gesangbuch* (1533)

Folget zum erſten die zehen gebot Gottes/auff dē thō/ Jn gottes namē farē wir

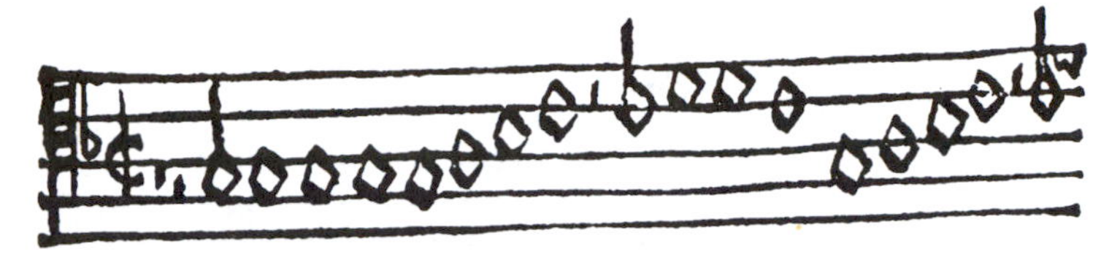

Dys ſynd die heylgen zehn gebot/die vnns gab vnſer herre Gott / durch Moſen ſeinen diener trew/hoch auff dem berg Sinay Kyrioleys.

Jch byn allein dein Gott der herr/ keyn Götter ſoltu habē meer. Du ſolt mir gantz vertrawē dich/ von hertzen grund lieben mich Kyrioleys.
Du ſoltt nicht brauchen zu vnehrn/dē namē gottes deines herrn/ du ſoltt nicht preyſen recht noch gnt/on was Gott ſelbs redt vnnd thut Kyrioleys.
Du ſolt heilgen den ſybend tag/ das du vnd dein hauß rugen mag/du ſoltt von deim thun laſſen ab/ das Gott ſeyn werck ynn dir hab kyrioleys.
Du ſolt ehrn vnd gehorſam ſeyn dem vatter vnd der mutter dein. Vn̄ wo dein hant yhn dienē kan/

—*continued*

From this setting and the version in the Vopelius chorale book (as well as Praetorius's Thuringian version of the tune) it seems clear that Bach knew the straight Mixolydian version of the chorale (that is, the version without the flattened third at the end). Georg Philipp Telemann's chorale book of 1730, which attempts to supply all the known variants of its five hundred chorale melodies, provides a slightly different "basic" version of the tune: unless Telemann was careless in proofreading

Example 7.1. (*continued*)

both the melodic accidentals and the *basso continuo* figures, which does not seem likely, his melody introduces b♭' as the melody ascends from g' to c'' at the beginning of the final phrase, then changes back to b'(♮) as it descends again to the final g'; that is, it is the opposite of the most common form of this phrase.[21] Telemann indicates only one variant version, the one that introduces the b♭' in the descent to the final g'—that is, Bach's version—an indication, perhaps, that the straight Dorian (minor) and straight Mixolydian (major) versions had disappeared from common usage, at least in some regions, by 1730.

If we consider why the modally anomalous version of "In Gottes Namen" / "Dies sind" should have ended up as the preferred one, we may well be led to the conclusion that, although there was precedence for b/b♭ (or f♯/f) variability in sixteenth-century settings of "In Gottes Namen," the version of the tune that alters the b to b♭ toward the end is associated particularly with "Dies sind die heil'gen zehn Gebot" rather than with "In Gottes Namen fahren wir." That version enters the picture very early in the history of the assignation of the old melody to Luther's hymn and gradually takes precedence over the others.

Turning now to the melody of "Dies sind die heil'gen zehn Gebot" in the form that Bach used in all his settings (and that is nearly identical to the one that appears in the Freylinghausen *Geistreiches Gesang-Buch* of his own time as well as to Telemann's principal variant version), we observe that it begins as if in Mixolydian G (in ordinary parlance G with f♮' rather than f♯' as an "essential" tone) and introduces the pitch b♭' twice in its penultimate phrase, placing that pitch in the context of the note g', on which the final phrase settles[22] (Ex. 7.2). This detail, which in historical terms suggests a shift from *cantus durus* to *cantus mollis*, had the most profound impact on Bach's conception of both the opening movement of Cantata 77 and the design of the cantata as a whole, which shifts overall from the *cantus durus* to the *cantus mollis*. And from this standpoint it might well suggest that Bach interpreted the b–b♭ shift as an "allegorical" device. That is, Bach perhaps felt that the preferred version of the melody in his time had come about as the result of an attempt to mirror the quality of Luther's chorale in tones. His setting suggests exactly that.

Bach might well have concluded that the melody of "Dies sind die heil'gen zehn Gebot" was carefully constructed from a series of interrelated elements, some of which suggest the dualisms of high and low, ascent and descent, sharp and flat, and even major and minor. Certainly he amplified all these qualities in the first movement of Cantata 77. The first phrase contains two such elements, the six initial repeated g's and the subsequent stepwise ascent of the major tetrachord from g' to c". The second phrase drops the tone repetition, replacing it by the introduction of a second element in its initial high tones, c", d", d", and c", after which it reiterates the g'–a'–b'–c" ascent of the first phrase. The third phrase then repeats the beginning of the second but now turns downward to close on the lowest tone of the chorale, f', instead of returning to c". This is a significant change that introduces the particular feature of the Mixolydian mode that in Kirnberger's view gave it its special worth: cadence a tone below the final—that is, on the pitch that differentiates the Mixolydian mode from the modern major key, reinforcing what many would call the subdominant character of the Mixolydian mode.[23] These three phrases are all of eight quarter-note beats in length. In the melody as it was normally presented in two centuries of chorale books there is only one further phrase, longer than the preceding ones and encompassing the *Kyrieleis* as its final cadence. Bach, however, always subdivides this phrase, either into two phrases, as in the version that appears in Cantata 77, or, as in the longer setting of *Clavierübung*, Part 3, into three phrases. In the five-phrase version that appears in Cantata 77, phrase 4 is necessarily considerably shorter than the preceding ones, simply reiterating the ascending major tetrachord from g' to c", without the tone repetitions, while phrase 5 is slightly longer than the first three, introducing the tone b♭' in alternation with g', then descending through a' to end with

Example 7.2. "Dies sind die heil'gen zehn Gebot" in the version used by Bach in Cantata 77, which is identical or nearly identical to that found in many seventeenth- and eighteenth-century hymnbooks (except for the division into five phrases)

three (or four) repeated g's. In this last detail the final phrase recalls the repeated tones at the beginning of the melody. Several verses of the chorale text, however, necessitate the singing of phrases 4 and 5 as a single unit (otherwise the line would have to pause in the middle of a phrase or even a word).[24] Singing the chorale in this way would result in the b♭'–g'–b♭' of phrase 5 becoming an appendage to phrase 4, so that the two phrases together would amplify the flattening effect introduced by the f' of phrase 3.[25] If the *Kyrieleis* is considered a part of this phrase as well, the melodic descent from b♭' to g' at the end may well suggest a G minor (or Dorian) context for the chorale ending. Within the melody as a whole, then, it is natural to perceive a progressive flattening from the G–C relationship of the initial two phrases to the F of the third and the B♭ of the fourth, even a potential G–g shift in the melody as a whole.[26]

In the tonal qualities just described, the version of the melody of "Dies sind die heil'gen zehn Gebot" that seems to shift from G Mixolydian to G transposed Dorian can be considered to match the way that Luther's text interprets the meaning of the Ten Commandments as a whole. That is, the progressive flattening of the melody, conceived as a *durus–mollis* shift (in both the archaic, sharp/flat, and modern German, major/minor senses of those terms), may well remind us of what Johann Melchior Göze said in his funeral oration for Andreas Werckmeister regarding God's wrathful and merciful natures as His *durus* and *mollis* sides and the harmonizing of major and minor as a symbol of the *Übereinstimmung* of God and humankind. Göze might well have remembered certain of Luther's own remarks on music's allegorical properties, such as that the Hypodorian mode was like the "poor weak sinner" (*infirmus peccator*) because of its variable mi–fa degree (b♮–b♭).[27] Göze's rather homely analogies describe how God does not always proceed from the *cantus mollis* in harmonizing melodies with humanity (i.e., He does not always show His merciful side), how God tunes the Dorian mode "belatedly, since the sun only shines for our pleasure" (presumably meaning that God's wrathful and merciful natures compare to the sun shining forth after a storm, an analogy that occurs in several of Bach's cantata texts), how the Mixolydian mode and the *cantus durus* are associated with God's wrath, the Ionian mode with human joy and pleasure, and the like.[28] Even Göze's remark that "He sometimes stretches the strings a little high" suggests qualities associated with the deity that humanity cannot live up to and that might be thought to have associations with the term *durus*.[29] We cannot make Göze's fanciful remarks the basis of an analytical or interpretative system, of course; it is enough to recognize that in certain respects the primary melody associated with "Dies sind die heil'gen zehn Gebot" was very well suited to Luther's poem, in which the dualism of God's demands from humankind (the Law) and humanity's need for mercy from a just and wrathful deity seem to be mirrored in the melodic qualities of the phrases and the shift from b♮' to b♭' toward the end, just before the final *Kyrieleis*.

Since twelve different stanzas are sung to the same melody, we cannot expect that the tune will match the individual words or strophes (or vice versa) with any degree of consistency. Nevertheless, there are points where the two coincide remarkably well. Thus, in the first verse the initial phrase with its six repeated tones and its perfect-fourth ascent from g' to c" projects an emphatic character that is owing in part to the tone repetition and in part to the sense of upward motion from dominant to tonic. (It may be mentioned that in certain versions of the melody the three-syllable word "heiligen" causes the first phrase to have ten tones instead of the usual nine that result from the two-syllable "heil'gen"; this difference, now with *seven* repeated g's, suggests a "counting" effect.) If this phrase seems well matched to the introductory line, "Dies sind die heil'gen zehn Gebot," then the second line—"die uns gab unser Herre Gott"—with its initial high tones (c"–d"–d"–c") and reiteration of the g'–c" fourth ascent of the first phrase seems to make an association between the upper pitch region of the melody and the sphere of God, after which the descent from those same initial high tones to f' in the third phrase—"durch Mosen, *seinen Diener treu*"—seems to match the idea of descent from the sphere of God to that of "Moses, His faithful servant." The fourth phrase then mirrors the words "hoch auf dem Berg" with a third iteration of the g'–c" ascent of phrases 1 and 2, after which the b♭'–g'–b♭', setting the word "Sinai," and the stepwise descent to the thrice-repeated final g', setting *Kyrieleis*, might be thought to mirror Moses' descent from the mountain with the commandments (or the more general idea of descent from God in His glory to suffering humankind, which is, in fact, the most compelling aspect of the melodic and tonal character of the melody as a whole).

Associations of a similar kind continue here and there throughout the twelve verses of the chorale. Thus, verse 5 associates the verb "dienen" again with the descent to f'; verse 12 associates the first two phrases with "Herr Jesus Christ" (as verses 2 and 3 associated them with "Gott und Herr"), setting phrase 3 with "es ist mit unserm Thun verlorn," and so on. Apart from such pitch associations, the chorale exhibits *tonal* text–music associations as well, and these are arguably the most fundamental ones. Certain phrases suggest attributes associated with the word *mollis* (soft), verse 6 setting "Geduld haben und sanften Muth" to phrase 3 (the words "sanften Muth" coinciding with the turn to F), and verse 8 setting "du solt aufthun dein' milde Hand den Armen in deinem Land" to phrases 3 and 4. The flattening effect toward the ending of the chorale melody was quite possibly perceived as analogous to Luther's view, developed from many passages in Paul, such as the one that formed the Epistle for the thirteenth Sunday after Trinity, that the role of the Law was to bring humankind awareness of its sinful nature, thereby prompting the appeal to God for mercy. Even though the individual elements of the chorale melody cannot always match up with the ideas of Luther's poem, the descent from b♭' to g' at the end always coincides with the plea for mercy, *Kyrieleis*, that ends all twelve verses. In this respect the modal-hexachordal shift in the tune fits perfectly with Luther's view that the Law, in making humankind aware of its sinfulness and inability to live up to

God's demands, humbles it, reinforcing its need to call upon God for mercy. Since the Law is a symbol of God's demand for perfect justice, which humanity cannot satisfy unaided, the prayer for God's mercy is added to the ending of every verse. In this context, the descent from b♭' to g' at the end of the melody contrasts strikingly with the ascent through b♮' to c" in lines 1, 2 and 4, creating the sense that the ending mirrors the human condition in need of God's aid (exactly the association of the "Soli Deo Gloria" and "Jesu Juva" that Bach placed on the manuscript pages of many of his cantata scores).[30]

The Text of Cantata 77

Occurring just at the midpoint of the 1723 Trinity season (the thirteenth Sunday after Trinity), the theological "message" of Cantata 77—love of God and one's neighbor as the meaning of the Law—can be taken not only to embody the principles underlying biblical hermeneutics, the reinterpretation of the Old Testament in terms of the New, the Law in terms of the Gospel, and the working of both on the believer but also to mirror the very purpose of music in the Lutheran tradition: to give glory to God and sustenance to one's neighbor. Together these themes have enormous potential to articulate a metaphoric statement regarding the role of music in the Lutheran tradition. In it the Law, embodied in the melody associated with Luther's Ten Commandments chorale, provided the principal thematic and tonal material for the movement and the basis for its well-known numerological features, while the New Testament reinterpretation of the Law contributed both the sung text and the conceptual basis for a sphere of "free" musical themes associated with it. In the movement as a whole, several levels of dualism—strict and free thematic procedures, major and minor tonalities, and presence and absence of *basso continuo*—aid in representing the basic theological ideas that lie behind the text: the relationship of Law and Gospel, love of God, and love of one's neighbor.

There are two principal scriptural sources for Jesus' reinterpretation of the Law in terms of love of God and one's neighbor, one of which, Luke 10:23–37, serves as the Gospel for the thirteenth Sunday after Trinity, while the other, Matthew 22:34–46, provides the Gospel reading for the eighteenth Sunday after Trinity.[31] Although occurring later in the liturgical sequence, Matthew's version is logically "prior" in that Jesus Himself speaks the words regarding the two great commandments in response to the question "Which is the greatest commandment in the Law?": "You shall love the Lord your God with all your heart, with all your soul, with all your mind. That is the first and greatest commandment. The second is like unto it: Love your neighbor as yourself. Everything in the Law and the prophets hangs on these two commandments" (37–40). In Luke's version the question put to Jesus (by a lawyer!) is: "What must I do to inherit eternal life?" and Jesus' answer is another question: "What is written in the Law? What is your reading of it?," prompting the reply: "You shall love the Lord thy God with all your heart, with all your soul, with all your strength, and with all your mind; and your neighbor as yourself," which

Jesus affirms as correct. Luke's version contains one further question: "And who is my neighbor?," which then elicits the parable of the Good Samaritan from Jesus. It is important, therefore, to recognize that the overall dynamic of the Gospel reading involves a "downward" progression, from the initial elevated themes of eternal life and love of God to love of one's neighbor and a practical illustration of what such love entails.

The text of the opening chorus of Cantata 77 is the excerpt from Luke, its musical and textual relationships to Luther's chorale (untexted) suggesting that it represents the "reading" or interpretation of the Law demanded by Jesus. After two movements in which the "heart" is associated with love of God, the second recitative refers to Luke's parable of the Good Samaritan, linking the believer's prayer for a *Samariterherz* to his hopes for eternal life. In this way the eschatological goal of the lawyer's question to Jesus receives its most concrete answer in terms of the believer's life in the world. Also, although it does not directly provide material for the text of Cantata 77, the Epistle reading for the thirteenth Sunday after Trinity, Galatians 3:15–22, takes up the meaning of the Law in a manner that was central to Luther's Pauline theology of justification. Paul speaks first of the promises made by God to Abraham and fulfilled in Christ. The Law, granted later in time, could not invalidate this "testament or covenant," which had been bestowed on Abraham's "issue" as a legal right. Instead, the Law was given later for the purpose of making wrongdoing a "legal offense." As a temporary measure, pending the arrival of Christ, it did not contradict God's promises to Abraham but reflected the view of the whole world as "prisoners in subjection to sin, so that faith in Jesus Christ may be the ground on which the promised blessing is given, and given to to those who have such faith." In this passage we have the Lutheran definition of the relationship of Law and Gospel: although the Law preceded the Gospel as revealed in Jesus, it was, in fact, preceded in turn by God's promise to Abraham, which was an expression of the Gospel. The purpose of the Law was to make humanity aware of its sinfulness, its inability to fulfill God's demands and justify itself before God; as Luther often expressed it, the Law is God's "alien work," leading ultimately to death, whereas the Gospel is God's "proper work," redemption through faith in Jesus Christ, leading to eternal life.[32] Understanding the Law in terms of the message of the revealed Gospel was therefore essential.[33]

Bach's text is a reworking of a cantata text by Johann Oswald Knauer that was published in Knauer's *Gott-geheiligtes Singen und Spielen des Friedensteinischen Zions* just three years before Bach produced Cantata 77.[34] Although Bach's text draws upon only seven of the twelve movements of Knauer's text, it derives much of its overall theological intent from that work. Movements 1 through 5 of Bach's six movements correspond closely to movements 6, 8, 9, 10, and 11 of Knauer's, while Knauer's twelfth movement, the last two verses of Luther's "Dies sind die heil'gen zehn Gebot"—that is, the two that articulate the purpose of the Law—undoubtedly provided the impetus for Bach's combining that chorale melody (untexted) with the excerpt from Luke (Knauer's sixth movement) in the opening movement of Cantata 77. Bach's opening movement thereby makes clear from the outset that the reinterpretation of the Law in terms of the Gospel is the principal theological theme of the work. And while Cantata 77 ends with a chorale of unspecified text sung to the melody of "Ach Gott, vom Himmel sieh' darein," its context suggests that it, too, came about as the result of the reworking of Knauer's text (see following discussion).

Knauer's movements 1 through 5 (i.e., those *not* used in Bach's text) constitute a distinct subdivision within his text to which his movements 6 through 12 respond. They begin from the twenty-fifth verse of Luke's Gospel (i.e., two verses before the one that begins Cantata 77), which is the question put to Jesus regarding eternal life: "Meister, was muß ich thun, daß ich das ewige Leben ererbe?" This question, which is reiterated in the three movements that follow, takes on the character of a petition to Jesus from one in tribulation, a representaton of the contemporary believer in search of *Trost.* In a sense, these three movements can be considered an introduction to the sequence of texts that follow, beginning with "Du sollt Gott, deinen Herren, lieben."

Aria (no. 2)

<table>
<tr><td>Wer will nach Eitelkeiten streben?
Man findet wenig Trost dabey.
Ich weiß schon, daß kein ewig Leben
Auf dieser Welt zu hoffen sey.
Da Capo</td><td>Who will strive after vanities?
One finds little comfort in that.
I know now, that no eternal life
Can be expected in this world.
Da Capo</td></tr>
</table>

[*Recitative*] (no. 3)

<table>
<tr><td>Nur Eins ist Noth.
Um eins nur will ich mich
bemühen.
Sonst will ich alle Sorgen fliehen.
Ich dencke nur daran,
Wie ich dort ewig leben kan.
Was soll ich mich mit eitlen Dingen
quälen,
Ich will allein das beste Teil erwehlen.
Es fliehen meine Tage
Hier wie Rauch und Nebel hin
Und sind nichts mehr als Kummer,
Angst und Plage.
Drum soll mein Sinn
Nur an das Ewige gedencken.
Dahin will ich mein Hertze stündlich
lencken.
Allein,
Der schmale Weg zum Leben
Will wohl gesuchet seyn:
Sonst kommt man leicht darneben.
Und wollt ich mich auch selber führen,
So würd ich mich gar bald verlieren.
Drum halt ich mich,</td><td>Only one thing is necessary.
For only one thing will I concern
myself.
Otherwise I will flee all cares.
I think only on this,
How I can live eternally up above.
Why should I torment myself with
vain things,
I will choose only the best part.
My days are fleeing
Away like smoke and fog
And are nothing more than trouble,
Anxiety and torment.
Therefore shall my mind
Only think on the eternal.
On that will I direct my heart
from hour to hour.
However,
The narrow path to life
Needs to be well sought out:
Otherwise one easily goes wrong.
And if I wanted to lead myself,
Then I would very soon lose myself.
Therefore I hold myself,</td></tr>
</table>

Mein Jesu, bloß an dich	My Jesus, solely to You
Du sollst mich deine Wege lehren,	You shall teach me your ways,
Ach, laß mich deine Stimme hören,	Ah, let me hear Your voice,
Und sage mir doch nun:	And say to me even now:
Was muß ich thun?	What I must do?

Aria (no. 4)

Du, mein Jesu, muß mir sagen,	You, my Jesu, must tell me,
Wie ich mich verhalten soll.	How I should conduct myself.
Daß ich einst nach meinem Sterben,	So that one day after my death,
Kan das rechte Leben erben,	I can inherit the true life,
Sonst verderb ich Kummer-voll.	Otherwise I will perish full of troubles.
Da Capo	Da Capo

This first part of Knauer's text ends with a chorale verse that urges the believer to hear Jesus' answer:

Chorus (no. 5)

Kommt, laßt euch den Herren lehren,	Come, let the Lord teach you,
Kommt und lernet allzumahl,	Come and learn particularly,
Welche die seynd, die gehören	Who they are, who belong
In der rechten Christen Zahl.	Among the number of true Christians.
Die bekennen mit dem Mund,	Who confess with their mouth,
Glauben fest aus Hertzens-Grund,	Believe firmly with all their heart,
Und bemühen sich darneben,	And concern themselves in addition,
Fromm zu seyn, so lang sie leben.	With being pious, so long as they live.

The sequence of movements that follows, and that constitutes the basis for Bach's text, thus functions as Jesus' answer (even though in Luke's version of the story it is a lawyer who answers Jesus' question regarding his understanding of the Law). After the "great commandment" as given in Luke (Knauer's sixth movement), Knauer places a recitative that Bach passed over in Cantata 77: "Hier hast du das Gesetz, das Gott dir vorgeschrieben: Du sollst zuförderst Gott, und dann den Nechsten lieben." In his analysis of the theological differences between Knauer's and Bach's texts Martin Petzoldt points out that Knauer's text emphasizes the "nacheinander" of one's love for God and for one's neighbor—that is, that love of God comes first, that of the neighbor second—whereas Bach's text emphasizes their simultaneity; Bach, therefore, not only omits the recitative just cited but also adds the word "zugleich" to Knauer's text for the tenth movement as well, thereby contradicting the "zuförderst . . . und dann" of Knauer's text: "Gib mir dabei, mein Gott! ein Samariterherz, daß ich *zugleich* den Nächsten liebe."[35] And in Petzoldt's view these changes fit with the musical character of the opening movement of Cantata 77, which likewise brings out the simultaneity of the two kinds of love, and suggests that Bach himself might have made or at least have had input into the textual revisions to the Knauer original.[36]

On the basis of his analysis of Bach's (or his librettist's) other revisions to Knauer's text Petzoldt argues very convincingly that in Bach's text the commandment to love God and one's neighbor is not exclusively "Law," as it is for Knauer, but "an expression of the will of God for community with humankind" (Bach's first recitative).[37] Apart from omitting Knauer's first recitative, Bach dispenses with Knauer's interrupting the first aria after its "A" section by the second recitative (the first in Bach's text), after which, in Knauer's text the "B" and "A" sections return. Bach produces instead a recitative–aria succession that emphasizes the role of God's Spirit in affecting the believer's ability to love God. In the seventh line of the recitative Bach substitutes "Geist" for Knauer's "Kraft":

So muß es sein!	So it must be!
Gott will das Herz vor sich alleine haben.	God will have the heart for Himself alone.
Man muß den Herrn von ganzer Seelen	One must choose the Lord with one's entire soul
Zu seiner Lust erwählen	For one's joy
Und sich nicht mehr erfreun,	And never rejoice more,
Als wenn er das Gemüte	Than when He ignites the spirit
Durch seinen *Geist* entzündt,	Through His Holy Spirit,
Weil wir nur seiner Huld und Güte	Because only through His favor and goodness
Alsdenn erst recht versichert sind.	Are we then completely secure.

Then in the aria Bach's text replaces the theologically neutral word "Glück" by "Gebot" —"Laß mich doch *dieses Glück* erkennen" (Knauer) versus "Laß mich doch *dein Gebot* erkennen" (Bach):

Mein Gott, ich liebe dich von Herzen,	My God, I love You from the heart,
Mein ganzes Leben hangt dir an.	My entire life depends on You.
Laß mich doch dein Gebot erkennen	Let me however recognize Your commandment
Und in Liebe so entbrennen,	And so burn with love,
Daß ich dich ewig lieben kann!	That I may love You eternally!

In Bach's setting the aria does not return to its opening lines but is through-composed, thereby placing its theological weight on the believer's prayer in the "B" section ("Laß mich doch dein Gebot erkennen . . ."), whose description of "burning" love follows from the "igniting" of the believer's soul ("Gemüte") by the Spirit in the recitative. Bach's changes therefore bring out that it is through God's Spirit that the believer receives the ability to recognize and carry out God's commandment of love—the "new law" given by Jesus—on which his salvation depends. As we will see, Bach's musical treatment of this movement mirrors the intent behind the text revisions.

In the second recitative Bach's (and Knauer's) text turns to love of one's neighbor, expressed in terms of the parable of the Good Samaritan and clearly set forth in the final lines as the key to the believer's hopes for eternal life:

Gib mir dabei, mein Gott!	Give me, my God!
Ein Samariterherz,	The heart of a Good Samaritan,
Daß ich zugleich den Nächsten liebe	That I may at the same time love my neighbor
Und mich bei seinem Schmerz	And in his pain
Auch über ihn betrübe,	Trouble myself also for him,
Damit ich nicht bei ihm vorübergeh	So that I do not pass him by
Und ihn in seiner Not nicht lasse.	And do not abandon him in his need.
Gib, daß ich Eigenliebe hasse,	Grant that I hate self-love,
So wirst du mir dereinst das Freudenleben	*Thus You will one day give me the life of joy*
Nach meinem Wunsch, jedoch aus Gnaden geben.	*According to my wish, but from Your grace.*

As Petzoldt points out, the principal changes in Bach's text are the aforementioned addition of the word "zugleich" and the replacing of Knauer's "einmahl" by "dereinst" in the penultimate line, a change that emphasizes the eschatological character of the final lines.[38]

In the aria that follows, Bach's changes further strengthen the idea that the believer's ability to fulfill God's commandment to love depends on God's helping him to overcome his human nature:

Knauer	*Bach*
Ach, es bleibt mit meiner Liebe	Ach, es bleibt *in* meiner Liebe
Lauter Unvollkommenheit.	Lauter Unvollkommenheit!
Oeffters hab ich wohl den Willen,	Hab ich oftmals gleich den Willen,
Doch das Gute zu erfüllen,	*Was Gott saget*, zu erfüllen,
Fehlet mir zu jederzeit.	Fehlt mirs doch *an Möglichkeit*.
Da Capo	Da Capo
(Alas, there remains with my love	(Alas, there remains in my love
Pure incompleteness.	Pure incompleteness!
Often I have certainly the will,	Even if I often have the will
But to accomplish the right thing	To accomplish what God says,
Is lacking to me at all times.	I am lacking, however, in the capacity.
Da Capo	Da Capo

The changes I have indicated in Bach's text emphasize that imperfection is a part of the nature of human love itself, that fulfilling God's commandment to love, just like fulfilling the Law in general, is beyond the human capacity. These last changes are of the utmost importance in the theology of Cantata 77 and all the more so in light of the ending of the work. That is, in choosing to end "Du sollt Gott, deinen Herren, lieben" with a chorale verse sung to the melody of "Ach Gott, vom Himmel sieh' darein," and especially in one that is set in the *cantus mollis* and with the particular harmonization that ends Cantata 77 (see the following chapter), Bach can be considered to have intended that the idea of human imperfection remain at the end. Even more than was the case with the final chorale of Cantata 46, the ending of Cantata 77 does not "overcome" its emphasis on humanity's need for God's intervention but ends with a prayer to God that is permeated by the idea of human weakness. Bach's use of the melody of "Ach Gott, vom Himmel sieh' darein" with a "weak" ending similar to that of the opening movement of Cantata 153 is very telling in this respect—especially since there are no further movements to provide a more optimistic character, as there are in the latter cantata.

Since Bach included the music of the final chorale without indicating the verse he intended as its text, we cannot be certain exactly how Cantata 77 would have ended. Two chorale verses have been supplied by the old and new Bach editions, respectively. The first is the eighth strophe of the chorale "Wenn einer alle Ding verstünd" by David Denicke (1657) and the second, also by Denicke (1657), the eighth strophe of the chorale "O Gottes Sohn, Herr Jesu Christ." The second line of the former verse is sometimes varied as indicated in my parentheses:

Du stellst, Herr Jesu, selber dich (Herr Jesu! du stellst selbsten dich) Zum Vorbild wahrer Liebe; Verleih', daß, dem zu folge, ich Die Lieb' am Nächsten übe; Daß ich bey allem, wo ich kan, Lieb', treu und hülfe Jedermann, Wie ichs mir wünsch, erweise!	Herr, durch den Glauben wohn in mir, Laß ihn sich immer stärken, Daß er sey fruchtbar für und für, Und reich in guten Werken: Daß er sey thätig durch die Lieb, Mit Freuden und Geduld sich üb, Dem Nächsten fort zu dienen.

Werner Neumann argues, on the basis of text–music relationships, that the first of these verses is not a good match and offers the second as substitute.[39] However, although the ending of "Herr, durch den Glauben wohn in mir" fits well with the remainder of the text of Cantata 77, the chorale from which it comes, "O Gottes Sohn, Herr Jesu Christ," deals with faith and not particularly with love of God or one's neighbor; it was categorized by Freylinghausen, for example, under the heading "Vom wahren Glauben." But "Du stellst, Herr Jesu, selber dich" belongs to the category "Von der brüderlichen und allgemeinen Liebe," which is more appropriate to Cantata 77.

In the theological context suggested by the aria "Ach, es bleibt in meiner Liebe lauter Unvollkommenheit," however, neither of these verses strikes the right tone, since neither contains any reference to God's commandment or to the inability of humankind to fulfill it. In keeping with the aforementioned parallel between the cantata's weak final cadence and that of the opening movement of Cantata 153, Bach must have intended that Cantata 77 end with a chorale verse that emphasized human weakness in its final line. And in this light a verse from another chorale suggested by Martin Petzoldt on the basis of the theological content of Cantata 77 fits perfectly. Petzoldt offers the eleventh strophe of the anonymous chorale "Herr, deine Recht und dein Gebot," a twelve-strophe chorale on the Ten Commandments that is metrically identical to "Ach Gott, vom Himmel sieh' darein," although it is not known to have been associated with that melody.[40] The verse in question goes as follows:

Ach Herr, ich wollte ja dein Recht Und deinen heilgen Willen,	Ah Lord, I would certainly fulfill Your right and Your holy will,

Wie mir gebührt, als deinem Knecht,	As befits me, as Your servant,
Ohn Mangel gern erfüllen,	Willingly and without lack,
So fühl ich doch, was mir gebricht,	But I feel, however, what fails me,
Und wie ich das Geringste nicht	And how I am unable to do
Vermag aus eignen Kräften.	The least thing of my own power.

In a brief but very perspicacious commentary on the theological suitability of this verse to Cantata 77 Petzoldt points out that its emphasis on God's "Recht und Willen" is mirrored in the text of Cantata 77 by changes to Knauer's original text such as the aforementioned substitution of "Gebot" for "Glück" in the first aria, while the progression of ideas toward the end of the cantata—especially the incompleteness of human love and the incapacity of the human will in relation to God's—continues from the aria to the verse in question. Even individual words of the chorale—"erfüllen" and "aus eignen Kräften"—echo from the preceding aria and the opening chorus, while the "Willen"/"erfüllen" rhyme also appears in the second aria. "Herr, deine Recht und dein Gebot" was closely associated with those Sundays in the liturgical year, including the thirteenth Sunday after Trinity, for which "Dies sind die heil'gen zehn Gebot" and "Es ist das Heil uns kommen hier" (two chorales that center on the fundamental relationship of Law and Gospel) were also designated. In the Freylinghausen *Geistreiches Gesang-Buch* it appears under the category "Vom Christlichen Leben und Wandel," which is the category of hymns that the Vopelius chorale collection indicates for the eighteenth Sunday after Trinity (i.e., the Sunday with the parallel Gospel reading from Matthew on the "great commandment"). We might speculate that in revising the Knauer text for Cantata 77 Bach, or his librettist, chose not to end the work with the last two verses of "Dies sind die heil'gen zehn Gebot," as Knauer's text did, because the ending had been conceived as emphasizing human weakness to a greater extent than Knauer's. Luther's chorale had already been made the basis of the opening movement, and in that movement, as we will see, Bach's setting brings out the simultaneity of God's demand for justice and humanity's innate weakness to an extraordinary degree. A setting of the same chorale, especially one that would have to be less complex than the opening movement, could never bring out the reality of human weakness to the same extent. But a minor-mode chorale with the capacity to confirm the believer's awareness of his weakness and inability to carry out God's will by means of an even greater disparity between the correct modal final and the perception of that final as an incomplete ending—that is, a dominant—would provide the perfect solution. And if that chorale were, like "Dies sind die heil'gen zehn Gebot," a multistrophe paraphrase of the Ten Commandments with a two-strophe summarizing conclusion, it would closely parallel the way that Knauer's original text had ended. Bach's not writing in the text for the final chorale might in that case reflect, inadvertently, the search for such a chorale—even a degree of uncertainty or ambiguity regarding the fact that the most suitable chorale would have to be sung to a melody not normally associated with it. Bach's beginning to write out another version of the final chorale immediately following the one we have might well have reflected a momentary degree of indecision regarding, one would guess, the prominent incompleteness of the ending. Perhaps he intended that the final *two* verses of "Herr, deine Recht und dein Gebot" be heard in succession, the latter with a somewhat different harmonization; ending the cantata with that verse would put the acknowledgment of human weakness of the preceding verse in the context of a prayer to God for aid in carrying out the commandment to love:

Drum gib du mir von deinem Thron,	Therefore, give me from Your throne,
Gott Vater, Gnad und Stärke;	God the Father, grace and strength;
Verleih, o Jesu, Gottes Sohn,	Grant, O Jesu, Son of God,
Daß ich thu rechte Werke;	That I do good works;
O heil'ger Geist, hilf, daß ich dich	O Holy Spirit, help that I
Von ganzem Herzen, und als mich,	From the whole heart, and as myself,
Ohn falsch, den Nächsten liebe.	Without falsehood, love my neighbor.

This verse has the great advantage of ending with three lines that place the paraphrase of the Ten Commandments on which its second through tenth verses center in the context of the "great commandment"; that is, it combines the Ten Commandments and the great commandment just as does the opening chorus of the cantata. That Bach's work ended in exactly this manner, appropriate though it is from the standpoint of the text, must, however, remain speculative. It is difficult to imagine that Bach would have repeated the unique harmonization of the final movement of Cantata 77 for a second successive verse (this might be the reason behind Bach's starting to copy the chorale a second time). In the final analysis, it is less important, perhaps, to discover the exact verse intended by Bach than to recognize that Cantata 77 describes, from beginning to end, a progression from God's commandment to love as the summary of the Law to humanity's awareness that carrying out that commandment lies beyond its unaided capacity; to the extent that humankind can emulate God's love it is inseparable from love of one's neighbor.

We have, in fact, arrived at the point at which Bach's music is needed in order for us to feel secure about the intended theological character of Cantata 77. And while the music may not provide unequivocal answers to questions such as the text of the final chorale, it certainly offers us an unusual amount of detail that must be considered to have been theologically motivated. In the contexts provided by the preceding chapters, analysis of the music and the text together will, I hope, reveal dimensions to Bach's intent for "Du sollt Gott, deinen Herren, lieben" that will enable us to reexperience its "message" both aesthetically and, in the best sense of the term, historically.

EIGHT

"Du sollt Gott, deinen Herren, lieben"

An Analysis of Cantata 77

OWING TO ITS PROMINENT NUMEROLOGICAL and canonic features, most of which involve the melody of the chorale "Dies sind die heil'gen zehn Gebot," the opening chorus of Cantata 77 has been the object of musicological attention for many years, whereas the remaining movements have not.[1] Bach, as is well known, set forth the melody associated with Luther's chorale as a canon in augmentation between the uppermost and lowermost instruments of the orchestra, the *tromba da tirarsi* and the *basso continuo*, the former in D Mixolydian (beginning from the pitch d") and moving basically in quarter notes and the latter in G Mixolydian (beginning from G) and featuring half-note motion. As described in the preceding chapter, Bach divides the melody into five rather than four or six phrases, beginning the fifth phrase at the point where the third degree of the Mixolydian scale is flattened, from f♯" to f♮" in the trumpet and B to B♭ in the *basso continuo*. This aspect of the movement not only separates the melodic ascent from d" to g" (G to c) from the remainder of the final phrase, so that its identity as a unit common to phrases 1, 2, and 4 is all the clearer but also provides the numerological basis for the augmentation canon between trumpet and *continuo*, whose ten phrases undoubtedly symbolize the Ten Commandments. And it emphasizes the minor character of the flattening effect toward the ending of the melody (in this five-phrase version of the chorale the final phrase simply moves between f" and d" [B♭ and G]). In addition, Bach follows each of the five canonic phrases of the chorale in the *tromba da tirarsi* by another trumpet solo made up of one or more phrases of the chorale; since these add an extra five (noncanonic) entrances of the trumpet, the trumpet alone also has ten solos. And Bach prolongs the final G of the last phrase of the chorale in the *basso continuo* for ten measures, bringing in the tenth of the trumpet solos above it; this time the trumpet plays the entire chorale without breaks between the phrases, and Bach adds two more repeated tones at the end, thereby extending the chorale for the full ten measures (plus an upbeat of three quarter notes). Each of the five "extra" or noncanonic

Table 8.1 Cantata 77, outline of opening movement.

Tromba da tirarsi (5+[5])	*Bassetchen* (5)	*Basso continuo* chorale (5)	Chorus (9? or 10?)	Key
	1) 1–8 (**R:** I)			C–G
1) **8–10: C1 (D)**		1) **9–15: C1 (G)**	8–15	G–C
2) [15–17]: C1 (C)				F
	2) 15–24 (**R:** I)			F–C
3) **22–24: C2 (D)**				
		2) **24–31: C2 (G)**		C
4) [28–30]: C1 (G)			22–31 (22–28 and 29–31)	C
	3) 31–39 (**R:** I/V) and 39–41			G–a
5) **39–41: C3 (D)**				C
			31–41	G–C
		3) **41–47: C3 (G)**	41–47	C–F
6) [43–47]: C1, 3 (G,C)				F
	4) 47–54 (**R:** I/V)		47–54	B♭–g
7) **53–54: C4 (D)**				g
8) [56–58]: C1 (G)		4) **54–58: C4 (G)**		c
	5) 58–63 (**R:** I/V)		54–63	g–d
9) **63–65: C5 (D)**				
		5) **64–77 [64–67 and 68–77]: C5 (G)**	63–67	c
10) [67–77]: C1–5 (D)			67–72	c
			72–77	G

Numbers in parentheses following column headings indicate the number of entries or sections. Thus in column 1 5+[5] indicates five canonic and five noncanonic entries of the *tromba da tirarsi.* Boldface in columns one and three indicates canonic entries. In columns 1 and 3 C1, C2, and so forth indicate choral phrases. The bracketed entries in column 1 are extra (noncanonic) choral phrases. Parentheses following the five entries in column 2 indicate that each of the sections in question contains a version of the ritornello material (mm. 1–8 of the movement), either for instruments alone (R: I) or for instruments and chorus (R: I/V). Tonalities in parenthesis in columns 1 and 3—for example, (D)—indicate the Mixolydian mode of the choral phrase(s) in question and not necessarily the key of the passage. Column 5 indicates tonal centers.

trumpet solos features a statement of the first phrase of the chorale, which therefore sounds five additional times; the first four of these (sometimes transposed) lend emphasis to important cadential points in the structure of the movement (to F in mm. 15–17, C in mm. 28–31, F in mm. 43–45, and C minor in mm. 56–58). Since the third of the "extra" trumpet solos features a statement of phrase 3 as well, and the fifth solo includes phrases 2 through 5, the five extra solos encompass a total of ten chorale phrases. And beneath the final trumpet solo Bach divides the chorus into two units of five measures each, the first one introducing the text that refers to love of one's neighbor and the second restoring the principal theme and tonal center of the movement after their absence in the preceding measures. As Table 8.1 makes clear, these permutational aspects of the movement control a great deal of its overall design.

In addition to the devices just described is another that has not been taken up in commentary on the movement: the regular alternation of high and low bass parts or, in the terms of the time, of *bassetchen* and *basso continuo*. Bach uses this device in a considerable number of works to represent both the idea of "above" and "below" as the spheres of God and humankind and the relationship of God's wrathful and merciful sides, His demand for justice and His love.[2] In Cantata 77 its use is one of the most distinctive in all his music. It was perhaps derived from the pitch (high/low) and melodic-directional (ascent/descent) qualities in the chorale melody. Since there are basically only two kinds of thematic material in the movement—the Ten Commandments chorale itself in the trumpet and *basso continuo* and the material derived from the chorale melody, which is shared by the chorus and the strings—the *bassetchen* line, played by the viola, is associated with the chorus/string material. Another aspect of the layout of the movement as a whole, therefore, is the alternation of five *bassetgen* segments with five that feature the chorale in the *basso continuo* (see columns 2 and 3 of Table 8.1).

But now there are differences from Bach's usual treatment of *bassetgen* lines. Normally such passages, and *all* those movements that feature the *bassetgen* texture throughout, are performed without *basso continuo*. When the *bassetto* alternates with the normal low bass, as in the first movement of Cantata 135, the latter always has a realized continuo part, while the former does not. In Cantata 77, however, when the chorale *cantus firmus* sounds in the *basso continuo* (i.e., in the instrumental bass line but not in the bass of the choir), its part contains no figured bass symbols and was presumably played by the violone and doubled at the unison by the organ. On the other hand, the first two *bassetgen* passages—the instrumental introduction to the movement (mm. 1–8) and the first instrumental interlude to appear between entrances of the chorale in the *basso continuo* (mm.15–24)—are both scored for two violins and viola, with the viola line doubled at the unison by a fully figured *bassetgen* organ part (Ex. 8.1). Since this eight-measure unit introduces the basic thematic material of the choral passages and recurs regularly, forming the core of the five *bassetchen* passages, it might almost be designated a ritornello.[3] For the first twenty-four measures of the movement, therefore, the differentiation of *bassetchen* and low *basso continuo* parts and the separation of instrumental and choral segments are greatest. And the realization of the *bassetchen* line by the organ and the (presumed) absence of such realization for the *basso continuo* chorale phrases represents a reversal of Bach's usual practice.

The third, fourth, and fifth *bassetgen* segments, however, sound along with the chorus (doubled by strings and utilizing the "ritornello" material). In them the *basso continuo* part is notated entirely in the alto clef *without* figured bass symbols. In these passages the *basso continuo* part doubles the viola even when the bass voice is present. Sometimes it provides a "free" bass line to the upper voices and instruments; sometimes it sounds in unison with the bass, sometimes an octave higher. As a result, when the *basso continuo* chorale is not sounding, the *bassetchen* version of the continuo becomes a high- or middle-register part in the texture. No other Bach work features a *bassetchen* part of this kind. Since the figured bass supplied for the two instrumental "ritornelli" is not carried forward to the remaining *bassetgen* passages, it is likely that in this movement Bach intended no continuo realization at all apart from the two places where the instruments play alone. And since the *bassetchen* line remains within the viola register even though the chorus intermingles

Example 8.1. Cantata 77: Beginning of opening movement

high and low registers, its role as a true bass part is clear only in the two instrumental passages that appear near the beginning of the movement (mm. 1–8 and 15–24). After that the *bassetgen* part and the ritornello merge into the ensemble as a whole and the exact definition of the ritornello and the bass line becomes less clear.

Precise interpretation of Bach's intention is elusive, yet the highly detailed nature of the various musical symbolisms in this movement suggests that a specific intent underlies the relationship of *bassetto* and *basso continuo*. Certainly, keeping the instrumental bass line at high pitch, except for those points where it plays the chorale, causes the latter to stand out clearly from the texture, lending greater audibility to the canonic, numerological basis of the structure. Since the low-pitch *basso continuo* line is confined to the rhythmically augmented chorale phrases and thus entirely independent of the choral basses, presumably it and the *tromba da tirarsi* (which is also entirely independent of the choral parts, with one very brief and significant exception just before the end) represent God's control of the spheres of "above" and "below" as well as His demand for strict justice (the canon). Whenever the chorale sounds in the *basso continuo*, therefore, an additional harmonic "foundation" is unnecessary. Since the choral passages all feature variations of the chorale melody as their principal thematic material, they mirror the fact that their text represents an interpretation or summary of the Law. That is, they depart from the "strictness" of the outermost parts in order to provide a more "human"—that is, variable—perspective. By separating the high and low bass parts and the vocal and instrumental textures at the outset, then merging them and casting the *basso continuo* in such an intermediary role Bach's texture suggests—as do the overlapping of canonic and free parts, even of formal divisions in the movement (see Ex. 8.1)—the increasing interaction or *Übereinstimmung* of God and humankind. This quality presumably relates to the fact that Bach's text represents what Martin Petzoldt calls the simultaneity of the two kinds of love and the "expression of the will of God for community with humankind."[4]

Since the canonic and numerological aspects of the first movement center around the Ten Commandments chorale, which appears without its text, they suggest an association with God's demand for strict, even abstract, justice. The text of the movement, from the twenty-seventh verse of Luke's Gospel for the day—"Du sollt Gott, deinen Herren, lieben von ganzem Herzen, von ganzer Seele, von allen Kräften und von ganzem Gemüte und deinen Nächsten als dich selbst"—affirms, however, that the more personal New Testament words of love for God and one's neighbor should be understood as a summary of the meaning of the Ten Commandments. Bach, therefore, expresses the relationship between the Law (i.e., the Ten Commandments) and its summary in the two principal commandments given by Jesus as one in which the Ten Commandments chorale and the various canonic and numerological devices associated with it in the instrumental parts constitute a framework and a background, so to speak, for the Gospel text and its "freer" musical treatment in the chorus. In this light, the form of the movement has two distinct aspects, the one defined by the canonic alternation of chorale phrases in D and G Mixolydian between the outermost voices—the abstract layout of the work, so to speak—and the other associated with the chorus, its variations of the chorale phrases, and deviations from their strict pattern. Instead of forming a succession in which the message of the Gospel replaces that of the Law (as in the "Actus Tragicus," for example), this movement represents the Law and the Gospel in a complementary simultaneous relationship, with Luther's chorale as their principal bond.

The Lutheran understanding of the roles of Law and Gospel in justification lies, of course, behind Bach's musico-theological intentions in Cantata 77.[5] In choosing the melody of the chorale "Dies sind die heil'gen zehn Gebot" as the basis of the opening movement of Cantata 77, and in setting it as a canon in augmentation between the highest and lowest voices of the instrumental ensemble, Bach perhaps intended to represent both God's all-encompassing nature and the role of the Law as the mirror of His demand for strict justice. At the same time, however, other aspects of the structure of the opening movement and of the design of the cantata as a whole reflect humanity's response to God's commandment. And in the Lutheran view, as given in the final two strophes of Luther's chorale, that response was first and foremost one of *Sündenerkenntnis* (recognition of sin). In this light, the "proper work" of the Law was to crush the sinner with the awareness of his inadequacy to justify himself before God. Only after that work was accomplished could he accept the meaning of the Gospel—the love that prompted Jesus' atonement on his behalf—and respond in turn with love of God. As we have seen, the dynamic of Law and Gospel, the destruction/restoration idea, was one that Bach often translates into one of descent followed by ascent or, in terms of key relationships, of modulation in the flat direction followed by restoration of the original key. And this is exactly the dynamic of the opening movement of Cantata 77, which begins in what was probably intended to be G Mixolydian and moves more and more into flat regions until it reaches G minor in measure 54 and C minor in measure 58, returning to G Mixolydian only in the final measures of the movement. Against the Mixolydian framework of the outermost voices the chorus seems to "drift" into flatter and flatter regions, turning to minor keys as well and substantially transforming the character of the original thematic material in the process. In this sense God's demands from humanity—represented in the canonic voices and their D/G Mixolydian-mode framework—are unchanging, while humanity's response is one that becomes "weaker" as the movement goes on, especially as the text speaks of the human attributes of heart, soul, strength, and spirit. The modulations to g and c represent the point where the disparity between God's demands and the human attributes that are required to fulfill them is greatest (see the following discussion). It might be viewed as simultaneously the climax and the "nadir" of the movement. The lessening of that disparity by means of the coming together of the canonic voices and the chorus to articulate the final cadence to G coincides with the shift to love of one's neighbor *as oneself.* It still leaves room for the view that the believer's "restoration" is not complete; thus, Alfred Dürr, in maintaining that the movement is in the key of C, and therefore that the final cadence is on the dominant, implies that not only are the aforementioned human qualities inadequate to lead to love of God, but also even loving one's neighbor as oneself does not fully provide for the believer's salvation.[6]

As the first recitative and aria make clear, only the "igniting" of the human spirit by that of God enables the believer to recognize God's *Gebot*—that is, the commandment to love God and one's neighbor—and to "burn" with the love that provides the key to his hopes for eternal life. The second recitative then specifies the inner love of one's neighbor—that is, the *Samariterherz*—and hatred of self-love (*Eigenliebe*) as the qualities that lead to salvation. The close of this recitative can be said to answer the believer's prayer in the first aria that he "recognize" God's commandment; it is, from the tonal standpoint, the most positive point in the cantata, providing for the only time in the work a secure and unquestioned close in G. This sequence of movements, therefore, completes the positive meaning behind the opening chorus. All three refer to the human heart, first as the human attribute that God demands ("So muß es sein! Gott will das Herz vor sich alleine haben"), second as the quality that most represents the bond between human nature and God ("Mein Gott, ich liebe dich von Herzen, mein ganzes Leben hängt dir an"—and third as the *Samariterherz*, love of one's neighbor, which is the proof, so to speak, of true love of God. From the C major of the first recitative, which echoes the human qualities of the opening movement as it confirms the "subdominant" tendency of its final cadence, the sequence of keys moves through A minor (the first aria), E minor, and B minor, before settling on G in association with the anticipated *Freudenleben* that God will grant those who overcome their *Eigenliebe*. The "ascending" tonal progression from a to G has a counterpart within the design of the first aria itself, as it, too, anticipates eternal life as the fulfillment of the believer's love: "daß ich dich ewig lieben kann."

After the G major of the second recitative, however, the second aria expresses sorrow over the incapacity of humankind to fulfill God's commandment. And the tonality now moves one degree flatter than the first aria: to D Dorian/minor. The stage is set, so to speak, for the shift to the *cantus mollis* of the final movement and what is surely the "weakest" of all Bach's cantata endings from the tonal point of view. Cantata 77 as a whole, therefore, describes a progression from God's demands from humanity, embodied in the paradoxical commandment to love, to the inability of humankind to carry this commandment out unaided. The ending of the cantata should undoubtedly be understood as a representation of humanity's need for that aid, and for that purpose no melody is better suited than that of "Ach Gott, vom Himmel sieh' darein." Bach's *cantus mollis* setting of the final chorale seems, therefore, to end Cantata 77 with renewal of the appeal for mercy (*Kyrieleis*) that ends every verse of Luther's chorale. As we will see, Bach foreshadows the dynamic of the cantata as a whole—a progression from God's *Gebot* to acknowledgment of human weakness—in that of the opening chorus.

COMMENTARY ON THE INDIVIDUAL MOVEMENTS

Chorus, "Du sollt Gott, deinen Herren, lieben": Tonal Design

Martin Petzoldt's remark that in Cantata 77 the simultaneity of love of God and love of one's neighbor represents the "expression of the will of God for community with humankind" is unconsciously reminiscent of Johann Melchior Göze's funeral oration for Werckmeister.[7] Göze's analogies of the consonance of major and minor and the harmony of God and humanity, of the Mixolydian mode and the *cantus durus* as

Example 8.2. Cantata 77: First choral segment, mm. 8–15 of first movement

manifestations of God's wrathful nature, the *cantus mollis* as the reverse, represent a simple form of musical punning on musical terms that crops up occasionally in nearly all eras of music history and that may or may not express something meaningful about either music in general or individual compositions. Composers have sometimes introduced such devices into their music without necessarily intending anything momentous. And Bach might or might not have read similar analogies; it is perhaps unlikely that he would have taken them very seriously. But, as it happens, the set of ideas that Göze alludes to has affinities with both the theological and the musical character of Cantata 77; and behind his naive-sounding remarks lie fundamental musical qualities that also underlie Bach's work. Those qualities derive, of course, from the modal and hexachordal theory of the sixteenth century and their reinterpretation in the seventeenth. In the first movement of "Du sollt Gott, deinen Herren, lieben" Bach seized on the opportunity of amplifying the motivic and tonal properties of "Dies sind die heil'gen zehn Gebot" so as to project a sense of the God/humankind, above/below dualisms that underlie its text and that of the cantata as a whole.

—*continued*

In Bach's interpretation of the Ten Commandments chorale the thematic and tonal qualities of the melody often interact so closely as to be virtually inseparable, deriving as they do from the aforementioned high/low, ascent/descent, and sharp/flat dualisms. To begin the ritornello and all the chorus entries except one (the point at which the text "und deinen Nächsten als dich selbst" enters in measure 67), Bach simply takes the rising diatonic fourth of the first phrase of the chorale melody and displaces its repeated tones from the initial pitch to the fourth one. At the outset this pattern is associated with the initial words of Luke's text: "Du sollt Gott, deinen Herren lie[ben]." This he follows by a decorated *descent* ("[lie]ben von ganzem Herzen"). The descent part of the theme begins with a circle-of-fifths pattern made up of rising fourths and falling fifths in alternation ("von ganzem Her[zen]"), at the end of which the word "Herzen" picks up on a melodic descent figure derived from "lieben von," extending it down the scale in intervals ranging from a third to a sixth (Ex. 8.2). In this respect the ritornello/chorus theme might be thought to mirror the manner in which love bridges the distance between God (the straightforward ascending fourth) and humankind (the decorated descent), especially since the first half of the

Example 8.2. (*continued*)

theme is directly derived from the chorale and is basically unvarying, while the latter half is generally variable in character.

Bach designed this theme very carefully so as to aid in articulating what is, along with the canonic and numerological aspects of the movement, its most striking large-scale feature: the progressive flattening of the tonality and its consequently turning to minor, so that by the time the fourth phrase of the chorale *cantus firmus* sounds in the trumpet the key on which it cadences is G *minor* (m. 54), after which the canonic augmentation of the same phrase in the *basso continuo* leads to C minor (m. 58). In this way Bach interprets the traditional "subdominant" tonal tendency of the Mixolydian mode in terms of the subdominant *minor*, making that shift to minor the outcome of the progressively flattening sequence of pitches in the melody of the Ten Commandments chorale and its amplification by the canon at the fifth below. In this Bach seized on a subtle allegorical potential within the theme itself. Its basis is the fact that the affirmative-sounding rising fourth with which it begins is at the same time a tonal motion from the "tonic" to the "subdominant," and it can be viewed, in fact, as initiating the flattening motion within the theme and the sugges-

tion of G minor at the end. In this light, the inability of the believer to live up to God's commandment is built into the chorale melody, so to speak, from the outset. After the cadence to the flat seventh degree of the scale at the end of phrase 3 (to F in the G Mixolydian melody), the return to the initial rising fourth in phrase 4 no longer projects the same tone of affirmation. In the chorale melody the change from b to b♭ with which it continues is the key to the shift in quality; the melody could be interpreted as ending in G minor or transposed Dorian or as turning toward F and ending on the dominant (depending on the harmonization). In other words, the descent from b♭ to g at the end of the melody may create the effect, by hindsight, that the b♮ of phrase 4 sounds like a *raised* pitch (i.e., a secondary dominant harmonically) rather than an essential tone of the scale, that role now taken over by the b♭. In the first movement of Cantata 77, Bach's shifting the tonality in the flat direction after the cadence to F at the end of phrase 3 (mm. 45–47) makes the point that the rising-fourth ascent of phrase 4 is now transformed, as it were, by the flattening of the harmony. The arrival at C minor is in a sense the climax of the movement, the point at which the trumpet reaches its highest tone and the rhythmic activity of the chorus is at its greatest. Its role in the allegorical design of the movement is to create a subdominant/minor region from which the restoration of G emerges at the last possible moment in conjunction with the insight that love of God and love of one's neighbor *as oneself* are inseparable.

In order to understand how Bach creates this design, we must trace its unfolding throughout the movement, beginning with the aforementioned variant of the chorale in the chorus/ritornello theme. The separate fifth levels suggested by the progressively flattening sequence of pitches within the chorale melody itself (i.e., d", g", c", and f" in the D Mixolydian of the trumpet, G, c, F, and B♭ in the G Mixolydian of the *basso continuo*) influenced not only the fact that Bach set his canon at the fifth below but also the manner in which he derived the principal theme of the instrumental and choral passages from the first phrase of the chorale and his decision to answer it in an imitative voice at the fourth above (or fifth below). In the chorus theme, Bach's displacing the repeated tones of the initial rising fourth from the first to the fourth tone emphasizes the role of the reiterated fourth tone as a point of arrival within the theme (a downbeat coinciding with the words "deinen Herren"), while its overlapping with the initial tone of the next entry, a fourth higher in the answering voice—g'–a'–b'–c" in the second violin followed by c"–d"–e"–f" in the first violin—outlines the G Mixolydian scale, bringing out the division of that scale into two identically patterned tetrachords (g–a–b–c' and c'–d'–e'–f'), the first moving from the "tonic" (G) to the fourth degree of the scale (C) and the second continuing from the fourth to the flat seventh (F).

The pattern just described is disarmingly simple, but Bach makes the tonal relationships it suggests serve elaborate structural purposes. The ritornello itself does not clearly articulate a single key but, rather, remains basically in a diatonic white-note region (analogous to the *cantus naturalis*) that nevertheless appears to lead toward G just as the trumpet enters with the first phrase of the chorale in D Mixolydian, sounding, of course, like a motion from dominant to tonic in G. Beneath it the bass voice begins the first chorus entry with the tones d–e–f♯–g and the tenor answers immediately with g–a–b–c' after the pattern of the ritornello but transposed at the fifth, just as the *basso continuo* begins its statement of the first chorale phrase in augmentation from the tone G. As the trumpet phrase moves upward through f♯" to g" the circle-of-fifths element in the chorus theme brings in the pitch f♮ in the bass (anticipated in the second violin) in preparation for a second set of chorus entries, now g'–a'–b'–c" in the soprano followed by c'–d'–e'–f' in the alto. This flattening of the harmony has the effect of amplifying the G–C–F motion of the initial set of entries in the ritornello. And to bring it out all the more Bach introduces the pitch b♭' in the soprano and b♭ in the tenor in measure 14 before the first chorus segment closes on C. Then he brings back the ritornello transposed at the fourth (i.e., from C to F) and reintroduces simultaneously with it the first phrase of the chorale in the trumpet (the first of the "free" trumpet entries), now transposed down a tone (i.e., two fifths) from D Mixolydian (or G) to C Mixolydian (or F).

Thus, Bach expands the rising fourth of phrase 1 into a broader circle-of-fifths motion than that of the thematic entries of the ritornello, utilizing *three* transpositional levels of the phrase, in D, G, and C Mixolydian, corresponding to the three hexachordal levels of the *cantus naturalis* (or to major scales on G, C, and F). The ritornello sounds at the two principal hexachordal levels, the *naturalis* and *mollis*. Overlapped with the ending of the second statement of the ritornello, Bach brings in phrase 2 of the chorale in the trumpet along with the second entrance of the chorus. Now the fifth relationship between the canonic voices articulates a return to C; and to confirm it Bach sounds the first phrase of the chorale in the trumpet again, now in G Mixolydian (i.e., ascending from g' to c", the second noncanonic trumpet solo), leading to a C major cadence on the first beat of measure 31. From this standpoint, the first thirty measures of the movement can be said to articulate a tonal equivalent of the *cantus naturalis*, beginning from the C hexachord and outlining a G–C–F motion that leads to the transposition of the ritornello to F (or C Mixolydian) before returning to C. Since these first two chorale phrases have the same cadence (motion from d" to g" in the trumpet, G to c in the *basso continuo*), Bach allows the fifth relationship of the canon to define G Mixolydian in the *cantus naturalis* as the principal mode (creating to this point the effect that C is the principal key).

For the first thirty measures of the movement, therefore, the G–C–F motion of the tonality is "contained" within the *cantus naturalis* and the key of C, whereas after measure 30 Bach widens the tonal scope so as to delineate a broad sharp–flat motion that leads to the *cantus mollis*. The impetus for this shift is, as we might expect, the third phrase of the chorale, which settles on the characteristic flat seventh degree of the Mixolydian scale: c" in the trumpet (m. 41), F in the *basso continuo* (mm. 45–47). We remember that Kirnberger described the most characteristic aspect of the Mixolydian mode as its cadencing on the flat seventh degree, lending it what we would call its "subdominant" tendency. The cadence to F in measure 47 is central to Bach's tonal design in this movement. From that point on Bach allows the flat shift just described to determine the course of events in the tonal structure, illustrating the idea of *durus–mollis* shift in both the archaic (sharp/flat) and modern (major/minor) meanings of those terms. In order to highlight the sharp–flat motion in terms of the two *cantus*, after the C cadence of measure 30 Bach reintroduces the ritornello material in the chorus in measure 31, transposing it now in the *sharp* direction to the G hexachord for the first time. On its previous two appearances the ritornello had shifted in the sharp direction at its close, the first time toward G to prepare the D and G Mixolydian entries of the first chorale phrase and the second time toward C to prepare the entries of the second phrase. Now, after its initial articulation of G, it shifts in the opposite direction, suggesting E minor and A minor (mm. 35–39) in preparation for the trumpet entry of the third phrase, which cadences on the flat seventh degree, C, of the D Mixolydian scale (m. 41). As it does, Bach introduces the pitch b♭' in the violins, increasing the tendency of the *basso continuo*'s answering phrase toward F (mm. 41–47). To lend added weight to this momentous event Bach brings in the first phrase of the chorale once again in the trumpet (i.e., the third noncanonic entry), transposed to C Mixolydian (i.e., F major, as in mm. 15–17, but an octave lower); its cadence to f' coincides with that of the *basso continuo* on F. And Bach holds the F in the bass for two measures, bringing in the *third* phrase of the chorale in the trumpet as well. Since he transposes it to G Mixolydian, so as also to end on f', it extends the F cadence for two additional measures (45–47). Introducing the pitch e♭' above the F harmony in measure 45, Bach anticipates the continuing motion to flats. And, beginning in measure 47, he transposes

Example 8.3. Cantata 77: First movement, mm. 47–54

the chorus/ritornello material to the two-flat (B♭) hexachord, also for the first time. The completion of this statement of the ritornello in measure 54 concides with the fourth phrase of the chorale in the trumpet, its d''–e''–f♯''–g'' ascent now cadencing in G minor (Ex. 8.3). After this, the canonic answer in the *basso continuo*, plus the return of the first phrase of the chorale in the trumpet (the fourth of the noncanonic entries, now transposed to G Mixolydian—i.e., C), leads, as mentioned, to C minor (m. 58).

In measures 1–24 Bach had used statements of the ritornello in the natural (C) and one-flat (F) tonal spheres to outline a G–C–F motion that was "contained" within the C framework of the first thirty measures. Now he uses transpositions to the one-sharp (G) and two-flat (B♭) tonal levels to amplify the sense of a broad *durus–mollis* shift leading to the minor modes of g and c. In this Bach indicates an awareness, even if purely intuitive, of the "hexachordal" background for the g–c–f–b♭ motion over the course of the G Mixolydian version of the chorale melody. That is, in the expanded harmonic view of the hexachords in the seventeenth century the basic two-system framework of the *cantus naturalis* and *cantus durus* together encompassed four hexachords, G, C, F, and B♭, the first and last of these unequivocally defining one *cantus* or the other.[8] Measures 31 to 58 of the

—continued

movement therefore expand the tonality beyond the *cantus naturalis* of the first 30 measures to the kind of *durus–mollis* shift that would in the seventeenth century have involved invoking the entire two-system framework. Behind it lies the double meaning of the two terms in Germany, sharp-major and flat-minor, the process in this movement inspired by the fact that the G Mixolydian/transposed Dorian interpretation of "Dies sind die heil'gen zehn Gebot" places the G–g shift in the context of the progressively flattening g–c–f–b♭ pitch sequence in the chorale melody.[9]

Until the C cadence of measure 31 the chorus text is confined to the line "Du sollt Gott, deinen Herren, lieben von ganzem Herzen." With the transposition of the chorus/ritornello material to G, however, Bach immediately brings in the words "von ganzer Seele," then introduces the entire part of the text that deals with love of God, "Du sollt Gott, deinen Herren, lieben von ganzem Herzen, von ganzer Seele, von allen Kräften und von ganzem Gemüte." Bach's reason for delaying the full text of the commandment to love God until this point was, perhaps, that he wanted to make an association between the list of human attributes with which it continues and the shift from the *cantus naturalis/durus* to the *cantus mollis.* The text is given complete to the word "Gemüte" at the point where the third phrase of the chorale cadences to C in the trumpet. And from the beginning of the two-flat transposition

Example 8.3. (*continued*)

of the chorus/ritornello material (m. 47) the text begins, for the only time, with "von ganzer Seele" continuing on to "Gemüte" for the G minor cadence (m. 54). Then, for the four measures in which the *basso continuo* and the trumpet lead the tonality on to C minor (mm. 55–58), Bach returns to "Du sollt Gott, deinen Herren, lieben," bringing in the first phrase of the chorale in the trumpet (mm. 56–58, the fourth of the noncanonic trumpet entries) in G Mixolydian, its rising fourth (g''–a''–b''–c''') continuing upward from the d''–e''–f♯''–g'' of the trumpet's fourth phrase to the only appearance of the highest pitch of the movement, c'''. I have described this point in the movement as simultaneously the climax and the "nadir" in part because the effect of this gesture, in combination with the arrival on C minor, is to underscore the disparity between the high ideal involved in love of God and the emphasis on human weakness that underlies the move to c. It may seem impossible to most musicians that an arrival on the minor subdominant be viewed as a climax; we are used to viewing points of climax more in conjunction with arrival on the dominant or some other, usually sharper, key that will cause the return to the tonic to effect a lessening of tension. This point in "Du sollt Gott, deinen Herren, lieben" is not of that type.

To better understand Bach's intention in shifting to C minor and the particular kinds of tension he *does* introduce at this point, we must consider an aspect of the

tonality that is implicit in a point I made in the overview of the movement. Bach intensifies the disparity between the unchanging D and G Mixolydian alternation of the canonic voices and the flatward motion of the chorus at certain points where pitch differences occur between the two. As the *basso continuo* and the C Mixolydian transposition of phrase 1 in the trumpet prepare to converge on the F major cadence of measure 45, the soprano and tenor begin the chorus theme in parallel sixths, on g' and b♭, the tenor supplying the pitch e♭' simultaneously with the arrival on F (m. 45) just after the *tromba da tirarsi* completes its ascent from c' through e♮' to f'. The effect is twofold: to point up the flattening of the harmony by causing the F to sound like a dominant and to hint at an e'/e♭' differentiation between the *tromba da tirarsi* and chorus (which will occur twice more in the movement, each one more "dissonant" than the preceding one, as the e♭" becomes more securely established). Tonally, the C Mixolydian transposition of phrase 3 in the trumpet continues, setting up the F major cadence of measure 47; but the intrusion of flat-minor qualities into the theme has taken its toll: Bach brings back the E♭ immediately afterward along with the shift to the *cantus mollis.*

E♭ remains as a fundamental pitch throughout this segment and, indeed, throughout most of the remainder of the movement. When, therefore, the fourth phrase of the chorale enters in the *tromba da tirarsi* in measures 54–55, cadencing to G minor, its e♮" sounds apart from the E♭-dominated tonality again (and to amplify that quality Bach prolongs the tone e♭" in the soprano line in measure 53, directly before the *tromba* begins its ascent, bringing it back after the cadence). Immediately following the G minor cadence (m. 54), the chorus begins what might almost be taken for the fifth statement of the ritornello/chorus material, except that the theme begins in minor rather than major and the chorus entries are built upon the fourth phrase of the chorale in the *basso continuo.* With the C minor cadence, however, the *bassetchen* texture returns for the fifth and last time (m. 58); and from here to the fifth set of canonic entries (mm. 63–64) we may speak of a greatly altered version of the ritornello material. Bach moves through g to a D minor cadence for the fifth phrase of the chorale, which begins with the f"–d"–f" alternation in the trumpet. The brief articulation of D minor lends support to the trumpet line, which for the only time in the movement sounds almost as though it might be in d, owing also to the replacing of its f♯" by f♮". But Bach forces the issue of the pitch clash by bringing in the canonic answering voice in the *basso continuo* at the distance of two quarter notes, rather than with the final tone of the trumpet, as in the previous statements. Its B♭–G–B♭ alternation then encourages him to bring back the pitch e♭" in the strings within the context of a brief B♭ canonic gesture in the violins (as well as an e♭ in the bass) immediately before the trumpet sounds its e♮" (m. 64). The effect, of course, is to render the e"–e♭" clash more dissonant than before, highlighting the independence of the trumpet from the flattening of the chorus harmony, which leads to a cadence on the dominant of C minor in measure 67, just as the tenth and last of the trumpet solos enters to play the chorale in its entirety.

From measure 67 to the end of the movement Bach holds the tone G as a ten-measure pedal in the *basso continuo*, above which the *tromba da tirarsi* plays the tenth of its solos, this time presenting the entire chorale melody in D Mixolydian, without breaks between the phrases, and with the addition of two extra d"s at the end (undoubtedly so as to make it fit within ten measures plus an upbeat). Up to measure 67 the text dealt solely with love of God; now, the canon completed, Bach introduces the second great commandment, love of one's neighbor. At the point where this takes place Bach, for the first time in the movement, begins a set of chorus entries not with the rising fourth but with a theme derived from the descent half of the principal chorus/ritornello theme for "und deinen Nächsten als dich selbst" (Ex. 8.4). That theme appears in slightly varied forms, all of which at first emphasize the semitone from b♭ to a on "Nächsten." Gradually, however, this theme changes to a form that encompasses a descent from d" through b♭' to g' for "und deinen Nächsten" followed by an ascending g'–c" fourth (through b♮', as in phrases 1, 2, and 4 of the chorale) for "als dich selbst." The descent–ascent shape of this theme mirrors the directional tendencies of the pitches b♭' and b', extending them to e♭ and e as well. This theme holds sway for the first of the two five-measure units into which Bach divides the final ten measures; it therefore comes to an end at exactly the midpoint of the third phrase of the chorale melody, its articulation of g/G coinciding with the high beginning of that phrase (g"–a"–a"–g"). The second five-measure unit (coinciding with the trumpet's drop in pitch to the flat seventh degree of the Mixolydian scale: d"–e"–d"–c") returns, as mentioned earlier, to the theme of "Du sollt Gott, deinen Herren, lieben" in its original form, but now with-

Example 8.4. Cantata 77: First movement, final eleven measures

—continued

out its descent half, and now sung to the words "und deinen Nächsten als dich selbst," thereby confirming the equivalence of love of God and love of one's neighbor as oneself.

Beneath the trumpet solo Bach contrives to make the return of the beginning of the chorus theme to its original form rise from the bass to the soprano, ascending by fifths through the tenor, alto, and soprano entries, so that the soprano sings the beginning ascent of the melody—d"–e"–f♯"–g"—simultaneously with its appearance in the fourth phrase of the trumpet. This is the only time in the movement when the chorale melody and the chorus theme derived from it coincide in this way. At this point, however, the G major harmony still sounds like the dominant of c/C; and the next two measures confirm that quality as the trumpet plays the f"–d"–f" of its final phrase (mm. 74–75) and the soprano leads the f" and d" down to c". As the trumpet settles on its final repeated d"s, however, Bach leads the harmonic coloring through the last sounds of the dominant of c/C and on to a close in G, introducing the dominant of G in the penultimate measure. On the downbeat of that measure the soprano sings a "fresh"-sounding f♯" ("als dich *selbst*"), triggering the final D–G

Example 8.4. (*continued*)

cadence with a return to the pitch it had sung along with the trumpet two measures earlier. Bach gives us only a single measure of dominant (D) harmony to offset the prolonged subdominant emphasis of the preceding thirty or more measures, yet it is enough to enable the ending to stand as a close in Mixolydian G, in part because the ascent of the voices in measures 72–74 had moved through an unbroken two-octave scale from g to g'', sounding the f♯'' at the end of the sequence, as the soprano came together with the trumpet. The subsequent contradiction of that pitch by f♮'' (on "selbst," m. 74) and its return on the first beat of the penultimate measure (again on "selbst," m. 76) in a melodic configuration that causes it to sound like the leading tone to g'' are gestures that emphasize the variability of the seventh degree of the G Mixolydian scale, enabling us for a time to "forget" that it represents the flattening of the third of the D Mixolydian scale. Bach does not want the G to sound perfectly secure, however, and not one of the F♯s that sound in the chorus parts in this measure resolves upward to G. The soprano itself ends on b'. We might, perhaps, interpret the ending as an expression of human weakness, the final cadence clearly not attaining the "high" tonal level of the D Mixolydian of the chorale, not even, in fact, repre-

senting a very strong G. Only the soprano's insight into the nature of human love, its reaching upward to make contact with the trumpet melody for one brief moment, enables the G to return as an acceptable final cadence. Ultimately, the remarkable subdominant tonal coloring of this movement, a progressive flattening that places the key of G in perspective, suggests at the end that Bach intended to bring out the distance between God and humankind—to highlight the weakening of G by the subdominant minor.

Chorus, "Du sollt Gott, deinen Herren, lieben": Thematic and Figurational Aspects

Much of what I have just described for the tonal design of this movement has counterparts in the ways that the themes unfold throughout the movement, especially after the shift to the *cantus mollis.* The flat–minor shift that dominates most of the last thirty measures of the movement is, in fact, prefigured in the initial chorus segment. When, for example, the descent half of the chorus theme turns to minor by

Example 8.4. (*continued*)

introducing a flattened pitch, as it does within the first choral segment (f♯ to f♮ in the bass, mm. 8–10; b to b♭ in the tenor, mm. 13–14), we perceive its relationship to the long final phrase of the chorale (i.e., the fourth and fifth phrases together in the version Bach uses in Cantata 77). That phrase begins with the rising fourth (with the pitch b♮), then returns downward, replacing b by b♭. In the *cantus firmus* of Cantata 77 Bach's dividing it into two phrases, separating the ascent and descent halves, and bringing in the commandment to love one's neighbor at the close of the latter clarify the division between God and humankind in the abstract layout of the movement, whereas the chorus theme, as we have seen, joins the two halves on the word "lieben." The chorus theme might also be taken as a conflation of the beginning and ending of the chorale (i.e., Bach's phrases 1 and 5 in the form used in Cantata 77), in which case the shift from the raised to the lowered third degree of the scale (see the bass of mm. 8–11 in Ex. 8.2) might have been intended to summarize the flat–sharp, major–minor shift in the melody of the Ten Commandments chorale. Above all, the directional dualism in the chorus theme mirrors the dualism of God and humankind (the neighbor), associated first with the shift from "Gott, deinen Herren"

to the human heart ("von ganzem Herzen") and later in the movement, as the flat-minor tonal qualities of the theme come ever more into the foreground, with the human attributes of heart, soul, strength, and spirit. Ultimately, its character represents a shift of perspective from God to humanity in general (the neighbor).

As the first choral passage of "Du sollt Gott, deinen Herren, lieben" comes to a close (in mm. 13–15), Bach introduces not only the tenor entry of the theme mentioned earlier, which changes from b to b♭ for its descent half, but also two additional variants of the chorus theme that will take on greater significance as the movement progresses. The soprano has a long melisma (on "Herzen") in which the descending half of the theme, now featuring the pitch b♭', precedes the ascending half, which features b♮' (see Ex. 8.2). The theme that Bach introduces for the first appearance of the commandment to love one's neighbor in measure 67 ("und deinen Nächsten als dich selbst") is an unmistakable variant of this line.[10] And simultaneously in the bass Bach brings in a minor version of the *ascending* fourth of "du sollt Gott, deinen Herren, lieben" (i.e., d–e–f–g in mm. 13–14). In comparison with the major version of this theme in the bass at the beginning of the choral segment (mm. 8–9), this gesture spells out the link between the flattening of the harmony and the turn from major to minor.

Although minor forms of the ascending fourth arise naturally when the major form is doubled at the third or sixth (the Dorian/Aolian form when it is doubled at the third below or sixth above and the Phrygian form when it is doubled at the third above or sixth below), Bach makes virtually no use of that fact until the point at which the shift to flats takes place.[11] In measures 42–45, however, he pairs first the tenors and basses, then the sopranos and tenors, the first pairing at the third and the second at the sixth; and in both cases the theme itself, rather than the doubling part, sounds the "Dorian" form of the fourth ascent, beginning from g (or g'). In fact, the tenor sings the doubling part twice, the first time ascending from b♭ but introducing e♮' as his fourth tone and the second ascending again from b♭ but now bringing in the e♭' that converts the F of the cadence in measure 45 into a dominant seventh. As the two-flat transposition of the ritornello-chorus material begins in measure 47, Bach doubles the major form of the fourth ascent in both the instrumental parts at the third above, thereby introducing the chorus entries with the ascending fourth in Phrygian form (i.e., a'–b♭'–c"–d" in the alto, d"–e♭"–f"–g" in the soprano; see Ex. 8.3). These passages make clear that the transformations of the theme are the result of the tonal shift, not the reverse. And from this point until the final set of choral entries in the movement (m. 72) the rising fourth will sound predominantly in minor forms.

Although the instrumental parts of this statement of the "ritornello" are nearly identical to those of the first two (transposed), Bach acknowledges that its text now centers on the human attributes of soul, strength, and spirit by associating the aforementioned Phrygian version of the rising fourth with "von ganzer Seele," introducing a new "leaping" idea in the lower parts for "von allen Kräften" and a scalar descending line in all parts for "von ganzem Gemüte." His meaning is clear: although the tenor and bass leap around for "von allen Kräften" (see mm. 49–50 of Ex. 8.3), their sudden bursts of activity coincide tonally with the first appearance of the pitch a♭' in the movement, hinting at the keys of g and c to come. Bach represents human strength as the "surface," so to speak, that covers human weakness, another reason for my calling this part of the movement simultaneously the climax and the "nadir."

In this passage, measures 48–54 in particular, Bach reveals that the descending part of the chorus theme (basically the pattern of the Phrygian tetrachord) is an inversion of the perfect-fourth ascent of the first, second, and fourth phrases of the Ten Commandments chorale (the Ionian/Mixolydian tetrachord). The upper instrumental parts have featured the scalar descent idea all along, of course, decorating it with the figure associated with "lieben" in the chorus theme. Now, following the ascending Phrygian form of the chorus theme in measures 47–48 Bach introduces the undecorated basic form of this descending line in the alto and soprano, then in all parts, descending from g' to g" and d" to d' in alternation, in the approach to the G minor cadence ("und von ganzem Gemüte"). Perhaps incidentally, the first four tones of these descending lines represent the descending Phrygian tetrachord (d'–c'–b♭–a or g'–f'–e♭'–d'), the pitches with which the melody of "Ach Gott, vom Himmel" ends. At the same time they form the exact inversion of the ascending fourth of phrase 4 of the chorale (d"–e"–f♯"–g"), which enters immediately in the *tromba da tirarsi*, producing the aforementioned e''–e♭'' clash, gestures that suggest an allegorical purpose, such as portraying the dualism of God and humankind (see the last four measures of Ex. 8.3). In measure 54 even the perfect-fourth ascent of the *tromba da tirarsi* sounds in descending form (retrograde) in the tenor, simultaneously with the trumpet ascent. Simultaneously, the music settles on the key of g, in which the segment closes (m. 54).

Although the move to C minor that follows immediately is the only point in the movement where the *tromba* reaches its highest tone, c''', Bach seems to suggest that the tonal flattening is a form of "descent" by introducing descending sixteenth-note scale patterns in the lower voices (first for the return of "von ganzem Herzen," then, as we might expect, for "von allen Kräften"). The pitch a♭', heard first in measure 50, reenters for two measures (55–56) before the C minor cadence. The dualisms of high and low, ascent and descent, associated with love of God and human weakness, are at their most intense here. In the measures that follow we hear the final clash between the e'' of the trumpet and the e♭'' of the violins, after which the shift from love of God to love of one's neighbor will eventually restore both the ascending major form of the principal theme and the G Mixolydian mode.

We cannot be certain just how much Bach might have known of the history of the melody of "Dies sind die heil'gen zehn Gebot," in particular concerning the fact that its origins as "In Gottes Namen fahren wir" were most likely as a Dorian, not a Mixolydian, melody. He almost certainly would have known that the melody existed in a form that did not introduce the flat third of the scale at the end (i.e., the b♭' in G Mixolydian); but the version that had the flat third all the way through and that therefore was minor rather than major appears to have been no longer current in his time. Nevertheless, his setting of the melody in "Du sollt Gott, deinen Herren, lieben" seems almost to "rediscover" something of the history of the melody as it was set by Isaac and Hofhaimer. The basis of that rediscovery lies in the potential of this particular melody to inspire affinities between the tonal fifth levels (hexachords) of the old *cantus durus* and *mollis* and the fifth levels (dominant, tonic, subdominant) of the untransposed system (or the *ambitus* of C) of Bach's time. The fact that its Mixolydian (subdominant) character is amplified by the introduction of the b♭ toward the end inspired Bach to create a tonal design in which the dominant of the primary mode (G) is not articulated at all but, perhaps, symbolized by the D Mixolydian chorale melody in the trumpet as an unattainable level (but one that is necessary in order for the G to be felt as a satisfactory final). The absence of the quality I have called the dominant dynamic—which after 1600 was increasingly perceived as the essential quality of tonal music—is a key to Bach's understanding of certain modes, especially those of the first and last chorales of Cantata 77. Bach was not attempting anything like a historical "revival," of course; rather, he was responding to an anomaly in the melody that quite possibly came about through some kind of historical "accident" such as the carrying over of the melody from a polyphonic setting in which either the major third of the initial phrases was introduced by *musica ficta* to a Dorian melody (i.e, as a *subsemitonium*, as in Isaac's setting of "In Gottes Namen") or the minor third at the end was introduced by a reverse process (to correct a tritone, as in Hofhaimer's setting). Bach's setting, like Hofhaimer's, features both minor and major forms of the initial phrase and, also like Hofhaimer's, centers on a canon at the fifth. Like Isaac's it presents the melody in D Mixolydian with f♯"s in phrases 1, 2, and 4 and f♮"s in phrase 5, while ending in G. But Bach's movement expands the tonal dimensions enormously in relation to the older settings even while it presents the melody unaltered in the double pitch levels of its canonic entries. And in its intermingling of high and low pitches, major and minor tonalities, sharp and flat transposition levels, ascending and descending forms of the first phrase, and strict (canonic) and free (variational) forms of the chorale elements, Bach's setting seems to have been intended to allegorize both the distance between God and humankind and the permeation of the human sphere by God's love. Theologically, the message Bach probably intended was that love of God is manifested in love of one's neighbor as oneself, which involves recognition and acknowledgment of human weakness.

The First Recitative and Aria

On the largest scale the tonal design of the remainder of the cantata, especially of movements 4 through 6, clarifies Bach's intention of delineating a progression from love of God to love of humankind by means of the change from major to minor and sharp to flat tonal regions. The recitative that follows the opening movement turns immediately to C, as if confirming the subdominant character of the opening movement. The ending of its first sentence even articulates a stepwise g–c' ascent that recalls the first phrase of the Ten Commandments chorale ("So muß es sein! Gott will das Herz für sich alleine haben") and reminds us of the principal C cadences at "von ganzem Herzen" (mm. 15, 28, and 31) in the chorus. References to "Herz," "Seelen," and "Gemüte" carry forward from the preceding movement, while the principal idea—that God's "igniting" or "inflaming" the mind through the Holy Spirit provides the surety of his grace and blessings—prepares for the aria that follows.[12]

That aria, "Mein Gott, ich liebe dich," deals with love of God in a form that is very unusual for Bach. The text is a straightforward da capo design that Bach sets in three divisions (framed by ritornelli), the second and third of which comprise the "B" section of the poem. There is no reprise of the text of the "A" section, a feature that Martin Petzoldt, as mentioned in the preceding chapter, interprets as an indication of Bach's intention to give greater weight to the believer's prayer that he will understand God's commandment and be "so inflamed with love" that he will attain eternal life ("Laß mich doch dein Gebot erkennen und in Liebe so entbrennen, daß ich dich ewig lieben kann!"). Since its progression from the Law, through the Spirit, to eternal life follows from the believer's initial proclamation of love in the "A" section ("Mein Gott, ich liebe dich von Herzen, mein ganzes Leben hangt dir an"), Bach did not utilize any contrast material in the aria but instead bound the first two sections together in a pattern of rising-third tonalities: A minor (ritornello, mm. 1–8), C major (m. 14), E minor (cadences in mm. 21 and 29), G major (half close in m. 33), and B minor (cadence in m. 42). That this design represents an "ascent" through the circle of keys seems an inevitable conclusion in light of its culminating on "daß ich dich ewig lieben kann." Lengthy melismas on "entbrennen" and "ewig" contribute to the increasing intensity toward the end of the progression. The constantly reiterated ritornello material increases the sense of continuity, while the fact that the two oboes

Example 8.5. Cantata 77: Beginning of third movement

play almost continually in parallel thirds and sixths lends the sonority the affective character of "sweetness" that was generally associated with love of God (Ex. 8.5).

In part so that the return to A minor for the third and final section will not seem anticlimactic after the lengthy sharpward motion that precedes it, Bach introduces a striking tonal effect: after the B minor cadence he shifts suddenly up another third, to D minor, introducing a dissonant-sounding b♭ in the *basso continuo* (enharmonic equivalent of the a♯ of the preceding measure). Since this gesture coincides with repetition of the text of the "B" section, rather than return of the opening lines, and since the rising-third progression does not continue on to D major, the effect that

Bach perhaps intended to project was that the rising progression to B minor represent an anticipation of something that was not present in the believer's life (as the key of B minor lies beyond the *ambitus* of a). As Petzoldt has pointed out, Bach's text revisions to the next movement, the second recitative, increase the sense of eschatological anticipation in relation to Knauer's original; and, as we will see, Bach mirrors that quality in the modulatory scheme of the recitative, which also features a prominent B minor cadence. In "Mein Gott, ich liebe dich" the momentary dissonance as a♯ changes to b♭ and the tonality returns to A minor through its subdominant (rather than the dominant, which could easily have followed) was probably intended as a shift in perspective, an allegory of the distance between the believer's hopes that his love of God will lead to eternal life and his present reality.

The Second Recitative and Aria

In order to link up the quasi-Pietistic emphasis on the feeling quality associated with love of God with the shift to love of the neighbor for the second half of the cantata, the fourth movement, an accompanied recitative for tenor, strings, and *basso continuo*, again outlines a progression that culminates with longing for eternity. The movement begins in e and, after a prominent internal cadence to B minor, closes in G. Up to the B minor cadence the recitative elaborates on the believer's prayer for the heart of a Good Samaritan (*Samariterherz*), thus giving more precise definition to the references to the human heart in the three preceding movements, while the turn to G coincides with his voicing the hope that God's gift of the ability to love one's neighbor (and to reject *Eigenliebe*) will lead him to eternal life: "so wirst du mir dereinst das Freudenleben nach meinem Wunsch, jedoch aus Gnaden geben" (Ex. 8.6). As the f' toward which the line moves on "Eigenliebe hasse" gives way to f♯' on "dereinst das Freudenleben," we may well remember the positive quality of the change from f" to f♯" in the soprano just before the end of the first movement (on "als dich selbst"). But now there is an important difference in the quality of the G major to which it leads. Following the B minor cadence that completes the first phase of the recitative, the f' of "Eigenliebe hasse" is not a fundamental pitch, and the word "dereinst" restores the f♯" immediately in a move toward the dominant of G. Whereas in the preceding aria the believer's anticipation of eternity as the result of his love of God had prompted a rising progression that led to B minor before returning through D minor to a, in this movement the E minor and B minor tonalities bring about a different outcome: that of rendering the G major cadence with which the movement ends perfectly secure in a way that the G ending of the first movement was not. As the sharpest key of the G–e *ambitus*, B minor legitimates the pitch F♯, and hence the key of G, in a manner that even the dominant does not. Only the brevity of the final G and the fact that subsequent events in the cantata do not confirm it indicate that it represents a hope for the afterlife ("dereinst"), not a present reality.[13] Centered on the believer's hope of eternal life, it leaps beyond the principal theme of the work, love of the neighbor as a manifestation of love of God. Bach chooses the Ionian mode that Göze and Werckmeister associated with joy to represent the goal of the believer's question to Jesus regarding eternal life in Luke's

Example 8.6. Cantata 77: Fourth movement

—continued

Example 8.6. (*continued*)

Gospel. The very optimistic G major ending of the recitative then serves as the background against which the subsequent events of the cantata must be measured.

After this pronounced sense of the believer's looking upward to eternity, the alto aria that follows, "Ach, es bleibt in meiner Liebe lauter Unvollkommenheit," returns to the sphere of human weakness with a flat-minor key, d (notated in the "Dorian" manner, without the flat key signature). And it features the *tromba da tirarsi* again as the instrumental voice. Now, however, that instrument, which is called upon not only to play in a minor key but also to play an array of pitches that are either not available or out of tune on the natural trumpet—c♯'', e♭'', g♯'', a'', and b♭', for example —is primarily a symbol not of the majesty of God but of the believer's fear that his ability to love adequately is contaminated by his human condition: "Ach, es bleibt in meiner Liebe lauter Unvollkommenheit! Hab ich oftmals gleich den Willen, was Gott saget, zu erfüllen, fehlt mirs doch an Möglichkeit." The idea of *Vollkommenheit* (perfection) and its opposite *Unvollkommenheit* was one with a particular resonance in

Example 8.7. Cantata 77: Aria "Ach, es bleibt in meiner Liebe lauter Unvollkommenheit" (no. 5), excerpt from bass of middle section

the writings of Werckmeister, whose allegorical schemes on the harmonic series and the harmonic numbers are rooted in those qualities as the fundamental distinction between God and humankind.[14] Of particular interest to the idea of *Unvollkommenheit* in this aria is Werckmeister's discussion of musical temperament and the numerical proportions it required as the mirror of human incompleteness and mortality, whereas the harmonic numbers represented completeness, the completed major scale of the clarino register enabling "not only a complete harmony, but also the building of a good *modulation*, which represents to us the good Christian life of the present as well as the eternal life and fulfillment to come, when we at last are admitted to heaven with God."[15]

Bach devises very particular means of representing both human imperfection and the anticipation of eternal life in this aria. Apart from the fact that the *tromba da tirarsi* melody gives prominence to the pitches that lend the melody line its "minor" character, the *basso continuo* introduces a variant of the *tromba da tirarsi* theme whose initial four tones are identical to the beginning of the theme associated with "und deinen Nächsten" in the opening movement (Ex. 8.7). This detail and the striking change in the character of the music assigned to the *tromba da tirarsi* from that of the opening movement might be understood to represent the imperfection and incompleteness of human love which, as mentioned, must not be directed toward the deity of God.[16] Beyond these features, Bach's notating the movement in the so-called Dorian notation might well have had additional symbolic meaning. Possibly the D minor/Dorian tonality was meant as a counterfoil to the D Mixolydian of the *tromba da tirarsi* chorale in the opening chorus—that is, as the mode that results when f♯ is changed to f. In several of his writings on music Martin Luther had made connections between theology and music's tonal elements; in one such remark, cited previously, he had viewed the Hypodorian mode as analogous to the "poor weak sinner," on account of its varying between the pitches b♭ and b♮.[17] Bach's aria makes much out of that variability, and his notating the movement without the flat in the key signature might well have been intended to make a point relating to the idea of *Unvollkommenheit*, especially since B♭ is clearly far more prominent than B♮ in the principal section of the movement. In that section the pitch b♭'' defines the upper limit of the trumpet register, so it seems, its D minor flat sixth character representing a boundary that even the final ascending-sixteenth-note flourishes do not exceed. In particular, the descending lines from b♭'' to c♯'' in the instrumental solos and on the expression "lauter Unvollkommenheit" seem to define a tonal space that gravitates toward d with an unusual sense of inevitability. The structure of the "A" section, in fact, is based upon a straightforward four-phrase periodic design (the sixteen-measure ritornello) that in itself suggests a closed framework and that simply repeats over again for the vocal part of the segment (another straight sixteen measures). The eight additional measures for trumpet and *continuo* that round out the segment (33–40) only serve to confirm, by outlining the same musical space from c♯'' to b♭'' and returning inexorably to d, the sense of confinement that underlies the believer's condition.

Within the aria's "B" section, however, Bach brings out the sense of disparity between b♭'' and b'', assigning the *tromba da tirarsi* a ten-measure solo in which it plays only the diatonic tones of the natural C trumpet in the clarino register, without a single accidental (mm. 52–61), a passage of remarkable optimism in which the *tromba* ascends to the high b♮'' and c''' twice. This solo perfectly matches the character of Werckmeister's allegorical view of the clarino register, as cited previously. That this passage follows directly on the believer's expressions of inability to carry out God's will and that those expressions themselves lead to a solid C major cadence seem to highlight the disparaties all the more. Then, at the close of the trumpet solo, in an equally remarkable juxtaposition of major and minor, Bach immediately counters the optimistic tone by introducing an e♭ in the *basso continuo* and making a sudden shift to G minor in preparation for the entrance of the voice with its reiterated acknowledgment of the human incapacity to carry out God's commandment. Bach now assigns the trumpet a line that brings virtually all the out-of-tune tones into prominence. And after a second phrase in g (ending on the dominant in m. 68), voice and trumpet together shift to the dominant, A minor, for the final ten measures of the "B" section. In this passage the high b'' and c''' reappear on the trumpet, while the voice sings diminished thirds (at "fehlt [mirs doch an Möglichkeit]"), an emphatic reiteration of the idea of imperfection. As the trumpet's final a'' carries over into the beginning of the reprise of the "A" section, the sense of the believer's inability to break out of the D minor framework returns like a dark shadow.

The Final Chorale

The b–b♭ wavering in "Ach, es bleibt in meiner Liebe" and the dominance of the flattened sixth degree of the scale over the key signature can be considered to bridge between the *cantus durus* of the first four movements of the cantata and the *cantus mollis* of the final chorale. Even though we do not know the text that Bach intended for the final chorale, it hardly seems far-fetched to claim that, especially in the context of the work as a whole, the musical setting itself further elaborates on the idea of human *Unvollkommenheit.* Drawing on the melody of "Ach Gott, vom Himmel sieh' darein," but transposing it to the one-flat signature so that it begins and ends on the tone a', Bach produced a setting that ends on what we hear as the dominant of G minor (Ex. 8.8). Of its seven phrases, the second, fourth, and sixth end with authentic cadences to g, phrase 5 with a cadence to F (rather than with the Phrygian cadence to A, or its transpositional equivalent, as in Bach's other settings), and phrases 1 and 3 with half closes to g. Phrase 7, after beginning in g, and sounding the harmonies of g and D as it outlines the g triad in the melody, closes on D. The approach to the final D is interesting on two counts. First, the penultimate and antepenultimate harmonies are both diminished chords with a distinctly pre-dominant character; and, second, the bass line moves up in register, with a stepwise ascent

Example 8.8. Cantata 77: Final chorale

from f♯ to d' that passes chromatically—c'–c♯'–d'—to the final tone. Thus, the final cadence of this setting closely resembles that of the setting of this melody that Bach would use nearly half a year later to begin Cantata 153, "Schau, lieber Gott, wie meiner Feind" (see Ex. 5.2). In the latter work Bach pitches the melody of "Ach Gott, vom Himmel" a tone higher, in the one-sharp signature, presumably intending that the mode be understood as E Aolian.[18] And the text of that setting as well as the context provided by the following movements and the design of the cantata as a whole leave no doubt that Bach's harmonization and especially his final cadence ("mich leicht in Unglück stürzen") were intended to convey a sense of human weakness and vulnerability. In Cantata 77 the principal differences from the ending of "Schau, lieber Gott" are the rising bass line (in "Schau, lieber Gott" the bass line is set in the lower octave and it begins with a prominent *descent*) and the absence of a comparable emphasis on the subdominant region before the cadence (i.e., the subdominant of the subdominant: c minor). In "Schau, lieber Gott" Bach's one-sharp key signature invites comparison between the very "weak" E ending of the chorale and the very secure E minor of the bass aria that sets God's words of *Trost.* And throughout that work, as we have seen, the flat or "subdominant" tonal area, represented mostly by the key of d, is associated with all that undermines the believer's confidence and resolve, whereas the final movements voice his hopes for eternal life in G and C. The ending of the first chorale of "Schau, lieber Gott" therefore represents something that is overcome throughout the course of the cantata. However, in Cantata 2, "Ach Gott, vom Himmel sieh' darein," Bach's settings of the chorale in the outer movements both make a point out of the weakening of the final, D, by means of substantial emphasis on the subdominant, c. Although the D is articulated by means of an authentic cadence, the complete absence of even the smallest articulation of the dominant of d in the opening chorale motet is very telling in this regard.[19] And the absence of the dominant of d elsewhere in the work in combination with the predominance of flat-minor modulations spells out the weakened character of the "tonic" throughout the work. In that light, Bach's ending both the outer movements with authentic cadences to D—thereby, in my opinion, indicating D as the true final—demands that the believer's reservoirs of hope and faith (D) be at their fullest in a world permeated by sin and tribulation (the flat modulations).

In comparison with the great majority of Bach's final chorales, the setting of "Ach Gott, vom Himmel" that ends Cantata 77 could hardly be more imperfect or incomplete. Whereas the G major ending of the fourth movement was associated with anticipation of eternal life, this final incomplete G minor was surely intended to represent an intensified awareness of human imperfection. But Bach probably intended that the very acknowledgment of human weakness go hand in hand with the orientation toward one's neighbor, the measure of both human and divine love. The text supplied by Werner Neumann in his edition for the *Neue Bach-Ausgabe*—"Herr, durch den Glauben wohn in mir," a prayer for God to enable the believer through faith to produce the good works of love, ending "den Nächsten fort zu lieben"—is not inappropriate, although it hardly seems to invite the passing augmented triad that appears near the beginning of the first phrase. In its reference to the "indwelling" of God in humanity through faith and its shift from God to the neighbor, it mirrors the dynamic of "descent" that pervades both the opening chorus and the cantata as a whole. And the rising chromaticism of the tenor and bass parts in their approach to the final cadence might have been intended to represent the word "fort" in the final line. The verse suggested by Martin Petzoldt, however, makes a statement that is far more consistent with the rest of the work. Also, its cry to God, "Ach, Herr," is matched by the initial harmonic progression and, above all, its final expression of human incapacity to fulfill God's Law is mirrored in the fundamentally "weak" ending.

It is possible, however, that Bach, despite the pronounced dominant quality of the ending of Cantata 77, intended the final cadence to be understood as representing the "correct" final, as he perhaps did in Cantata 2 and in the case of the setting of "O grosser Gott von Macht" that ends Cantata 46. In addition, we may note that the *tromba da tirarsi* plays the melody of the final chorale, doubling the soprano. Possibly, therefore, Bach intended that the instrument be associated with D modes in movements 1, 5, and 6: D Mixolydian in the first movement, D Dorian in "Ach, es bleibt in meiner Liebe," and D Aolian in the final chorale. In the first and last of these movements, however, the tonal centers are G and g, respectively, not D. In the first movement the D Mixolydian melody stands apart from the tonality of the chorus, the latter even tending greatly toward the major and minor subdominant of G. And in the final movement the melody played by the *tromba*, taken on its own, is "in" A, whereas the "correct" modal final was presumably intended as D and the tonal "feel" of the final cadence as the dominant of g. It is as if the D on which Cantata 77 ends is an "ideal" that can never be attained, as the D Mixolydian tonality of the melody in the *tromba da tirarsi* is at the end of the first movement, whereas the D "Dorian" of "Ach, es bleibt in meiner Liebe" expresses the reality of human imperfection. More important than the question of mode, however, is the fact that in the opening chorus the pitch B♮ is the primary pitch of the mode, even though it is undermined by the final B♭s of the chorale melody and still more so by all that Bach introduces into the harmony in terms of the tonal flattening effect toward the end of the movement. In "Ach, es bleibt in meiner Liebe lauter Unvollkommenheit" B♮ and B♭ represent the variable "mi" and "fa" of the mode that Luther associated with the *peccator infirmus* on that very account. Although the movement is notated in the *cantus durus*, B♭ is more prominent than B by virtue of its dominance in the "A" section. Then in the final chorale B♭ emerges as a "basic" pitch in the key signature and the question of mode centers on whether or not E♭ is a fundamental pitch. The disparity between the e♮' of the melody and the many E♭s of the harmonization reminds us of the E/E♭ disparities between the D Mixolydian chorale and the chorus in the first movement. In this sense Cantata 77 can be said to shift from a *cantus durus* G that is already weakened in the opening movement to a *cantus mollis* g that is the "real" tonality at the end. The situation is analogous to the "reality" of A minor in Cantata 153 in which the aria in that key expresses the believer's acceptance of worldly persecution. In Cantata 77 the "reality" represented in the final chorale is the acknowledgment of human inability to fulfill God's commandments unaided. In this chorale we might conclude that the very quality of tonal hearing (*sensus*) is an allegory of the inevitability of human weakness, while the modal viewpoint represents an unattainable ideal.

In fact, in assigning the *tromba da tirarsi* to play in three D modes, only one of which (the one that directly voices the idea of human imperfection) constitutes the tonal center of the movement in which it appears, Bach might well have intended an allegory of the human inability to love God except through love of the neighbor. If such an interpretation sounds fanciful from the musico-allegorical standpoint, it is certainly not from the standpoint of the Lutheran theology that underlies the message of Cantata 77. For Luther love of God was love of God in the flesh, not anything that might invite a distinction between "spiritual" and earthly love.[20] In both outer movements of Cantata 77 the "tonal" character of the music undermines or weakens the modal character of the chorale melody, quite possibly an allegory of the kind that Werckmeister intended in speaking of tempered music as a mirror of the mortality and incompleteness of human life.

In its overall design Cantata 77 can be said to delineate a shift from major to minor from the first to last movements and, in terms of their key signatures as well, from the *cantus durus* to the *cantus mollis*. This shift is strikingly prefigured in the tonal design of the opening movement, where it derives directly from the progressive flattening, especially the b'–b♭' shift, in the Ten Commandments chorale, "Dies sind die heil'gen zehn Gebot." Bach's keeping that chorale at its usual untransposed pitch (G Mixolydian) meant that many of the tonal features of the movement (and ultimately of the cantata as a whole) echoed what I have called elsewhere the "modal-hexachordal" system of the early seventeenth century and resonated with certain writings of an older generation of music theorists, such as Andreas Werckmeister. In that sense Bach's reflection on the past in this work is very closely bound up with the roles of the pitches B and B♭, symbols for centuries of the sharp (hard) and flat (soft) hexachords and the transpositional shifting between fifth levels they brought about, as well as of the affective states that derived from their names. Within the diatonic framework of the traditional presentations of the modes in the *cantus durus* and *mollis*, the kinds of modal anomalies identified by Werckmeister, as well as the presence of B♭ in "Dies sind die heil'gen zehn Gebot," had far greater expressive and tonal significance than they have had for later generations, much less accustomed to reflect on the historical features of the melodies per se. Thus, not only Werckmeister but also Johann Melchior Göze, Kirnberger, and even Luther described B♭/♮ (or "fa" and "mi") differences in modes, melodies, and their harmonizations in ways that still resound in several movements of Cantata 77. The first movement is as much a virtuoso piece in that respect as it is in its better-known numerological and canonic aspects. These different sides of the movement, and the regular alternation of *bassetchen* and low bass, go hand in hand to articulate the sense of "above" and "below," bounded by God's Law (the *tromba da tirarsi* and *basso continuo* canon). Although the harmony is subdivided into the spheres of the divine and the human, those spheres nevertheless interrelate and intermingle throughout the movement (the *bassetchen* and low bass textures as well as the derivation of the thematic material of the former from the chorale within the latter).

In summary, within the opening chorus there is a basic sense of flatward tonal motion that, I think, should be viewed as a "downward" motion through the circle of fifths; in historical terms it should probably be conceptualized as a *durus–mollis* shift, whereas a modern tonal approach would describe it as a very strong subdominant tendency. The confirming of that subdominant (C) in the first recitative may, perhaps, be viewed as a continuing descent, a further motion in the direction of the human sphere. Along with the first aria, in A minor, it describes love of God very much in terms of human feeling, expressed in the Pietistic tone of the verbs "entzünden" (ignite) and "entbrennen" (inflame).[21] If the basic key sequence of the first three movements may be considered a "descent" pattern, then the striking series of "ascending" third modulations in the aria perhaps represents the believer's looking upward toward eternal love of God, as expressed in the text. If so, then the rising modulation probably depicts, as I suggested, a hope that lies beyond the normal range of the key. That this key sequence leads to B minor may reflect Bach's perception of the role of that key in establishing the secure G major of the following recitative. It and the single b♭ that immediately turns the tonality back toward d and a may be conceptually rather than "structurally" connected to the b♮/♭ of the opening movement; that is, they may constitute an "allegorical" thread that runs through several movements of the cantata. The sequence of keys in the second recitative—e–b–G—culminates in an expression of the believer's hopes for eternity, the final G cadence harking back to the tonal center of the opening movement. We remember that the Knauer original text on which Bach's is based began with the question of the lawyer in the Gospel for the day: "Master, what must I do to inherit eternal life?" In this light, the second recitative is the "answer," completing the message of the opening chorus as it articulates the strongest G cadence in the cantata. After the pronounced role of b in setting up that G in the recitative, the aria "Ach, es bleibt in meiner Liebe lauter Unvollkommenheit" makes a great deal out of the b♭/♮ dualism in the ways I have described. Its *cantus durus* (Dorian) key signature then gives way to the *cantus mollis* (the b♭ signature), within which the chorale harmonization confirms a transposition level that is, in fact, one degree flatter still (the two-flat system, owing to the prominence of E♭ in the movement). The progressive flattening lends the final chorale much of its affective character and theological meaning, just as it does in the opening chorus. In this sense the cantata as a whole might be said to describe a "descent" pattern, from major to minor, sharp to flat, articulating a motion from the sphere of God and the perfection of the major triad to that of the neighbor and the minor triad as symbol of human imperfection and incompleteness.

NINE

Cantata 60

"O Ewigkeit, du Donnerwort"

ONE OF THE RUNNING THEMES OF this book has been that the endings of many Bach cantatas—above all their sense of completeness or incompleteness—reflect the extent to which their theological concerns are oriented toward eschatological or present perspectives. In this respect, the tonal "directions" of Cantatas 21 and 77 can be considered opposite each other. In Cantata 21 the overall C minor–major shift and the pattern of increasing "sharpness" in the movement keys that leads to the C major of its final chorus mirror the idea of a progression from worldly tribulation to the anticipation of eternity. In contrast, the change from a weakened G major to a real but incomplete G minor over the course of Cantata 77 delineates a downward progression from God to humankind that expresses the hope of eternity in terms of life on earth. The final chorus of Cantata 21 is one of the closest approaches Bach ever made to the representation of eschatological fulfillment, whereas the final chorale of Cantata 77 is, as we saw, tonally incomplete and most likely associated with the idea of human imperfection. In terms of traditional hermeneutics, the one work represents transcendence of the Old Testament framework (part 1 of Cantata 21) by means of the message of the Gospel (part 2 of that work), while the other centers on the meaning of the Law as given in the Old and New Testaments, building its entire design around the inability of humanity to fulfill it and the acknowledgment of that inability as the prerequisite to salvation.

The idea of completeness versus incompleteness, or eschatological versus earth-centered perspectives, can be represented by a variety of means, tonal or otherwise. Cantatas that begin in major and end in the "tonic" minor, or vice versa, are extremely rare. But those that end "higher" (i.e., sharper) on the circle of fifths than they begin are, in fact, not uncommon at all. And even when there is not such a stage-by-stage progression toward the final key as there is in Cantata 21 (or Cantatas 12, 61, and 27 and a host of other "ascent" cantatas), shift of key at the end of a cantata, or even just for the final phrase of the final chorale, may be associated with ideas such as the juxtaposition of the old and new years (Cantatas 121 and 41 and the chorale "Das alte Jahr vergangen ist") or the old and new "man"—that is, Adam and Jesus ("Durch Adams Fall")—or some other (related) theological idea such as the opposition of death and resurrection (Cantata 127) or the "new life" given by Baptism (Cantata 7).

In this book I have emphasized tonal qualities that arise as the result of the conflict or disparity between modal and tonal finals in chorale settings, above all the sense that certain chorale melodies encourage harmonizations that do not confirm the modal final as what we call the "tonic" key. Sometimes there is a sense that such harmonizations, and hence entire cantatas, end on the dominant. When the designs of whole cantatas are considered, the question of modal versus tonal harmonization may involve shift from the one compositional style to the other over the course of a multimovement sequence, such as those of Cantatas 25 and 153. In this respect the cantatas discussed in chapter 5 all reflect issues that Andreas Werckmeister had taken up in relation to the correct modal finals of particular chorales. Analyzing these works in their musico-theological contexts enables us to advance hypotheses regarding Bach's intent with respect to the relative completeness or incompleteness of their final cadences. In Cantata 46 Bach perhaps intended a degree of ambiguity regarding the tonality of the final movement, a tension or balance between the modal final, D, and the strong sense of G minor in the harmonization. In Cantata 77 it appears virtually certain that the final D should be understood as an incomplete cadence, an ending on the dominant of g in order to represent the imperfection of human nature. In Cantata 121 the whole-tone (e–F♯) shift in the chorale settings of the outer movements does not suggest anything of incompleteness, despite Werckmeister's view that that shift represented a falsification of the true modal final and despite the fact that the final F♯ retains something of a "dominant" character. Rather, the ending is a perfect reflection of the shift from a physical to an eschatological perspective within the text itself. In Cantata 109, however, Bach went to great pains to indicate that the shift from d to a in the final chorale should really be understood not just as a change of tonal center but also as one that resolved all doubt regarding the key of the cantata as a whole, just as the emergence of faith put an end to the believer's wavering uncertainty regarding the outcome of his fears and hopes.

And some other cantatas whose final chorales shift from the tonic to the dominant —such as "Christ, unser Herr, zum Jordan kam" (BWV 7) and "Herr Jesu Christ, wahr' Mensch und Gott" (BWV 127)—derive important aspects of their tonal designs from those shifts. I have described this aspect of Cantata 127 in chapter 6. In the case of Cantata 7 the shift from E minor to B minor on the final phrase of the chorale "Christ, unser Herr" can be thought of as Dorian shifting to Aolian or as Dorian ending on the dominant (or simply as a modulation from e to b). In this case the shift of key or mode was perhaps intended to mirror the final line of its first verse, "Das galt ein neues Leben," which expresses the central idea of the chorale, that Baptism represents rebirth into a new life.[1] In the opening movement Bach absorbs the e–b shift in the melody into a chorale fantasia that remains in e (set by Bach in the one-sharp signature), whereas in the final chorale he realizes the shift of mode in tonal terms, ending the movement and therefore the cantata in b and notating the chorale in two sharps. And other aspects of the modulatory character of the

Table 9.1 Cantata 60, "O Ewigkeit, du Donnerwort." Leipzig, 1723. Twenty-fourth Sunday after Trinity.

Movement	Genre	Instrumentation	Text incipit	Key
1	Dialogue aria with chorale	Alto, tenor, hrn., ob. d'am. 1, 2, str., b.c.	Fear: O Ewigkeit, du Donnerwort Hope: Herr, ich warte auf dein Heil	D
2	Recitative dialogue	Alto, tenor, b.c.	Fear: O schwerer Gang zum letzten Kampf und Streite! Hope: Mein Beistand ist schon da	b–G
3	Dialogue aria	Alto, tenor, ob. d'am., vln. 1 solo, b.c.	Fear: Mein letztes Lager will mich schrecken Hope: Mich wird des Heilands Hand bedecken	b
4	Recitative dialogue	Alto, bass, b.c.	Fear: Der Tod bleibt doch der menschlichen Natur verhaßt Jesus: Selig sind die Toten, die in dem Herren sterben, von nun an	e–D
5	Chorale	SATB chorus, plus all instruments, b.c.	Es ist genung	A

cantata as a whole reflect Bach's associating not only the dominant region with the new life of the spirit but also the subdominant region with the idea of the incarnation —that is, God's taking on human or physical form. The latter quality emerges with particular clarity in the D minor ending of the first recitative, associated with Jesus' "niedriger Gestalt," His taking on the "Fleisch und Blut der Menschenkinder," and the A minor aria that follows, which tells how the Trinity appeared at Jesus' Baptism in "word" (the voice of God the Father) and "picture" (the Holy Spirit in the form of the dove) so as to be comprehensible to humankind. In this context the shift to b at the end of the final chorale, setting the line "auch von uns selbst begangen," refers to the "new life" of the opening movement, the elevation of humankind through Jesus' incarnation and Baptism.

The wavering qualities that emerge in Cantata 109 (for the twenty-first Sunday after Trinity, 1723) characterize the Trinity season in general, and especially so toward the end, as the opposition of fear and hope, or doubt and faith, intensifies to the level of a double perspective on the coming judgment. The work from late Trinity 1723 that most embodies those oppositions, leading them toward an eschatological vision that in its way is every bit as impressive as that of Cantata 21, is Cantata 60, "O Ewigkeit, du Donnerwort," for the twenty-fourth Sunday after Trinity (November 7). In this work, as in Cantata 77, the relationship of the beginning and ending chorale settings articulates a very meaningful change of key at the end, now, as in Cantata 109, to the dominant of the original key, for the purpose of representing an inner change associated with the believer's increasing confidence and faith (see Table 9.1). And once again an "irregularity" in one of the chorale melodies stimulated Bach to devise a very daring chorale harmonization for the final movement and to direct the course of the cantata toward that point.

Cantata 109 had suggested a dialogue between fear and hope in the antithetical relationship of the alternating phrases of its first recitative and in the juxtaposed keys, styles, and affects of its two arias. Cantata 60 makes that dialogue character explicit, designating the alto soloist "Fear" and the tenor soloist "Hope" in its first three movements, then replacing the figure of "Hope" by that of Jesus (bass) in the fourth movement. I have already referred (chapter 1) to the fact that the words from Revelation (14:13) that are assigned to Jesus in the fourth movement ("Selig sind die Toten, die in dem Herren sterben, von nun an") constitute a response to the words of Jacob. "Herr, ich warte auf dein Heil"(Genesis 49:18) given to "Hope" in the first movement. Jacob's words embody one of the most widespread ways in which the "time of Israel" was interpreted in traditional hermeneutics: as a time of waiting for what would be fully revealed only at a later stage of salvation history. Translated via Luther's "analogy of faith" into the time frame of the contemporary believer, such a time of waiting becomes an expression of the individual's doubt and tribulation concerning the experience of faith. As in Cantatas 106, 21, and 61, the coming of Jesus represents the pivotal event in the believer's shift from a worldly to a spiritual outlook on life, from doubt to faith, from fear to hope; the final chorale of Cantata 60 makes this clear in its fourth, fifth, and sixth lines: "Mein Jesus kömmt; / nun gute Nacht, o Welt! / Ich fahr ins Himmelshaus" (My Jesus comes; / now good night, O world! / I journey to the heavenly home). In Cantata 60, therefore, we have another progression in which the stages of traditional hermeneutics and of chronological eras parallel the inner experience of faith, the work as a whole ending with the anticipation of eternity. Cantata 21 had represented that experience in terms of the extended nature of the shift from C minor to major, whereas Cantata 109 had associated the confirmation of the believer's faith after a period of waiting with the shift from d to a in the final chorale (analogously, perhaps, to the theological association of the phrase "In fine videbitur cujus toni"). In Cantata 60 Bach represents the progressive nature of that revelation in the fourth and fifth movements, presenting it first in three distinct stages in the final dialogue of the cantata (movement 4). In the first of those stages Jesus responds to the believer's (Fear's) cries of torment with the phrase "Selig sind die Toten," in the second with "Selig sind die Toten, *die in dem Herren sterben*," and in the third with the complete line "Selig sind die Toten, die in dem Herren sterben, *von nun an*." The response of "Fear" to this message—"Wohlan! soll ich von nun an selig sein: so stelle dich, o Hoffnung, wieder ein! Mein Leib mag ohne Furcht im Schlafe ruhn, der Geist kann einen Blick in jene Freude tun" (Well then! if I shall be blessed from now on: then restore yourself, O hope! My body may rest in sleep without fear, the Spirit can take a glance into that joyful state)—makes clear that the final words of Jesus' promise, "von nun an," enable the believer to live in the hope of eternal life and even to experience a vision of that life in the present through the Spirit. The famous setting of "Es ist genung" with which Bach ends Cantata 60 represents that vision, drawing upon some very daring as well as some very subtle tonal qualities in order to depict the return of "Hope" in the believer's consciousness.

The fear with which Cantata 60 deals is that of death, the ultimate cause of the believer's loss of hope in the penultimate movement, which begins "Der Tod bleibt doch der menschlichen Natur verhaßt und reißet fast die Hoffnung ganz zu Boden" (Death remains hateful, however, to human nature and casts hope almost completely to the ground). As a result, human life itself becomes what the first recitative of Cantata 60 describes as a "schwerer Gang zum letzten Kampf und Streite," a hard passage to the final struggle that threatens to destroy all hopes. Death is terrifying, however, not only of itself but also because of the believer's fear of God's judgment and the possibility of eternal damnation. The chorale "O Ewigkeit, du Donnerwort," sung by the figure of "Fear" in the opening movement, encapsulates that fear in all its verses, demanding that the sinner envisage an afterlife of torment as a perpetual beginning without end: "O Ewigkeit, du Donnerwort, o Schwert das durch die Seele bohrt, o Anfang sonder Ende" (O eternity, word of thunder, O sword that bores through the soul, O beginning without end). Against that possibility the believer must, like Jacob, hold to God's promise of salvation ("Herr, ich warte auf dein Heil"), recognizing its fulfillment in Jesus; only that recognition enables him to overcome fear with hope so that life in the present becomes a time of peace instead of a "schwerer Gang."

The theological meaning of Cantata 60 hinges on the change in the believer's outlook on eternity that takes place from the first to the last movement, whose chorales, as I have described elsewhere, relate to one another in revealing ways.[2] In the opening movement the first line of the melody "O Ewigkeit, du Donnerwort" outlines an ascending D major scale, in which the initial progression through the tones of the D major triad is aligned with "O Ewigkeit" and the rising a'–b'–c♯''–d'' tetrachord that ends the phrase with "du Donnerwort." Bach separates the line into two parts in the opening ritornello by beginning the movement with the rising tetrachord in the unison strings (i.e., the second half of the phrase) and following it by the rising pentachord from d' to a' (the first half of the phrase). As the ritornello leads into the first entrance of the alto with phrase 1 of the chorale (mm. 13–16), Bach clarifies the relationship between the two halves of the chorale phrase by ending the ritornello with the tetrachord (Ex. 9.1). This gesture and Bach's accompanying the tetrachord by a *stile concitato* tremolo pattern in the strings indicate the dominance of fear at the beginning of the cantata. Throughout the movement the first half of the phrase does not appear as a separate idea; instead, Bach reiterates the rising tetrachord, associated with the words "du Donnerwort," as the principal motif.

But for the beginning of the following recitative, proclaiming the aforementioned "schwerer Gang," Bach makes reference to the first phrase, sharpening its third and fourth tones so as to outline melodic progressions of a tritone and an augmented rather than a perfect fifth. The "schwerer Gang" is the transformation of two successive tones from "fa" to "mi": first the fourth degree of the scale, g', becomes g♯'; then, as we expect it to move to a' (a new "fa" degree), it takes another "difficult step," to a♯', the third successive "mi" degree (Ex. 9.2b). This gesture distorts the melodic unit associated with "O Ewigkeit" with the aid of a musico-rhetorical device known as the *passus duriusculus*, of which the German "schwerer Gang" is, in fact, a near-literal translation.[3] In this light, the fact that the pitches are sharpened is probably an indication that the harshness of the progression puns not only on the word *durus*

Example 9.1. Cantata 60: First movement. (a) mm. 1–3; (b) mm. 12–15

—*continued*

Example 9.1. (*continued*)

Example 9.2. Cantata 60: Excerpts from first, second and last movements

but also on the German word for the sharp sign, *Kreuz.* That is, the difficult path is the way of the cross, embodied in a life of tribulation, which the believer undergoes as the route to the "letzter Kampf und Streite."

There is much more than mere rhetorical punning going on here, however, as the final chorale, "Es ist genung," reveals. As Alfred Dürr has pointed out, the very provocative melodic tritone that begins that chorale (a'–b'–c♯"–d♯") can be considered as a distortion of the last four tones of the first phrase of "O Ewigkeit, du Donnerwort" in just the same way that I have described the transformation of the *first* four tones of that phrase into the "schwerer Gang" of the first recitative—that is, an exceeding of the normal tone sequence by the transformation of "fa" (d") into "mi" (d♯")[4] (Ex. 9.2). And that beginning functions, in Bach's network of tonal and theological relationships, as the means by which not only the principal motivic element in the opening movement but also the key of that movement give way to new interpretations at the end. The crucial point is the change of the key of the cantata from its original D, on which it settles at the end of the penultimate movement, to an A that is associated with the final "Es ist genung." That point now represents a completely satisfying close in which "Hope" returns to transform the believer's understanding of death.

The manner by which Bach brings about this final outcome is particularly revealing in relation to the various "weak" endings I have considered throughout this book. Those endings were all owing to the absence of the aforementioned "dominant dynamic" in the chorale melodies in question (especially the Mixolydian and "Hypophrygian" melodies) as well as to the unusual degree of subdominant emphasis given them by Bach's harmonizations. That subdominant emphasis extended, as I have endeavored to show, to a preponderance of flat-side modulations in the tonality of those works in general. And the principal association of those flat modulatory regions was with human weakness, the quality that Werckmeister associated with tempered music as a representation of "our incompleteness and mortality in this life." Motion in the flat modulatory direction, conceived in terms of seventeenth-century hexachord theory as a progressive transformation of "mi" into "fa" (or the changing of the leading tone into the flat seventh degree of the scale and, by extension, other major intervals, such as the third, into their minor counterparts), underlay the character of the chorale melody that was most widely associated in Bach's time with "Dies sind die heil'gen zehn Gebot," as we have seen. And Bach did not fail to perceive its potential to articulate the theological message of human weakness that underlay the chorale text. In addition, he linked that subdominant character with the "Hypophrygian" melody of "Ach Gott, vom Himmel sieh' darein," placing those chorales at the beginning and ending of Cantata 77 and transposing the latter into the *cantus mollis.* In this he brought out the impact of the flattened pitches and "subdominant" harmonizations on the tonal-affective character of the modal melodies as well as on the musico-theological character of the work as a whole.

In the case of "Es ist genung" Bach dealt with the opposite effect, that of sharpened pitches, and their suggesting a very strong "dominant dynamic," one that would, in the end, shift the tonal center of Cantata 60 in the sharp rather than the flat direction, and that would create an unusually satisfying rather than an unusually weak ending. Much of that quality is directly attributable to J. M. Ahle's melody for "Es ist genung," to which Bach adheres closely and which is ingeniously constructed so as to highlight the relationship between its tonic, A, and dominant, E, in terms of the directional tendencies of the pitches d♯" and d" (Ex. 9.3). The ten phrases of "Es ist genung" (three in each of the *Stollen,* four in the *Abgesang*) are all contained within the range of the perfect fifth from a' to e", which appears in full within a single phrase only in the melodic e"–c♯"–b'–a' descent of the last two phrases. Those final phrases, both setting the words "Es ist genung," seem to be an obvious response to the first (and the fourth) phrase, the ascending a'–b'–c♯"–d♯" tritone, which also sets the words "Es ist genung." The pitch a' appears only as the first and last tones of the chorale (i.e., the first note of phrases 1 and 4 and the final tone of phrases 9 and 10), initiating the ascending motion that leads to the dominant at the beginning and serving as the goal of the descent from dominant to tonic at the end. If the first four notes of the chorale can be considered a distortion of the ending of the first phrase of "O Ewigkeit, du Donnerwort," then its last four can be viewed as the inversion of the beginning of "O Ewigkeit," as if to make the point that the two halves of that phrase come to rest in the final descent to the new tonic.

The tonal "dynamic" of "Es ist genung" is one in which the two *Stollen* articulate a very secure shift to the dominant, E, after which the *Abgesang* prepares and completes the chorale's only point of tonic closure, in the A major cadence of the final phrase. In the *Stollen* the basic melodic direction is that of ascent to e", initiated in the rising tritone of the first phrase and completed in the E cadence of the third. The *Stollen* are, in fact, perfectly constructed so as to juxtapose the tendency of the pitch d♯" ("mi") to progress upward to e" and that of d" ("fa") to move down to c♯". The beginning of the second phrase leads the provocative d♯" of phrase 1 upward to e", while the ending of that phrase places the d"–c♯" of its A major cadence entirely within the context of E; the third phrase then emphatically confirms the E. That is, in phrase 2 the ascending "mi–fa" semitone, d♯"–e", gives way to the "fa–mi" semitone, d"–c♯", in a manner that makes clear not the sense of a return to A but exactly the opposite—the subordination of A to E—after which the third phrase restores the d♯"–e" semitone, now in the context of the rising b'–e" tetrachord and the very strong E cadence. The next two phrases (7 and 8) then prepare for the resolution of

Example 9.3. Cantata 60: Final chorale

this E to the final A by articulating the range of the minor third, b'–c♯"–b"–d"–c♯"–b', ascending and descending, to pause on the tone above the final. After all this, the range of the melody expands outward in both directions to describe a descent through the perfect fifth from dominant to tonic for the reiterated final phrase. The melody thus controls and delays the return to a', phrases 2 and 5 outlining a descending third motion from e" to c♯" that gives way in phrases 3 and 6 to the ascent to e", phrases 7 and 8 ending with a third descent from d" to b' and phrases 9 and 10 finally supplying the third descent from c♯" to a'. In phrases 2 and 5 A is the subdominant of E, in phrases 7 and 8 it becomes the tonic of the half close on E, and in phrase 10, after a deflection of phrase 9 to the relative minor, it finally sounds as the tonic of a full close. Although withheld until the end, the A cadence, when it finally comes, is unusually satisfying.

Although "Es ist genung" is, in fact, a tonal, not a modal, melody, its beginning with a quasi-Lydian gesture highlights tonal qualities that underlie the way that the modes were perceived for many centuries and that remained beyond the time of Bach even though modal composition itself declined drastically.[5] "Es ist genung," that is, begins with the tetrachord that was traditionally corrected in the Lydian mode because of its introduction of the tritone or, in hexachordal terms, its confusing the placement of the "mi" and "fa" degrees. And it is not coincidental that when we arrange the spectrum of six modal finals (and four tetrachord types) as defined by a single hexachord in a circle-of-fifths pattern—F, C, G, d, a, and e in the case of the *cantus naturalis* and *cantus durus*—the Lydian mode is the flattest, followed by the Ionian/Mixolydian (major) and the Dorian/Aolian (minor), with the Phrygian as the sharpest.[6] The "fa" and "mi" degrees of the hexachord, that is, express a flat–sharp opposition that translates readily into tonal terms. Owing to the fact that its lower tetrachord describes a tritone, the Lydian mode tends toward the mode a fifth above; it was traditionally corrected, therefore, by the substitution of b♭ for its fourth tone, b, a modification that rendered the mode into the more stable Ionian mode but at the same time shifted it into the flat hexachord or system. The Phrygian mode, however, tended tonally toward the mode a fifth below; owing to the widespread avoidance of the sharp system, however, its "correction" to the key of E minor, with the substitution of f♯ for f (Kircher's "other" Hypophrygian mode), came much later in time.[7] The one mode, therefore, involved tonal expansion from the *cantus naturalis* to the *cantus mollis* and the other expansion from the *cantus naturalis* to the *cantus durus*.

The chorales that begin and end Cantatas 77 and 60 embody fundamental melodic qualities of the kind just described that Bach expands on in the settings as a whole, relating those qualities to the "directional" qualities in the cantata texts (heaven/earth; God/humankind, etc.). "Dies sind die heil'gen zehn Gebot" begins with the Ionian/Mixolydian (major) tetrachord, which changes to the Dorian/Aolian (minor) and the Phrygian as the tonality of the opening movement of Cantata 77 expands in the flat direction. "Ach Gott, vom Himmel sieh' darein" ends the cantata with the Phrygian tetrachord in the *cantus mollis*. The first phrase of "O Ewigkeit, du Donnerwort" ends with the Ionian/Mixolydian tetrachord, which changes to the Lydian tetrachord via the raising of its fourth tone, d'', to d♯'' at the beginning of "Es ist genung." The upward or sharpward tendency of the Lydian tetrachord and its final resolution into the Ionian/Mixolydian tetrachord of the mode a fifth higher at the end of Cantata 60 can be considered to mirror the fact that "Es ist genung" represents the believer's glimpse of eternity in the present life, while the downward or flatward tendency of the Phrygian tetrachord and its lack of resolution at the end of Cantata 77 can be considered to represent the believer's cry to God from a state of weakness (although we cannot be sure if the chorale text that ended Cantata 77, "Ach Gott, vom Himmel sieh' darein," itself is an appeal for God to look down upon a world in which the believer is beset by evil and torment). The anomalous flattened and incomplete ending of the final chorale of Cantata 77 may be compared with the anomalous sharpened beginning of "Es ist genung" and its resolution into one of Bach's most satisfying endings.

In Cantata 60 the first phrase of "Es ist genung," harmonizing the rising melodic tritone, introduces one of the most striking gestures in all Bach's music. For others at the time, however, the melodic tritone was problematic: the Vopelius collection alters it to the perfect fourth, featuring d'' instead of d♯'', while Telemann's version of the melody, for example, simply begins on the tonic and ascends by step to the third, repeating the third tone instead of continuing the line upward; Telemann harmonizes the phrase by a simple tonic–dominant–tonic progression. And Telemann, who provides variant versions for the great majority of his melodies, has none in the case of "Es ist genung." The Freylinghausen collection, however, ends the first phrase on the raised fourth degree and retains the motion from tonic to dominant it implies but replaces the initial a' by c♯'', after which the line outlines a stepwise ascent from b' to d♯''.

In contrast, Bach's opening phrase not only retains but also harmonically amplifies the qualities of the tritone. After the initial A major chord, Bach duplicates the rising whole tones of the melody line at the minor tenth (third) below in the bass ([a], g♯, a♯, b♯), changing "fa" into "mi" twice in succession, by raising what we expect to be a second a to a♯ and following it by b♯. The two successive whole tones recall the effect of the "schwerer Gang" of the first recitative. And after the E^6 chord that appears beneath the second melody tone, b', Bach's harmonizing the third tone, c♯'', not with the tonic or any other diatonic harmony but with an $F♯^6$ chord, and his following that in turn not by the normal V of V harmony (B) but by V^6_5 of iii (i.e., a $G♯^6_5$ chord), duplicates the rising whole-tone progression in a sequence of ascending dominant harmonies, thus rendering the entire passage much sharper than we expect. Against this, however, Bach has the alto voice move downward by step from its initial e' through the tone d♮', which sounds on the beat simultaneously with the penultimate $F♯^6$ chord, before reaching the harmony tone c♯' on the second half of the beat. The alto then leaps up a fifth to the root of the $G♯^6_5$ chord, rather than making the much more straightforward motion to b♯ (which has, of course, been preempted by the whole-tone motion to b♯ in the bass). How much easier it would have been had the bass moved back from a (or even a♯) to g♯ rather than pushing upward from a♯ to b♯! But this progression was obviously intended to represent the quintessential "schwerer Gang." The clash of c♯'' and d' on the beat, followed by the c♯''–d♯'' motion of the soprano, suggests that the pitches that constitute the "mi" and "fa" of the scale, their relationship suddenly altered by the sharpening of the "fa" (d'') to "mi" (d♯''), represent an essential relationship whose displacement demands resolution.

The phrase that follows provides a provisional resolution in that the G♯ dominant harmony shifts into root position and moves to the root-position c♯ chord, after which the bass makes a long scalar descent to A and the soprano's d'' resolves to c♯'' for the cadence to A. The cadential c♯–B–A descent in the bass line places the dominant in $^4_2$ position, introducing another passing c♯–d'' clash on the beat just before the cadence. Owing in part to the absence of a strong dominant–tonic bass progression, but even more to the sharpness of the first phrase, the A major cadence sounds like the subdominant of E. The third phrase then reintroduces the still provocative melodic d♯'' and the bass the still provocative a♯, those two pitches leading the phrase to a very strong E cadence. The dynamic of this third phrase represents a "crescendo" to the A♯ diminished-seventh chord with which Bach harmonizes the initial arrival on e''. Its resolution involves one of the most interesting events of the setting, as the tenor, in the highest part of its register, sings the falling semitone, g'–f♯', and is echoed immediately at the cadence by the alto's a'–g♯' semitone. The effect of this brief "dialogue" between the vocal ranges that represent Fear and Hope in the first three movements (which, incidentally, spells the tones B-A-C-H transposed) is that of tension release, as the B^7 chord settles on the cadential E harmony. The alto's initial leap up to g#' now comes to rest, as it were, in the upward melodic curve of the alto line from g#' to c#" (the latter pitch coming within the "dissonant" central harmony of the phrase) and back to g#'; the melodic figure that highlights its final a'–g#' motion lends the cadence a particularly satisfying character that is prophetic, as we will see, for the ending of the chorale.

In Cantata 60 one of Bach's most important goals is to render the dominant of the final A into such a strong point of arrival that the establishing of the new tonic itself, when it comes, will not only be very secure but will also draw earlier tonal events into its perspective. To bring this about Bach provides an "extra" degree of sharpening in the first phrase of "Es ist genung." His exact choice of harmonies is not casual, however, but a greatly compressed version of tonal procedures that had become established in the early seventeenth century in conjunction with the emergence of the "sharp dynamic" and the opening up of the formerly "difficult" sharp system. As Carl Dahlhaus recognized, the dynamic of modulation in the sharp direction, which appeared much later historically than did that in the flat direction, was bound up with articulation of the sharpest of the harmonies that comprised the harmonically conceived hexachord—that is, the "mi" or Phrygian degree, e/E in the case of the C or natural hexachord.[8] Preceding that degree by its dominant involved the encroachment of pitches from the sharp hexachord: F# in the case of the natural hexachord. We have already encountered this "problem" in Athanasius Kircher's Hypophrygian E minor. Once that dominant or sharp dynamic had become established, however, the way was open for the closed circle of keys and a fully transpositional system that would render simultaneously the integrity of the modes and of the single system to which they belonged virtually irrelevant, even to modal composition, which now became a "historical" exercise. Instead of the "Phrygian" degree of the system or hexachord (now the *ambitus*), the dominant of the dominant (or even *its* dominant) became the normal means of securing a shift in the sharp direction. In the opening phrase of "Es ist genung," however, Bach perceived that a swift tonal motion to the dominant of iii, the G#$^{6}_{5}$ chord with which the phrase ends, and especially a motion that emphasized the whole-tone ascent from the dominant (the E^6 chord) to the dominants of ii and iii in turn, would "legitimate" the dominant (sharp) region in a very intensified manner. As the fifth of the harmony, the d#" would be more secure than as the leading tone to E (the role of the *subsemitonium* in older music, which was not taken to be indicative of modulation in the sharp direction), although it would, of course, be heard in the latter role at the E major cadence, two phrases later. We have already seen that one of Bach's means of stabilizing a major tonic, new or otherwise, especially when it is approached from a subdominant context and when it is is associated with the anticipation of eternity, is to move to its mediant degree beforehand. The roles of G# minor in Cantatas 8 and 9 (chapter 6) and of B minor in Cantata 77 (Chapter 8) provide cases in point. The harmonies of the first phrase of "Es ist genung," daring as they are in themselves, have the larger function of immediately and decisively eradicating the tonal framework of D major, renewed at the close of the preceding recitative. They, in fact, "signal" the shift to a sharper frame of reference in a manner that is, once again, "opposite" to the passing augmented triad that sounds in the first phrase of the final chorale of Cantata 77 or the dominant thirteenths in the first four phrases of "Das alte Jahr" in the *Orgelbüchlein.* The tension of the leading tone and the minor third, heard simultaneously in such harmonies, reinforces the downward motion to the minor tonic, whereas the series of raised pitches at the beginning of "Es ist genung" contains an excess of energy that pushes upward to the major mediant. The psychological effect of the one beginning is to suggest a quality of inevitability—ultimately of mortality—and that of the other just the opposite. The one can be considered to project a *mollis* quality, while the other, especially within the musico-theological context of the cantata as a whole, is certainly *durus.*[9]

Obviously, after such a beginning, the second *Stollen* of "Es ist genung" could have no need of a comparable tonal-harmonic event. On the repeat of phrase 1 as phrase 4, therefore, Bach introduces a chromatic descent in the bass that enables him to bring in the dominant of D directly before the melody moves to its d♯'', then to harmonize the d♯'' with vii^6 of E (a dominant substitute). After the chromatic rise from a to a♯ to b in the bass of the preceding phrase, one of the means by which Bach confirms the key of E, the a–g♯–g♮–f♯ descent has, certainly a passing tendency toward the subdominant of A. But the D♯ diminished chord lays it immediately to rest, after which the B–e bass motion at the beginning of the next phrase reconfirms E major in no uncertain terms. Phrase 6 then reabsorbs the pitch G♮ into the E major frame of reference, introducing E minor to darken but in no way undermine the tonality before the E major cadence of phrase 6. Thus, the aforementioned "dialogue" between the tenor g'–f♯ and alto a'–g♯' in phrase 3 returns, now with a slight displacement in the alto line that renders the cadence even more secure. At the end of phrase 6, E major bids fair to be considered the "tonic" key.

There are so many astonishing effects in the harmony and voice leading of this piece that to detail them all would occupy several more pages. The principal point to which they all contribute is the immensely satisfying character of the final cadence. That quality is owing to the fact that after the very strong dominant emphasis in the two *Stollen* and Bach's retaining the pitch d♯' in the harmony of the E cadences of the first phrases of the *Abgesang,* the final A cadence has the effect of resolving the dualism of upward d♯''–e'' and downward d♮''–c♯'' motion, which runs throughout the setting. The first phrase of the *Abgesang* (phrase 7) turns the tonality toward A by introducing the subdominant, D, below the melodic d'' that initiates the descent to the half close on E; the return of d♯' and the dominant of E in the harmony of the cadence give way before this pivotal gesture. In fact, every phrase except the last emphasizes the presence of D♯. But after this sounding of the subdominant for the first time in the piece all subsequent emphasis on E merely prepares for the final A. In this respect, nothing could surpass phrases 8 and 9. Although phrase 8 begins and ends with dominant–tonic progressions to E, between them Bach introduces one of the most mysterious harmonic passages in his output. The chromatic descent of the bass is routine enough; it is the expiring effect of the third, fourth, and fifth chords of the phrase that opens up unsuspected levels of meaning for "mein großer Jammer." Spelled differently, the third chord might have functioned as an augmented-sixth chord, confirming the key of E. But Bach draws it into the chromatic descent pattern so that even the F♯ dominant seventh chord to which it moves (potentially V of V in E) drifts downward to what we must hear by hindsight as ii^6_5 in a/A. With the arrival on the dominant seventh (E^7) beneath the melodic d" that had formerly hosted the subdominant, however, all ambiguity is over, and the D♯s of the half close on E ("bleibt danieden") aid in restoring the believer's confidence in preparation for the final reiterated "Es ist genung." Bach's harmony on the first of the final pair of phrases brings back the whole-tone ascent in the bass, raising the fourth and fifth degrees of the scale to lead the cadence into the relative minor.[10] In itself it is not unusual; its significance lies in its relationship to the following phrase. After this gesture, the bass simply continues its rising line upward through g♯ to a for the beginning of the final phrase; from there it moves solidly downward to the dominant, e, and the lower tonic, A, the harmonies of the final phrase settling on the tonic and dominant only for the first time in the setting.

Most of all, however, the final phrase makes its deeply satisfying effect by virtue of the simple stepwise passage of the tenor from the dominant, e', through d', to c♯', in parallel sixths with the 3–2–1 descent from c♯" to a' in the soprano. We hear this gesture in relation to the rising, sharpened c♯–d♯–e♯–f♯ motion in the bass of the preceding phrase. Bach decorates the tenor d' exactly as he had the a' of the alto as it settled on the g♯' of the very strong E cadence of phrase 3, making the point that this A cadence finally resolves the dominant emphasis at the beginning of the setting. The tenor's e'–d'–c♯' descent also recalls the alto's e'–d'–c♯' descent in the first phrase, suggesting, perhaps, that Fear's dissonant motion is replaced by Hope's satisfying close. The expression "it is enough" can have two virtually opposite meanings, the one indicating longing for release from the fear and tribulation of life and the other representing the transforming quality of the believer's glimpse of eternity on his life in the world—in the terms of Cantata 60, the return of Hope. In fact, that double meaning is prominent in the original text of "Es ist genung," written by Franz Joachim Burmeister. There the third verse clearly articulates the idea of the cross as a "schwerer Gang," just as it appears in Bach's text (the appearance of the word "hart" twice is revealing):

Es ist genug des Kreuzes, das mir fast	It is enough of the cross, that
Den Rücken wund gemacht.	Almost cripples my back.
Wie schwer, o Gott, wie hart ist diese Last!	How heavy, O God, how hard is this burden!
Ich schwemme manche Nacht	Many a night I soak
Mein hartes Lager durch mit Thränen.	My hard bed through with tears.
Wie lang', wie lange muss ich sehnen!	How long, how long must I yearn!
Wenn ist's genug?	When is it enough?

Burmeister's "Wenn ist's genug" was frequently altered to "Es ist genug" (as was the "Des ist genug" of verse 2) so as to render all the verse endings uniform. The original formulation, however, makes clear that the message of this particular verse is dissatisfaction with life, while the two subsequent verses, both of which end with "Es ist genug," make equally clear the transformation effected by Jesus' presence (which comes in verse 4) and the altered meaning of "Es ist genug." Bach's setting of the last strophe of the hymn retains the antithesis between the beginning and ending phrases, the latter of which accomplishes the aforementioned transformation. There is, however, nothing inherently remarkable about the final cadence of "Es ist genung" itself; and the tenor motion described previously is a conventional cadential gesture. What makes it special is that it resolves the d♯–d disparity once and for all. It is possible, in fact, to feel at the close of this chorale that the entire harmonization exists for the satisfying quality of the tenor's d' resolving to c♯', an allegory of the replacing of the troubled "schwerer Gang" of earthly life by the peace and certainty of Jesus' promise.

The final cadence of Cantata 60 not only puts the initial "Es ist genung" in perspective but also fulfills certain tonal-harmonic tendencies of a provocative nature in the preceding two movements. "Es ist genung" is a direct response to the preceding dialogue (movement 4), at the end of which the believer ("Fear"), finally consoled by Jesus' promise of the blessedness of eternal life in the present, had called for "Hope" to return: "Wohlan! soll ich von nun an selig sein: so stelle dich, o Hoffnung, wieder ein! Mein Leib mag ohne Furcht im Schlafe ruhn, der Geist kann einen Blick in jene Freude tun." The ending of this dialogue returns, as mentioned earlier, to the key of D, cadencing in that key with the rising tetrachord from a' to d" as if recalling the principal motif of "O Ewigkeit, du Donnerwort" (Ex. 9.4). The words "[der Geist kann einen Blick] in jene Freude tun," however, prepare for the startling transformation of that gesture at the beginning of "Es ist genung."

The return to D at the end of the final dialogue is a gesture that must be interpreted in light not only of the unusual tonal-modulatory scheme of the movement as a whole but also of the recurrences of D throughout the cantata. After the opening dialogue D is heard solely in association with the response of Hope to Fear's expressions of angst. In the first recitative, for example, Hope answers Fear's initial phrase—"O schwerer Gang zum letzten Kampf und Streite!" (O hard route to the final struggle and combat!)—in D, with "Mein Beistand ist schon da, mein Heiland steht mir ja mit Trost zur Seite" (My assistance is already here, my Savior stands by my side to comfort me). In the first aria dialogue, in b, Hope answers Fear's "Des Glaubens Schwachheit sinket fast" with a strong D major—"Mein Jesus trägt mit mir die Last" (My Jesus bears the burden with me)—after which the ritornello sounds in D. In this particular instance Fear picks up immediately after the ritornello by turning the D into E minor, replacing the hopeful-sounding high d" of its line, and the positive-sounding D major arpeggio with which it begins, by shifting to a low d♯' and deflecting the tonality toward e: "Das offne Grab sieht *greulich* aus" (The open grave has a gruesome appearance). Gestures of this kind appear, in fact, throughout the cantata, but in this case Hope's response is to turn Fear's motion to E minor into major by reintroducing the arpeggio figure a tone higher than before and leading it toward A: "Es wird mir doch ein Friedenshaus" (It becomes, however, a house of peace for me). Fear reiterates its former gesture, converting the A to f♯, after which Hope turns to F♯ major and attempts to lead Fear on to B major. Fear, however, converts the d♯' into the leading tone of e again, breaking the pattern. Hope has the last word, resolving Fear's doubts into a secure B minor cadence, but the tendency toward a rising whole-tone sequence of major keys is unfulfilled. Something more than Hope is required.

Example 9.4. Cantata 60: Ending of penultimate movement (no. 5)

In the next movement the figure of Jesus replaces Hope, as we know. This dialogue begins in e with a prominent d♯ in the bass, which shifts a tritone to a after two measures, the alto shifting from its initial a' to d♯' with a diminished-seventh-chord arpeggio line that has been heard several times in both the preceding movements. Then, as if recalling the rising whole-tone pattern of the preceding dialogue, the alto shifts up to F♯ minor, closing in that key: "Der Tod bleibt doch der menschlichen Natur verhaßt und reißet fast die Hoffnung ganz zu Boden." Now Jesus answers in arioso style and in D major, with the first phrase of the words of Revelation: "Selig sind die Toten." The major-third shift downward from f♯ to D has a comforting quality to offset the tension of Fear's rising whole-tone modulation. And not only is the D very secure, but Jesus' line seems to recall the D major arpeggio line of the preceding movement. Fear, however, cannot accept the words of promise as yet, entering with a g♯' above the d of the *basso continuo* and returning the tonality to f♯: "Ach! aber ach, wieviel Gefahr stellt sich der Seele dar, den Sterbeweg zu gehen" (Ah! but ah, how much danger presents itself to the soul, to take the path of death). And with the next line, Fear once again shifts up a whole tone, now to g♯ (a tritone modulation in relation to Jesus' D), closing in that key as its torment increases: "Vielleicht wird ihr der Höllenrachen den Tod erschrecklich machen, wenn er sie zu verschlingen sucht; vielleicht ist sie bereits verflucht zum ewigen Verderben" (Perhaps the rage of hell will make death frightening to it [the soul], when it attempts to devour it; perhaps it is already cursed to eternal destruction). On "verflucht" Fear leaps a tritone from c♯' to f double sharp (a *saltus duriusculus* to confirm the meaning of the earlier "schwerer Gang"), the double-sharp sign reminding us of St. Paul's (and Luther's) description of the cross as a "Fluch" (curse). Fear has reached the apex of its torment, introducing the sharpest key of the cantata.[11] The ascending e–f♯–g♯ progression in the alto can be considered to prefigure the harmonies of the first phrase of "Es ist genung." And Jesus responds to Fear's g♯, as He had to its f♯, by shifting to the major key a major third below, E, and with the same comforting phrase (now extended by the addition of "die in dem Herren sterben") and the same secure tonal character: "Selig sind die Toten, die in dem Herren sterben." Fear now appears to accept something of the meaning of Jesus' words: its initial question—"Wenn ich im Herren sterbe, ist denn die Seligkeit mein Teil und Erbe?" (If I die in the Lord, is then blessedness my share and inheritance?)—takes on a rhetorical character, and the verb "scheinen" in its final line: "da ich ein Kind des Todes heiße, so schein ich ja im Grabe zu verderben" (since I am a child of death, I certainly appear to disintegrate in the grave) indicates a weakening of its former pessimism. This solo, therefore, reverses its earlier modulatory pattern, beginning in f♯ and moving down a whole tone to end on the dominant of e (the half close leaving the tonality open for Jesus' answer); the bass of the cadence even returns to the a–d♯ tritone with which the movement had begun.

Jesus' answer, again, shifts down the major third, to C, as the bass completes the line from Revelation. Already in the first recitative Bach had introduced a tendency for Hope to respond to Fear's anguished outcries by shifting in the subdominant direction. There Hope's final solo had responded to Fear's tormented shift to f♯ by turning to a and ending in a hopeful-sounding G. Now in Jesus' third solo Bach moves further in the flat direction, introducing the first (and only) flat accidentals in the work in conjunction with the subdominant of C. Although the passage is comforting and basically in major, as before, Bach does not avoid the reality of death that lies behind Jesus' words. For the final "sterben, von nun an" he therefore settles on the dominant of e and cadences in that key after a final threnodic prolonging of the word "sterben." This confirmation of the key in which Fear's solos had begun and ended can be considered to complete an upward–downward tonal curve in which Fear moves upward by whole tones (e–f♯ and f♯–g♯) to the apex of its torment, g♯, and back (f♯–e), while Jesus responds in D, E, and C, ending in e in confirmation of the reality of death but placing that e in a hopeful context. Whole-tone and major-third relationships predominate in keeping with Bach's intent to depict both the "schwerer Gang" of earthly life and the message of comfort that enables the believer to overcome it. Fear now concludes the dialogue with the words cited previously, modulating down one final whole tone, to D, and cadencing in that key with the aforementioned association of the rising tetrachord of the key and the glimpse into eternity. The beginning of "Es ist genung" then immediately intensifies and transforms that gesture by means of the most revealing rising-whole-tone progression in the work.

The chorale, as we saw, deals with the relationship between D and D♯, the latter pitch impelling the strong articulation of E that enables the cantata not only to end a fifth higher than it began but also to invest the new tonic key with associations of peace. The dialogue aspect of this and other Bach cantatas is, of course, a symbol of a divided human nature, an inability to find rest from doubts regarding death in particular. Lutheran eschatology emphasized the peace that faith provided by interpreting death in terms of sleep; Luther's paraphrase of the canticle of Simeon, the *Nunc dimittis*, as the chorale "Mit Fried und Freud ich fahr' dahin" poeticized the "sleep of death" in terms of the believer's ability to view death in peace and joy. The ending of the last dialogue of Cantata 60 refers to the believer's glimpse into the joyful hereafter (the rising D tetrachord), after which the task of "Es ist genung" is to render that vision of the world above into the source of peace for the believer. Earlier in the cantata Hope (movement 4) and Jesus (movement 5) had attempted to lead Fear's vision upward, by whole tones, into the sphere of the sharp major keys, especially the E of Jesus' second solo, and back. Hope's answer to Fear in the final exchange of movement 4 had interpreted the grave (Fear's "Das offne Grab sieht greulich aus") as a "house of peace" (Hope's "Es wird mir doch ein Friedenshaus"). Now, in "Es ist genung" we hear an echo of the believer's longing for peace, as the second *Stollen* closes with two phrases cadencing in A and E, respectively: "Nun gute Nacht, o Welt!" (phrase 5) and "Ich fahr ins Himmelshaus" (phrase 6). The completed E major of phrase 6 thus represents the vision of the world above, to which the world below is subordinated (the A of phrase 5), while the gradual move back toward A over the subsequent phrases represents the return of the believer's viewpoint to the world below as one that has been transformed by that vision into a new sense of peace and security: "Ich fahre sicher hin mit Frieden, mein großer Jammer bleibt danieden. Es ist genung" (I journey securely forth in peace, my great misery remains here below. It is enough).

Alban Berg's choosing this chorale setting as the principal musical symbol behind the eschatological program for his 1935 violin concerto was an action permeated by a profound understanding of what the movement represented for Bach.[12] From that standpoint the concerto is a milestone in the area of Bach reception. Berg, as is well known, incorporated the first phrase of the chorale into the tone row of the concerto, its four pitches, transposed up a whole tone, serving as the last four of the set. The transposition was owing, of course, to the fact that the other nine pitches of the row outline a rising-third progression that passes through a series of triads formed on the open strings of the violin (the first, third, fifth, and seventh pitches): g, b♭, d', f♯', a', c'', e'', g♯'', b'', c♯''', d♯''', e♯'''. Thus, the row outlines an alternating set of minor and major triads over its first nine pitches—g, D, a, E—after which the whole-tone sequence borrowed from "Es ist genung" suggests, if we refer to its original context (transposed, of course), the keys of B and its dominant, F♯. In other words, the row is an ascending circle of fifths that favors minor triads at the beginning and major toward the end; and if we transpose it down the whole tone, so that the final four pitches correspond with the first four of Bach's chorale (an octave higher, of course)—a", b", c♯''', and d♯'''—then the last six tones (d", f♯", a", b", c♯''', and d♯''') would correspond to the beginning of the first phrase of "O Ewigkeit, du Donnerwort" (the D major triad) followed by the beginning of "Es ist genung." And the sequence of triads in the row as a whole, including the keys implied by the ending of the series, would be f, C, g, D, A, and E. Taken as a series of pitches, this pattern corresponds to the natural hexachord, which would be very unlikely for Berg to have had in mind at all. Taken as a series of triads or even keys, it traverses a much wider tonal range, the one, in fact, that corresponds, in abbreviated form, to the flat/sharp limits of the movement keys of Bach's cantatas and passions—F minor to E major. Berg has arranged his row so that it embodies an essential feature of the Western tonal system, and one that many composers after 1600 drew upon for musico-allegorical purposes, despite the great style differences among their works. The fifth- or fifth-plus-third-based principle behind pitches, triads, modes, and keys tended very much to view flatward progressions as descending motion and sharpward ones as the reverse. In the nineteenth century, when forms of "religious aesthetics" came into existence, especially in Germany, we find no dearth of works, among which Wagner's *Tristan und Isolde* is, of course, the prime example, that polarize the "deep" flat and sharp keys, even merge them via wide-ranging enharmonicism, for the purpose of creating an aura of transcendence. The beginning and ending keys of the third act of *Tristan*—F minor and B major—offer the most outstanding example, but other endings, such as the B major of the Lizst B minor sonata and Strauss's *Also sprach Zarathustra* and the E major ending of Mahler's Fourth Symphony, seem also to make an association between their very sharp keys and the elevated or transcendental spheres those ending keys represent. We might say that Berg is reflecting on fundamental properties of the tonal system within a new atonal context just as Bach and many Baroque composers before him reflected back on what they viewed as the *stile antico* of the sixteenth century within the context of the new tonal system.

In the foregoing description I have, despite the considerable detail, merely sketched the qualities, tonal or otherwise, that might be brought to bear on the question of musical allegory in Cantata 60. I have intended basically to indicate that Bach's musical language, in the cantatas at least, is conditioned in major ways by the Lutheran thought world in which he lived and produced his many masterworks. If Bach's works are nevertheless "universal" in their expressive content, that quality is owing to the fact that neither Lutheranism nor any other conceptual system has a monopoly on the kinds of expression of which music is capable. Music such as Bach's, that is, deals with analogues of religious ideas and affective qualities that underlie the human experience in general. Nevertheless, understanding the particular, or historical, aspects of Bach's work—its various contexts—is, I believe, essential to fully appreciating the nature of Bach's genius. Bach's progressiveness has, in my view, little or nothing to do with his putting on the mantle of contemporary styles such as the *galant* manner but is owing to a much more interesting quality: a complexity of thought (whether manifested purely in tone relationships or in musico-allegorical procedures) that sets him apart from his surroundings. While his contemporary Johann Mattheson made an issue out of publicly rejecting the church modes, solmization, all that he deemed unnatural in the area of text setting, the role of *ratio* and received theoretical opinion on questions of consonance versus dissonance, and the like, Bach perceived the potential of all those ways of understanding music for composition. His dissonances, for example, are amazingly rational and even capable of being conceptualized in terms of solmization; they are nonetheless affective on that account. Whereas Mattheson's outlook is unquestionably progressive, it is just as surely locked in its own time. In developing and intensifying traditional, even archaic, ways of understanding music, however, Bach carried them far into the future, opening up questions for the analysis, interpretation, and composition of music that are very much with us and are probably timeless.

Notes

Chapter One

1. See Paul Althaus, *The Theology of Martin Luther*, trans. Robert C. Schultz (Philadelphia: Fortress Press, 1966), pp. 72–78.

2. See Heinrich Bornkamm, *Luther and the Old Testament*, trans. Eric W. Gritsch and Ruth C. Gritsch, ed. Victor I. Gruhn (Philadelphia: Fortress Press, 1974).

3. In fact, the opposition of Law and freedom accounted for the only place in the Bible where the process of allegorizing scripture was applied directly (by St. Paul) and even with the term "allegory." The passage in question, Galatians 4:21–31, is a central focus for the subject matter of Paul's Epistle, as Paul's interpretation of the relationship of Law and Gospel was for Luther's theology. Luther's commentary on Galatians 4: 21–31 (see Martin Luther, *Lectures on Galatians, Chapters 1–4*, vol. 26 of *Luther's Works*, ed. Jaroslav Pelikan [St. Louis: Concordia, 1963], pp. 432–61) provides an excellent summary of his attitude toward allegory, including his rejection of the medieval four senses of scripture (pp. 433, 440) because of its traditional application to Law and works rather than faith, grace, and Christ. In this passage, as in his commentary on Isaiah, Luther describes the interpretation of scripture according to the analogy of Law (destruction) and Gospel (revival) as the only true form of allegory—that is, the interpretation of historical events according to their internal or tropological meaning. See Philip Rollinson, *Classical Theories of Allegory and Christian Culture* (Pittsburgh: Duquesne University Press and Harvester Press, 1981), pp. 30–32.

4. Martin Luther, *Lectures on Isaiah, Chapters 1–39*, trans. Herbert J. A. Bouman, vol. 16 of *Luther's Works*, ed. Jaroslav Pelikan (St. Louis: Concordia, 1969), p. 327.

5. See Eric Chafe, "Luther's 'Analogy of Faith' in the Bach Cantatas," *dialog* 24 (Spring 1985): 96–101, and Chafe, *Tonal Allegory in the Vocal Music of J. S. Bach* (Berkeley: University of California Press, 1991), p. 13.

6. That work, Cantata 46, "Schauet doch und sehet ob irgendein Schmerz sei," for the tenth Sunday after Trinity, 1723, takes up the theme of the destruction of Jerusalem in the time of Jeremiah, drawing a parallel between that event and Jesus' prediction in the New Testament of the destruction of Jerusalem in A.D. 70. It then interprets the destruction of Jerusalem in terms of the believer's spiritual condition. In the Middle Ages, as Stephen L. Wailes points out

(*Medieval Allegories of Jesus' Parables* [Berkeley: University of California Press, 1987], pp. 10–11), the particular example of Jerusalem was so widespread as to be a "commonplace" in discussions of the several levels of hermeneutics, undoubtedly a factor behind Luther's choice of the destruction and rebuilding of Jerusalem as the example for the "analogy of faith." In such explications, Jerusalem was understood literally as a city, but spiritually as the church (the allegorical sense), the soul (the tropological sense), and the Kingdom of Heaven (the eschatological sense). In this light, it may be mentioned that the story of the destruction of Jerusalem in A.D. 70, as told by the Roman historian Josephus, was read annually in Leipzig, as in other places, on the tenth Sunday after Trinity. See Robin A. Leaver, "Bach, Hymns and Hymnbooks," *The Hymn* 36, no. 4 (October 1985): 7–13.

7. The Calov Bible that Bach possessed contains many examples of Luther's allegorical interpretations of scripture, and several were underlined or marked by Bach himself. See, for example, Howard H. Cox, ed., *The Calov Bible of J. S. Bach* (Ann Arbor: UMI Research Press, 1985), pp. 40 (three wells), 405 (precious stones), 406 (spices), and 410 (the parts of the Law).

8. Jaroslav Pelikan, *Bach among the Theologians* (Philadelphia: Fortress Press, 1986), p. 4

9. Although Neumeister's treatise speaks of the *threefold* advent of Jesus, whereas Cantata 61 describes a fourfold advent, it is clear that the sequence is the same in both cases. The first recitative (no. 2) describes Jesus' taking on human flesh ("Der Heiland ist gekommen, hat unser armes Fleisch und Blut an sich genommen"), the first aria (no. 3) represents "word" and "sacrament" in its final lines, "Erhalte die gesunde Lehre und segne Kanzel und Altar," the second recitative (no. 4) extends the sacramental advent to the *Abendmahl* that Jesus shares with the believer ("Siehe, ich stehe vor der Tür und klopfe an. So jemand meine Stimme hören wird und die Tür auftun, zu dem werde ich eingehen und das Abendmahl mit ihm halten und er mit mir"), and the second aria interprets Jesus' knocking and entering as His dwelling within the believer ("Daß ich seine Wohnung werde"). In other words, the stage that represents "word" and "sacrament" becomes a twofold one, describing a progression from word as doctrine (*Lehre* and *Kanzel*) through the internalizing of the word via the sacrament (*Altar, Abendmahl,* and *Wohnung*). The appropriateness of the four stages of hermeneutics for Advent was underscored by the fact that the Gospel reading for Advent Sunday (Matthew 21:1–9) described Jesus' entry into Jerusalem; behind the text of Cantata 61, therefore, lies the traditional interpretation of Jerusalem according to the four senses, to which Cantata 61 corresponds exactly (see note 6). Matthew's narrative of the entry into Jerusalem culminates with the words that constitute the Hosanna and Benedictus of the Mass, thereby reinforcing the association between Jesus' entering the human heart (the tropological sense) and the communion. Thus, as Alfred Dürr points out (*Die Kantaten von Johann Sebastian Bach* [Kassel: Barenreiter, 1971], 1:103), the "high point" of Cantata 61 is the accompanied recitative in which the bass, functioning as the *vox Christi,* refers to sharing the *Abendmahl* with the believer. The symbolic or "spiritual" interpretation of Jesus' birth as His entry into Jerusalem has parallels, of course, with the liturgical occasion on which the entry into Jerusalem was the direct (literal) subject matter, Palm Sunday, for which Paul's description of the Last Supper (1 Corinthians 11:23–32) was an alternate Epistle reading. In Cantata 61 the overall textual pattern is one of increasing intimacy with Jesus, which, as Dürr has pointed out for this and other early Bach cantatas, is represented by a pattern of decreasing instrumentation in the closed movements, the second aria being for voice and *basso continuo* alone. See Alfred Dürr, *Studien über die frühen Kantaten Johann Sebastian Bachs* (Wiesbaden: Breitkopf & Härtel, 1977), pp. 213–16. On the theme of darkness/light in Cantata 61 and its association with the turning of the liturgical year see "Aspects of the Liturgical Year." On the key plan of Cantata 61 see Chafe, *Tonal Allegory*, pp. 142–43.

10. Chafe, *Tonal Allegory*, pp. 91–123. The levels of organization in question involve Old Testament/New Testament parallels, chronological sequences of Old Testament, New Testament, and chorale texts, patterns of reduction and expansion in scoring, motivic interrelationships, and tonal plan. Most of the texts of the individual movements were, as Renate Steiger has shown, to be found in prayer books of the time, where they were organized into "catenas of both biblical sayings and hymns, used for the pastoral care of the dying"; on a single page (130) of Johann Olearius's *Christliche Bet-Schule auff unterschiedliche Zeit/Personen/Verrichtungen/Creutz/Noth und Zufälle im Leben . . . Die dritte Ausfertigung* (Leipzig, 1668), for example, the sequence of texts that correspond to four successive movements of the "Actus Tragicus" (from "Bestelle dein Haus" through "Heute wirst du mit mir im Paradies seyn") appear in order, with the only difference from the cantata being that instead of the chorale text whose melody Bach assigns to the instruments in the central movement of the cantata ("Ich hab' mein Sach' Gott heimgestellt"), Olearius provides the biblical text "Ich habe Lust abzuscheiden und bey Christo zu seyn." Later in the book (p. 715), the texts "Heute wirst du mit mir im Paradies seyn" and "Mit Fried und Freud ich fahr dahin" appear in immediate succession, as they do in the cantata (Renata Steiger, "Symbol and Musical *Inventio*: Biblical and Emblematic Imagery in the Vocal Works of Johann Sebastian Bach," a paper given at the annual conference of the Internationale Arbeitsgemeinschaft für theologische Bachforschung at the Newberry Library, Chicago, in September 1997, and "Actus tragicus und ars moriendi. Bach's Textvorlage für die Kantata 'Gottes Zeit ist die allerbeste Zeit' [BWV 106]," *Musik und Kirche* 59 [1989]:11–23). In this light, Bach's work presents us with a multifaceted reflection of the coordination of devotional texts of various kinds for the purpose of meditation. The most prominent overall musical means that Bach uses to coordinate all these are the well-known symmetrical arrangement of the movements and the tonal plan of modulation from E♭ to b♭ and back. The numerous compositional choices involved (of style, instrumentation, solo versus choral settings, major/minor keys, etc.) attest to Bach's intention of mirroring the principles behind Lutheran hermeneutics, the progression from scripture to the consolation of faith in the believer. The modern interpreter of Bach's cantata texts needs to be alert to the variety of forms that the reflections of traditional hermeneutics may take in the Bach cantatas. In the present study I have attempted to indicate patterns of various kinds in the discussions of Cantatas 21, 18, 153, 121, 9, 77, and 60.

11. Bornkamm, *Luther and the Old Testament*, p. 120.

12. See Pelikan, *Bach among the Theologians*, pp. 91–101; and Althaus, *The Theology of Martin Luther*, pp. 202–8.

13. For a different, and controversial view see Gustaf Aulén, *Christus Victor: An Historical Study of the Three Main Types of the Idea of Atonement*, translated by A.G. Hebert (New York: Macmillan 1969), pp. 101–122. I have summarized Aulén's views in "Aspects of the Liturgical Year."

14. Elke Axmacher, *"Aus Liebe will mein Heyland sterben": Untersuchen zum Wandel des Passionverständnisses im Frühen 18. Jahrhundert* (Neuhausen-Stuttgart: Hänsller, 1984), pp. 170–85. See also Chafe, *Tonal Allegory*, pp. 343–54.

15. As Friedrich Smend argued convincingly many years ago ("Bachs Matthäus-Passion," *Bach-Jahrbuch* 25 [1928]? 60–71), the part of the trial scene of the *St. Matthew Passion* that centers around the aria "Aus Liebe will mein Heiland sterben" constitutes a centerpiece ("Herzstück") or focal point for the opposition between Jesus' innocent sufferings and the demand for His death from the mob. The middle section of "Aus Liebe" makes clear that Jesus' death, motivated by love for the believer, removes both the eternal contamination of humanity by sin and God's judgment ("Aus Liebe will mein Heiland sterben, von einer Sünde weiß er nichts, *daß das ewige Verderben und die Strafe des Gerichts nicht auf meiner Seele*

bliebe"). And shortly before "Aus Liebe," and also forming part of the aforementioned centerpiece, the chorale "Wie wunderbarlich ist doch diese Strafe" describes Jesus' judgment as His paying the sinners' debts: "Die Schuld bezahlt der Herre, der Gerechte, für seine Knechte." "Wie wunderbarlich" and "Aus Liebe" connect up theologically and musically with the scene at Gethsemane in part 1, where the arioso "O Schmerz" and chorale verse "Was ist die Ursach aller solchen Plagen" take up the imagery of Jesus suffering before God's court of judgment on behalf of the sinner. By virtue of its *bassetchen* setting (i.e., without *basso continuo*), "Aus Liebe" also links up with other Bach movements in which the opposition of God's judgment and mercy figures prominently. On Bach's use of the *bassetchen* texture see chapter 5, "'O grosser Gott von Macht' in Cantata 46," the introduction to chapter 8.

16. The chorale was written by Paul Sperontes in 1523–24 and published in the latter year. I have discussed Cantata 9 in "'Es ist das Heil uns kommen hier' (Cantata 9)" in chapter 6; see also Chafe, *Tonal Allegory*, pp. 163–64.

17. Klaus Düwel, ed., *Gedichte 1500–1600*, vol. 3 of *Epochen der deutschen Lyrik* (Munich: Deutsche Taschenbuch, 1978), pp. 71–75. As Düwel indicates, the fourteen verses of "Es ist das Heil uns kommen hier" are followed by fourteen paragraphs headed with the letters of the German alphabet from *A* to *O*, each paragraph listing the scriptural references that underlie the corresponding verse of the chorale. The practice of constant allusion to scripture in chorales and even cantata texts was well established, of course. Among modern scholars, Martin Petzoldt has developed the interpretation of such texts according to their scriptural "concordances" as a means of understanding their theological intentions. See Martin Petzoldt, "Studieren zur Theologie im Rahmen der Lebengeschichte J. S. Bachs," unpublished *Habilitationsschrift*, Leipzig, 1985.

18. In the present study see, for example, the discussions of Cantatas 21 (chapter 3), 18, 109 (chapter 5), 9 (chapter 6), and 77 (chapters 7 and 8).

19. These alignments are in some cases approximate, of course, especially since the date of Easter fluctuated over a period of longer than a month. But the intent that the liturgical, geophysical, and civil years parallel one another is an ancient one that gave rise to many metaphoric correspondences between the physical world (e.g., light/darkness) and religious life. The literature on the liturgical year is very large. A useful summary of its origins can be found in Thomas Talley, *The Origins of the Liturgical Year*, 2d ed. (Collegeville, Minn.: Liturgical Press, 1991).

20. This interpretation of Pentecost can be found in Cantata 68, "Also hat Gott die Welt geliebt," for the second day of Pentecost, 1724, all the movements of which refer not to the coming of the Holy Spirit but to the incarnation of Jesus: "Also hat Gott die Welt geliebt, daß er uns seinen Sohn gegeben" (no. 1); "Mein gläubiges Herze, frohlocke, sing, scherze, dein Jesus ist da!" (no. 2); and "Du bist geboren mir zugute" (no. 4). Without knowing the occasion for which the work was composed, we might well conclude that it was a Christmas cantata.

21. Another form of ordering was to begin with the chorales for the Temporale followed by those for the few other fixed feast days in the year, such as those of John the Baptist, the Visitation, and the feast of St. Michael, then either to continue with chorales that centered on doctrine (but not necessarily with the catechism chorales), ending with eschatological chorales and miscellaneous chorales (this is the ordering of Johann Anastius Freylinghausen, *Geistreiches Gesang-Buch* and *Neues geistreiches Gesang-Buch*, ed. G. A. Francke [Halle, 1741), or to follow the ordering of the Trinity season (this is the pattern of Gottfried Vopelius, *Neu-Leipziger Gesangbuch* [Leipzig, 1682]), ending with miscellaneous chorales.

22. That certain of the chorales on these two subjects overlapped can be seen in Vopelius, *Neu-Leipziger Gesangbuch*, for example, which includes the chorales on justification (among which "Es ist das Heil" appears) under those for the Lord's Supper.

23. See Christoph Wolff, ed., *The Neumeister Collection of Chorale Preludes from the Bach Circle* (New Haven and London: Yale University Press, 1986).

24. In addition, the chorale cantata that Bach supplied in later years for the fourth Sunday after Trinity in the chorale cantata cycle, "Ich ruf' zu dir, Herr Jesu Christ" (Cantata 177, 1732), centers on a penitential chorale (see Dürr, *Die Kantaten,* 2: 475). On the cantatas for the early weeks of Bach's first Leipzig cantata cycle see later in this chapter.

25. I discuss Cantata 60 in greater detail in chapter 9.

26. Dürr, *Die Kantaten,* 2: 714–15.

27. "Freu' dich sehr" was normally set in quadruple meter, as, for example, in the final movement of Cantata 25, where it culminates a change from torment to optimism in the cantata as a whole (see later in this chapter). In "Wachet! betet! betet! wachet!" the change from quadruple to triple meter for this movement (a device utilized by Bach in many cantatas) amplifies the positive tone of the chorale; and, in fact, that quality took precedence over correct text declamation, since in triple meter the final syllable of the word "Seele" is accented in the line "*Freu'* dich *sehr,* o *mei*ne See*le*."

28. Helene Werthemann, *Die Bedeutung der alttestamentlichen Historien in Johann Sebastian Bachs Kantaten* (Tübingen: J. B. Mohr, 1960), p. 19. Werthemann cites expressions from the texts of four movements: "*diesen* Tag" (1), "O selger Tag, o ungemeines *Heute* (2), "So kehret sich nun *heut* das bange Leid" (4), and "Was Gott hat *anheut* getan" (5). It may be added that the third movement also emphasizes the present, now in terms of the image of all that is contrary to but nevertheless subordinate to God's will, "Gott, du hast es wohl gefüget, was uns *itzo* widerfährt."

29. Dürr (*Die Kantaten,* 1:121) points out that the construction of Cantata 63 is one of "astonishing symmetry."

30. The aria in question is the fifth movement of Cantata 190, "Singet dem Herrn ein neues Lied." For an instance of ending/beginning symbolism in Bach's cantata for New Year's Day 1725, see Eric Chafe, "*Anfang und Ende*: Cyclic Recurrence in Bach's Cantata *Jesu, nun sei gepreiset,* BWV 41," *Bach Perspectives* 1 (spring 1994): 103–34.

31. See the discussion of Cantata 153 in chapter 5.

32. Aulén, *Christus Victor,* pp. 1–60.

33. Althaus, *The Theology of Martin Luther,* p. 222.

34. Jaroslav Pelikan (*Bach among the Theologians,* pp. 91–101) was the first to set forth this idea, which I have elaborated upon in relation to the structures of Bach's two passions in *Tonal Allegory,* pp. 275–423.

35. Helene Werthemann (*Die Bedeutung der alttestamentlichen Historien,* p. 16) brings out the important point that Bach's cantatas for Christmas, the Passion, and Easter are linked by the *Christus victor* theme.

Chapter Two

1. The most sustained study of the themes and theorists of this tradition is Rolf Dammann, *Der Musikbegriff im deutschen Barock* (Cologne: Arno Volk, 1967). Dammann does not use the expression "metaphysical tradition," although many of his discussions tend in that direction.

2. Werckmeister's title page, after setting forth the purpose of his treatise, continues: "auch andern Gott und Kirchen-Music liebenden zum weitern Nachdencken Mathematicè, Historicè, und Allegoricè, durch die Musicalischen Proportional-Zahlen entdecket . . ."

3. Monteverdi's views were set forth by his brother Giulio Cesare as the afterword to Claudio Monteverdi's *Scherzi musicali* of 1607 in the form of a "declaration concerning the letter published in the fifth book of his madrigals" ("Dichiaratione della lettera stampata nel

quinto libro de suoi madrigali"). English translation in Oliver Strunk, ed., *Strunk's Source Readings in Music History*, revised edition, Leo Treitler, general editor (New York: Norton, 1998), pp. 535–544.

4. Manfred Bukofzer, *Music in the Baroque Era* (New York: Norton, 1947), pp. 3–4.

5. Virtually all Werckmeister's treatises state this purpose not only once but several times, sometimes in slightly different forms (that is, exchanging "usefulness" to one's neighbor for edification or recreation). See, for example, *Musicae mathematicae hodegus curiosus* (Frankfurt and Leipzig, 1686; facsimile ed., Hildesheim: Georg Olms, 1972), dedication p. 2, text pp. 3, 152, 154; *Musicalische Temperatur* (Quedlinburg, 1691; ed. Rudolf Rasch, Utrecht: Diapason Press, 1983), pp. v, xiii, 91; *Hypomnemata Musica* (1697), p. 44, together with *Erweiterte und verbesserte Orgel-Probe* (1698), p. 82; *Cribrum Musicum* (1700), p. 58; *Harmonologia Musica* (1702), pp. 6, 7 (unnumbered) of the dedication, p. 3 (unnumbered) of the preface, pp. 71, 142 of the text; and *Musicalische Paradoxal-Discourse* (1707), title page, text p. 11 (facsimile ed. [5 vols. in 1], Hildesheim, Georg Olms, 1970). Also, the oration written by Johann Melchior Göze for Werckmeister's funeral (1706) and published in 1707 (see later in this chapter) describes the goal of music in terms of giving honor to God and pleasure to human spirits ("zu Gottes Ehre und der menschlichen Gemüther Vergnügung"). Even Johann Mattheson, whose opposition to the more conservative branch of the Lutheran musical tradition (represented by Johann Heinrich Buttstedt) is well-known, had a deep affinity for many aspects of that tradition. Mattheson describes the purpose of his treatise "Geist- und Weltlichen Harmonien" in *Der musicalische Patriot* (Hamburg, 1728; facsimile ed., Leipzig: Zentralantiquariat der Deutschen Demokratischen Republik, 1975), as to promote "the glory of God, the common good and the edification of each particular reader" (title page), adding that its "proper order" and "best use," which "every school boy knows how to sing," is "for the praise of God and the use and service of the neighbor" (p. 11).

6. As is well-known, Bach described the purpose of music on the title page of the *Orgelbüchlein* as "to honor almighty God alone and to instruct the neighbor" ("Dem höchsten Gott allein zu Ehren, dem Nächsten, draus sich zu belehren"). The excerpts from Friedrich Niedt's *Musicalische Handleitung* that Bach used in teaching thoroughbass to his students described the thoroughbass as producing a "well sounding *Harmonie* for the Honour of God and the permissible delight of the soul," adding that "the ultimate end or Final Goal of music, including the thorough-bass, shall be nothing but the Honour of God and recreation of the Soul" (see Hans T. David and Arthur Mendel, eds., *The New Bach Reader*, revised and enlarged by Christoph Wolff (New York: Norton, 1998), pp. 16–17, and Werner Neumann and Hans-Joachim Schulze, eds., *Bach-Dokumente*, vol. 1: *Schriftstücke von der Hand Johann Sebastian Bach* [Kassel: Bärenreiter, 1963], p. 214, and vol. 2: *Fremdschriftliche undgedruckte Dokumente zur Lebensgeschichte Johann Sebastian Bachs 1685–1750* [Kassel: Bärenreiter, 1969], p. 334). Bach, like Niedt, was describing the purpose of music in a way that is encountered over and over again in the writings of the Lutheran "metaphysical" tradition in music theory. That this view of the purpose of music derived from the commandment to love God and one's neighbor is clearly evident in a passage from Werckmeister's *Harmonologia Musica*, where Werckmeister speaks of "Gottes Ehre und die Liebe des Nechsten" in conjunction with the necessary training of organists, leading that topic directly into the necessity of understanding the modes (p. 71).

7. See Neumann and Schulze, *Bach-Dokumente*, 1: 19–20; and David and Mendel, *The New Bach Reader*, pp. 57, 80–81. Gunther Stiller (*J. S. Bach and Liturgical Life in Leipzig*, trans. Herbert J. A. Bouman, Daniel F. Poellot, and Hilton C. Oswald, ed. Robin Leaver [St. Louis: Concordia, 1984], pp. 208–11) makes the case that Bach's statement of Glory to God and service to the neighbor is an expression of "final purpose" (*Endzweck*) that relates to his well-known statement regarding his goal of producing a "well regulated church music to the glory of God" in the 1708 letter of resignation to the Mühlhausen town council.

8. See Eric Chafe, "Bach's First Two Leipzig Cantatas: A Message for the Community," in *A Birthday Offering: Essays in Honor of William H. Scheide*, ed. Paul Brainard and Ray Robinson (Kassel: Bärenreiter, and Chapel Hill: Hinshaw, 1993), pp. 71–86.

9. See Eric Chafe, "Allegorical Music: The 'Symbolism' of Tonal Language in the Bach Canons," *Journal of Musicology* 3 (fall 1984): 340–62.

10. Bach's canons on the harmonic triad (*Trias harmonica*) and the catchphrases "Mi fa et fa mi est tota musica" and "In fine videbitur cujus toni" all represent tonal aspects of music that Werckmeister (and others in the Lutheran "metaphysical" tradition of music theory) associated with both the basic elements of music—the triad as basis of harmony, the "mi/fa" semitone as basis of diatonic music, and the final cadence as determinant of the mode—and music's mirroring of the divine order. On the triad see, for example, Werckmeister, *Musicae mathematicae*, pp. 3–4, 104–5; on the "mi/fa" catchphrase see *Musicalische Paradoxal-Discourse*, p. 45. In the case of Bach's canon on "In fine videbitur cujus toni" only the inscription has survived, without the music. For Werckmeister's and Luther's use of that expression, see chapter 4, "Durch Adams Fall'—Andreas Werckmeister on the Hypophrygian Mode." In "Allegorical Music" (pp. 353–54), I discuss the possibility that one of the fourteen canons notated in Bach's hand in a copy of the *Goldberg Variations* was the lost "In fine videbitur cujus toni" canon. The canon in question obscures its key (G) at the beginning and, owing to Bach's harmonization and the perpetual circling, can only end with all parts together in a cadence on the dominant (D). Bach's only other canon that is headed with the word "Symbolum" appears among the fourteen, without its heading. In addition, Bach might also have derived the titles *Wohl-temperirtes Clavier* and *Kleines harmonisches Labyrinth* from Werckmeister, whose *Erweiterte und verbesserte Orgel-Probe* he perhaps used when testing organs.

11. For a survey of those meanings, see Carl Dahlhaus, "Die termini 'dur' und 'moll,'" *Archiv für Musikwissenschaft* 12 (1995): 289–91.

12. I have taken up these questions in *Monteverdi's Tonal Language* (New York: Schirmer, 1992); see pp. 112–17, 188–91.

13. See my discussion of the first printed circle of keys (in Johann David Heinichen, *Neu-erfundene und Gründliche Anweisung* [Hamburg, 1711]), and its relation to hexachord theory in *Tonal Allegory in the Vocal Music of J. S. Bach* (Berkeley: University of California Press, 1991), pp. 65–70, and *Monteverdi's Tonal Language*, pp. 45–47.

14. Theodor W. Adorno, "Bach Defended against His Devotees," in *Prisms*, ed. and trans. Samuel Weber and Shierry Weber (Cambridge, Mass.: MIT Press, 1981), pp. 135–46; see p. 141. Behind Adorno's remark lies, of course, Walter Benjamin's pathbreaking study of allegory in the dramas of seventeenth-century Lutheran Germany, *The Origins of German Tragic Drama*, trans. John Osborne (London: New Left Books, 1977).

15. Werckmeister, *Musicalische Paradoxal-Discourse*, pp. 50–51.

16. Friedrich Erhardt Niedt, *The Musical Guide*, trans. by Pamela L. Poulin and Irmgard C. Taylor (Oxford: Clarendon Press, and New York: Oxford University Press, 1989), pp. 28–29.

17. I have discussed several such works in *Tonal Allegory* (see pp. 134–44, 187–201. The a–C–e–G key sequence of Cantata 61 provides a particularly clear example. A close parallel to the key sequences Niedt describes can be found in the aria "Mein Gott, ich liebe dich" from Cantata 77, which presents its basic thematic material in the following sequence: a–C–e–G–b–d; see the introduction to chapter 8.

18. Kuhnau's prefaces to his *Musikalische Vorstellung Einiger Biblische Historien* (Leipzig, 1720; vol. 4 of *Denkmäler deutscher Tonkunst*, ser. 1, ed. Karl Päsler (Leipzig: Breitkopf 8 Härtel, 1901), and his Leipzig cantata cycle of 1709–10 (reprinted in B. F. Richter, "Eine Abhandlung Joh. Kuhnau's," *Monatshefte für Musik-Geschichte* 34:148–54) are of particular interest in this respect. In the latter preface, Kuhnau makes an explicit analogy between biblical hermeneutics and composition with the aid of a wide range of musico-allegorical devices.

Werckmeister's outlook is more theoretically and speculatively oriented than Kuhnau's, of course, but the bond between such speculation (in the scholastic sense of the word) and musical practice was shared by both men. The spiritual link of such writings to Bach is profoundly evident throughout Bach's work, although that does not mean, of course, that their conception of music completely defines Bach's.

19. Johann Kuhnau, *Six Biblical Sonatas, for Keyboard, 1700*, with the original preface and introductions in German (facsimile) and English, trans. and annotated by Kurt Stone (New York: Broude Brothers, 1953), pp. xii–xiv.

20. Ibid., p. xiv.

21. Ibid.

22. See Richter, "Eine Abhandlung Joh. Kuhnau's"; Chafe, "Key Structure and 'Tonal Allegory' in the Passions of J. S. Bach: An Introduction," *Current Musicology* 31 (1981): 39–54. The conception of modulation in terms of "mi–fa" shifting can have more than one meaning. In Lorenzo Penna's discussion of key signatures, for example, the addition of flats is described as changing "mi" into "fa" and vice versa for sharps (*Li Primi Albori Musicali* [Bologna, 1672], pp. 34–35). But enharmonic changes were also described as changing "mi" into "fa." By using the word *verwandeln* (transform) Kuhnau may mean modulation to a distant key or at least to one that is not adjacent on the circle of keys. On the association between the word *verwandeln* and major–minor shift in Cantata 21, see the introduction to chapter 3.

23. Chafe, *Tonal Allegory*, p. 261, n. 5.

24. *Der Weit-berümte MUSICUS und ORGANISTA wurde bey Trauriger Leich-Bestellung des weyland edlen und Kunst-hoch-erfahrnen Herrn ANDREAE WERCKMEISTERS, treu-verdient-gewesenen Organistens bey unserer St. Martini-Kirche, und Königl. Preuss. wohl-bestallt-gewesenen Inspectoris über alle Orgel-Wercke in Fürstenthumb Halberstadt, welcher am abgewichenen 26. Octob. des 1706ten Jahres in JESU seelig verstorben, in einer Stand-Rede dargestellet von Johann Melchior Gözen, SS. Theol. Doct.* (1707). Göze's oration has been reprinted in facsimile along with five of Werckmeister's treatises by Georg Olms (Hildesheim, 1970).

25. Ibid.: p. 3 "Denn gleich wie alle gute Gabe und alle vollkommene Gabe von oben herab kombt, so ist vor allen die Music eine herrliche Gabe Gottes, und kömt der *Theologischen* Wissenschafft sehr nahe. Ich wolte nicht, schreibt *Lutherus*, um was grosses mich derselben begeben."

26. Ibid., pp. 3–4.

27. Ibid., p. 4: "Und freylich klingt es nicht allein im gemeinen Wesen wohl, wenn Obrigkeit und Unterthanen in einer feinen Einträchtigkeit beysammen leben, sondern wenn auch wir sterbliche Menschen nach dem Willen unsers Gottes uns gehorsamst schicken lernen, und fein geduldig mit einstimmen, ob er uns gleich die Saiten bisweilen ein wenig hoch spannet. Die Lieder Gottes, die Er mit uns anstimmet gehen nicht allemahl aus einem *B molli*. Der *Tonus Jonicus*, da es nur immer auf Freude und wollust hinnaus läufft, will nicht allezeit erschallen, so wird auch der *Tonus Dorius*, da die Sonne nur nach unsern Gefallen scheinet, offte sehr späte angestimmet. Vielfältig hingegen läst sich der *Tonus Mixolydius* hören, da man muß aus der Tieffe ruffen und fragen: Hat denn Gott vergessen gnädig zu seyn, und sein Angesicht im Zorn verborgen? O wie sehr offte ist dem Seeligen nach Gottes willen dergleichen begegnet, da sein lieber Gott manchmahl aus dem *B. duro* ein Lied mit ihm angestimmet. als Er Ihm seine erste Frau sterben lassen nebst einem Kinde, als Er Ihm viele wehrte Muths-Freunde unvermuthet durch den Todt entrissen . . ."

28. In Monteverdi's music and that of many of his contemporaries the qualities associated with the terms *durus* and *mollis* in the old hexachord theory expanded to the level of music's harmonic-tonal aspects; as a result texted musical compositions often mirrored qualities associated with "hardness" and "softness" in their texts at the level of local as well as large-

scale harmonic-tonal events. In many of Monteverdi's works the qualities of *durezza* (hard-heartedness) and *pieta* (compassion) were juxtaposed, sometimes even serving as the pivots in the design of entire compositions. See Chafe, *Monteverdi's Tonal Language*, pp. 21–37, 112–117.

29. "Christus ist ein freundlicher HERR, und seine Rede sind lieblich, darumb wollen wir *Sextum Tonum* zum Evangelio nehmen, und weil S. Paulus ein ernster Apostel ist, wollen wor *Octavum tonum* zur Epistel ordnen." Luther's remark was preserved by Johann Walther (see Michael Praetorius, *Syntagma Musicum* (Wolfenbüttel, 1619; reprint, ed. Wilibald Gurlitt, Kassel: Bärenreiter, 1959), 1: 451–52.

30. One of the central ideas of the Lutheran "metaphysical" tradition in music theory, the concept of *Harmonie*, probably underlay Bach's allegorical intention in the first movement of Cantata 77. Not only Werckmeister's treatises and Göze's oration but also even Johann Mattheson's *Der musicalische Patriot* saw the *Übereinstimmung* of God and humanity as a central theme of music. On the concept itself see Walter Blankenburg, "Der Harmonie-Begriff in der lutherisch-barocken Musikanschauung," *Archiv für Musikwissenschaft* 16 (1959): 44–56; and Dammann, *Der Musikbegriff im deutschen Barock*, pp. 23–92.

31. The bass recitative begins with this theme, setting the line "So herrlich stehst du, liebe Stadt." In the seventh movement it sounds first (somewhat modified) in the instrumental introduction and conclusion, then again in the middle section, punctuating the words "Er seh' die teuren Väter an und halte auf unzählig' und späte lange Jahre 'naus in ihrem Regimente Haus, so wollen wir ihn preisen," first in unison strings, then unison oboes, and finally (again slightly modified) unison recorders. We have already encountered this theme in the opening movement of Cantata 70, where it represents God's coming in glory to judge the world. For further instances of its use in Bach's work see chapter 3, note 34.

32. In Werckmeister's time the old hexachordal meanings of *durus* and *mollis* had yielded to the German terms *dur* and *moll* as the two genera under which tonality was grouped. For a survey of the changing meanings of *durus* and *mollis* through the centuries see Carl Dahlhaus, "Die termini 'dur' und 'moll,'" pp. 289–91. In the *Musicae mathematicae* (p. 81) Werckmeister still refers to the C major and minor triads as *cantus durus* and *cantus mollis*, thereby alluding to the hexachordal meanings, and in that treatise (p. 125) he still resists the association of the word *dur* with the major triad, although he admits that the usage is so widespread as to be unavoidable; the association of *mollis* and minor, however, he finds tolerably appropriate.

33. As is well-known, the principal exponent of the new hermeneutics, Johann August Ernesti, was the person with whom Bach had a famous confrontation in the 1730s. See Paul Minear, "J. S. Bach and J. A. Ernesti: A Case Study in Exegetical and Theological Conflict," in *Our Common History as Christians: Essays in Honor of Albert C. Outler*, ed. John Denschner, L. T. Howe, and K. Penzel (New York: Oxford University Press, 1975), pp. 131–55 for the view that the differences between the two men expressed conflicting outlooks.

Chapter Three

1. Walther von Loewenich, *Luther's Theology of the Cross*, trans. Herbert J. A. Bouman (Minneapolis: Augsburg, 1976), pp. 77–88; Paul Althaus, *The Theology of Martin Luther*, trans. Robert C. Schultz (Philadelphia: Fortress Press, 1966), pp. 55–63.

2. See, for example, the frontispiece to August Pfeiffer's *Antimelancholicus* of 1684, a book that Bach had in his library (facsimile in Robin A. Leaver, *Bach's Theological Library* [Neuhausen-Stuttgart: Hänssler, 1983], p. 148). The page in question is set up symmetrically with the allegorical figure of "melancholicus" seated despondent between the standing figures of an armed antagonist, a seductress, and a demon (i.e., the world, the flesh, and the devil) on

the one side and Jesus on the other. Beneath this picture medallions on the left and right sides contain the verses "Ich habe solches offt gehöret, ihr seyd allzumahl leidige Tröster" (Job 36:2) and "Ich hatte viel Bekümmernisse in meinem Herze, aber deine Tröstungen erquicken meine Seele" (Psalms 94:19).

3. See note 6. For a summary of the source situation pertaining to the three basic versions of Cantata 21 (Weimar 1714, Köthen c. 1720, Leipzig 1723) see volume 1 of Hans-Joachim Schulze and Christoph Wolff, eds., *Bach Compendium: Analytisch bibliographisches Repertorium der Werke Johann Sebastian Bachs* (Leipzig and Dresden, 1985–), pp. 405–6. And for a fuller discussion of the question of the possible earlier history of the work see Martin Petzoldt, "'Die kräfftige Erquickung unter der schweren Angst-Last.' Möglicherweise Neues zur Entstehung der Kantate BWV 21," *Bach-Jahrbuch* 79 (1993): 32–46.

4. Martin Petzoldt points out that the designation "per ogni tempo" appears to take precedence over the remark, also found on the cover page, that the work was *performed* on (i.e., not necessarily written for) the third Sunday after Trinity (on which occasion it was performed in Leipzig as well), also that Cantata 21 would be best suited to Jubilate Sunday (whose theme is the transformation of suffering into joy), with the sixteenth and seventeenth Sundays after Trinity as possible other candidates (Petzoldt, "'Die kräfftige Erquickung,'" pp. 34–35, p. 37, n. 22, p. 42). I discuss later in this chapter the affinities between certain ideas in its text and the Gospel reading for the second Sunday in Epiphany.

5. See Eric Chafe, *Tonal Allegory in the Vocal Music of J. S. Bach* (Berkeley: University of California Press, 1991), pp. 140–41.

6. The text of the first chorus of part 1 is Psalms 94:19, that of the final chorus of part 1 is Psalms 42:12, that of the first chorus of part 2 (no. 9) combines Psalms 116:7 with two verses from the chorale "Wer nur den lieben Gott läßt walten," and that of the final chorus of part 2 is Revelation 5:12–13. In addition, Helene Werthemann argues ("Zum Text der Bach-Kantate 21, 'Ich hatte viel Bekümmernis in meinem Herzen'," *Bach-Jahrbuch* 51 [1965]: 139) that the overall text of the cantata, apart from the first and last choruses, is also indebted to an eighteen-strophe poem from Johann Rist's *Himmlische Lieder, das dritte Zehn* (1642), of which strophes 1–9 center on tribulation and 10–18 on *Trost.* As Werthemann points out (p. 139), the imagery that surrounds the transformation of tears into "floods" and "waves" in the aria "Bäche von gesalznen Zähren" derives from the fourth and eighth verses of Psalm 42 (whose twelfth verse provides the text of the following chorus). Also, the lines "Verwandle dich, Weinen in lauteren Wein! Es wird nun mein Ächzen ein Jauchzen mir sein" from the aria "Erfreue dich, Seele" show the influence of Paul Gerhardt's poem "Ach trauer Gott, barmherziges Herz," whose sixteenth strophe contains the lines "Da wird mein Weinen lauter Wein / mein Ächzen lauter Jauchzen sein" (Werthemann, "Zum Text," p. 141). It may be pointed out as well that Gerhardt's use of the expression "ewger Lust" in the opening line of the aforementioned strophe ("Dasselbst wirst du in ewger Lust aufs süßte mir mir handeln") is echoed in "Erfreue dich, Seele" ("weil Jesus mich tröstet mit himmlischer Lust"), while his use of the verb "wandeln" to indicate the change from suffering to joy ("Mein Creutz, das dir und mir bewußt, in Freud und Ehre wandeln") perhaps gave rise to the "verwandle" of the aria. Martin Petzoldt (see n. 22 of "'Die kräfftige Erquickung'") expands on Werthemann's discovery by pointing out that Gerhardt's poem itself paraphrases a passage from Johann Arndt's *Paradiesgärtlein* that articulates the "eschatological topos of the transformation of degradation into glorification in the two forms of the *visio beata* and the *gaudium aeternum.*" Arndt's (and Gerhardt's) objectives are thus exactly paralleled in Bach's overall structure. At the end of his article (pp. 45–46) Petzoldt cites the texts of movements 2–6 and 9 of Cantata 21 with a set of concordances to the Bible passages they refer to.

7. As I have pointed out elsewhere (*Tonal Allegory*, p. 78), the key structure of Cantata 21

fits with the modulatory principles set forth by Johann David Heinichen in his *Neu-erfundene und gründliche Anweisung* (Hamburg, 1711). Heinichen (p. 266) speaks of modulation between A minor and A major in terms of what he calls *toni intermedii,* that is, the intervening keys on the *musicalischer Circul.* In other words, Heinichen conceives of such modulation as a progression through adjacent key-signature levels.

8. Petzoldt's concordances for part 1 (see the end of note 6) identify references to ten different psalms.

9. In the early eighteenth century the term *ambitus* took on *tonal* connotations in addition to its traditional melodic ones in the writings of certain German music theorists. I follow Johann David Heinichen's use of the word *ambitus* (see *Neu-erfundene und Gründliche Anweisung*) to designate the six most closely related keys to any given major or minor "tonic": that is, A♭, f, E♭, c, B♭, g, in the case of C minor/E flat (see the introduction to chapter 4). For Niedt's use of the term see chapter 2.

10. Cantata 155 contains the line "Das Tränenmaß wird stets voll eingeschenket" (The measure of tears is continually full) and Cantata 13 the line "Mein Jammerkrug ist ganz mit Tränen angefüllet" (My cup of sorrow is completely full of tears). Although Cantata 21 does not draw directly on this imagery, there are other affinities with Cantatas 155 and 13. Cantata 155, for example, makes reference to the same psalm text that appears in the ninth movement of Cantata 21. Throughout the cantata the antithesis of tears and *Trost* is constantly in the foreground (featuring the rhyme *Weinen/erscheinen* in two movements). Also, as Werthemann indicates ("Zum Text," p. 141, n. 4),the penultimate movement contains the words "Ächzen" and "Weinen" in a single line.

11. See Raymond Brown, The Gospel according to John XIII–XXI, *Anchor Bible* (Garden City, N.Y.: Doubleday, 1970), 29A: 541–42.

12. It thus articulates the idea of the transformation of "Schmach" into "Herrlichkeit" that came into Cantata 21 via Gerhardt's paraphrase from Arndt's *Paradiesgärtlein* (see n. 6).

13. Brown, The Gospel according to John I–XII, *Anchor Bible* (Garden City, N.Y.: Doubleday, 1966), 29: 517–18.

14. "Du mußt glauben, du mußt hoffen, du mußt Gott gelassen sein! Jesus weiß die rechten *Stunden,* dich mit Hülfe zu erfreun, wenn die trübe Zeit verschwunden, steht sein ganzes Herz dir offen!" (Cantata 155). "Mein liebster Gott läßt mich annoch vergebens rufen und mir in meinem Weinen noch keinen Trost erscheinen. Die *Stunde* lässet sich zwar wohl von ferne sehen, allein ich muß doch noch vergebens flehen" (Cantata 13).

15. See, for example, my discussion of Bach's eschatological canon "Christus Coronabit Crucigeros" in *Tonal Allegory,* pp. 16–19.

16. Werthemann, "Zum Text," p. 138.

17. In the seventeenth and eighteenth centuries the "feeling quality" that was most associated with the "realization" of faith was often described as "sweet." The believer, in accepting the fact that Jesus' death was undertaken from love for him personally, experienced an inner transformation analogous to the transmutation of bitterness into sweetness or tears into wine ("bitter tears" in Cantata 155, "salty tears" in Cantata 21). In this sense Jesus' death had "sweetened" the believer's eschatological hopes. The *St. Matthew Passion* contains many instances of this association, one of the most prominent being the metaphor of Jesus' accepting the "cup" (i.e., the necessity of the Passion) at Gethsemane: the arioso/aria pair "Der Heiland fällt vor seinem Vater nieder"/"Gerne will ich mich bequemen" interprets Jesus' action as His "sweetening" the bitterness of death for the believer: "Er ist bereit, den Kelch des Todes Bitterkeit zu trinken" (arioso), "Gerne will ich mich bequemen, Kreuz und Becher anzunehmen, trink ich doch dem Heiland nach. Denn sein Mund, der mit Milch und Honig fließet, hat den Grund und des Leidens herbe Schmach durch den ersten Trunk versüßet" (aria). The idea that the

believer drank from the cup from which Jesus had previously drunk refers, of course, to the Holy Eucharist as the symbol of the believer's acceptance of Jesus' sufferings on behalf of humanity.

18. See Althaus, *The Theology of Martin Luther*, pp. 446–58 (appendix 2, "Love and the Certainty of Salvation": Luther's interpretation of 1 John 4:17a).

19. Elke Axmacher, "Bachs Kantatentexte in auslegungsgeschichtlicher Sicht," in *Bach als Ausleger der Bibel*, ed. Martin Petzoldt (Göttingen: Vandenhoeck & Ruprecht, 1985), pp. 16–17; Helene Werthemann, *Die Bedeutung der alttestamentlichen Historien in Johann Sebastian Bachs Kantaten* (Tübingen: J. B. Mohr, 1960); Paul Minear, "J. S. Bach and J. A. Ernesti: A Case Study in Exegetical and Theological Conflict," in *Our Common History as Christians: Essays in Honor of Albert C. Outler*, ed. John Deschner, L. T. Howe, and K. Penzel (New York: Oxford University Press, 1975), pp. 131–55.

20. Chafe, *Tonal Allegory*, pp. 92–102.

21. Ibid., pp. 27–63.

22. For Johann Kuhnau's use of the word *verwandeln* to describe a "structural" modulation in which "mi" changes to "fa" or vice versa see chapter 2.

23. See note 6. Petzoldt, "'Die kräfftige Erquickung,'" p. 38.

24. Mattheson's criticism was published in the eighth part of his periodical *Critica Musica* in 1725. See Werner Neumann and Hans-Joachim Schulze, eds., *Fremdschriftliche und gedruckte Dokumente zur Lebensgeschichte Johann Sebastian Bachs 1685–1750*, vol. 2 of *Bach-Dokumente* (Kassel: Bärenreiter, 1969), pp. 153–54. English translation in Hans T. David and Arthur Mendel, *The New Bach Reader*, p. 325. As Petzoldt points out ("'Die kräfftige Erquickung,'" pp. 31–33), Mattheson is not criticizing Bach pejoratively, as is often believed, but using Bach's work as an example of musical text setting as distinct from the purely rhetorical principles that might be applied to verbal texts per se.

25. As I have pointed out elsewhere (*Tonal Allegory*, p. 107), the ground-bass solo "Herr, lehre uns bedenken, dass wir sterben müssen" from the "Actus Tragicus" (BWV 106) breaks with both the repeating bass pattern and the key of c as it turns to the words "auf dass wir klug werden," which shift in a very optimistic fashion to E♭ before returning to c (and restoring the ground bass). Both the "Actus Tragicus" and Cantata 12 set up frameworks that represent the inevitability of worldly tribulation, then offset those frameworks by turning to major in ascending key sequences that mirror the hope of eternal life. Part 1 of Cantata 21 uses the key of E♭ in relation to c in much the same way as the ground-bass aria of the "Actus Tragicus," as a momentary point of hope within a movement of basically pessimistic tone.

26. See, for example, the discussions of Cantatas 2, 46, and 77 following.

27. Von Loewenich, *Luther's Theology of the Cross*, pp. 93–95; Althaus, *The Theology of Martin Luther*, pp. 446–58.

28. See the discussion of Cantata 121 in chapter 6.

29. Luther's remarks are cited in von Loewenich, *Luther's Theology of the Cross*, p. 106.

30. See Alfred Dürr, *Die Kantaten von Johann Sebastian Bach* (Kassel: Bärenreiter, 1971), 2: 463.

31. Chafe, *Tonal Allegory*, pp. 137–39.

32. In this movement the text repetitions that Mattheson cited once again reflect the basic insecurity of the soul, which now seeks consolation directly from Jesus.

33. Von Loewenich, *Luther's Theology of the Cross*, p. 94.

34. Perhaps the best-known occurrence of this theme in Bach's work is as the horn call of the first movement of the first Brandenburg Concerto, where Bach assigns it a triplet rhythm that stands apart from the quadruple meter of the other parts and the movement as a whole. Bach used a version of the first movement of this concerto as introductory Sinfonia to the

final cantata of the Trinity season in 1726, Cantata 52, "Falsche Welt, dir trau ich nicht," for the twenty-third Sunday after Trinity. In Cantata 127 ("Herr Jesu Christ, wahr'r Mensch und Gott," for Quinquagesima, 1725) Bach introduces this theme at the beginning of the apocalyptic bass solo "Wenn einstens die Posaunen schallen," a representation of the Last Judgment; there its C major arpeggio juxtaposes to the C minor (with recorders and other "soft" devices, such as pizzicato bass) of the preceding movement, "Die Seele ruht in Jesu Händen," a representation of the "sleep of death." Other prominent appearances of this theme occur in Cantata 119 for the changing of the Leipzig town council in 1723 (in association with the majesty of Leipzig, interpreted allegorically as Jerusalem) and Cantata 130, for St. Michael's Day, 1724 (as principal theme of the aria "Der alte Drache brennt vor Neid"); closely related forms of this theme occur in Cantata 147 for the Visitation of Mary, 1723 (as principal theme of the aria "Ich will von Jesu Wunden singen," whose Weimar original text for the fourth Sunday of Advent, 1716, "Laß mich der Rufer Stimme hören," has a character that is comparable to the first movement of "Wachet! betet!"). All the latter movements are in C. Versions of the theme also appear in the other trumpet key, D, generally with associations of majesty and/or victory: Cantata 172, the aria "Heiligster Dreieinigkeit"; Cantata 214, on the words "Erschallet, Trompeten"; the *St. John Passion*, in the middle section of the "Es ist vollbracht" on "Der Held aus Juda siegt mit Macht"; Cantata 249, later the *Easter Oratorio*, at "Wir sind erfreut [daß unser Jesum wieder lebt]." The first appearance of this theme that is known to me is in the setting of Psalm 136 from Heinrich Schütz's *Psalmen Davids* of 1619, where it is associated with God's majesty. It appears also in the *Intrada* first movement of Heinrich Biber's string suite, titled *Trombet und musicalischer Tafeldienst* (around 1673–74), where it is played by solo violin in imitation of the trumpet (headed "Tromba luditur in violino solo") above a sustained C major chord on the lower strings.

35. On this quality see Manfred Bukofzer, *Music in the Baroque Era* (New York: Norton, 1947), pp. 365–69.

36. See "Aspects of the Liturgical Year" in chapter 1.

37. See Chafe, *Tonal Allegory*, pp. 92–102.

Chapter Four

1. Johann Philipp Kirnberger, *Die Kunst des reinen Satzes in der Musik* (Berlin and Königsberg, 1776–79, facsimile ed., Hildesheim: Georg Olms, 1968), part 2, p. 49: "Ich kann auch noch anführen, daß der delicateste der neuern Componisten, J. S. Bach, die Methode, nach den alten Kirchentönen zu setzen, vor nothwendig gehalten hat, wie aus dessen Catechismus: Gesängen zu sehen ist, deren so viele auf diese Weise gesetzet sind." The "Catechismus:Gesängen" in question refers to Bach's *Dritter Teil der Clavierübung* (1739), from which Kirnberger then cites a series of chorale settings in various modes. All translations in this chapter are mine. For another translation see Johann Philipp Kirnberger, *The Art of Strict Musical Composition*, trans. David Beach and Jurgen Thym (New Haven: Yale University Press, 1981).

2. On Bach's use of the *stile antico* see Christoph Wolff, *Der stile antico in der Musik Johann Sebastian Bachs* (Wiesbaden: Breitkopf & Härtel, 1968), pp. 13–16.

3. Kirnberger, *Die Kunst des reinen satzes*, pp. 63–66. I do not mean to suggest, however, that the qualities of "charm" and "variety" Kirnberger prized were shared by Bach or intended for his setting of "Das alte Jahr vergangen ist." It is interesting to compare the meanings that "completeness" (*Vollkommenheit*) had for Werckmeister and Kirnberger, which were opposite in some respects. The "completeness" of "Das alte Jahr" for Kirnberger was distinctly related to its harmonic richness; its featuring all twelve semitones of the chromatic scale makes it a perfect example of "tempered music," which Werckmeister viewed as an allegory of the im-

perfection and *in*completeness of human life. For Werckmeister music's completeness or incompleteness was determined by musico-theological qualities, while for Kirnberger it was a purely pragmatic matter involving only the notes.

4. Kirnberger's version of this setting differs very slightly from that published by him and C. P. E. Bach in their posthumous collection of chorales by J. S. Bach, and in the penultimate measure the latter version contains a passing-note b♭ as well.

5. Because of Bach's emphasizing the pitch f♯ in the final phrase, I feel that the ending at least should be designated an E mode, even though to the modern ear the ending may well sound like the dominant of a. In his treatise Kirnberger follows Bach's setting by an anonymous composition in a that almost seems to have been introduced to compensate for the ending of "Das alte Jahr."

6. Georg Philipp Telemann, *Fast allgemeines Evangelisch-Musicalisches Lieder-Buch* (Hamburg, 1730; facsimile ed. Siegfried Kross), Hildesheim: Georg Olms, 1977, p. 51.

7. I have discussed these matters in *Monteverdi's Tonal Language* (New York: Schirmer, 1992), pp. 38–55.

8. Osiander's collection has been published as *Das erste evangelische Choralbuch* (1586; reprint, ed. Friedrich Zelle (Berlin: Weidmannsche Buchhandlug, 1903) and, along with selected facsimiles, in Louis Eugene Schuler, Jr., "Lucas Osiander and his *Fünfftzig Geistliche Lieder und Psalmen*: The Development and Use of the First Cantional," Ph.D. diss., Washington University, 1986, pp. 120–97.

9. I am speaking now of Monteverdi's earlier works (up to the Fourth Book of Madrigals of 1605), as I have described their tonal character in *Monteverdi's Tonal Language* (pp. 21–104). This almost classic phase in his work, however, serves as the basis for expansion of the modal-hexachordal system throughout the rest of Monteverdi's work. I have traced that expansion (which involves primarily the increasing use of sharps) in the book just cited.

10. Normally only the four sharpest triads in either *cantus* may appear in both minor and major forms, but occasionally the next degree in the flat direction—C in the *cantus durus*, F in the *cantus mollis*—may be heard in its minor form.

11. Osiander's setting of "Der Herr ist mein getreuer Hirt" begins in G Hypomixolydian, and its first two phrases end with authentic cadences to G. The third phrase appears about to end with an authentic cadence to D but substitutes B♭ as the final chord. The fourth and fifth phrases feature b♭'s rather than b♮'s in the melody, and Osiander harmonizes both phrases with B♭ and g harmonies throughout, creating a shift to the transposed Hypodorian mode (g) and ending with the *Tierce de Picardie* (G). The textual motivation is the description of God's leading the believer into green pastures. In terms of the hexachords, however, the pitch content is perfectly consistent with the one-flat hexachord in the *cantus durus*. This occurence, in fact, is strikingly indicative of the priority of hexachordal and major/minor perceptions over the integrity of mode.

12. That is, the final f'–e' semitone of the melody is harmonized with F, then an a–E plagal cadence (both these last two harmonies sounding beneath the final e').

13. A generation later Monteverdi reserves the key of E minor and the sharp system for one point in *Orfeo*, assigning it an association, loss of hope, that is opposite to the one place in which the key of B♭ appears (in association with the allegorical figure of Speranza). For this and other instances of Monteverdi's and Marco da Gagliano's reserving E minor for moments of special significance see Chafe, *Monteverdi's Tonal Language*, pp. 152–53, 361–70.

14. More than a century later, Bach joins two chorales in the opening movement of Cantata 95, the first, "Christus, der ist mein Leben," in G major, triple meter, and fast tempo, the second, "Mit Fried und Freud," in G minor (Dorian), quadruple meter, and slow tempo, bridging the two with a tenor recitative that modulates to C minor as it anticipates the believer's death. The effect is of a *durus–mollis* shift in which neither quality is treated pejora-

tively. I have described the work in greater detail in *Tonal Allegory in the Vocal Music of J. S. Bach* (Berkeley: University of California Press, 1991), pp. 172–73.

15. See Carl Dahlhaus, "Die termini 'dur' und 'moll,'" Archiv für Musikwissenschaft 12 (1955): 289–91.

16. Andreas Werckmeister, *Musicae mathematicae hodegus curioses* (Frankfurt and Leipzig, 1686; facsimile ed., Hildesheim: Georg Olms, 1972), pp. 81, 120–25.

17. See my introduction to these questions in *Monteverdi's Tonal Language*, pp. 24–55. That Werckmeister omits the sharpest (Phrygian) and flattest (Lydian) modes from his grouping of the major and minor types reflects the process of modal reduction. As I discuss later, these two modes tended to be "corrected" into the Aolian and Ionian, respectively, through the process of borrowing either F♯ or B♭ from the adjacent hexachord.

18. See Johann David Heinichen, *Neu-erfundene und gründliche Anweisung* (Hamburg, 1711), pp. 261–67; and Johann Mattheson, *Das beschützte Orchestre* (Hamburg, 1717; facsimile ed., Leipzig: Zentralantiquariat der Deutschen Demokratischen Republik, 1981), title page.

19. Carl Dahlhaus (*Studies on the Origin of Harmonic Tonality* [*Untersuchungen über die Entstehung der harmonischen Tonalität*, Kassel: Bärenreiter, 1968], trans. Robert O. Gjerdingen [Princeton: Princeton University Press, 1991], pp. 291–323) uses the term "Teiltonarten" (translated as "component keys") to describe the manner in which the cadence degrees of the hexachords came to function as temporary articulations (or representations) of the modes associated with those degrees (often for only a single phrase). Viewed as the degrees of the hexachord, the "Teiltonarten" formed a modal "society" in which the chosen mode was often no more than the "primus inter pares" of the set. Such a concept will work, however, only for the transitional phase between modal and tonal composition, and I have preferred to speak in terms of circles or spectra of cadences within the system or *cantus* (*Monteverdi's Tonal Language*, pp. 69–70).

20. Chafe, *Monteverdi's Tonal Language*, pp. 50–53.

21. Athanasius Kircher, *Musurgia universalis sive Ars magna consoni et dissoni in X. libros digesta* (Rome, 1650; facsimile ed., ed. Ulf Scharlau [Hildesheim: Georg Olms, 1970], part 2, pp. 51, 64). See my discussion of these questions in *Monteverdi's Tonal Language*, pp. 39–43, 362–64.

22. Carl Dahlhaus emphasizes the importance of the B–E cadence in opening up the sharp system in *Studies on the Origin of Harmonic Tonality*, p. 316.

23. On Banchieri see Walter Atcherson, "Key and Mode in Seventeenth-century Music Theory Books," *Journal of Music Theory* 17 (1973): 205–33. In Banchieri's scheme of what Atcherson calls the eight "pitch-key modes," each of the modal pairs except that comprising the third and fourth involves a fifth relationship between two modes, one of which is in the *cantus durus* and the other in the *cantus mollis* (i.e., d/g, a/e, C/F, and d/G). In this system authentic/plagal and untransposed/transposed modes seem to merge or overlap, so that the available modal spectrum is divided between two *cantus* rather than one. The third and fourth modes (i.e., the Phrygian/Hypophrygian pair, on a and e, although Banchieri does not use the Greek names) represent somewhat of an anomaly here, as they do in Kircher's system, in that they appeared in the same *cantus* and the plagal mode was a fourth rather than a fifth below the authentic. That difference was owing in part to the fact that the third, or Phrygian, mode had become widely associated with what we call the key of A minor (owing to the dominant character of the widespread Phrygian d^6–E and plagal a–E cadences in that mode), so that the fourth, or Hypophrygian, mode was often associated with E; and it had, as we saw, a pronounced subdominant character. In order for that mode to exist independently, with its own authentic cadence, it was sometimes reinterpreted as E minor; and that reinterpretation opened up the sharp system or the true *cantus durus*, as described previously.

24. Heinichen, *Neu-erfundene und gründliche Anweisung*, pp. 261–67.

25. Johann Kuhnau, *Six Biblical Sonatas, for Keyboard, 1700,* with the original preface and introductions in German (facsimile) and English, trans. and annotated by Kurt Stone (New York: Broude Brothers, 1953), p. viv.

26. Bach's canon on the "mi/fa" idea (see chapter 2, n. 10) uses the tones f', a', b♭' and e' (i.e., "fa," "mi," "fa," and "mi") as its ground bass, thereby expressing the three forms of "mi–fa" interaction within a single major key (F).

27. Kircher (*Musurgia universalis,* part 1, p. 672) describes *mutatio toni* (shift of mode within the same system or *cantus*) from *mutatio modi* (shift of system or transposition level); see Chafe, *Monteverdi's Tonal Language,* p. 23.

28. Mattheson, *Das beschützte Orchestre.*

29. Kirnberger's view of the modes was harmonically oriented, as his comparison of two settings of an unnamed melody, one Dorian and the other Aolian, makes clear (*Die Kunst des reinen Satzes,* p. 62). The two settings in question are at the same pitch, both cadencing with full closes to d. But although the melody contains a b♭' and no b♮', Kirnberger explains that the first one is Dorian because it utilizes B♮ throughout in the harmonization while the second (now notated in the one-flat key signature), utilizes B♭ throughout. Kirnberger adds: "This has the effect that the first example appears much more dignified and proper than the second, and the second much softer and more tender than the first." In attributing such qualities to the presence or absence of B♭ Kirnberger was, perhaps unconsciously, alluding to the traditional qualities of hardness and softness that had been associated for centuries with the hard and soft hexachords and systems (the *hexachordum durum* and *cantus durus* versus the *hexachordum molle* and *cantus mollis*). It is unlikely, however, that Kirnberger was simply assigning such qualities in deference to tradition. He does not mention the *cantus durus* and *cantus mollis* in relation to his two key signatures, which suggests that he perceived the affective differences he assigned the two settings as real ones, directly audible and attributable to the presence or absence of the B♭. In any case, by the late eighteenth century, when he wrote his treatise, even the debate between Mattheson and Buttstedt over the validity of the modes and hexachords was long in the past, and the terms *durus* and *mollis,* concerning which there had been a similar debate in the early eighteenth century, had been adopted in Germany to mean major and minor for several decades. As early as 1708 Mattheson had spoken out against the common belief held by some musicians of his time that the flat keys were "soft and tender" and the sharp keys "hard, fresh and gay" (*Das neu-eröffnete Orchestre* [Hamburg, 1713], pp. 231–53). And Mattheson, likewise, did not refer to that perception in terms of the hard and soft hexachords or systems, although it certainly appears to underlie his remarks.

30. Chafe, *Monteverdi's Tonal Language,* pp. 56–102.

31. Besides the setting cited by Kirnberger and that of the *Orgelbüchlein,* one other, for organ, appears in the Neumeister Collection at Yale University and another in the collection of chorales published after Bach's death by Kirnberger and C. P. E. Bach; the origin of the latter setting, if any, in Bach's cantata oeuvre is unknown.

32. This phrase resembles somewhat the ascending part of Bach's allegorical canon "Christus Coronabit Crucigeros," which, as its *Symbolum* indicates, was intended to represent the believer's reward in the afterlife for his tribulations in this one; in that canon the intermingling of descending and ascending chromatic tetrachords and the dualism of tonal directions—now toward c, now toward G—convey the sense that the believer lives in tribulation and hope simultaneously, a perfect representation of Luther's famous catchphrase, "simul justus et peccator." See Paul Althaus, *The Theology of Martin Luther,* trans. Robert C. Schultz (Philadelphia: Fortress Press, 1966), pp. 242–45.

33. See the discussions of Cantatas 18, 109, 121, and 77 in the following chapters. More generally, Bach often derives large-scale cantata designs from ideas that are latent in their chorale

melodies. Thus, cantatas that feature the Phrygian chorale "Herzlich tut mich verlangen" often emphasize C major, which is prominent in the melody; compare Cantatas 161, 25, and 135. See also the discussions of Cantatas 135 and 38 in chapter 6. In Cantata 60, discussed in chapter 9, the tonal anomaly appears at the beginning of the final chorale; its impact on the design of the whole is, nevertheless, unmistakable.

34. The change was from quadruple to triple meter, a type of shift that was undoubtedly intended to suggest that the change would be a joyful one. In terms of the metaphoric dimension of the change from old to new year (see the following paragraph) shift from quadruple to triple meter often signified anticipation of eternity. In Bach's cantatas that is a very frequently encountered allegory. See, for example, the final line of the chorale (by Johann Rosenmüller) that ends Cantata 27 and that was undoubtedly introduced by Bach to fit in with the allegorical idea expressed in the catchphrase "Ende gut macht alles gut" (which appears in the opening chorus and the first recitative). Rosenmüller's final lines, "In dem Himmel allezeit Friede, / Freud und Seligkeit," indicate the meaning clearly.

35. I have taken this matter up in greater detail in "*Anfang und Ende*: Cyclic Recurrence in Bach's Cantata *Jesu, nun sei gepreiset*, BWV 41," *Bach Perspectives* 1 (spring 1994): 103–34.

36. The fourth cantata of the *Christmas Oratorio*, as is well-known, was parodied in part (the opening and closing choruses in particular) in Cantata 213, which is in F. That fact, however, did not (as some would argue) cause Bach to "accidentally" introduce a new key to the oratorio, without any regard for what preceded and followed. Bach transposed the other movements from Cantata 213 as necessary to their new contexts. But that he retained the key of F (and the F horns of the cantata) for the two choruses is an indication of what led him to parody that particular cantata in the first place.

37. The Gregorian melody on which this hymn was based was traditionally classed as Phrygian. It seems natural, therefore, to view Bach's version of the chorale as shifting from Dorian to Phrygian as, for example, Alfred Dürr does (*Die Kantaten von Johann Sebastian Bach* [Kassel: Bärenreiter, 1971), 1: 142.

38. Andreas Werckmeister's description of the ending of this chorale (*Harmonologia Musica* [1702] (in facsimile ed. [5 vols. in one], Hildesheim: Georg Olms, 1972), p. 61–62. is that it ends on the second degree of the Dorian scale; and that was a traditional perception. The Freylinghausen chorale collection, for example, harmonizes the final melody tone, e', with an A major chord—that is, the dominant (Johann Anastasius Freylinghausen, *Geistreiches Gesang-Buch*, ed. G. A. Francke [Halle, 1741], p. 23). Telemann (*Fast allgemeinis Evangelisch-Musicalisches Lieder-Buch*, p. 2) likewise ends his setting with a half close to the dominant. Bach's settings, however, shift *to* the dominant key and end on *its* dominant, which might well have been viewed as a plagal cadence to the mode of the final chord—that is, as a shift from D Dorian to E Phrygian.

39. We remember that Cantata 61, for Advent Sunday, is also "open" tonally, its key sequence suggesting an allegory of the beginning of the liturgical year.

40. Chafe, *Tonal Allegory*, pp. 218–23.

41. Werckmeister, *Harmonologia Musica*, p. 62: "Der Gesang: durch Adams Fall ist ganz verderbt; ist ebenfalls auch *Hypophrygii*, aber man *Clausuliret* mehrentheils auf den *Dorium*, da doch der *Dorius* im D. Schliesset."

42. On Werckmeister's use of the term "Clausula minus principali" to indicate the dominant see p. 60 of *Harmonologia Musica*. On his use of "minus principali" to indicate the plagal mode see *Musicae mathematicae*, p. 115.

43. Werckmeister, *Harmonologia Musica*, pp. 62–63: "So kan es nicht *Dorii modi* seyn, denn kein Gesang schliesset in *Clausula minus principali*, wiewohl in diesen Liede deswegen keine sonderliche *confusiones* verursachet werden, weil dessen melodey etwas verändert wird. Denn ich habe auch in uhralten Gesang-Büchern gefunden, daß die *Formal-Clausulen*

zu diesen Liede ganz anders *formiret* werden, als sie bishero gemachet worden, denn das ♮ wird nicht darinnen gefunden, das b. aber wird ganz anders und traurig angebracht, weil es ein Trauer-Lied, von der Verderbung menschlicher Natur ist. Also: Ach Gott vom Himmel sieh darein: *Item*, O grosser Gott von Macht: und dergleichen mehr. Diese müssen alle mit einen traurigen *Affect* durch den *Hypophrygium exprimiret* werden, wie es ihr Text erfordert . . . "

44. Johannes Zahn, *Die Melodien der Deutschen Evangelischen Kirchen lieder* (Gütersloh, 1889; reprint, Hildesheim: Georg Olms, 1963).

45. In that passage (*Harmonologia Musica*, p. 62) Werckmeister, speaking of "Du Friedefürst, Herr Jesu Christ," which he also considered to be in the Hypophrygian mode, says: "Da doch dies Lied *Hypophrygii transpositi* ist, und man aus dem a. wie sonst aus dem *Phrygio transp.* gebräuchlich *Clausuliren* solte." In the principal chorale books of Bach's time, however, "Du Friedefürst" is treated as transposed Ionian, and all Bach's settings of the melody (in Cantatas 67, 116, and 143) follow that usage. Presumably Werckmeister felt that the final line should end on a' instead of f', as the two *Stollen* do and as the final line does in the Vopelius chorale book (ending on e'' in the *cantus durus*).

46. See the discussions of Cantatas 153 and 2 in the following chapter; also Dürr, Die Kantaten, 1: 198.

47. Since, however, "Durch Adams Fall" was widely classified as Dorian in the seventeenth and eighteenth centuries, it is possible that Werckmeister is reacting to classifications that were, in fact, describing the other melody associated with that chorale, the one we know from Bach's settings, which begins in D Dorian in the *cantus durus* and ends on A (see later in this chapter).

48. Robert L. Marshall, ed., *Kritischer Bericht* to *Johann Sebastian Bach*, vol. 19 of *Neue Bach ausgäbe sämtlicher Werke*, ser. l. Kassel: Bärenreiter, 1989), p. 156. See " 'Oh grosser Gott von Macht' in Cantata 46" in chapter 5; also, Ex. 5.8.

49. See chapter 7, n. 33

50. That Werckmeister speaks of the erroneous interpretation of the mode as Dorian rather than Hypodorian is because at that point he is speaking about the *cantus durus* version of the mode, in which the *ambitus* was that of the D Dorian mode, but ending on A. Later, when he refers to the *cantus mollis* A Hypophrygian version, the mode is plagal, and if he had referred to an erroneous harmonization of this version it would have been *Hypo*dorian.

51. See chapter 5, n. 13.

52. See Mattheson, *Das beschützte Orchestre*, title page, and *Das forschende Orchestre* (Hamburg, 1721), title page.

53. Theodor W. Adorno, "Bach Defended against His Devotees," in *Prisms*, ed. and trans. Samuel Weber and Shierry Weber (Cambridge, Mass.: MIT Press, 1981), pp. 133–46.

54. This is why Kirnberger speaks of Bach's varying the sixths and sevenths in his harmonization of "Das alte Jahr." With the grouping of modes under the two types of *keys* the question of whether the third was major or minor was central, whereas that of the sixths and sevenths (the only other variable pitches between the major and minor keys) was not.

55. See Martin Luther, *Tischreden*, vol. 1, no. 76, of *D. Martin Luthers Werke. Gesamtausgabe* (Weimar: H. Buhlau, 1912). The theological context in which Luther introduces the widely known catchphrase is closely related to that of the text of "Durch Adams Fall ist ganz verderbt." Luther discusses the idea that scripture cannot be fully explained or comprehended because of the limitations of human nature, especially human reason: "Noch sehen wir, wie böse, verderbt und vergiftet des Menschen Herz sei, dieweil die Erbsünde so tief in uns eingewurzelt ist. So ist auch Gottes Wille viel höher, denn wir mit unsern fünf Sinnen begreifen oder verstehen können" (p. 27). God's will, as it is manifested in scripture, often runs

contrary to the world and human reason. In the end, however, God's will becomes manifest: "Im Auskehrich (wie man saget) wird sichs aber wol finden, denn *in fine videbitur, cuius toni*" (p. 28). Interestingly, the antithesis of original sin and God's will, which is prominent in "Durch Adams Fall ist ganz verderbt," is described in terms of the antithesis of the deep-rootedness of the former in humanity and the higher nature of the latter. Since the latter (God's will) is revealed at the end the musical metaphor suggests a new key that is "higher" than the original. It may be mentioned that an edition of Luther's *Table Talk* (in which the most interesting of Luther's remarks on music appear) was among the contents of Bach's library (see Robin A. Leaver, *Bachs theologische Bibliothek* [Neuhausen-Stuttgart: Hänssler, 1983], pp. 59–60). On Luther's writings on music in general see Paul Nettl, *Luther on Music*, trans. Frida Best and Ralph Wood (New York: Russel and Russel, 1948).

56. In saying this I do not mean that Bach intended the *Orgelbüchlein* as a cycle in the sense that its separate settings should be played through in order. But it sometimes appears here, as in other cycles, such as the six cantatas of the *Christmas Oratorio*, which were assuredly not heard on the same day, that Bach's imagination was stimulated by the possibilities afforded by the sequential aspect, even though it might never be heard as such. In the three Easter chorales, "Erstanden ist der heil'ge Christ," "Erschienen ist der herrliche Tag," and "Heut' triumphiret Gottes Sohn," from the *Orgelbüchlein*, we might be tempted to view their shared time signatures and final (d) as evidence of cyclic intent. The first of the three is in D major, the second in D Dorian (i.e., d in the *cantus naturalis*), and the third in D Aolian (i.e., d in the *cantus mollis*). What is interesting is that "Heut' triumphiret Gottes Sohn" begins in B♭ and until the middle of its sixth phrase favors E♭ over E in the harmonization and the melody, turning to E♮ just before the authentic cadence to D that ends phrase 6. The seventh and final phrase then harmonizes the four reiterated d''s of its melody ("Alleluia") with what is basically a long-drawn-out plagal cadence to D (g–D). The setting as a whole thereby creates the impression that the D final (which was sometimes harmonized in B♭, as in Freylinghausen, *Geistreiches Gesang-Buch*, for example) and, even more, the shift from E♭ to E in the harmony served as an allegory of Jesus' triumph over death. In the three settings as a group the first makes its triumphant effect by means of the D major tonality, the second by means of its canon between the outermost voices, and the third by means of the aforementioned tonal shift.

57. See chapter 2.

58. The two cantatas "Wer weiß, wie nahe mir mein Ende" (BWV 27) and "Ich steh mit einem Fuß im Grabe" (BWV 156) both begin with anticipation of death. Cantata 27 delineates a progression toward the anticipation of eternity, while Cantata 156 is the prayer of one near death first for release from the sickbed of punishment for sin, then for God's aid with the sickness of the soul. In the one (27) readiness for death and in the other (156) acceptance of God's will leads to the awaited "blessed end." Cantata 27 begins in c and ends, after a rising-third sequence of keys, in B♭; Cantata 156 begins in F and ends, after first modulating in the subdominant direction in association with the theme of sickness, in C. I have discussed both cantatas in *Tonal Allegory*, pp. 187–90 and 167, respectively.

59. See the discussions of Cantatas 18 and 109 in the following chapter.

60. Zahn, *Die Melodien der Deutschen Evangelischen Kirchenlieder.*

Chapter Five

1. Theodor W. Adorno, "Bach Defended against His Devotees," in *Prisms*, ed. and trans. Samuel and Shierry Weber (Cambridge, Mass.: MIT Press, 1981), pp.

2. Manfred Bukofzer, *Music in the Baroque Era*, (New York: Norton, 1947), pp. 260–305.

3. Johann Philipp Kirnberger, *Die Kunst des Reinen Satzes in der Musik* (Berlin and Königsberg, 1776–79; facsimile ed., Hildesheim: Georg Olms, 1968), part 2, p. 49.

4. Alfred Dürr, *Die Kantaten von Johann Sebastian Bach*, (Kassel: Bärenreiter, 1971), 1:268–72.

5. See "Basic Principles" in chapter 1.

6. Paul Minear, "J. S. Bach and J. A. Ernesti: A Case Study in Exegetical and Theological Conflict," in *Our Common History as Christians: Essays in Honor of Albert C. Outler*, ed. John Deschner, L. T. Howe, and K. Penzel (New York: Oxford University Press, 1975), pp. 131–55.

7. Kuhnau describes his utilizing continuous modulation (calling it a "*Verführung* des Gehörs") to represent Laban's deceit in one of his biblical sontatas. In the most widely modulatory part of Cantata 18 Bach's text is "So sehr *verführet* sie [Seelen] die Welt."

8. The setting in question is, as mentioned earlier, an exact transposition down a tone of the setting in d/a described in the final section of the preceding chapter.

9. Eric Chafe, *Monteverdi's Tonal Language* (New York: Schirmer, 1992), pp. 31–37. In the *St. John Passion* Bach utilizes this effect for the two choruses set to the words "Jesum von Nazareth"; their harmonic pattern is confined to a circle of fifths that begins on the dominant and returns to end on it via the Phrygian cadence. The chorus is of great symbolic meaning in the passion since it deals with the question of Jesus' identity; Bach repeats its music three more times, always to texts that reveal the adverse reaction of the crowd to Jesus. See my discussion in *Tonal Allegory in the Vocal Music of J. S. Bach* (Berkeley: University of California Press, 1991), pp. 286–301.

10. It may be worth mentioning that within the *ambitus* of C–a as Heinichen set it forth the keys of the two arias of Cantata 109, e and F, constitute the sharpest and flattest, or the "mi" and "fa" degrees if the *ambitus* is viewed as the descendant of the hexachord. And that fact might have been related to the polarized affective qualities of the two arias. For a very similar situation between the two arias of Cantata 121 see "Cantata 121, 'Christum wir sollen loben schon'" in chapter 6.

11. See, for example, Helene Werthemann, *Die Bedeutung der alttestamentlichen Historien in Johann Sebastian Bachs Kantaten* (Tübingen: J. B. Mohr, 1960). One of the means by which Bach represents the destruction/restoration dynamic in his cantatas is that of tonal descent followed by ascent. That procedure led Bach, in his cantata for the Sunday after the New Year 1725, to devise one of the most conspicuously symmetrical designs in his cantata oeuvre, one in which parallel chorale-plus-recitative settings of "Ach Gott, wie manches Herzeleid" in C frame a recitative–aria–recitative sequence that modulates "down" by thirds to d for the "central" aria and back to C for the final movement (i.e., C, a–F, d, F–a, C). In that work, "Ach Gott, wie manches Herzeleid" (BWV 58), parallels between the outer movements set the *Angst* and *Geduld* of the present life (no. 1) in opposition to the *Herrlichkeit* and *Trost* of the "Himmels Paradies," the believer's "rechtes Vaterland" (no. 5), reinforcing the metaphoric interpretation of the old year as the time of Israel and the new year as the time of Christ. The first recitative draws explicit parallels, first between the believer's plight in the world and Herod's persecution of Jesus, then between both those events and the flight of the Israelites from Egypt in the time of Joseph. Then, following the central aria, "Ich bin vergnügt in meinem Leiden," the second recitative narrates God's hand pointing to "ein andres Land," ending with the believer's longing for eternity: "Ach! könnt es heute noch geschehen, daß ich mein Eden möchte sehen!" See the discussion in Chafe, *Tonal Allegory*, pp. 154–55.

12. Dürr, *Die Kantaten*, 1: 198.

13. In Kirnberger, *Die Kunst des Reinen Satzes*, the setting of "Ach Gott, vom Himmel sieh' darein" to which I have referred has been incorrectly identified as Phrygian rather than Aolian (pp. 320–21), an error that is carried forward by Lori Anne Burns in her valuable book, *Bach's Modal Chorales* (Stuyvesant, N.Y.: Pendragon Press, 1995, p. 116) and that causes her to argue,

somewhat unnecessarily, against what she believes to be Kirnberger's interpretation (pp. 115–19). In fact, Burns argues that the setting in question is Aolian ending on the dominant—that is, A Aolian—whereas Kirnberger may have intended the setting to be understood as E Aolian. Nevertheless, the setting certainly *sounds* as though it ends on the dominant of a as Burns argues.

14. See "The Seventeenth-century Background" in chapter 4.

15. We may note that the endings of both "Schau, lieber Gott" and "Und obgleich alle Teufel" feature chromatic four-semitone ascent patterns in the bass. In the former setting, however, the sequence articulates motion toward the final chord, no more than "nominally" the tonic, rendering it into a dominant ending, whereas in the latter one it leads toward the penultimate chord of a plagal cadence.

16. See "Aspects of the Liturgical Year" in chapter 1.

17. I have completed a chapter on the relationship between Cantatas 105 and 46 that I hope to publish in a future study of Bach hermeneutics.

18. See chapter 1, n. 6.

19. Robin A. Leaver, "Bach, Hymns and Hymnbooks," *The Hymn* 36, no. 4 (October 1985):7–13.

20. Ibid., p. 7.

21. Leaver points out also (ibid., p. 8) that the two passages in Bach's *St. John Passion* text in which that text borrows from Matthew's account both "occur in the same sequence in Bugenhagen's harmony of the passion, and thus it may have influenced Bach—or his librettist—at these points, since it was available in this *Leipziger Gesang-Buch* of 1724, as in many other hymn books of the time."

Chapter Six

1. A version of this chapter was given at the annual conference of the Internationale Arbeitsgemeinschaft für theologische Bachforschung at the Newberry Library, Chicago, in September 1997; and on that occasion I benefited from comments made by Martin Petzoldt in the question period afterward, in particular those that presented his view that the central theme as I had articulated it in both cantatas was that of the incarnation. See n. 18.

2. See A. S. Walpole, *Early Latin Hymns*, (Cambridge: Cambridge University Press, 1922; reprint, Hildesheim: Georg Olms, 1966), pp. 149–58.

3. Ibid., p. 149.

4. Andreas Werckmeister, *Harmonologia Musica* (1697), in facsimile ed. (5 vols. in 1) (Hildesheim: Georg Olms, 1972), pp. 61–62.

5. Alfred Dürr (*Die Kantaten von Johann Sebastian Bach* [Kassel: Bärenreiter, 1971], 1:142) speaks of the text of this cantata as dividing into two parts, the first part dealing with the mystery of the incarnation (emphasizing wonder rather than understanding) and the second dealing with the human response to that event.

6. "Christum wir sollen loben schon, / der reinen Magd Marien Sohn, / so weit die liebe Sonne leucht't, / und an aller Welt Ende reicht" (strophe 1); "Lob, Ehr, und Dank sei dir gesagt, / Christ, geborn von der reinen Magd, / samt Vater und dem heil'gen Geist, / von nun an bis in Ewigkeit" (strophe 8).

7. Christoph Wolff, *Der stile antico in der Musik Johann Sebastian Bachs* (Wiesbaden: Breitkopf & Härtel, 1968), pp. 111–12. The special character of this instrumentation may be gathered from the fact that Bach's entire cantata oeuvre includes only ten works in which it figures, in addition to Bach's arrangement of the Kyrie of Palestrina's *Missa à 6 voci* (score in Wolff, pp. 210–12). See the discussions of Cantatas 2 and 25 in the preceding chapter.

8. The aria deals with the idea of humanity as a "creature elevated by God" by means of its various directional qualities, such as the initial falling fifth on "O du," the rise of a fifth for

"erhöhte Creatur," the free transposition of the entire phrase up from b to D for the second line of text ("begreife nicht, nein, nein, bewund're nur"), and the rising melisma and modulation to D that ends the first phase of the text: "Gott will durch Fleisch des Fleisches Heil erwerben."

9. Werckmeister, *Harmonologia Musica*, p. 43.

10. I have argued elsewhere (*Tonal Allegory in the Vocal Music of J. S. Bach* [Berkeley: University of California Press, 1971], pp. 16–17) that one of the allegorical devices in Bach's canon bearing the heading "Symbolum. Christus Coronabit Crucigeros" (Symbol. Christ will crown the crossbearers) is its polarizing within a scant four measures the harmonies of F♯ and c. In that canon Bach intensifies the idea of antithesis (descent–ascent, chromatic–diatonic, major–minor, sharp–flat, and the like) for the purpose of representing the opposition indicated in the *Symbolum*: between those who "bear the cross" in life and the reward they will receive in eternity. Another of Bach's "allegorical" canons, the modulating canon *per tonos* from the *Musical Offering* (which Bach dedicated to Frederick the Great with the inscription "as the modulation ascends so may the glory of the king") provides in microcosm the minor keys of the circle of keys (c, g, d, a, e, etc., and back to c) as a mirror of increasing glory and an all-encompassing framework; the minor key, however, and the chromatic theme ensure that the composition is, in fact, limited to the kind of representation that Andreas Werckmeister (and, I think, Bach as well) would have viewed as "a nice moral of our mortality and incompleteness in this life" (*Musicae mathematicae hodegus curioses* [Frankfurt and Leipzig, 1686; fascimile ed., Hildesheim: Georg Olms, 1972], p. 145). Werckmeister, from whose writings Bach may have derived the title of the *Well-tempered Clavier*, viewed the necessity of tempered music as a mirror of God's having created a "tempered" universe. In this way the circle of keys became a symbol of the inevitable finiteness of the human perspective and an enharmonic tritone modulation would represent the human perception of all that was totally opposed, such as the divinity and humanity of Christ.

11. On pages 40–44 of the *Harmonologia* Werckmeister discusses enharmonic modulations, especially that from E major to F minor (centering on the reinterpretation of G♯ as A♭), of which he generally disapproves, although he admits that others use them and leaves each to his own taste. Werckmeister's view of such modulations is that their numerical proportions are too far from the ideal of equality for ordinary use; they should be confined to the tempered keyboard (pp. 43–44). In describing the G♯ as losing its "nature" (p. 43), in speaking of "metamorphosis," of "falling in an instant from one *genus* into another" (p. 40), of the difficulty the ear has in judging such progressions (p. 43), and of their running "contrary to reason and nature" (p. 44), Werckmeister describes some of the very miraculous, suprarational qualities that underlie Bach's enharmonic change in Cantata 121.

12. Extending the seasonal aspect of these associations leads to that between the spring equinox and the date of the annunciation as well. In that connection we may remember that March 25 was celebrated as the beginning of the new year in England as late as the eighteenth century. In Bach's cantatas the connection between the new beginning of the annunciation and that of the liturgical, geophysical, and civil new years is apparent, for example, in his basing his best-known cantata for the annunciation, "Wie schön leuchtet der Morgenstern" (BWV 1), on a hymn usually assocated with Advent (and whose *Abgesang* serves as the final chorale of the advent cantata "Nun komm, der Heiden Heiland," BWV 61).

13. The characterization of C major cited in the text is that of Johann David Heinichen, *Neu-erfundene und gründliche Anweisung* (Hamburg, 1711). Quite possibly the enharmonic modulation was conceived by Bach as a "mi"/"fa" *Verwandlung*, with the keys of b and C in the two arias representing another "mi" (b)–"fa" (C) shift. In his preface to his Leipzig cantata cycle of 1709–10 (reprinted in B. F. Richter, "Eine abhandlung Joh. Kuhnau's," *Monatshefte für Musik-Geschichte* 34: 148–54), Johann Kuhnau describes a modulation in his setting of the

first psalm as a place where "[the music] should proceed entirely from a different key, with Mi transformed into Fa or Fa into Mi" ("Da soll es . . . gantz aus einem andern *tono* gehen, und das Mi in Fa, oder das Fa in Mi verwandelt werden"). If representing unmediated awareness of the incarnation in C was a part of Bach's intent, then the chorale was undoubtedly transposed up a tone from its usual pitch so as to end on the dominant of b and to create a context for the tritone modulation from f♯ to C in the recitative.

14. In this connection we might compare the ending of "Christum wir sollen loben schon" with that of Cantata 148, "Bringet dem Herrn Ehre seines Namens," for the seventeenth Sunday after Trinity, 1723. The latter work features a "descending" sequence of movement keys from its initial D major (chorus), through B minor (aria) and G major (recitative and aria), to E minor (recitative beginning), in conjunction with the idea of the "indwelling" of God in humankind: "Denn Gott wohnt selbst in mir" (ending of first recitative); "Mund und Herze steht dir offen, Höchster, senke dich hinein!" (second aria); "Bleib auch, mein Gott, in mir" (second recitative). After the arrival on e, the prayer for God to give His Spirit leads to the anticipation of eternity: "Damit ich nach der Zeit in deiner Herrlichkeit, mein lieber Gott, mit dir den großen Sabbat möge halten," at which point Bach shifts to f♯ for the remainder of the recitative, remaining in that key for the final chorale as well. The descent by thirds up to the penultimate movement mirrors the indwelling of God through the Spirit, while the shift from e to f♯ mirrors the anticipation of eternity. In contrast with Cantata 121, however, the ending of Cantata 148 is a securely established F♯ *minor*, whose final harmony is altered to major.

15. We might speak of the literal-historical sense of the cantata as the narrative of the incarnation (the first "half" of the cantata), the allegorical sense as the idea of the incarnation as a turning point initiating a new era in salvation history as well as corresponding to the liturgical, geophysical, and civil new years (the ending of the first "half"), the tropological sense as the believer's acceptance of the meaning of the incarnation for him personally (the second aria and recitative, in which the believer holds the infant Jesus symbolically with the "Glaubensarm" of faith), and the eschatological sense as his hopes for eternal life (the ending of the second recitative and the final chorale).

16. Telemann, however, provides two versions of the melody, the first (no. 52) in Ionian (major), pure and simple, with the seventh degree raised in phrase 1 (but with the flat seventh degree listed as a variant), and the other (no. 423) with the flat seventh degree in phrase 1 (in this version the raised seventh degree is not listed as a variant in phrase 1).

17. The association of flat (subdominant) modulations and of shifts from major to minor keys with the incarnation and with the shift of focus from God to humankind is so common in Bach's work that it is, I hope, unnecessary to cite many instances. Suffice it to say that the device may appear almost as an incidental harmonic coloring (as in the very expressive b♭ on the word "uns" in the line "Denn der Herr hat grosses an *uns* getan" in the opening movement of Cantata 110, where the "grosses" referred to is the incarnation), as a more extended tonal or modal shift (as in the duet "Et in unum Dominum" from the Credo of the *Mass in B minor*, where the music shifts from G major to G minor for the last eight measures of the vocal part, on "qui propter *nos* et propter nostram salutem descendit de coelis"), or as a large-scale tonal-structural device (as in the shift from love of God to love of one's neighbor in the opening movement of Cantata 77, discussed in chapter 8). In the case of the "Et in unum Dominum," Bach's intention is particularly clear from the fact that originally (i.e., in the autograph score) this movement incorporated the text of the "Et incarnatus" as well, at the end: "Et incarnatus est de Spiritu Sancto ex Maria virgine et homo factus est." In that version Bach turned to G minor at "et homo factus est" and remained in g until the end of the texted part of the movement.

18. I am grateful to Martin Petzoldt for pointing this out in the discussion period follow-

ing my presentation of this chapter as a spoken paper (see n. 1). I have discussed the very similar three-stage idea of the "Actus Tragicus" (BWV 106) in relation to the idea of salvation history in *Tonal Allegory*, pp. 92–102.

19. That is, as I have set forth elsewhere (*Tonal Allegory*, p. 396), in the *St. Matthew Passion* the E major movements, "Erkenne mich, mein Hüter" and "O Mensch, bewein dein Sünde gross," represent, respectively, a prayer to the *resurrected* Jesus to look favorably on the believer and the first verse of a very long chorale summary of Jesus' work of salvation (which is not at all apparent from its first line). In the passion "O Mensch, bewein" represents a positive point of culmination since it expresses *acknowledgment* of sin, not sin itself. The E minor movement toward the end of the *St. Matthew Passion*, part 1, is the soprano/alto duet "So ist mein Jesus nun gefangen" and chorus "Sind Blitze, sind Donner in Wolken verschwunden," which contains the line "Eröffne den feurigen Abgrund, O Hölle." The E minor aria of Cantata 9 is the aria "Wir waren schon zu tief gesunken, der Abgrund Schluckt uns völlig ein." In both cases the basic tonal context is E major, in which the shift to E minor and the imagery of the *Abgrund* represent a contrary aspect (Judas's betrayal in the passion, humanity falling into sin in the cantata).

20. See "The Seventeenth-century Background," in chapter 4.

21. For translations of the texts of this cantata see "Basic Principles" in chapter 1.

22. See the discussion of the arioso "Der Heiland fällt vor seinem Vater nieder" from the *St. Matthew Passion* in "Cantata 18, 'Gleichwie der Regun und Schnee'" in chapter 5.

23. On the role of the mediant, or Phrygian degree, in establishing a secure tonic, see later in this section, also chapter 9.

24. This outlook is, of course, the theology of the cross—the cross as emblem of God's revealing His purpose in a manner that is directly contrary to human expectations; on that basis Luther called the cross "God's allegorical work." See Walther von Loewenich, *Luther's Theology of the Cross*, trans. Herbert J. A. Bouman (Minneapolis: Augsburg, 1976), p. 128.

25. In fact, ending the cantata with this verse might have been central to the conception of the cantata; the chorale itself has an additional two verses (basically a doxology based on the Lord's Prayer) that were not used in the cantata.

26. We must remember, however, that in the case of the melody of "Es ist das Heil" it was Bach's own decision to bring out the "subdominant" or Mixolydian quality I have described here, not something that was demanded of him by the chorale melody. Bach wrote a second chorale cantata that uses the same melody, now set to the text "Sei Lob und Ehr' dem höchsten Gut" (Cantata 117), which centers on praise of God and therefore has nothing of the theological qualities associated with the flat seventh degree of the scale in "Es ist das Heil." And Bach neither harmonizes the chorale with the extravagant subdominant effect of the first phrase of "Es ist das Heil" nor derives a descent–ascent tonal design from it. In other words, it was the connection between the flat seventh degree of the scale and the theological content of "Es ist das Heil" that stimulated his imagination in Cantata 9.

27. Lothar and Renate Steiger, *"Sehet! Wir gehn hinauf gen Jerusalem": Johann Sebastian Bachs Kantaten auf den Sonntag Estohimi* (Göttingen: Vandenhoeck & Ruprecht, 1992).

28. Dürr, *Die Kantaten*, 2: p. 568.

Chapter Seven

1. See Martin *Luther, Luthers geistliche Lieder und Kirchengesange*, vol. 4 of *Archiv zur Weimarer Ausgabe der Werker Martins Luthers*, ed. Marcus Jenny (Cologne: Bohlau, 1985), pp. 55–56.

2. Theodore G. Tappert, trans. and ed., *The Book of Concord* (Philadelphia: Fortress Press, 1959), p. 361.

3. See "Aspects of the Liturgical Year" in chapter 1.

4. The second commandment (Exodus 20:4–6; Deuteronomy 5:8–10), after expressing God's wrath toward the succeeding generations of those who serve other gods, turns to God's promise of mercy to those that love Him and keep His commandments: "For I the Lord thy God am a jealous God, visiting the iniquity of the fathers upon the children unto the third and fourth generation of them that hate Me [Exodus 20:5]; And showing mercy unto thousands of them that love Me, and keep My commandments" [v. 6].

5. On the theological background of "Dies sind die heil'gen zehn Gebot" see Johachim Stalmann and Johannes Heinrich, eds., *Handbuch zum Evangelischen Kirchengesangbuch*, vol. 3, part 2 (Göttingen: Vandenhoeck & Ruprecht, Wilhelm Hoppe, 1990), pp. 171–74.

6. Paul Althaus, *The Theology of Martin Luther*, trans. Robert C. Schultz (Philadelphia: Fortress Press, 1966), pp. 44–45, 132.

7. Ibid., pp. 133–34.

8. Ibid., pp. 130–36.

9. Luther, *Luthers Geistliche Lieder*, p. 55). As Jenny points out, "In Gottes Namen" was associated not only with pilgrimage to Jerusalem but also with the idea of pilgrimage and procession generally. See note 14; also Stalmann and Heinrich, *Handbuch zum Evangelischen Kirchengesangbuch*, vol. 3, part 2, pp. 527–30.

10. Johann Leisentrit, *Gesangbuch von 1567*, facsimile ed. (Kassel: Bärenreiter, 1966), pp. 147, 152. The Leisentrit collection, however, is a Catholic chorale book and therefore has a modified text for "Dies sind die heil'gen zehn Gebot."

11. A parody version of "In Gottes Namen" exists under the heading "Der Christen Schiffart"; see *Jahrbuch für Liturgik und Hymnologie*, ed. Konrad Ameln, Christhard Mahrenholz, and Karl Ferdinand Müller, 10:79.

12. One of these settings appears in Trent Codex Tr. 89 (see *Denkmäler der Tonkunst in Österreich* 14–15, edited by Guido Adler and Oswald Koller (Graz: Akademische Druck- und Verlagsanstalt 1959), pp. 266–68; Helmut Federhofer (MGG, 9:670) dates it 1459–75. The other appears in Thomas Nablitt, ed., *Der Kodex des Magister Nicolaus Leopold: Staatsbibliothek München, Mus. ms. 3154*, vol. 80 of Das Erbe deutscher Musik (Kassel: Bärenreiter, 1987), pp. 104–7.

13. Heinrich Isaac, *Weltliche Werke*, vol. 28 of *Denkmäler der Tonkunst in Osterreich* ed. Johannes Wolf (Graz: Akademische Druck–v. Verlagsanstalt, 1959), pp. 14–15; Heinrich Finck, Ausgewählte Werke, vol. 70 of *Das Erbe deutscher Musik*, 1955), ed. Lothar Hoffmann-Erbrecht and Helmut Lomnitzer (Frankfurt: C. F. Peters 1981) pp. 134–35; Hans Joachim Moser, *Paul Hofhaimer: Ein Lied- und Orgelmeister des deutschen Humanismus*, 2d ed. (Hildesheim: George Olms, 1966), appendix, pp. 63–65.

14. This part of the text extends the final *Kyrieleis* to an appeal to the Trinity, adding a reference to death as the final pilgrimage: "das wir frölich farn von hyn." And, interestingly, Johann Walther produced a version of "In Gottes Namen fahren wir," titled "In Gottes Namen scheiden wir," whose text incorporates Lutheran beliefs and whose final strophe borrows its first two lines—"Das helf uns der Herr Jesu Christ, / der unser Mittler worden ist"—from the final strophe of "Dies sind die heil'gen zehn Gebot." The words "Das helf uns [der Herr Jesu Christ]" in Luther's final strophe are indebted to phrases such as "Des helf uns die Goteskraft" and "Das helff uns der heylig geyst" in the oldest surviving versions of "In Gottes Namen." See Johann Walhter, *Geistliches Gesangbüchlein* (Wittenberg, 1551), vol. 1 of *Samtliche Werke* (1953), p. 122. It may be noted that "In Gottes Namen scheiden wir," in G Mixolydian with b♭s written in the last phrase, is followed by a straightforward setting of "In Gottes Namen fahren wir," in g transposed Dorian. Elsewhere in the collection (pp. 49–51) are two settings of "Dies sind die heil'gen zehn Gebot," the former in *cantus mollis* g and the latter in *cantus durus* G with b♭s in the final phrase.

15. Moser, *Paul Hofhaimer*, appendix, p. 65, n. 23.

16. Johann Walther, *Wittembergische Geistliche Gesangbuch von 1524*, vol. 7 of *Publikation Älterer Praktischer und Theoretischer Musikwerke* (1878, ed. Otto Kade [New York: Broude Bros., 1966], pp. 35–37.

17. Johannes Zahn, *Die Melodien der Deutschen Evangelischen Kirchenlieder*, 6 vols. (Gütersloh, 1889; reprint, Hildesheim: Georg Olms, 1963).

18. For example, Kirnberger *Die Kunst der reinen Satzes*, (p. 49) cites Bach's two settings of "Dies sind die heil'gen zehn Gebot" from *Clavierübung*, vol. 3, as examples of his ingenious treatment of the Mixolydian mode.

19. Friedrich Blume, ed., *Gesamtausgabe der Musikalischen Werke von Michael Praetorius, Musae Sioniae* 7 (1609): 5–8, 9 (1610): 76–78.

20. See Christoph Wolff, ed., *The Neumeister Collection of Chorale Preludes from the Bach Circle*, (New Haven and London: Yale University Press, 1986), pp. 56–57.

21. See Georg Philipp Telemann, *Fast allgemeines Evangelisch-Musicalisches Lieder-Buch* (Hamburg, 1730; facsimile ed. Siegfried Kross (Hildesheim: Georg Olms, 1977), p. 14.

22. The chorale itself introduces the b♭' in its fifth, penultimate, phrase; but Bach's version compresses the fifth and sixth phrases into one, apparently for symbolic reasons. See the discussion of Bach's version of the melody in the following paragraph.

23. Kirnberger, *Die Kunst der reinen Satzes*, p. 53.

24. In verse 1, for example, lines 4 and 5 together are "hoch auf dem Berg / Sinai"; in verse 7 they are inseparable, "mit Zucht und Mäßigkeit sein."

25. In this connection we may note that in the longer chorale prelude setting of "Dies sind die heil'gen zehn Gebot" from *Clavierübung*, vol. 3, Bach divides the chorale melody (now treated in canon at the unison) into six phrases. The distance between canonic entries, however, is greatly reduced toward the end of the setting: six measures between phrases 1 and 2, eight measures between 2 and 3, five between 3 and 4, two and a half between 4 and 5, and less than a measure between 5 and 6. Phrases 5 and 6 in particular almost sound as one, a quality that is enhanced by the increased flattening that takes place just before phrase 5 and the fact that Bach adds a passing tone, a, between the tones g and b♭, thereby increasing the resemblance between phrases 5 and 6.

26. The ending of "Dies sind die heil'gen zehn Gebot" does not sound like G minor, of course; rather, the effect produced by the b♭' is to intensify the already pronounced subdominant coloring of G Mixolydian—that is, to increase the tendency toward C. Alfred Dürr (*Die Kantaten von Johann Sebastian Bach* [Kassel: Bärenreiter, 1971], 2:568) even places the first movement of Cantata 77 in C.

27. See Martin Luther, *Tischreden*, in *D. Martin Luthers Werke. Gesamtausgabe* (Weimar: H. Buhlau, 1883–4), vol. 1 (1912), no. 816; vol. 3 (1914), no. 2996.

28. See chapter 2.

29. That is, the word *durus* originally referred to the greater string tension that accompanied higher pitches, in relation to the lesser (*mollis*) tension of low pitches. See Carl Dahlhaus, "Die termini 'dur' und 'moll,'" *Archiv für Musikwissenschaft* 12 (1955): 289–91. I have related this quality to Monteverdi's *stile concitato* in *Monteverdi's Tonal Language* (New York: Schirmer, 1992). pp. 237–38.

30. In the longer setting of "Dies sind die heil'gen zehn Gebot" from *Clavierübung*, vol. 3, Bach adds the chromatic descending minor tetrachord to the final line of the chorale melody, a device that underscores the flat-minor quality of the ending as a symbol of the human condition.

31. The work that Bach performed on the latter occasion in 1723 is unknown; owing to the unusually close relationship between the theological messages of the two occasions the absence of a cantata for the latter occasion might be no coincidence. Possibly, that is, Bach reper-

formed Cantata 77 on the latter occasion. There is, admittedly, no evidence for that notion, and Bach is not known ever to have reperformed a cantata soon after its initial production.

32. See Althaus, *The Theology of Martin Luther*, pp. 120, 165–68, 171–72, 251–73.

33. Luther even expressed the relation of Law and Gospel with the aid of a musical allegory. He described the "mi/fa" semitone of the musical scale as analogous to the Gospel and the other tones as analogous to the Law; the "mi/fa" semitone (which he called the "lieblichste" of intervals) gave the others their meaning in analogy to the way that the placement of the semitone determined the mode. Luther also described the second (i.e., Hypodorian) mode as analogous to a "poor weak sinner" (*peccator infirmus*) because it wavered between mi and fa (i.e., it utilized the tones B and B♭). See n. 27. I suggest below that something of this latter association underlies Bach's setting of the aria "Ach es bleibt in meiner Liebe lauter Unvollkommenheit" and its "Dorian" notation.

34. Knauer's collection was published in Gotha in 1720–21. Martin Petzoldt has done a close comparison of the Knauer and Bach texts and their theological content ("Studieren zur Theologie im Rahmen der Lebensgeschichte J. S. Bachs," unpublished *Habilitationsschrift*, Leipzig, 1985, pp. 80–91, 100–105; also appendix 1).

35. Petzoldt, "Studieren zur Theologie," pp. 83–87.

36. Ibid., pp. 83–87, 102.

37. Ibid., p. 88.

38. Ibid., p. 90.

39. See Werner Neumann, ed., *Kritischer Bericht to Johann Sebastian Bach*, vol. 21 of *Neue Bach Ausgabe sämtlicher werke*, ser. 1 (Kassel: Barenreiter, 1959), pp. 11–12.

40. In the category of brotherly love Freylinghausen offers two additional chorales that were sung to the melody "Ach Gott, vom Himmel sieh' darein," both of which contain verses that might be suitable for Cantata 77: "O himmlische Barmherzigkeit" (whose first, fourth, seventh, and tenth verses might be considered) and "O Vater der Barmherzigkeit" (whose third and sixth verses might come into question). It might also be mentioned that the chorale "O Gott, der du die Menschenkind," a paraphrase of Psalm 110 that was traditionally sung to the melody of "Ach Gott, vom Himmel sieh' darein," ends with a prayer to the Trinity for aid in loving God and one's neighbor: ". . . dein Segen sich vermehre, daß wir fort spüren deine Güt, und stets mit willigem Gemüth dir und dem Nächsten dienen." None of these verses, however, is as appropriate to the text of Cantata 77 as the one suggested by Petzoldt.

Chapter Eight

1. Arnold Schering, "Bach und das Symbol, insbesondere die Symbolik seines Kanons," *Bach-Jahrbuch* 22 (1925):53–59; Manfred Bukofzer, "Allegory in Baroque Music," *Journal of the Warburg Institute* 3 (1939–41):15–18; Gerhard Herz, "Thoughts on the First Movement of Johann Sebastian Bach's Cantata No. 77, 'Du sollst Gott, deinen Herren, lieben,'" in *Essays on J. S. Bach* (Ann Arbor: UMI Research Press, 1985), pp. 205–17.

2. On the *bassetchen* practice see Frank T. Arnold, *The Art of Accompaniment from a Thorough-Bass* (London: Oxford University Press, 1931; reprint, New York: Dover, 1965), pp. 224, 233, 373–81. The German spellings *bassetchen* and *bassetgen* were used interchangeably. The Italian form of this term is *bassetto* and the French *petit basse*. I have prepared a full study of this phenomenon (considering more than thirty instances in Bach's work) under the title "Bach's Use of the *Bassetto*: A Theological Interpretation."

3. In using that term I intend only the idea of a recurring musical unit, whether instrumental or vocal, not that of the traditional instrumental ritornello of the Bach arias or its model in the instrumental concerto, and I do not intend to imply any connection to the formal types that are associated with the instrumental ritornello.

4. See chapter 7, n. 4.

5. In this connection it may be noted that in Leipzig on certain occasions during the Trinity season two particular chorales were assigned, the one, Luther's "Dies sind die heil'gen zehn Gebot," not only summarizing the Ten Commandments but also placing them clearly within the Lutheran-Pauline perspective and the other, Paul Speratus's "Es ist das Heil uns kommen hier," treating of the subject of justification as a whole. While Vopelius assigned each of these chorales separately to several different points in the liturgical year, he assigned both to just three Sundays in the Trinity season, the sixth, thirteenth, and eighteenth (Gottfried Vopelius, *Neu-Leipziger Gesangbuch* [Leipzig, 1682]). Thus, there was a particular association between the Law and justification on the two Sundays that center on the two great commandments.

6. See chapter 7, n. 26.

7. See chapter 2.

8. See Eric Chafe, *Monteverdi's Tonal Language* (New York: Schirmer, 1992).

9. In *Monteverdi's Tonal Language* (pp. 112–17, 188–91) I take up madrigals and even a madrigal cycle in which Monteverdi shifts from the *cantus mollis* to the *cantus durus* (beginning in g and ending in G), making clear associations of the two *cantus* to the qualities associated with the words *mollis* and *durus*. His choice of the g/G modes as the framework for shift of cantus was undoubtedly bound up with the fact that G is both major and sharp, while g is both minor and flat (the only other pairing of modes on the same final to which both dualisms would apply is d/D, and at the time D major was not yet a common feature of Monteverdi's music). In his later music, however, several forms of d/D mode could be found within a single piece. The dualisms in question are central to the understanding of *Orfeo* as well (see pp. 126–58).

10. As we will see, the variant theme that begins the segment "und deinen Nächsten als dich selbst" will even reappear in the aria "Ach, es bleibt in meiner Liebe lauter Unvollkommenheit" (see Ex. 8.7).

11. The only exception occurs in measures 26 and 27, as the tenor doubles the alto's g' version of the theme at the sixth below (i.e., beginning from b); this is clearly heard as a shadowing of the major form of the theme, not as an independent entry.

12. It may be remembered at this point that the fourth of the human attributes, "Kräften," does not appear in this recitative. But Knauer's original text referred to *God's* strength ("Kraft"), which Bach (or his librettist) changed to God's *Spirit* ("Geist"; see "The Text of Cantata 77" in chapter 7). Apart from the fact that the aria that follows develops the "fire" imagery associated with the Holy Spirit, Bach's text also acknowledges in the change from "Kraft" to "Geist" the fact that in the preceding movement human *weakness* had received unusual emphasis.

13. See Martin Petzoldt, "Studieren zur Theologie im Rahmen der Lebengeschichte J. S. Bachs," unpublished *Habilitationsschrift*, Leipzig, 1985, for Petzoldt's analysis of the eschatological character of this movement. In Cantata 77 the eschatological framework is more future-oriented ("contained" within an earthly framework) than in Cantata 21, which attempts to visualize eternity in its final movement.

14. Andreas Werckmeister, *Musicae mathematicae hodegus curioses* (Frankfurt and Leipzig, 1686; facsimile ed., Hildesheim: Georg Olms, 1972), p. 145, and *Musicalische Paradoxal-Discourse* (1707; in facsimile ed. [5 vols. in 1], Hildesheim: Georg Olms, 1970), pp. 114–20. As noted in chapter 2, the final sections of those two treatises are allegorical treatments (in both cases specified as such) of the diatonic-harmonic and tempered tonal materials of music.

15. Werckmeister, *Musicae mathematicae*, p. 149.

16. See Paul Althaus, *The Theology of Martin Luther*, trans. Robert C. Schultz (Philadelphia: Fortress Press, 1966), pp. 133–34.

17. See Martin Luther, *Tischreden*, in *D. Martin Luthers Werke*. Gesamtausgabe (Weimar: H. Buhlau, 1883–), vol. 1 (1912), no. 816; vol. 3 (1914), no. 2996.

18. See "Cantata 153, 'Schau, lieber Gott, wie meine Feind" in chapter 5.

19. As an indication of the principal affect Bach intended for this movement, we may note that he introduced a chromatic descent (c"–b♮'–b♭'–a'–g') into the second and fourth phrases of the chorale *cantus firmus*, and the "free" parts, as the text takes up the cries to God for mercy from humanity in grave need ("und lass dich's doch *erbarmen*" and "verlassen sind *wir Armen*").

20. Althaus, *The Theology of Martin Luther*, pp. 152–56, 268–73.

21. On the feeling qualities associated with love of God see, for example, Johann Arndt, *True Christianity*, trans. Peter C. Erb (Ramsey, N.J.: Paulist Press, 1979), pp. 123–28, 187.

Chapter Nine

1. In fact, "Christ, unser Herr" is constructed so as to highlight the final line of each of the seven strophes as if it were an "extra" line. Each strophe has nine lines, following the rhyme scheme ababcdcde, according to which the final line stands apart. And the melody reflects this quality closely, the eighth line closing in the original tonic at low pitch, after which the ninth line begins an octave higher and closes in the dominant. In some strophes the final line sounds like an afterthought or an amplification of the content of the strophe.

2. Eric Chafe, *Tonal Allegory in the Vocal Music of J. S. Bach* (Berkeley: University of California Press, 1991), pp. 193–96.

3. See, for example, Christoph Bernhard's discussion of the *passus duriusculus* in terms of chromatically ascending and descending lines and melodic patterns in which augmented seconds and diminished thirds replace their normal counterparts; Bernhard adds that other intervals, such as the ascending augmented fourth, were "nowadays too easily used" ("heutiges Tages zu gelassen"). Bernhard's "Tractatus compositionis augmentatus" has been reprinted in Joseph Müller-Blattau, *Die Kompositionslehre Heinrich Schützens in der Fassung seines Schülers Christoph Bernhard* (Kassel: Bärenreiter, 1963), pp. 40–131; see pp. 77–78.

4. Alfred Dürr, *Die Kantaten von Johann Sebastian Bach* (Kassel: Bärenreiter, 1971), 2:519–20. Bach himself perceived—but did not create, of course—that relationship, since his version of "Es ist genug" is nearly identical to J. M. Ahle's 1662 melody. Ahle's melody was altered, however, in many subsequent collections, and, in fact, the Vopelius collection of 1682 began with the tones a', b', c♯", and d".

5. Thus, the slow movement of Beethoven's A minor String Quartet, Opus 132, as is well-known, was considered by Beethoven to be in F Lydian, which meant, basically, F major with B♮ rather than B♭.

6. That is, the lower tetrachords of the modes comprise a sequence of ascending fourths according to the circle of fifths: F–G–A–B (Lydian), C–D–E–F (Ionian), G–A–B–C (Mixolydian), D–E–F–G (Dorian), A–B–C–D (Aolian), and E–F–G–A (Phrygian). The next tetrachord, B–C–D–E, would complete the Phrygian mode.

7. See chapter 4, "The Seventeenth-Century Background."

8. See Carl Dahlhaus, *Studies on the Origin of Harmonic Tonality*, translated by Robert O. Gjerdingen (Princeton: Princeton University Press, 1991).

9. In this light, it may be mentioned that one of the ancient associations of the terms *durus* and *mollis* was that of the opposite qualities of the whole tone and the half tone (see Carl Dahlhaus, "Die termini 'dur' und 'moll,'" *Archiv für Musikwissenschaft* 12 [1955]:), which relate to a spectrum of other associations that are best summarized in terms of the qualities of the raised versus the flattened fourth degree of the Lydian scale—that is, the motion from "mi" to "mi" versus that from "mi" to "fa."

10. The second through the fifth tones in the bass pitch sequence g♯–a–c♯–d♯–e♯–f♯ recall those of the "schwerer Gang" of the first recitative, transposed at the fifth.

11. Behind this modulation may lie something akin to Heinichen's describing the sharpest and flattest keys of the *musicalischer Circul* as "difficult" and "hardly usable" Hans T. David and Arthur Mendel, eds., *The New Bach Reader*, revised and enlarged by Christoph Wolff (New York: W.W. Norton, 1998) pp. 16–17.

12. Unfortunately, however, Berg must have used a faulty source for Bach's harmonization since the version used in the *Violin Concerto* displaces the accented passing tone in its first measure, thereby eliminating the most biting dissonance in the setting.

Bibliography

Adorno, Theodor W. "Bach Defended against His Devotees." In *Prisms*, edited and translated by Samuel Weber and Shierry Weber, pp. 133–46. Cambridge, Mass.: MIT Press, 1981.

Althaus, Paul. *The Theology of Martin Luther.* Translated by Robert C. Schultz. Philadelphia: Fortress Press, 1966.

Arndt, Johann. *True Christianity.* Translated by Peter C. Erb. Ramsey, N.J.: Paulist Press, 1979.

Arnold, Frank T. *The Art of Accompaniment from a Thorough-Bass.* London: Oxford University Press, 1931. Reprint. New York: Dover, 1965.

Atcherson, Walter. "Key and Mode in Seventeenth-Century Music Theory Books." *Journal of Music Theory* 17 (1973): 205–33.

Aulén, Gustav. *Christus Victor: An Historical Study of the Three Main Types of the Idea of the Atonement.* Translated by A. G. Hebert. New York: Macmillan 1969.

Axmacher, Elke. "*Aus Liebe will mein Heyland sterben*": *Untersuchungen zum Wandel des Passionsverständnisses im frühen 18. Jahrhundert.* Neuhausen-Stuttgart: Hänssler, 1984.

———. "Bachs Kantatentexte in auslegungsgeschichtlicher Sicht." In *Bach als Ausleger der Bibel*, edited by Martin Petzoldt, pp. 15–32. Göttingen: Vandenhoeck & Ruprecht, 1985.

———. "Erdmann Neumeister: Ein Kantatendichter J. S. Bachs." *Musik und Kirche* 60 (1990): 249–302.

Bach, Johann Sebastian. *Orgelbüchlein.* Facsimile edition of the autograph score, edited and with a preface by Heinz-Harald Löhlein. Vol. 11 of *Documenta Musicologica*, ser. 2. Kassel: Bärenreiter, 1981.

Benjamin, Walter. *The Origins of German Tragic Drama.* Translated by John Osborne. London: New Left Books, 1977.

Bernhard, Christoph. "Tractatus compositionis augmentatus." MS treatise. In Joseph Müller-Blattau, *Die Kompositionslehre Heinrich Schützens in der Fassung seines Schülers Christoph Bernhard*, pp. 40–153. Kassel: Bärenreiter, 1963.

Blankenburg, Walter. "Der Harmonie-Begriff in der lutherisch-barocken Musikanschauung." *Archiv für Musikwissenschaft* 16 (1959): 44–56.

Bornkamm, Heinrich. *Luther and the Old Testament.* Translated by Eric W. Gritsch and Ruth C. Gritsch, edited by Victor I. Gruhn. Philadelphia: Fortress Press, 1974.

Brainard, Paul. "Cantata 21 Revisited." *Festschrift for Arthur Mendel* (1974): 231–42.

———, ed. *Kritischer Bericht to Johann Sebastian Bach.* Vol. 16 of *Neue Bach Ausgabe sämtlicher Werke*, ser. 1. Kassel: Bärenreiter, 1984.

Brown, Raymond. The Gospel according to John I–XII and XIII–XXI. *Anchor Bible*, vols. 29 and 29A. Garden City, N.Y.: Doubleday, 1966, 1970.

Bukofzer, Manfred. "Allegory in Baroque Music." *Journal of the Warburg Institute* 3 (1939–41): 1–21.

———. *Music in the Baroque Era.* New York: Norton, 1947.

Burns, Lori Anne. *Bach's Modal Chorales.* Stuyvesant, N.Y.: Pendragon Press, 1995.

Chafe, Eric. "Allegorical Music: The 'Symbolism' of Tonal Language in the Bach Canons." *Journal of Musicology* 3 (fall 1984): 340–62.

———. "*Anfang und Ende*: Cyclic Recurrence in Bach's Cantata *Jesu, nun sei gepreiset*, BWV 41." *Bach Perspectives* 1 (spring 1994): 103–34.

———. "Aspects of Durus/Mollis Shift and the Two-System Framework of Monteverdi's Music." In *Schütz-Jahrbuch 1990*. Kassel: Bärenreiter, 1991, 171–206.

———. "Bach's First Two Leipzig Cantatas: A Message for the Community." In *A Birthday Offering: Essays in Honor of William H. Scheide*, edited by Paul Brainard and Ray Robinson, pp. 71–86. Kassel: Bärenreiter, and Chapel Hill: Hinshaw, 1993.

———. *The Church Music of Heinrich Biber.* Ann Arbor: UMI Research Press, 1987.

———. "Key Structure and 'Tonal Allegory' in the Passions of J. S. Bach: An Introduction." *Current Musicology* 31 (1981): 39–54.

———. "Luther's 'Analogy of Faith' in Bach's Church Music." *dialog* 24 (spring 1985): 96–101.

———. *Monteverdi's Tonal Language.* New York: Schirmer, 1992.

———. *Tonal Allegory in the Vocal Music of J. S. Bach.* Berkeley: University of California Press, 1991.

Cox, Howard C., ed. *The Calov Bible of J. S. Bach.* Ann Arbor: UMI Research Press, 1985.

Dahlhaus, Carl. *Studies on the Origin of Harmonic Tonality.* (*Untersuchungen über die Entstehung der harmonischen Tonalität.* Kassel: Bärenreiter, 1968.) Translated by Robert O. Gjerdingen. Princeton: Princeton University Press, 1991.

———. "Die termini 'dur' und 'moll.'" *Archiv für Musikwissenschaft* 12 (1955): 289–91.

Dammann, Rolf. *Der Musikbegriff im deutschen Barock.* Cologne: Arno Volk, 1967.

David, Hans T. and Arthur Mendel. *The New Bach Reader* revised and enlarged by Christoph Wolff. New York: Norton, 1998.

Dreyfus, Laurence. *Bach's Continuo Group: Players and Practices in His Vocal Works.* Cambridge: Harvard University Press, 1987.

Dürr, Alfred. *Die Kantaten von Johann Sebastian Bach.* 2 vols. Kassel: Bärenreiter, 1971.

———. *Studien über die frühen Kantaten Johann Sebastian Bachs.* Wiesbaden: Breitkopf & Härtel, 1977.

Düwel, Klaus, ed. *Gedichte 1500–1600.* Vol. 3 of *Epochen der deutschen Lyrik.* Munich: Deutsche Taschenbuch, 1978.

Finck, Heinrich. *Ausgewählte Werke*, Part Two. Vol. 70 of *Das Erbe deutscher Musik*, edited by Lothar Hoffmann-Erbrecht and Helmut Lomnitzer. Frankfurt: C. F. Peters, 1981.

Freylinghausen, Johann Anastasius. *Geistreiches Gesang-Buch* and *Neues geistreiches Gesang-Buch.* Edited by G. A. Francke. Halle, 1741.

Heinichen, Johann David. *Der General-Bass in der Composition.* Hamburg, 1728. Facsimile ed. Hildesheim: Georg Olms, 1969.

———. *Neu-erfundene und gründliche Anweisung.* Hamburg, 1711.

Herz, Gerard. "Thoughts on the First Movement of Johann Sebastian Bach's Cantata No. 77, 'Du sollst Gott, deinen Herren, lieben.'" In *Essays on J. S. Bach*, pp. 205–17. Ann Arbor: UMI Research Press, 1985.

Isaac, Heinrich. *Weltliche Werke.* Vol. 28 of *Denkmaler der Tonkunst in Österreich.* Edited by Johannes Wolf. Graz: Akademische Druck– u. Verlagsanstalt, 1959.

Jansen, Martin. "Bachs Zahlensymbolik, an seinen Passionen untersucht." *Bach-Jahrbuch* 34 (1937): 96–117.

Kircher, Athanasius. *Musurgia universalis sive Ars magna consoni et dissoni in X. libros digesta.* Rome, 1650. Facsimile ed. Edited by Ulf Scharlau. Hildesheim: Georg Olms, 1970.

Kirnberger, Johann Philipp. *The Art of Strict Musical Composition.* Translated by David Beach and Jurgen Thym. New Haven: Yale University Press, 1981.

———. *Die Kunst des reinen Satzes in der Musik.* Berlin and Königsberg, 1776–79. Facsimile ed. Hildesheim: Georg Olms, 1968.

Krausse, Helmut K. "Erdmann Neumeister und die Kantatentexts Johann Sebastian Bachs." *Bach-Jahrbuch* 72 (1986): 7–32.

Kuhnau, Johann. *Musikalische Vorstellung Einiger Biblische Historien.* Leipzig, 1720. Vol. 4 of *Denkmäler deutscher Tonkunst,* ser. 1. Edited by Karl Päsler. Leipzig: Breitkopf & Härtel, 1901.

———. *Six Biblical Sonatas, for Keyboard, 1700.* With the original preface and introductions in German (facsimile) and English, translated and annotated by Kurt Stone. New York: Broude Brothers, 1953.

Leaver, Robin A. "Bach and Hymnody: The Evidence of the Orgelbüchlein." *Early Music* 13, no. 2 (May 1985): 168–73.

———. "Bach, Hymns and Hymnbooks." *The Hymn* 36, no. 4 (October 1985): 7–13.

———. "Bach Kirchenlieder und Gesangbücher." *Musik und Kirche* 57 (1987): 169–74; 58 (1988): 8–12.

———. *Bachs theologische Bibliothek.* Neuhausen-Stuttgart: Hänssler, 1983.

Leisentrit, Johann. *Gesangbuch von 1567.* Facsimile ed. Kassel: Bärenreiter, 1966.

Lipphart, Walther. "Das Wiedergefundene Gesangbuch: Autograph von Adam Reißner aus dem Jahre 1554." *Jahrbuch für Liturgik und Hymnologie* 10 (1965): 55–86.

Loewenich, Walther von. *Luther's Theology of the Cross.* Translated by Herbert J. A. Bouman. Minneapolis: Augsburg, 1976.

Luther, Martin. *The Bondage of the Will (De servo arbitrio).* In *Luther and Erasmus: Free Will and Salvation,* translated and edited by Philip S. Watson, pp. 99–334. Philadelphia: Westminster Press, 1969.

———. *Lectures on Isaiah, Chapters 1–39.* Translated by Herbert J. A. Bouman. Vol. 16 of *Luther's Works,* edited by Jaroslav Pelikan. St. Louis: Concordia, 1969.

———. *Luthers geistliche Lieder und Kirchengesänge.* Vol. 4 of *Archiv zur Weimarer Ausgabe der Werker Martins Luthers,* edited by Marcus Jenny. Cologne: Bohlau, 1985.

———. *Luther's Works.* 55 vols. Edited by Jaroslav Pelikan and Heinz Lohmann. St. Louis: Concordia, and Philadelphia: Fortress Press, 1955–86.

———. *Tischreden.* In *D. Martin Luthers Werke. Gesamtausgabe* (Weimar: H. Buhlau, 1833–19), vol. 1 (1912), no. 76, no. 816; vol. 3 (1914), no. 2996.

Marshall, Robert, ed. *Kritischer Bericht* to *Johann Sebastian Bach.* Vol. 19 of *Neue Bach Ausgabe sämtlicher Werke,* ser. 1. Kassel: Bärenreiter, 1989.

Mattheson, Johann. *Das beschützte Orchestre.* Hamburg, 1717. Facsimile ed. Leipzig: Zentralantiquariat der Deutschen Demokratischen Republik, 1981.

———. *Critica Musica. Des fragende Componisten/Erstes Verhör/über eine gewisse Passion* . Hamburg, 1724. Facsimile ed. Amsterdam: F. Knuf, 1964.

———. *Das forschende Orchestre.* Hamburg, 1721.

———. *Der musicalische Patriot.* Hamburg, 1728. Facsimile ed. Leipzig: Zentralantiquariat der Deutschen Demokratischen Republik, 1975.

———. *Das neu-eröffnete Orchestre.* Hamburg, 1713.

McCracken, James. "Die Vedrwendung der Blechblasinstrumente bei J. S. Bach unter besonderer Berücksichtigung der Tromba da tirarsi." *Bach-Jahrbuch* (1984): 59–90.

Minear, Paul. "J. S. Bach and J. A. Ernesti: A Case Study in Exegetical and Theological Conflict." In *Our Common History as Christians: Essays in Honor of Albert C. Outler*, edited by John Deschner, L. T. Howe, and K. Penzel, pp. 131–55. New York: Oxford University Press, 1975.

Monteverdi, Giulio Cesare. "Dichiaratione della lettera stampata nel quinto libro de suoi madrigali." In Claudio Monteverdi, *Scherzi musicali* (1607). Reprinted in G. Francesco Malipiero, *Claudio Monteverdi*, pp. 83–84. Milan: Fratelli Treves, 1929. Translated in Oliver Strunk, *Source Readings in Music History*, pp. 411–12. New York: Norton, 1950.

Moser, Hans Joachim. *Paul Hofhaimer: Ein Lied- und Orgelmeister des deutschen Humanismus.* 2d ed. Hildesheim: Georg Olms, 1966.

Nettl, Paul. *Luther and Music.* Translated by Frida Best and Ralph Wood. New York: Russel and Russel, 1948.

Neumann, Werner, ed. *Kritischer Bericht* to *Johann Sebastian Bach.* Vol. 21 of *Neue Bach Ausgabe sämtlicher Werke*, ser. 1. Kassel: Bärenreiter, 1959.

Neumann, Werner, and Hans-Joachim Schulze, eds. *Fremdschriftliche und gedruckte Dokumente zur Lebensgeschichte Johann Sebastian Bachs 1685–1750.* Vol. 2 of *Bach-Dokumente.* Kassel: Bärenreiter, 1969.

———. *Schriftstücke von der Hand Johann Sebastian Bach.* Vol. 1 of *Bach-Dokumente.* Kassel: Bärenreiter, 1963.

Niedt, Friedrich Erhardt. *The Musical Guide.* Translated by Pamela L. Poulin and Irmgard C. Taylor. Oxford: Clarendon Press, and New York: Oxford University Press, 1989.

———. *Musicalische Handleitung zur Variation des Generalbasses.* 2d ed. Hamburg, 1721. Facsimile reprint. Vol. 32 of *Bibliotheca Organologica.* Buren: Frits Knuf, 1976.

Noblitt, Thomas, ed. *Der Kodex des Magister Nicolaus Leopold: Staatsbibliothek München, Mus. ms. 3154.* Vol. 80 of *Das Erbe deutscher Musik.* Kassel: Bärenreiter, 1987.

Osiander, Lucas. *Das erste evangelische Choralbuch.* 1586. Edited by Friedrich Zelle. Berlin: Weidmannsche Buchhandlung, 1903.

Pelikan, Jaroslav. *Bach among the Theologians.* Philadelphia: Fortress Press, 1986.

Penna, Lorenzo. *Li Primi Albori Musicali.* Bologna, 1672.

Petzoldt, Martin., ed., *Bach als Ausleger der Bibel: Theologische und musikwissenschaftliche Studien zum Werk Johann Sebastian Bachs.* Göttingen: Vandenhoeck & Ruprecht, 1985.

Petzoldt, Martin. *Gleichnisse Jesu und christliche Dogmatik.* Berlin: Evangelisches Verlagsanstalt, 1983.

———. "'Die kräfftige Erquickung unter der schweren Angst-Last.' Möglicherweise Neues zur Entstehung der Kantate BWV 21." *Bach-Jahrbuch* 79 (1993): 32–46.

———. "Schlußchoräle ohne Textmarken in der Überlieferung von Kantaten J. S. Bachs." *Musik und Kirche* 59 (1989): 235–40.

———. "Studien zur Theologie im Rahmen der Lebengeschichte J. S. Bachs." Unpublished *Habilitationsschrift.* Leipzig, 1985.

———. "Zur Frage der Textvorlagen von BWV 62, 'Nun komm der Heiden Heiland.'" *Musik und Kirche* 60 (1990): 302–10.

Praetorius, Michael. *Gesamtausgabe der Musikalischen Werke.* 21 vols. Wolfenbüttel, 1619. Edited by Friedrich Blume. Wolfenbüttel: Bärenreiter, 1958.

———. *Syntagma Musicum.* 3 vols. Wolfenbüttel, 1619. Edited by Wilibald Gurlitt. Kassel: Bärenreiter, 1959.

Richter, B. F. "Eine Abhandlung Joh. Kuhnau's." *Monatshefte für Musik-Geschichte* 34: 148–54.

Rollinson, Philip. *Classical Theories of Allegory and Christian Culture.* Pittsburgh: Duquesne University Press and Harvester Press, 1981.

Schering, Arnold. "Bach und das Symbol, insbesondere die Symbolik seines Kanons." *Bach-Jahrbuch* 22 (1925): 53–59.

Schuler, Louis Eugene, Jr. "Lucas Osiander and his *Fünfftzig Geistliche Lieder und Psalmen:* The Development and Use of the First Cantional." Ph.D. diss., Washington University, 1986.

Schulze, Hans-Joachim, ed. *Dokumente zum Nachwirken Johann Sebastian Bachs.* Vol. 3 of *Bach-Dokumente.* Kassel: Bärenreiter, 1972.

Schulze, Hans-Joachim, and Christoph Wolff, eds. *Bach Compendium: Analytischbibliographisches Repertorium der Werke Johann Sebastian Bachs.* 4 vols. (Leipzig and Dresden, Peters 1985–).

Schweitzer, Albert. *J. S. Bach, le musicien-poète.* Paris, 1905. German ed. 1908. English translation from the German by Ernest Newman with alterations and additions by the author. London: Breitkopf & Härtel, 1911. Reprint. Boston: Bruce Humphries, 1962.

Smend, Friedrich. "Bachs Matthäus-Passion." *Bach-Jahrbuch* 25 (1928): 1–95.

———. *Johann Sebastian Bach bei seinem Namen gerufen: Eine Notenschrift und ihre Deutung.* Kassel: Bärenreiter, 1950.

Smithers, Don. "Die Verwendung der Blechblasinstrumente bei J. S. Bach under besondere Berücksichtigung der Tromba da tirarsi. Kritische Anmerkunggen zum gleichnamigen Aufsatz von Thomas G. MacCracken." *Bach-Jahrbuch* 76 (1990): 37–52.

Stalmann, Johachim, and Johannes Heinrich, eds. *Handbuch zum Evangelischen Kirchengesangbuch,* vol. 3, part 2. Göttingen: Vandenhoeck & Ruprecht, Wilhelm Hoppe, 1990.

Steiger, Lothar and Renate. *"Sehet! Wir gen hinauf gen Jerusalem": Johann Sebastian Bachs Kantaten auf den Sonntag Estomihi.* Göttingen: Vandenhoeck & Ruprecht, 1992.

Steiger, Renate. "Actus tragicus und ars moriendi. Bachs Textvorlage für die Kantate 'Gottes Zeit ist die allerbeste Zeit' (BWV 106)." *Musik und Kirche* 59 (1989): 11–23.

———. "'Amen, amen. Komm, du schöne Freudenkrone': Zum Schlußsatz von BWV 61." *Musik und Kirche* 59 (1989): 246–51.

Stiller, Gunther. *J. S. Bach and Liturgical Life in Leipzig.* Translated by Herbert J. A. Bouman, Daniel F. Poellot, and Hilton C. Oswald, edited by Robin Leaver. St. Louis: Concordia, 1984.

Strunk, Oliver, ed. *Strunk's Source Readings in Music History,* rev. ed., Leo Treitler, General editor. New York: Norton, 1998.

Talley, Thomas. *The Origins of the Liturgical Year.* 2d. ed. Collegeville, Minn.: Liturgical Press, 1991.

Tappert, Theodore G., trans. and ed. *The Book of Concord.* Philadelphia: Fortress Press, 1959.

Telemann, Georg Philipp. *Fast allgemeines Evangelisch-Musicalisches Lieder-Buch.* Hamburg, 1730. Facsimile ed. Edited by Siegfried Kross. Hildesheim: Georg Olms, 1977.

Vopelius, Gottfried. *Neu-Leipziger Gesangbuch.* Leipzig, 1682.

Wailes, Stephen L. *Medieval Allegories of Jesus' Parables.* Berkeley: University of California Press, 1987.

Walpole, A. S. *Early Latin Hymns.* Cambridge: Cambridge University Press, 1922. Reprint. Hildesheim: Georg Olms, 1966.

Walter, Meinrad. "Cogitatio aeternitatis als Ars moriendi in J. S. Bachs Kantaten 'O Ewigkeit, du Donnerwort' (Dialogus BWV 60) und 'Liebster Gott, wenn werd ich sterben? (BWV 8)." In *Die Seelsorgliche Bedeutung Johann Sebastian Bachs: Kantaten zum Thema Tod und Sterben,* bulletin 4, pp. 133–80. Heidelberg: Internationale Arbeitsgtemeinschaft für theologische Bachforschung, 1993.

———. *Musik-Sprache des Glaubens. Zum geistlichen Vokanwerk Johann Sebastian Bachs.* Frankfurt: Verlag Josef Knecht, 1994.

Walther, Johann. *Geistliches Gesangbüchlein.* Vol. 1 of *Sämtliche Werke* (1953). Wittenberg, 1551. Edited by Otto Schröder. Kassel: Bärenreiter, 1953.

———. *Wittembergische Geistliche Gesangbuch von 1524.* Vol. 7 of *Publikation Älterer Praktischer und Theoretischer Musikwerke.* 1878. Edited by Otto Kade. New York: Broude Brothers, 1966.

Werckmeister, Andreas. *Hypomnemata Musica* (1697), together with *Erweiterte und verbesserte Orgel-Probe* (1698), *Cribrum Musicum* (1700), *Harmonologia Musica* (1702), and *Musicalische Paradoxal-Discourse* (1707). Facsimile ed. (5 vols. in 1). Hildesheim: Georg Olms, 1970.

———. *Musicae mathematicae hodegus curiosus.* Frankfurt and Leipzig, 1686. Facsimile ed. Hildesheim: Georg Olms, 1972.

———. *Musicalische Temperatur.* Quedlinburg, 1691. Edited by Rudolf Rasch. Utrecht: Diapason Press, 1983.

Werthemann, Helene. *Die Bedeutung der alttestamentlichen Historien in Johann Sebastian Bachs Kantaten.* Tübingen: J. B. Mohr, 1960.

———. "Zum Text der Bach-Kantate 21, 'Ich hatte viel Bekümmernis in meinem Herzen.'" *Bach-Jahrbuch* 51 (1965): 135–43.

Wolff, Christoph, ed. *The Neumeister Collection of Chorale Preludes from the Bach Circle.* New Haven and London: Yale University Press, 1986.

———. *Der stile antico in der Musik Johann Sebastian Bachs.* Wiesbaden: Breitkopf & Härtel, 1968.

Zahn, Johannes. *Die Melodien der Deutschen Evangelischen Kirchenlieder.* 6 vols. Gütersloh, 1889. Reprint. Hildesheim: Georg Olms, 1963.

Index